AN INTRODUCTION TO GLOBAL FINANCIAL MARKETS

An Introduction to Global Financial Markets

An extensively revised edition of

An Introduction to Western Financial Markets

STEPHEN VALDEZ

Published 1993 as *An Introduction to Western Financial Markets*
Reprinted twice
This extensively revised edition published 1997

Published by
MACMILLAN PRESS LTD
Houndmills, Basingstoke, Hampshire RG21 6XS
and London
Companies and representatives
throughout the world

ISBN 0–333–69584–4 hardcover
ISBN 0–333–69394–9 paperback

A catalogue record for this book is available
from the British Library.

This book is printed on paper suitable for recycling and
made from fully managed and sustained forest sources.

10 9 8 7 6 5 4 3
06 05 04 03 02 01 00 99 98

Printed and bound in Great Britain by
Antony Rowe Ltd, Chippenham, Wilts.

Contents

Wholesale
Clients

Private Clients &
Asset mgmt

Consumer &
Commercial Clients

Preface

The idea of a book on global financial markets came to me when I hit the problem of recommended reading for candidates coming from the continent of Europe to one of our courses.

Since the course in question was about the markets in general, books called 'How the City of London Works' (or similar titles) did not exactly answer the problem. This was particularly true when we found ourselves facing audiences from the former Russian republics and from East Europe.

It seemed to me that there was a need for a more general book about the global markets as a whole, as opposed to one about markets in one particular country such as the US or the UK. In any case, the financial world is becoming more integrated and global in its operations. A parochial knowledge of just one country is proving less and less satisfactory. This book attempts to answer this need.

Having said that, the book does not attempt a systematic coverage of the markets in all countries. Such a book would be far bulkier than this one and, probably, unreadable! Instead I have usually concentrated on examples from the US, UK, Germany, France and Japan. From time to time, illustrations will also be given from markets such as the Netherlands, Spain, Italy and Switzerland. The aim is not only to give a basic idea of how the markets work, but also to show the diversity of customs and practices within a common theme.

The book should prove useful for those preparing for a variety of examinations (MBA, banking, finance, economics and business studies), those working in banking and financial institutions in a support role (computer staff, accountants, personnel, public relations, back office and settlement) and, finally, staff in the many suppliers of information and computer services to the financial markets (computer manufacturers and software houses, Reuters, Telerate and so on).

In preparing the second edition, I have acted on suggestions from readers that a summary at the end of each chapter would be useful and that the scope of the book would be improved by more coverage of the Japanese markets. I have also followed up useful suggestions for additions to the glossary.

I have, of course, brought all the statistical tables up to date and included more recent events such as international bank mergers (for example, the Bank of Tokyo/Mitsubishi and Chemical/Chase Manhattan), the spate of changes in the UK building society movement, the Nick Leeson affair, the BIS 1995 survey of OTC derivative markets, the Lloyd's of London recovery plan and developments in the European Union, especially the moves towards a single currency in 1999.

Extra subjects now included in the text are a mention of credit unions in the banking chapter, a widening of the topics discussed in money markets and bonds to cover repos, asset backed securities, coupon stripping and dragon bonds and, in the equity chapter (Chapter 9), the addition of bought deals, share buy backs, GDRs as well as ADRs and the increasingly popular scrip dividend.

Finally, after much heart searching and discussions with my publisher, we have decided that *An Introduction to Global Financial Markets* is a slightly more apposite title than that used in the first edition.

Stephen Valdez

Acknowledgements

Many organisations kindly gave permission for copyright material to be used and these were:

Association for Payment Clearing Services
Acquisitions Monthly
The Banker
Bank of England
Bank for International Settlements
Datastream International
Euromoney Publications plc
European Association of Cooperative Banks
Federal Trsut
Financial Times
London Stock Exchange
Organisation for European Cooperation and Development
PDFM
SBF – Paris Bourse
Society for Worldwide Interbank Financial Telecommunications
Technimetrics Inc.
Union Bank of Switzerland

Once again, as with the first edition, my thanks to Tina Shorter of Firm Focus for her excellent work in preparing the text, including camera-ready copy.

1 The Debt Merry-Go-Round

RAISON D'ÊTRE OF THE MARKETS

The beginning is always a good place to start. Let's go straight to the heart of the matter and ask the most fundamental question of all – what are the financial markets *for*? What is their purpose? What is the raison d'être?

The markets are all about the raising of capital and the matching of those who *want* capital (borrowers) with those who *have* it (lenders).

How do the borrowers find the lenders? Clearly, with difficulty but for the presence of intermediaries, such as banks. Banks take deposits from those who have money to save and bundle it up in various ways so that it can be lent to those who wish to borrow.

More complex transactions than a simple bank deposit require markets in which borrowers and their agents can meet lenders and their agents, and existing commitments to borrow or lend can be sold on to other people. Stock exchanges are a good example. Companies can raise money by selling shares to investors and existing shares can be freely bought and sold.

The money goes round and round, just like a carousel on a fairground (see Table 1.1).

Table 1.1   *The debt merry-go-round*

Lenders	Intermediaries	Markets	Borrowers
Individuals	Banks	Interbank	Individuals
Companies	Insurance companies	Stock Exchange	Companies
	Pension funds	Money market	Central government
	Mutual funds	Bond market	Municipalities
			Public corporations

Lenders

Let's have a look at some of those who might be lenders:

Individuals   Individuals may have conscious savings in banks of various kinds. Individuals also may not think of themselves as conscious savers at all but, nevertheless, pay monthly premiums to insurance companies and contributions to pensions. Regarding pensions, there are different traditions. The US, UK, the

1

Netherlands, Switzerland and Japan have a strong tradition of pension funds. They invest the money paid into either private pension plans or employers' pension schemes. In France, the state takes care of most pensions and pays them out of current taxation, not out of a fund. In Germany, company pensions are important but the company decides on the investment, which may be in the company itself. Where pension funds exist, these funds of money, along with those of insurance companies, are key determinants of movements in the markets. They have to look ahead to long-term liabilities, and will assist the borrowers of capital by buying government bonds, corporate bonds, corporate equities and so on. The shortage of such funds in many of the newly emerging economies is a major reason for the slow growth of local securities markets there.

Companies We think of commercial companies as borrowers of capital. However, even if the company is a borrower, if some of the money is not needed for a short period of time, it will seek to make money by lending in the short-term markets called 'money markets' (that is, transactions of up to 1 year in duration).

There are also companies whose cash flow is strong and who tend to be lenders rather than borrowers. A major company in the dissemination of financial information is Reuters. Their Annual Report for 1995 showed liquid funds in excess of £850m.

Borrowers

Who, then, are the borrowers of capital?

Individuals Individuals may have bank loans for domestic purchases or longer-term mortgages to fund house purchase.

Companies Companies need money short-term to fund cash flow. They need money longer term for growth and expansion.

Governments Governments are typically voracious borrowers. Their expenditure exceeds their receipts from taxes and they borrow to make up the deficit. They may also borrow on behalf of municipalities, federal states, nationalised industries and public sector bodies generally. The total is usually called the 'Public Sector Borrowing Requirement' (PSBR). The cumulative total for all the borrowing since they started is called the 'National Debt'. The first surprise for many of us is that governments don't pay off the national debt, it just gets bigger. Of this, more in Chapter 3.

Municipalities and similar bodies Apart from the government borrowing on behalf of various local authorities, these bodies may borrow in their own name. This would cover municipalities like Barcelona, counties like Berkshire in the UK, federal states like Hesse in Germany.

Public corporations This might include nationalised industries, like SNCF in France or the German railways and post office authorities, or general public sector bodies like Crédit Local de France or the German Unity Fund.

Within an economy, many of the above will not be nationals but foreigners, with implications for the *foreign exchange* market.

cash flow / P/L /

Securities

When the money is lent, it may simply be a deposit with a bank. Most of the time, however, the lender will issue a receipt for the money, a promise to pay back. These pieces of paper are, in the most general sense, what we call *securities*. There are, unfortunately for the beginner, masses of different names – Treasury Bills, certificates of deposit, commercial paper, bills of exchange, bonds, convertibles, debentures, preference shares, Eurobonds, floating rate notes and so on. At least we can console ourselves with the thought that they are essentially all the same – promises to pay back which show key information:

❏ HOW MUCH is owed
❏ WHEN it will be paid
❏ THE RATE OF INTEREST to reward the lender.

A major characteristic of the markets is that these securities are freely bought and sold. This makes life easier for the lender and helps the borrower to raise the money more easily.

For example, a young American wanting to save for old age spends $5000 on a 30 year government bond which has just been issued. After 5 years, he decides that this was not such a good idea and wants the money now. What does he do? He simply sells the bond to someone else. This is crucially important, as it means that he is more willing to put the money up in the first place, knowing that there is this escape clause. It also gives great velocity to the 'Debt Merry-Go-Round' as the same security is bought and sold many times.

Let's tackle the market jargon here. The first time the money is lent and changes hands, the first time the security is issued, is the *primary market.*

All the buying and selling that takes place thereafter we call the *secondary market.*

The secondary market is very significant as the flexibility it gives makes the primary market work better – it's the oil that helps the wheels to turn round.

Let's look at other terminology used (see Figure 1.1).

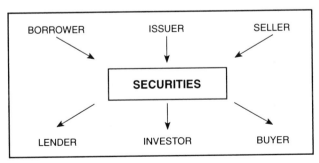

Figure 1.1   *Market terminology*

Suppose the government announces a new bond. We can say the government is *issuing* a new bond. We could just as easily say that the government is *selling* a new bond. We might see it as a sign of the government's need to *borrow* more money.

If you hear of the new bond, you may tell a friend that you've decided to *invest* in it. You might alternatively say you've decided to *buy* the new bond. You probably won't think of it that way, but you are the *lender* of money to a, no doubt ungrateful, government.

It may seem an obvious point, but all those terms might be used. Sometimes newcomers need to be reminded that whoever buys a security is directly or indirectly lending money.

RAISING CAPITAL

Let's look at an example. Suppose a commercial company needs $200m to finance building a new factory. We have just explained that the financial markets are all about the raising of money. What, then, are the choices?

Bank Loans

One obvious source of money when we need it is the *bank*. These days, with large sums of money, it may be a syndicate of banks to spread the risk. The banks are taking deposits lent to them and relending the money to the commercial company. It's their classic role as intermediary. The money will not be lent at a fixed rate but at a variable rate according to market rates from time to time. This is called the *floating rate*. The banks may lend at a basic rate (such as the prime rate in the US or the interbank rate in Europe) plus a given margin such as ¾%. The bank will re-adjust the rate, say, every 3 months. The rate is fixed for 3 months but then changed for the next 3 months. Note that this creates *risk*. If rates fall, the lender loses income. If rates rise, the borrower pays more.

Bonds

Another choice would be to issue a *bond*. A bond is just a piece of paper stating the terms on which the money will be paid back. For example, it may be a 10 year bond, paying interest at 7% in two instalments per year. The word 'bond' implies that the rate of interest is fixed. If it's floating, then we have to find another name, such a *'floating rate note'*. The bond may be bought by a bank as another use for depositors' money, or it might be bought directly by an investor who sees the bond notice in the paper and instructs their agent to buy.

There is a strong obligation to meet the interest payments on the bond. If an interest payment is missed, the bond holders acquire certain rights and might even be able to put the company into liquidation.

Equity

A final choice would be to raise the money by selling shares in the company. Shares are called '*equity*'. If it's the first time the company has done this, we call it a '*new issue*'. If the company already has shareholders, it may approach them with the opportunity to buy more shares in the company, called a '*rights issue*'. This is because, under most EU law, the existing shareholders must be approached first if any new shares are to be offered for cash. These rights are not protected as strongly in the US.

The reward for the shareholders by way of income is the *dividend*. However, the income is usually poorer than that paid on a bond and the shareholders look to *capital gains* as well, believing that the share price will go up as time goes by.

Our three choices are shown in Figure 1.2.

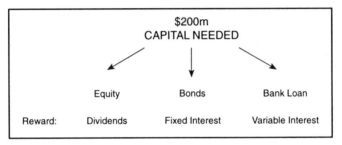

Figure 1.2   *Raising capital*

We must recognise that the equity choice is fundamentally different from the other two. The shareholder is part owner along with the other shareholders. There is, thus, no date for paying the money back (the shares may be sold on a stock exchange to someone else, but that's quite different). The shareholder accepts risk – they could prosper if the firm prospers, or lose some or all of their money if the firm goes into liquidation. If the latter sad event happens, the shareholders are the last to receive a share of any money left. In addition, if the firm hits trouble, the dividend can be cut or even missed altogether.

In the case of bonds and bank loans, the money must eventually be paid back and there are strong legal obligations to meet the interest payments – they are *debt* not *equity*. Equity is the exception in the 'Debt Merry-Go-Round' in that it is not debt at all.

Gearing

There's nothing wrong in principle with borrowed money. It enables the company to do more trading than it could on the shareholders' equity alone. The danger comes when too much money is borrowed, especially if boom times are followed (as they usually are) by recession. The firm may be unable to pay the interest out of its reduced profits, apart from the problem of repaying the principal sum itself.

Stock market analysts, therefore, look at firms' balance sheets and look at the ratio of long-term debt to equity. However, let's note here that when we say 'equity', we don't just mean the money raised by selling shares originally and by subsequent rights issues. The firm (we hope) will make profits. Out of the profits it will pay tax to the government and dividends to the shareholders. The remaining profit is retained for growth and expansion. This money also belongs to the shareholders. As a result, the phrase *shareholders' funds* is used for the total equity of the shareholders:

> Original equity
>
> \+   Rights issues
> \+   Retained profit
>
> \=   Shareholders' funds

Analysts, then, look at the ratio between the long-term debt and the shareholders' funds. The relationship is called *gearing* or *leverage*.

The metaphor is from mechanics. A gear enables more work to be done with a given force. The lever is a similar idea. Remember Archimedes' saying 'give me a fulcrum and I will lever the world'? The shareholders are doing more trading than they could with their money alone. How? By borrowing other people's money. The general idea behind gearing or leverage is to make a given sum of money go further. In this context, we do it by borrowing someone else's money. We shall also meet other contexts in this book.

The ratio between long-term debt and shareholders' funds is thus the *gearing ratio*. What ratio is safe? Frankly, this has become a matter of some controversy. Generally, people worry if the ratio reaches 100%, but that's only a crude guideline. For example, if the business is cyclical, analysts will worry more than if it's a steady business from one year to the next. They will also worry less if there are assets that can easily be realised, rather than assets which may not be easy to dispose of, especially during a recession (for example, property).

In 1991, the Bank of England produced a report on the deterioration in the financial position of many UK companies as recession came at the end of the 1980s and published its findings in the *Quarterly Bulletin* for May 1991. High gearing was identified as a common feature of a number of company failures.

Having looked at the three key choices for new capital – equity, bonds and bank loans – we should also be aware that, in Western financial markets generally, probably 50% of the money needed for growth and expansion comes from retained profits. 'Profit' can be a sensitive topic and, in some people's eyes, a pejorative term – for example, 'they are only in it for the profit'. However, profit provides not only rewards for the shareholders and taxes for the government, but funds for expansion which create further employment and a more secure environment for the employees.

Looking at international markets, the Organisation for Economic Cooperation and Development (OECD) analyses the raising of capital. Looking at long-term capital, they produced the figures which are shown in Table 1.2.

Table 1.2 *Raising capital on international markets*

	1994 *$bn*	*1995 (9 months)* *$bn*
Bonds	428.6	343.7
Equities	45.0	22.4
Syndicated loans	236.2	264.7

Source: OECD, *Financial Market Trends* (November 1995).

We shall look at the concept of *international* markets in Chapter 6. Briefly, we are talking about equity raised across national boundaries; bonds issued in, say, London in dollars and sold to international investors; international banks getting together to syndicate a large loan.

In addition to the above would be capital raised in purely *domestic* markets. The table also refers to *long-term* capital. There is the raising of *short-term* capital, for meeting cash flow needs rather than growth and expansion. Equity is not applicable here but there are various securities and types of bank loan which meet this need.

The above international figures could be misleading, as the emphasis may be quite different in *domestic* markets. Each country has its own traditions. The US is a big market for company bonds, as well as a large equity market. German companies have a long tradition of close relationship with banks and use of bank finance. (For an interesting analysis, see J. Edwards and K. Fischer, *An Overview of the German Financial System*, Cambridge University/CEPR, 1991.) Equity finance is strong in the UK and the corporate bond market weak.

CONCLUSION

We have seen that the raison d'être of the financial markets is the raising of capital. Our examination of the choices for finding capital shows us the financial markets in action, and also the themes which we study in this book:

Banking In Chapters 2–5 we look at banking in all its aspects.

Money and Bond Markets In Chapter 6 we examine the domestic and international markets. We look at raising money short-term (money markets) and long-term (bond markets).

Foreign Exchange The international character of the markets today and gradual deregulation create strong demand for foreign currencies. This is considered in Chapter 7.

Finance for Trade   World trade is, of course, extremely important. The need for capital to back trade transactions and the need to control the risk pose special problems. These are discussed in Chapter 8.

Equities   Stock markets, brokers, market makers, institutions are explained in Chapter 9.

Derivative Products   Interest rates, currency rates, bond prices and share prices all go up and down, creating *risk*. There are financial products which are, paradoxically, used both to exploit risk and to control risk. These are called *derivative products* and are, possibly, the fastest growing sector of the financial markets today. This complex but fascinating subject is looked at in Chapters 10–12.

Insurance   The insurance market is one of the oldest world financial markets. Domestic and business risks create the need for insurance. The premiums paid in advance are a major factor in creating funds for lending to those who need capital, until such time as these funds are required to meet insurance claims. This is explained in Chapter 13.

Key Trends   Finally, in Chapter 14, we analyse the key trends in the financial markets today.

SUMMARY

The purpose of the markets is to facilitate the raising of capital and match those who want capital (borrowers) with those who have it (lenders).

Typically, the borrower issues a receipt promising to pay the lender back – these are *securities* and may be freely bought and sold.

Money may be raised by a bank loan (commercial banking) or by the issue of a bond or equity (the capital markets). The first two represent debt. The relationship between debt and equity on a balance sheet is known as *gearing*.

There are domestic markets and international (cross-border) markets.

2 Banking (I) – Background

Money and the use of metal coins as money has a long history – going back at least 10 centuries. Banking, certainly in today's sense, is rather more modern.

In many ways, the origins of capitalism as we see it today lie in the operations of Italian merchanting and banking groups in the 13th, 14th and 15th centuries. Italian states, like Lombardy and Florence, were dominant economic powers. The merchants had trading links across-borders and used their cash resources for banking purposes.

The bankers sat at formal benches, often in the open air. The Italian for bench is 'banco', giving us the modern word for bank. (If you happen to be in Prato, Italy, look in the Chapel of San Francisco for a fresco showing the money-changers' *banco,* or counter.) If the bank went into liquidation, the bench would be solemnly broken, giving us the *bancorupto* or bankrupt, as we say today. The early associations were partnerships, as shareholding companies did not begin until 1550. As a result, people might write to the 'Medici e compagni', the 'Medici and their partners'. It gives us the modern word – the *company.* It is the Italians who claim the oldest bank in the world, Monte dei Paschi of Siena (1472).

For a long period, Florence was a major centre. As a result, many coins ended up with names based on Florence. The UK had a 'florin' until the coinage was decimalised in 1971; Dutch guilders have the abbreviation FL – florins; the Hungarian currency is the 'forint' and so on.

Italian bankers had a long relationship with the British crown. The first bankers to lend money in London came from Lombardy and London still has 'Lombard Street' at the heart of the financial area. Bankers lent money to Edward I, Edward II and Edward III (naturally, to finance their various wars). Edward III, however, defaulted on the loan in 1345 and the proud families, the Bardi and the Peruzzi in Florence, crashed into liquidation as a consequence. Presumably this was the world's first (but not last!) international banking crisis.

Those bankers were very advanced for their time. They used bills of exchange (to be explained in Chapter 5), letters of credit, book entry for money instead of physically transporting it and double entry bookkeeping. The first textbook on double entry bookkeeping was published in 1494 by a Franciscan monk, Luca Pacioli. They experimented with marine insurance and evolved a body of mercantile law. The Bardi operated 30 branches in Italy and overseas and employed more than 350 people.

S. D. Chapman, *The Rise of Merchant Banking* (Allen & Unwin, 1984) shows how the Medici bank helped an Italian firm in Venice sell goods to a firm in London using a bill of exchange. The Medici bank in London would collect the money and the bank would take care of the foreign exchange conversion and risk. The goods were invoiced at £97.18s.4d (in old pounds, shillings and pence). This was the equivalent of about 535 ducats. The Medici branch in Venice paid the local firm 500 ducats on the bill of exchange, making 7% on money they would not receive for 6 months, that is, about 14% p.a. The date? 20 July 1463.

The bill above was not 'discounted' in the modern sense, since this would imply charging interest on money and this was forbidden by the Roman Catholic Church as 'usury'. The bill represented a service to facilitate trade and change foreign money – it could not appear to involve the lending of money. On the deposit side, no formal interest could be paid for the same reason. Depositors received a share of profits paid at discretion. Thus the liabilities side of the balance sheet was headed, 'Discrezione'. Islamic banking faces similar problems due to the Koran's rejection of the concept of interest as such. Today there are some 60 Islamic banks which follow the principal that the reward for deposits is not fixed but based on the profit from the use of the money.

The one thing the Italians didn't invent was banknotes. For this, we look to goldsmiths in the UK. There, merchants would keep money for safe keeping in the Royal Mint. Charles I had many arguments with Parliament about money and solved one of them by marching down to the Royal Mint and stealing £130 000! Although the money was replaced later, confidence in the Royal Mint had gone. It was good news for goldsmiths who had secure vaults for gold and silver coins and began an era of goldsmiths as bankers for some 150 years. Coutts Bank, still going today, began in 1692 as a goldsmith bank. The goldsmiths found it convenient to give out receipts for a deposit of gold coins made out to 'the bearer' and to issue 10 receipts for a deposit of 10 coins. In this way, if the bearer owed someone else three gold coins, they could pass on three bearer receipts. Even better, if someone wanted to borrow five gold coins, the goldsmiths could lend them five of these nice pieces of paper and not give gold coins. We are now very much into modern banking traditions, except that today the notes aren't backed by gold or silver anyway! By the end of the 17th century, the goldsmiths' receipts had become banknotes in a formal sense, the first being issued by the Bank of Sweden in 1661.

Internationally, the emphasis in banking, which had been in Florence, moved to Genoa, as gold and silver were flooding in from the New World. Outside Italy, the Fugger family of Augsburg created a financial dynasty comparable to the Italians. They were originally wool merchants, but turned to precious metals and banking. They had gold, silver and copper mines in Hungary and Austria and became principal financiers to the Hapsburg empire in Germany, the Low Countries and Spain (see E. Green, *Banking, an Illustrated History*, Phaidon Press, 1989).

Later still, we have the rise of the two great rivals, the Dutch and British Empires and Amsterdam and London as rival financial centres. Amsterdam, for example, is Europe's oldest stock exchange.

We also see merchant banking (or investment banking) in the modern sense. Francis Baring was a textile merchant from Exeter and started Baring Brothers in 1762. In 1804, Nathan Mayer Rothschild opened up for banking business in London, after a brief spell in textiles in Manchester. In Holland, we had Mees & Hope and Pierson, Heldring & Pierson – both still in business today as subsidiaries of the ABN–AMRO Bank.

The merchant bankers had two key activities – financing trade, using bills of exchange and raising money for governments by selling bonds. Baring Brothers financed the huge reparations imposed on France after the Napoleonic wars with a large international bond issue. (As a consequence, the Duc de Richelieu dubbed them 'Europe's 6th super-power'!) In 1818, Rothschild's raised a large loan for Prussia, to be redeemed after 36 years. They arranged to pay dividends to shareholders in their local currency. The bonds were sold to merchants, private subscribers and the aristocracy. Prussia paid 7½% of which 5% was paid to bondholders and 2½% was used to create a 'sinking fund' to redeem the bond after 36 years (see Chapman, *The Rise of Merchant Banking*). The Dutch Bank Mees, together with Baring Bros, helped the American states finance the purchase of Louisiana from Napoleon in 1803.

In the second half of the 1700s and into the 1800s there was a large growth in Europe's population (from 180 million in 1800 to 450 million by 1914). This period also saw the growth of industrialisation and urbanisation. As a result, the spread of banking followed. While private banks continued to flourish in many cases, the gradual change in legislation to allow joint stock banks (that is, banks with shareholders) paved the way for the growth of larger commercial banks with many branches and a strong deposit taking function.

In the US, the Bank of New York and the Bank of Boston (later First National Bank of Boston) opened in 1800. The water company, the Manhattan Company, became a bank around about the same time. (It became Chase Manhattan in 1955.) The 'City Bank' opened in 1812, becoming the National City Bank later and merging with First National Bank to form today's Citibank in 1955.

In Europe, we see the Société Générale of Belgium formed in 1822; the Bayerische Hypotheken und Wechsel Bank in 1822; Creditanstalt in Austria in 1856; Crédit Suisse also in 1856; UBS in 1862; Crédit Lyonnais in 1863 and the Société Générale (France) in 1864 (by 1900 they had 200 and 350 branches respectively); Deutsche Bank in 1870 and Banca Commerciale Italiana in 1894.

In the UK, the Bank of England's monopoly of joint stock banking ended in 1826. There were 1700 bank branches in 1850, 3300 by 1875 and nearly 7000 by 1900. The Midland Bank opened in 1836 and the forerunners of National Westminster in 1833–6. Private banks, threatened by the greater resources of the new joint stock banks, were either bought out or merged. One such merger formed the Barclays we know today. One of the earliest of such private banks was Child & Co, at No. 1 Fleet Street since 1673 and nowadays part of the Royal Bank of Scotland. By 1884, the London Clearing House was clearing cheques worth £6 billion.

There is one interesting point about the UK. Although Rothschild's on the continent had a hand in setting up some of the commercial banks (Creditanstalt and Société Générale of France are examples), in the UK, the merchant banks ignored the new developments and stuck to that which they knew and did best (international bonds and trade finance). As a result, the British tradition has been one of looking at two types of bank – the 'merchant' bank on the one hand and the 'commercial' bank on the other (we shall examine the differences later in this chapter). It was only in the 1960s and later that the large commercial banks thought it necessary to open merchant bank subsidiaries or buy one (for example, Midland Bank buying Samuel Montagu).

On the continent of Europe, especially in Germany, Austria and Switzerland, the pattern became that of banks who did all types of banking – both 'merchant' and 'commercial'. This is the 'universal' bank tradition – banks like Deutsche Bank and the Union Bank of Switzerland.

These developments take us into this century and the age of computers, communications, automated teller machines (ATMs), credit cards, bank mergers and electronic funds transfer at the point of sale (EFT-POS).

BANKING SUPERVISION

Let's start with the question: 'Who is in charge of the banks?' If you were in the Netherlands, Italy or the UK, you might reply, 'The Central Bank', and you would be correct. However, this is by no means always the case. Indeed, it is more common to find that the supervisory body is separate. Even the mighty Bundesbank is not responsible legally for supervision – that is the task of the 'Federal Banking Supervisory Office'. It does, of course, consult the Bundesbank and the latter collects detailed reports from all the country's banks. However, if any action is to be taken, it will be taken by the Federal Banking Supervisory Office.

There is a Banking Commission in France and Belgium and a Federal Banking Commission in Switzerland.

In Japan, the Ministry of Finance is in charge and, in the US, the picture is very mixed with differing roles played by the Federal Reserve, individual states, the Federal Deposit Insurance Corporation (FDIC), the Comptroller of the Currency and the Savings and Loan Associations reporting to the Federal Home Loan Bank System. For example, when Chicago's Continental Illinois Bank hit trouble in 1984, it was rescued by the FDIC and not the Federal Reserve. The US Congress has been promising to simplify this confusion for some time but has, so far, failed to do so.

Having decided who is in charge, what general rules will they lay down? Usually, the following:

- ❏ Conditions of entry
- ❏ Capital ratios
- ❏ Liquidity rules
- ❏ Large exposure rules
- ❏ Foreign exchange control
- ❏ Rights of inspection.

(The meaning of the more technical terms here will be explained within the banking chapters.)

TYPES OF BANK: DEFINITIONS

There are many different terms used, not all mutually exclusive. Let's examine the following:

❑   Central banks
❑   Commercial banks
❑   Merchant/Investment banks
❑   Savings banks
❑   Cooperative banks
❑   Mortgage banks
❑   Giro banks and National Savings banks
❑   Credit unions.

Central banks   Typically, an economy will have a central bank, like the Federal Reserve in the US or the Bundesbank in Germany. The role of the Central Bank will be examined in detail in Chapter 3.

Commercial banks   These are banks in the classic business of taking deposits and lending money. There are two further relevant terms here – *retail* banking and *wholesale* banking. Retail banking involves high street branches, dealing with the general public, shops and very small businesses. The use of cheques and cheque clearing is normally of crucial importance (for example, 3250 million cheques were written in the UK in 1995). We are talking here of high volume but low value. Wholesale banking involves low volume and high value. It covers dealings with other banks, the central bank, corporates, pension funds and other investment institutions. Cheques are not so important here, but electronic settlement and clearance is – systems like CHIPS (Clearing House Interbank Payments) in New York, CHAPS (Clearing House Automated Payments) in the UK and SIT (Système Interbancaire de Télécompensation) in France. The dealings in the money markets which we describe in Chapter 6 are wholesale banking activities. Retail banking and other wholesale activities like corporate loans are discussed in Chapter 4. Foreign exchange may be retail (a member of the public going on holiday) or wholesale (a French corporate wants DM10m to buy German imports). Foreign exchange is discussed in Chapter 7.

A special subset of retail banking is *private* banking. This involves handling the needs of high net worth individuals – deposits, loans, fund management, investment advice and so on. Historically, it is a key Swiss speciality!

Merchant/Investment banks   *Merchant* bank is a classic UK term; *Investment* bank is the US equivalent and perhaps the more general and modern term. We shall use them interchangeably (but beware use of the term 'merchant banking' in the US, where it is applied to taking an active part with the bank's own capital in takeover/

merger activities). If commercial banking is about lending money, merchant banking can be summarised as 'helping people to find the money'. For example, in Chapter 1 we examined three choices for raising capital – bank loan, bond issue or equity. Sometimes the choice is not necessarily clear. For example, in 1989, Sulzer Brothers from Switzerland issued $100m 3 year bonds at 8¾%. The comment in the *Financial Times* was: 'Traders said the terms were very generous and speculated that Sulzer could have borrowed the funds more cheaply by going direct to the banks for a loan' (see *Financial Times*, 28 November 1989). We quote this simply to illustrate that the choice is not necessarily obvious. Equally, in September 1993, an article in London's *Evening Standard* criticised corporates for their fondness that year for rights issues, arguing that bonds would have been better value in the long run. Merchant or investment banks will give advice on this aspect. If the choice is bonds or equities, they will help the issuer to price them, will assist in selling them and, with other associates, *underwrite* the issue, that is, they will buy the securities if the investors do not.

There are other activities of merchant or investment banks and we will cover these in Chapter 5.

Savings banks   What we have to distinguish here is the historical, traditional role of savings banks and their more modern role today. In the modern world they are looking more and more like ordinary commercial banks due to (a) growing mergers of previously autonomous savings banks, (b) deregulation, removing restrictions on their activities and giving them powers to act like commercial banks. In spite of (a) and (b), what might still make them a little different is their ownership structure – usually they are 'mutuals', that is, owned by the members.

There are strong savings bank movements right across Europe with terms like:

❏ Sparkasse   Germany/Austria
❏ Cassa di Risparmio   Italy
❏ Caja de Ahorros   Spain
❏ Caisses d'Epargne   France/Belgium.

In the US, they are known as 'Savings and Loan Associations' or 'Thrifts' and in the UK (historically, but not today) – 'Trustee Savings Banks'.

There are about 750 savings banks in Germany with some 19 000 branches. As it is a federal republic, each federal state or county within a state guarantees the deposits and there is a central bank for the savings banks called the *Landesbank*. The biggest of these is the Westdeutsche Landesbank. It is also house bank to the government of North-Rhein Westphalia and Germany's third largest bank.There is also an overall central authority to coordinate activities, the Deutsche Girozentrale Deutsche Kommunalbank. Deregulation means that the Sparkasse have more or less normal banking powers. More than 60% of German citizens have a Sparkasse account. They are said to handle 65% of loans to local authorities, 60% of loans to small businesses and 40% of personal loans. Their numbers have increased since unification with the addition of the savings banks in the former GDR.

Having some form of central bank for savings banks is not uncommon. In Austria it's the Girozentrale Vienna (now called GiroCredit Bank). In Finland, prior to its financial collapse in September 1991, it was the Skopbank. It was reorganised as the Savings Bank of Finland. Widespread mergers are taking place in Spain and Italy and even mergers with other banks. For example, in Italy the Cassa di Risparmio di Roma has merged with Banco di Roma and Banco di Santo Spirito to form a large bank to be called (curiously) Banca di Roma. In Spain the two largest savings banks have merged to form a major force in Spanish banking called La Caixa, using its short Catalan title. In neither Spain nor Italy has deregulation of powers gone as far as in Germany.

In the UK, the movement was started in 1810 in order to accept small deposits (the minimum deposit for a normal bank was quite large). In 1817, the government passed a law that the banks must be run by trustees to protect the depositors, hence 'Trustee Savings Banks'. In 1976, they were deregulated and given normal banking powers. From a large number of distinct autonomous banks, the movement eventually came together as one bank, simply known as 'TSB Bank'. In 1986 the government sold shares to the general public and it lost its mutual status. In April 1991, TSB left the European Association of Savings Banks on the grounds that it was no longer a savings bank in any real sense. This is the most extreme example of a change in status. Finally, in 1996, it was taken over by Lloyds Bank.

In France, too, the movement is coming together and sells and markets itself as 'Caisse Nationale des Caisses d'Epargne et de Prévoyance' (Cencep). This central body has embarked on a programme of mergers leading to a reduction in savings banks from 468 in 1984 to less than 200 today (with over 400 branches). They have normal banking powers, and have expanded into bancassurance (see Chapter 4), lending to local authorities, leasing, venture capital, property investment and collective investment sales (UCITs). They account for some 20% of deposits in France and are allowed to run special tax exempt accounts (as is the National Savings Bank).

In the US, deregulation of the Savings and Loan Associations in 1981 was a total disaster leading to a mixture of fraud and mismanagement. It has created one of America's biggest banking crises.

In Japan, the mutual savings banks are called *sogo* banks and there are 70 of them. They take retail deposits and are important lenders to small businesses.

A list of Europe's top savings banks is shown in Table 2.1

Cooperative banks   These are banks which are owned by the members and with maximum profit not necessarily the main objective – they may aim, for example, to give low cost loans to members.

Usually, the membership derives from a trade or profession. Much the most common is agriculture which gives us Crédit Agricole, in France (Europe's largest bank in asset terms), the Rabobank in the Netherlands and the Norinchukin bank in Japan. In Table 2.2 we show the share of deposits in the EU accounted for by cooperatives. From this we see that they are significant in Finland, France, Austria, the Netherlands and Germany.

Table 2.1   *Top European savings banks, 1994*

Bank	Non-bank deposits Ecu bn
Cariplo	44.2
Caixa	33.5
ASLK–CGER	32.2
Landerbank Bank Austria – Linz	23.0
Caja de Madrid	19.0
Sparbanken Sverige	17.7
Caixa Geral de Depositos	15.1
Caisse d'Epargne Ile-de-France	13.4
Hamburger Sparkasse	13.3
Landesgirokasse Stuttgart	10.8

Source: *European Savings Banks Group.*

Table 2.2   *Cooperative banks' share of deposits, 1994*

	%
Finland	34.3
France	33.0
Austria	30.5
Netherlands	25.0
Germany	21.0
Spain	7.2
Italy	7.1
Belgium	6.5
Eire	2.8
Sweden	2.0
UK	2.0
Denmark	0.5
Greece	—
Luxembourg	—
Portugal	—

Note: — Figures not available
Source: European Association of Cooperative Banks.

Germany, in particular, has a strong cooperative tradition drawn from all sorts of trades and professions. There is, for example, the 'Chemists and Doctors' Bank' (Apotheker und Ärztebank). There are over 3000 Cooperative banks with some 15 000 branches. There exist regional cooperatives and a single central bank acting as a clearing house and using central funds for international activities; this is the Deutsche Genossenschaftsbank or DG Bank.

The Crédit Agricole (CA) has 65 local banks and a central Caisse Nationale de Crédit Agricole. The latter was owned by the government, but has since been sold to the whole movement. There are 5700 branches and 67 000 employees. It has 15 million customers and accounts for 25% of all deposits in France. The bank at one time had a monopoly on farm loans. It lost this in 1990, but won the right to lend to corporates. Mortgages are important and CA handles about 30% of the mortgages in France.

There are other cooperative organisations in France, although much smaller – Banques Populaires and the Crédit Mutuel.

The Rabobank in the Netherlands is the name for the central body which acts for about 800 local agricultural cooperative banks. It is the second biggest bank in Holland. Rabobank is one of the world's few banks with an AAA rating from the two largest rating organisations. It has 2500 branches and accounts for 40% of savings deposits and 25% of domestic mortgages. It took control of a Dutch insurance company called Interpolis and later another company called AVCB, making the group the second biggest in the Netherlands. It has also entered into a joint venture with the leading Dutch fund management group Robeco. It has 19 offices abroad in ten countries and is active in international banking generally.

In Japan, there are cooperative banks in agricultural fishery and forestry. There is a Central Cooperative bank for Agriculture and Forestry called the Norinchukin Bank. There are also a large number of commercial credit cooperative banks.

In the UK, there is only one cooperative bank, called the Cooperative Bank. It works closely with the general retail cooperative movement and has normal banking facilities. However, its share of total UK bank deposits is less than 1%.

Outside the EU, Finland has many cooperative banks (over 300) with their own central bank, the Okobank.

Mortgage banks   Some economies have a special sector dealing with mortgages and some do not.

The most obvious example of a special sector is the UK's *Building Societies*. Originally they were associations which came together to build houses and then disbanded. Gradually, they became permanent mutual organisations, collecting small high street savings and using the money to fund domestic mortgages. There were over 2000 in 1900, but only about 80 today in a movement dominated by the larger societies. The Building Societies Act of 1986 deregulated them to the extent of allowing them to offer cheque accounts and unsecured loans as well as a variety of other services. However, the amount of such business that they can do is strictly limited. The Act also allowed them to become a public limited company if the members agreed. Abbey National took advantage of this and went public in 1989, becoming the UK's fifth biggest bank in asset terms. By 1995–6 the movement was undergoing considerable change. Lloyds Bank acquired the Cheltenham and Gloucester, Abbey National acquired National and Provincial and the merged Halifax/Leeds Societies, along with the Alliance and Leicester, the Woolwich and Northern Rock, all revealed plans to go public and become a bank. Others, like the Britannia, defended the 'mutual' principle and announced loyalty bonuses for their longer term members.

Germany has mortgage banks (Hypothekenbanken), often subsidiaries of other banks, and a few building societies (Bausparkassen). The mortgage banks fund the mortgages with a special bond – the Pfandbriefe. The Netherlands has several mortgage banks which are subsidiaries of other banks (for example, Rabobank) or of insurance companies. Denmark has a small number of Mortgage Credit Associations which sell bonds on the Stock Exchange and hand the proceeds to the borrower whose property is security for the bond.

The specialists in mortgages in the US are the Savings and Loan Associations who were deregulated in 1981. Unlike the UK's 1986 Building Societies Act, however, prudent restrictions on new powers were not imposed and the movement has hit serious trouble, as mentioned earlier.

Giro banks   Let's start by considering this word 'Giro'. It comes from the Greek 'Guros', meaning a wheel or circle. The circle in finance is the passing round of payments between counterparties.

We find references to this term in early Italian banking. In the Middle Ages there were important trade fairs for the cloth industries of France and Flanders. Merchants would incur debts and any not settled could be carried forward to the next fair. Gradually, the merchants who were bankers began to offer a clearing system. One can imagine the circle of debt as – trader *A* owes *B* who owes *C* who owes *D* who also owes *A* (see Figure 2.1).

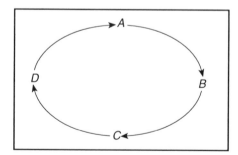

Figure 2.1   *The circle of debt*

The bankers set up a clearing system known as 'giro di partita' – the giro of ledger entries. In 1619, the state of Venice set up a Banco del Giro to speed up payments to the state's creditors. The bank also issued interest bearing bonds to creditors and a secondary market gradually developed.

In the modern age, the word *giro* crops up in two connections. In the first case, it simply refers to money transfers by which an individual sends a giro slip to their bank instructing them to pay a sum of money to, say, the electricity or gas company. In Germany and Holland this is far more likely than sending a cheque directly to the company.

The second use is in the term *Giro bank* and the use of post offices to help those without a bank account pay their bills. The idea began in Austria in 1883. Those without bank accounts could pay a variety of bills at post offices and the money was then transferred to the payee. There is a Post Office Giro in Belgium and the UK set up a Girobank in 1968 which was sold to a building society in 1990. It is difficult to separate out postal giro from the general concept of a *postal bank*. This itself may be known instead as the *National Savings Bank*. In the UK, the Post Office Savings Bank, which was set up in 1861, became the National Savings Bank in 1969. The general idea is to encourage small savings rather than letting the bank engage in lending. France has a 'Caisse Nationale d'Epargne'; Ireland has a Post Office Savings Bank; in Finland we find the very important Postipankki, which handles much of the government's finances and Spain, too, has a Post Office Savings Bank. In the Netherlands, the Post Office Bank and the National Savings Bank merged to become Postbank, itself later merging with the NMB Bank and now known as ING Bank.

Due to the trend for deregulation, post office banks are flexing their muscles and seeking expanded powers. In May 1992, some German commercial banks took the Postbank to court, accusing it of unfair competition. The Belgian Bankers' Association has claimed that the post offices' financial activities are subsidised and, in France, opposition from the banks has stopped the Post Office from offering a form of current account. However, the Post Office there has sold mutual funds (SICAVs) very successfully. Spain's Caja Postal has gone into leasing, asset management and property consulting. It has now been drawn together with other state-owned financial institutions into a single body called Argentaria.

Credit unions The idea of credit unions goes back to 1849 in Germany when a local mayor formed a union to help people cope with debt and poverty. By the early 1900s, the idea had spread to Australia, Canada, New Zealand, Ireland, the UK and the US. The general idea is that a local credit union has some common bond – possibly membership of a church or place of work. The members save money and are allowed to borrow a sum of money, usually a multiple of the money saved. There may be tax privileges. For example, in the US, credit unions don't pay federal income tax. There are 15 000 credit unions in that country and 60 million members. In the UK, there are 400 credit unions with 50 000 members, including British Airways and the London Taxi Drivers. In Ireland, 23% of the population are members. In Japan, there are some 460 credit associations. They also enjoy tax privileges.

OTHER BANKING TERMINOLOGY

There are one or two other terms which, perhaps, should also be explained.

Clearing banks   This term is applied to the banks which are most involved in the system for clearing cheques. They will be the large domestic banks who are heavily into retail banking. Banks which offer cheque book facilities and have smaller volumes will arrange for one of the larger clearing banks to handle clearing of their cheques. Usually, each bank will clear its own cheques, that is, cheques drawn by a customer of the branch in favour of another customer of the same bank. Cheques drawn in favour of other banks are sent to a central clearing system where they can be gathered together and sent to each bank for posting to individual accounts. The customer account number, bank branch code and cheque number are already encoded on the bottom line of the cheque. It only needs the amount to be encoded for the cheques to be sorted using electronic sorting machines.

Electronic clearing is becoming increasingly important for direct debits, standing orders, salary payments, supplier payments and high value payments made electronically by banks for corporate customers.

State or public banks   This term is used for banks owned by the state which are not central banks but carry out some public sector activity. State-owned Post Office or National Savings Banks are one example. Sometimes others are set up to lend to industry sectors or local authorities or provide finance for exports and imports. Germany has Kreditanstalt für Wiederaufbau, which was set up in 1948 to help finance reconstruction after the war and is now a general development bank for small to medium size companies. France has Crédit Local de France, which makes loans to local authorities, and Crédit Foncier, which finances house purchase and property development. Italy has Crediop which finances public utilities and makes other industrial loans. In Spain, a major change has taken place which has resulted in the formation of one body from various state banks:

❏	Banco Exterior	the finance of foreign trade
❏	Banco Hipotecario	subsidised loans for social housing
❏	Banco de Credito Agricola	loans for agriculture and forestry
❏	Banco de Credito Local	loans for local authorities
❏	Banco de Credito Industrial	loans for industry
❏	Caja Postal de Ahorros	post office savings banks.

These were all united in 1991 as Corporacion Bancaria de Espana which operates under the marketing name of 'Argentaria'.

The position regarding state banks is changing somewhat as full or partial privatisation takes place (for example, Crédit Local de France and Argentaria).

Banks which have a role in lending to specialist industries are also known as *industrial banks*.

International banking This involves a variety of activities such a deposits/loans to nationals in foreign currencies and to non-nationals in the domestic currency. It also covers cross-border operations, trade finance, foreign exchange, correspondent banking, international payments' services, international finance with syndicated loans and/or Euromarket instruments, dealing in precious metals, international corporate advice and corporate risk management facilities on an international basis.

Clearly, the terms we have been using are not mutually self-exclusive – they overlap. International banking with a syndicated loan, for example, is commercial wholesale banking. International banking through a Eurobond issue is investment banking and largely wholesale, but with sales at times aimed at *retail* investors.

A BANK'S BALANCE SHEET

Before proceeding any further into this chapter, we must look at a bank's balance sheet and the terminology which is used. Then we will be in a position to explain concepts like 'creation of credit', 'liquidity' and 'capital ratio'.

In this section and later, we use the terms 'assets' and 'liabilities'. A liability in accountancy does not have the meaning 'disadvantage' as it does in everyday English. It is money for which the entity concerned is *liable*, for example, if money is borrowed, the borrower is *liable* to repay it, hence it is a liability.

Looking at a bank, the *liabilities* show us where the money comes from.

There are three key sources:

❏ Shareholders' equity plus additions from retained profit
❏ Deposits (the largest figure)
❏ Borrowings (for example, a bond issue).

The liabilities, thus, represent claims *against* the bank.

The first category is called 'shareholders' funds' and is the main source for a bank's *capital*. This is the part of the liabilities that can be relied upon because, being the owner's money, there is no date for paying it back. The bank has the indefinite use of the money. If times are hard, even the dividend may be passed. Deposits, on the other hand, can be withdrawn, a large part without notice, and borrowings have to be repaid and interest payments met.

Assets represent how this money has been used, for example:

❏ Notes, coin
❏ Money market funds
❏ Securities
❏ Lending (the largest figure)
❏ Fixed assets, for example, property.

The assets, thus, represent claims by the bank against others. Assets and liabilities will always balance.

Banks list assets in descending order of liquidity:

❑   Cash
❑   Balances at the central bank
❑   Money at call and short notice
❑   Bank and trade Bills of Exchange
❑   Treasury bills
❑   Securities
❑   Advances to customers
❑   Premises and equipment.

Its liabilities would be:

❑   Ordinary share capital
❑   Reserves
❑   Retained profits
❑   Customers' deposits
❑   Bond issues
❑   Other borrowing
❑   Trade creditors
❑   Tax.

The balance sheet is laid out with assets on the left and liabilities on the right (see Figure 2.2).

The profit and loss account shows how a bank has traded during a particular *period*, such as 1 month, 3 months, or a year – for example: 'Profit and Loss Account for the year ended 31 December 1992'. Note that the balance sheet shows what the bank is worth at a particular *point* in time, for example: 'Balance Sheet as at 31 December 1992'.

Revenue is contrasted with costs and the resulting difference is the profit or loss. After paying dividends and tax, the remaining profit is transferred to the balance sheet and added to the shareholders' funds, thus *increasing capital*. Equally, a loss will *reduce capital*.

One of the assets listed above was 'Balances at the central bank'. Most central banks insist that banks within the country maintain certain reserves with it. Usually, these are substantial sums and help the central bank in its control of monetary policy and what is called the 'money supply'. We shall examine this in more detail in Chapter 3.

Even where the reserves are very tiny (for example, in the UK only 0.35% of eligible liabilities), the main clearing banks have to maintain far higher working balances and *must not fall below these*. These balances are to cover things like the daily settlement for cheque clearing and the daily settlement for Treasury bill and bond purchases for themselves and clients for whom they are acting. There is also the total net payment by the bank's clients of taxes to the government. The government's balance at the central bank will rise – the individual bank's balance will fall.

SUMMARY BALANCE SHEET A. N. OTHER BANK As At 31/12/96

ASSETS	LIABILITIES
(that is, how liabilities have been *used*)	(that is, where the money *comes from*)
Cash	Shareholders' funds
Money market funds	Deposits
Other securities	Borrowings
Lending	

Figure 2.2 *Summary balance sheet*

THE CREATION OF CREDIT

As only a small proportion of deposits is drawn in cash, it follows that banks have considerable facilities to 'create credit'.

Imagine approaching a bank (not your own) to request flexible lending facilities up to $2000. The bank opens an account and sends you a cheque book. You wander down the high street writing cheques to the value of $2000. The recipients pay the cheques into their accounts and the amounts are credited to them 3 days later and debited to you. The bank has created $2000 of expenditure that did not exist 1 week earlier. The suppliers of the goods have $2000 in bank accounts – disposable money. Where did it come from? Not from you, because you didn't have any. It came from the bank that allowed you to overdraw to the value of $2000 – the bank has created money. Bank lending = spending and excessive spending may mean unacceptable inflation and imports the nation can't afford.

Banks' credit creation has several implications:

1. A reminder that banking depends on confidence
2. Governments and central banks will want to control it in view of the implications for inflation and imports
3. Banks will need internal controls called 'liquidity ratios'
4. An external control enforced by bank supervisors called 'capital ratios' is required.

Banking Depends on Confidence

The system works because we have confidence in it and accept cheques in payment of debt. Where is the gold and silver behind this? Of course, there isn't any. Money is as much an entry on a computer disk as anything else.

The Money Supply

Governments and central bankers will want to control credit and measure the 'money supply'. This figure is a measure of bank deposits as being the best guide to bank lending. The figure for deposits sounds like a motorway – M3 or M4, depending on the country. Another measure is M0 – notes and coin in circulation, plus banks' till money and balances with the central bank. Add to this the private sector's deposits at banks and you have the essential elements of M3 or M4. Control of inflation by controlling these monetary aggregates is part of what is meant by 'monetarism', the economic doctrines of the American economist, Milton Friedman. In the UK, the Conservative government of 1979 used them as a rather rigid instrument of government policy in the early 1980s. (Charles Goodhart, one time economic adviser to the Bank of England, has coined 'Goodhart's Law'. This says that 'when an economic indicator is used as an instrument of government policy, its behaviour then changes'!)

It was concern over failure to control the money supply that led the Bundesbank to raise interest rates in December 1991 and then raise the discount rate further in July 1992. Later, rates fell as inflation came under control.

The central bank has a number of weapons – raising mandatory reserves which banks must deposit with it, raising interest rates and general 'open market operations', for example, selling more government paper than it needs to in order to drain credit and keep monetary conditions tight. It may also not be as quick as usual to help banks' liquidity when acting as 'lender of last resort' (see Chapter 3).

Liquidity Ratios

Bankers have internal controls based on 'liquidity ratios'. They know that it would be folly to take their deposits and lend 100% as 3 year personal loans. They have internal rules on what percentage of deposits should be held as cash, what percentage at call and short notice, what percentage as short-term securities (Treasury bills, bills of exchange) and so on. The controls may also be *external* and laid down by the central bank as they are in Spain, where they are called *Coeficientes*. This is why banks list assets in *descending* order of liquidity, that is, the most liquid assets (cash) are first. Cash is particularly important as banks must keep a given percentage to meet cash withdrawals. In the case of the new bank accounts totalling $2000 which we discussed above, if cash withdrawals average 5%, then the bank must have $100 cash to back these accounts.

The Capital Ratio

Capital ratio is the external control imposed by bank supervisors in the interests of prudence. It is a major issue in banking and we need to look at it in more detail.

CAPITAL RATIO

The Basic Concept

The basic concept has been around for hundreds of years. Bankers lend money and some people will default. Does this mean that the banks cannot repay depositors? The buffer, the money the bank can rely on, is its capital. Thus, there should be a prudent relationship between capital and lending – that is the capital ratio.

All this assumes that the bank has not made things worse by an excessive exposure to a few key borrowers. In 1984, for example, it was found that Johnson Matthey Bank in the UK had lent the equivalent of 115% of its own capital to just two borrowers. This loophole was plugged in the 1987 Banking Act. If exposure to one borrower exceeds 10% of capital, the Bank of England must be informed. Before exposure can exceed 25%, Bank of England permission must be obtained. Exposure to industry sectors (for example, textiles) and countries is also monitored. All central banks have 'large exposure' controls.

The older idea of relating capital to *lending* has to be extended to capital to *assets* in the modern age. However, all assets are not the same for this purpose – for example, what is the default risk with cash? Surely the answer is 'none'. Thus we end up with the concept of 'risked weighted assets'. A normal bank loan is, therefore, weighted 100%, that is, a loan of $500 000 counts as $500 000 for this purpose. However, cash is weighted at 0%, and a cash balance of $10m thus becomes $0 for risk weighting purposes. Secured lending has a weight of 50% (see Table 2.3).

The capital ratio is thus determined by applying the ratio to the figure of risk weighted assets. If the agreed ratio were 10%, then, from the figures in Table 2.3, capital must be $10\% \times \$1260m = \$126m$.

The Basle Committee

However, every central bank had different rules. The Group of 10 nations (see Chapter 3) together with Luxembourg, set up a 'Committee on Banking Regulations and Supervisory Practices' to draw up uniform rules. The Committee meets at Basle in Switzerland under the auspices of the Bank for International Settlements (BIS). It is thus typically (but not accurately) called the 'Basle' Committee or 'BIS' Committee. In 1988, after several years of discussion, the Committee announced agreement on uniform rules for capital ratio.

Table 2.3   *Risk weighting example*

Assets	Value $m	Risk weighting %	Risk weighted value $m
Cash	50	0	—
T. Bills	100	10	10
Mortgages	500	50	250
Loans	1000	100	1000
Total	1650		1260

The first stumbling block was the definition of 'capital'. The Committee came to a compromise – the 'best' capital is called 'Tier 1' and must be at least half the necessary figure. It consists of:

❑   Shareholders' equity
❑   Retained profits
❑   *Non-cumulative* perpetual preference shares.

'Tier 2' capital is the remainder and would include:

❑   *Cumulative* perpetual preference shares
❑   Revaluation reserves
❑   Undisclosed reserves
❑   Subordinated term debt.

(For a discussion of preference shares, see Chapter 6. Subordinated debtors come after other debtors in the event of liquidation.)

The capital ratio itself is 8% and applies from 1 January 1993.

The risk weighting figures were agreed and we gave examples of some of these above. While unsecured loans are 100%, loans to or claims on OECD governments and sometimes other governments as well are weighted 0%. Thus loans to Saudi Arabia have not been given the full 100% weighting, but Kuwait, in raising a large syndicated loan for reconstruction of $5.5bn in Autumn 1991, was weighted 100%.

The risk weightings are not only applied to balance sheet items, but to *off-balance sheet* items that involve risk – loan guarantees, standby letters of credit, documentary letters of credit, derivative products such as options, futures, swaps and FRAs (all explained in later chapters).

The banks are very conscious of capital ratio rules and have tightened up the discipline regarding profit as a return on capital. If a transaction needs capital backing under the new rules, then the profit on the transaction must meet the bank's target for profit on capital employed. Some consultants call this 'RORAC' – 'return on risk adjusted capital'. While there is a capital requirement for off-balance sheet items, it is not as onerous as for on-balance sheet items and thus adds to the attraction of these transactions. For example, documentary letters of credit backed by documents giving title are weighted at 20%. A general standby letter of credit not related to a specific transaction is weighted 100%, but a standby letter of credit which is so related is weighted at 50%. As capital has a cost, the bank will ensure that the charges to the client cover the *cost of capital* as well as any other costs.

For their results for the year ending March 1996, Japanese banks finally recognised their true position regarding bad debts and began to write these off against profit. The three long-term credit banks, the seven trust banks and seven out of the top eleven city banks all declared a loss. As a result, some of the capital ratios were close to the minimum.

Increasing Capital Ratio

If a bank does not have enough capital to meet the new requirements, what can it do? There are essentially only two possibilities:

(a) Find more capital
(b) Reduce assets.

(a) *Finding more capital* could involve a rights issue, reducing dividends (to increase retained profit), raising money through other forms of capital, for example, *non-cumulative* perpetual preference shares or perpetual variable rate notes. Tier 1 capital must, of course, be 4% and there is a limit to the value of certain Tier 2 items that can be used. Examples of the above include the rights issue by Midland Bank in 1987, followed by selling 14.9% of new shares to the Hongkong and Shanghai Bank. We have also had non-cumulative perpetual preference share issues from National Westminster, the Bank of Scotland and the Royal Bank of Scotland (in dollars). Several German banks have issued their own type of cumulative preference share (genusscheine) to count as Tier 2 capital. National Westminster, NAB, Banco Santander, the Royal Bank of Scotland, Crédit Lyonnais and others have all issued perpetual variable rate notes to count as Tier 2 capital.

(b) *Reducing assets* could involve selling off subsidiaries, selling off loans to other banks or converting assets into securities – *securitisation*.

Examples of selling subsidiaries include Midland Bank selling the Clydesdale in 1987, the British banks owning the Yorkshire Bank selling it in 1990 (they had owned it since 1911!) and Citicorp selling several overseas subsidiaries.

We shall meet the word 'securitisation' again in Chapter 6. In that context it means the change in emphasis in international banking markets from 1982, by which borrowers began to borrow on the capital markets by issuing bonds rather than by having a bank loan. The usage in our current context is similar, but here we take an existing loan off the balance sheet by converting it into securities. The best and most common example is selling off mortgage loans as mortgage bonds (pioneered by Salomon Bros in the US). Other examples include converting car loans into notes or bonds and converting credit card receivables into bonds (frequent issues by Citicorp). Another possibility is simply to bundle bank personal loans together and sell them as bonds or shorter-term notes, with the loans as the assets backing the security. The legalities are difficult, usually involving a separate purpose vehicle to issue. Guarantees from insurance companies or other financial entities are involved and the idea is for the original lender to so weaken the link to the loan that it no longer counts for capital ratio purposes. The issuer usually continues to administer the loan, and will receive a fee for doing so.

CENTRAL BANK REPORTING

All banks operating within a country make detailed reports to the central bank as part of its supervisory role, even if any action to be taken will be carried out by a separate supervisory body.

Reports will be sent at varying frequencies – monthly, quarterly, 6 monthly, annually – and will cover the following items:

- ❑ Maturity of assets, that is, liquidity
- ❑ Large exposures
- ❑ Foreign exchange exposure
- ❑ Capital expenditure
- ❑ Assets/liabilities for overseas residents
- ❑ Assets/liabilities by foreign currencies
- ❑ Balance Sheet
- ❑ Profit and Loss.

Foreign banks operating in a country operate as either branches or as legal entities. If only operating as a branch, no reports on capital will be made as the capital is held by the parent company.

THE SECOND BANKING DIRECTIVE

This came into effect on 1 January 1993. The original intention of the Community had been to achieve a full harmonisation of banking legislation throughout the EU. This has now been abandoned. Instead, under the Second Banking Directive, banks in the EU will continue to be authorised and regulated by their own national authority. This will be accepted as adequate for granting them freedom to operate throughout the Community. They will thus acquire a *European Banking Licence* or *Passport*. This will allow them to engage in investment as well as commercial banking, since 'universal banking' has always been the tradition in Europe. In countries where this has not been so, their banks will now be free to engage in activities throughout the Community that they may still be prevented from doing in their own country. (The specific Investment Services Directive is discussed in Chapter 9.)

Third country banks can operate within the EU if 'reciprocal treatment' is afforded in their country to EU member banks. At first this was taken to mean that they must be allowed to engage in the same activities as third country banks are permitted to do within the Community. This led to protest from America (where commercial and investment banks are traditionally separated). In response to this, reciprocity is now defined as equal 'national treatment' – that is, EU banks being treated the same as local banks in third countries. But, in individual cases, the Community may still insist on 'equal/comparable access'.

The EU's Banking Federation has drawn up a list of 26 non-EU countries which impose restrictions on the operation of foreign banks within their country. Should these countries continue to withhold 'equal national treatment' they may find their banks banned from operating within the Community.

MAJOR WORLD BANKS

The UK *Banker* magazine for July 1996 published an analysis of the world's largest banks. Although 'large' was defined by holdings of Tier 1 capital, the asset figures were also disclosed.

We shall, therefore, first look at a 'Top 20' sequence of the world's biggest banks in *asset* terms (Table 2.4).

The Japanese provide nine of the world's Top 20 (and seven out of the top 10!). Just as they have become powerful internationally in consumer durables and motor cars, they have also become dominant in world finance. Looking at the figures in Table 2.5, it can be seen that the Japanese accounted for 25% of international bank lending in 1994, although in 1991 the figure was as high as 31%.

Looking at *nationality* in the Top 20 we find the following:

Country	Banks
Japan	9
Germany	2
France	4
UK	1
Netherlands	1
China	1
Switzerland	2

Table 2.4   *Top 20 world banks, by assets, 1996*

Bank	Rank	Assets $bn
Bank of Tokyo/Mitsubishi	1	713
Deutsche	2	503
Sanwa	3	501
Sumitomo	4	499
Dai Ichi Kangyo	5	498
Fuji	6	487
Sakura	7	478
Norinchukin	8	429
Crédit Agricole	9	386
Industrial and Commercial Bank of China	10	373
IBJ	11	361
CS Holdings	12	359
HSBC Holdings	13	351
ABN–Amro	14	341
Crédit Lyonnais	15	339
Union Bank of Switzerland	16	336
Dresdner	17	332
Société Générale	18	326
BNP	19	325
Tokai	20	298

Source: *The Banker* (July 1996).
(Includes Bank of Tokyo/Mitsubishi; not merged in original table)

The Japanese have a high propensity to save (remember the 'Debt Merry-Go-Round' in Chapter 1?) and a huge balance of payments surplus. Until recently, the Japanese were even more dominant than they are today. Their share of international bank lending was 37% in 1989. The collapse of the Stock Exchange index and falling property values have caused them to withdraw a little from the international scene.

Table 2.5 *International banking shares, by nationality of bank, end 1994*

	%
Japan	25.0
Germany	15.3
US	11.1
France	10.3
Switzerland	6.6
Italy	6.0
UK	5.6
Netherlands	3.5
Others	16.6
	100.0

Source: BIS Basle.

The other surprise, looking at Table 2.5, is to see the US not providing any bank out of the Top 20. We have to realise that banking is very fragmented in the US where there are no less than about 12 000 banks! Unlike Europe, branch banking across the US is unknown. The McFadden Act of 1927 limited banking activities to within a single state; some local state legislation limits it to one branch in one *city* within the state! The Act, however, was repealed in 1994 by the US Interstate Banking and Banking Efficiency Act which will permit full interstate banking by 1997 unless local state laws prevent it. Many states did not wait for Congress but changed their laws and allowed reciprocal banking facilities with other states. This has led to a growth in so-called 'Regional Banks'. A good example is Bank One in Columbus, Ohio, which now operates in twelve states due to a variety of acquisitions and taking advantage of new state laws. Another example is the NCNB from Carolina which, due to mergers and acquisitions, has become NationsBank and one of the biggest in the US with 1700 offices in nine states.

(The merger of Chemical Bank with Chase Manhattan is not included in the above figures as it took place legally in March 1996, after the closing date for *The Banker* figures. The assets of the combined bank are £304 billion.)

Having looked at international bank lending by nationality of bank, it may be interesting to see it by *centre* – that is, from where did the loan emanate? (Table 2.6)

Table 2.6   *International banking shares, by centre, end 1994*

	%
UK	16.9
Japan	14.2
US	7.5
France	7.4
Germany	6.6
Switzerland	5.7
Asian Centres	14.6
Offshore – Caribbean	9.0
Other	18.1
	100.0

Source: BIS Basle.

We see that, although the UK banks' share was only 5.6%, London accounts for slightly more international bank lending activity than Tokyo. It has a huge population of foreign banks – 541 at the end of 1995.

Finally, we can look at the original sequence of banks in *The Banker* magazine, that by *capital* (Table 2.7).

The change of sequence to capital (it used to be assets) came about because of the so-called Basle Agreement in 1988. *The Banker* magazine decided that capital was the important thing for the future, and not assets.

There is an interesting change of sequence. Citicorp is fifth and the Swiss Bank Corporation is 17th, but neither appear in the top 20 by assets at all. The Union Bank of Switzerland is fourth, but only 16th by assets.

Table 2.7   *Top 20 world banks by capital*

Ranking		Strength: Tier 1 Capital $m
1	Bank of Tokyo/Mitsubishi	27 836
2	HSBC Holdings	21 445
3	Crédit Agricole	20 836
4	Union Bank of Switzerland	19 908
5	Citicorp	19 239
6	Dai Ichi Kangyo	19 172
7	Deutsche	18 937
8	Sumitomo	18 605
9	Sanwa	17 676
10	Sakura	15 961
11	Fuji	15 443
12	BankAmerica	14 820
13	CS Holdings	13 751
14	ABN–Amro	13 372
15	Groupe Caisse d'Epargne	12 667
16	IBJ	12 497
17	Swiss Bank Corporation	11 773
18	National Westminster	11 501
19	BNP	11 453
20	Chemical	11 436

Source: *The Banker* (July 1996).
(Includes Bank of Tokyo/Mitsubishi; not merged in the original table.)

SUMMARY

Supervision of banks may be carried out by the central bank (UK) or other supervisory bodies (France, Germany, Japan, US).

Central banks, commercial banks and investment banks are the main types of bank. There are also savings banks, cooperative banks and mortgage banks but, with increasing deregulation, the differences are generally weakening. Finally, there are credit unions.

On a bank's balance sheet, the *liabilities* are shareholders' equity, deposits and borrowings. The *assets* are cash, money market deposits, securities, loans and fixed assets like buildings.

The shareholders' equity (including retained profits) is at the heart of the bank's *capital*.

International rules limit the amount of a bank's lending to the capital it has.

In an era where money is no longer tied to gold or silver, the ease with which a bank can advance money is called *creation of credit*. It is limited by liquidity rules, capital ratio rules and central bank monetary policy.

The Second European Banking Directive allows banks in the EU to open branches anywhere in the EU under licence from their *home* central bank.

Appendix 1

MAJOR BANKS ACROSS THE WORLD

Main European Banks

AUSTRIA	Creditanstalt Bankverein
	GiroCredit Bank
	Bank Austria
BELGIUM	Generale De Banque
	Banque Bruxelles Lambert
	Kredietbank
	ASLK–CGER
DENMARK	Den Danske Bank
	UNI Bank Denmark
FINLAND	Merita Bank (the merger of Kansallis and UBF)
	Postipankki
FRANCE	Banque Nationale De Paris
	Crédit Agricole
	Crédit Lyonnais
	Société Générale
GERMANY	Deutsche Bank
	Dresdner Bank
	Westdeutsche Landesbank
	Commerzbank
GREECE	National Bank of Greece
	Commercial Bank of Greece
	Agricultural Bank of Greece
	National Mortgage Bank of Greece
HOLLAND	ABN–AMRO
	Rabobank
	ING Bank

| IRELAND | Allied Irish |
| | Bank of Ireland |

ITALY	Banca Nationale del Lavoro
	Banca Commerciale Italiana
	Istituto Bancario San Paolo di Torino
	Cariplo

| LUXEMBOURG | Internationale à Luxembourg |
| | Générale du Luxembourg |

NORWAY	Den Norske Bank
	Christiana Bank
	Union Bank of Norway

PORTUGAL	Caixa Geral de Depositos
	Banco Portugues do Atlantico
	Banco Totta e Acores
	Banco Espirito Santo & Commercial

SPAIN	Banco Central – Banco Hispano Americano
	Banco Español de Credito
	Banco Bilbao Vizcaya
	Banco Santander
	La Caixa
	Corporacion Bancaria de España – Argentaria

SWEDEN	S. E. Banken
	Svenska Handelsbanken
	Nordbanken

SWITZERLAND	Union Bank of Switzerland
	Swiss Bank Corporation
	Crédit Suisse

TURKEY	TC Ziraat Bankasi
	Turkiye Is Bankasi
	Turkiye Emiak Bankasi
	Akbank

UNITED KINGDOM   HSBC Holdings
                      National Westminster Bank
                      Barclays Bank
                      Lloyds Bank
                      Abbey National

US and Japan

UNITED STATES   Chase Manhattan (merged with Chemical Bank)
                      Citicorp
                      Bank America
                      J.P. Morgan
                      Bankers Trust
                      NationsBank
                      First Chicago/NBD
                      First Union/First Fidelity
                      Bank One
                      Wells Fargo

JAPAN   Bank of Tokyo/Mitsubishi
                      Dai Ichi Kangyo
                      Fuji
                      Sumitomo
                      Sanwa
                      Norinchukin
                      Industrial Bank of Japan
                      Tokai
                      Sakura
                      Long Term Credit Bank

Appendix 2

INTERNATIONAL BANKING COOPERATION AND MERGERS

(Some of the following are full-scale mergers; some are merely arrangements to cooperate)

1   Deutsche Bank–Morgan Grenfell

2   Mitsui–Taiyo Kobe (now Sakura)

3   Banco de Bilbao–Banco de Vizcaya

4   La Caixa–Barcelona Savings Bank

5   ABN–AMRO Bank (acquired Hoare Govett later)

6   NBM–Postbank (now ING Bank, acquired Baring Bros later)

7   Hongkong and Shanghai Bank–Midland Bank

8   Bank of Yokohama–majority stake in Guinness Mahon

9   Cassa di Risparmio di Roma–Banco di Santo Spirito; then a merger with Banco di Roma to form Banca di Roma.

10 National Australia Bank–Yorkshire Bank

11 Bergen Bank–Den Norske Creditbank

12 Den Danske Bank–Copenhagen Handelsbank–Provinsbanken to form the Danske Bank

13 Privatbanken–SDS–Andelsbanken to form UNI Bank, Danmark

14 Svenska Handelsbanken–Skanska Banken

15 PK Banken–Nordbanken

16 Banco Central–Banco Hispano Americano

17 Crédit Suisse–Bank Leu

18 Swiss Bank Corporation–Banc della Svizzera Italiana

19 Barclays Bank–Merck Finck

20 Barclays Bank–Européene de Banque (subsidiary of Crédit Commercial de France)

21 Chemical Bank–Manufacturers Hanover to form Chemical Banking Corporation. Later merged with Chase Manhattan, using the Chase name.

22 NCNB–C & S/Sovran to form NationsBank

23 Banco Exterior, Caja Postal and Instituto de Credito Oficial form Corporacion Bancaria de España (now trading as Argentaria)

24 Bank of America–Security Pacific

25 Austria–Österreichische Landerbank and Zentral Sparkasse to form Z-Landerbank (now Bank Austria)

26 Girozentrale–Österreichisches Credit-Institut to form GiroCredit Bank.

27 Crédit Lyonnais–BfG Bank

28 Crédit Suisse Group–Swiss Volksbank

29 CCF/BHF Bank–Charterhouse

30 Dresdner Bank–Kleinwort Benson

31 Swiss Bank Corporation–S G Warburg

32 Lloyds Bank–TSB

33 First Chicago–NBD

34 First Union–First Fidelity

35 Merrill Lynch–Smith New Court

36 Bank of Tokyo–Mitsubishi

37 Banco Santander–60% of Banesto

38 Union Bank of Finland–Kansallis (now Merita Bank, later merged with Nordbanken)

39 Bank Austria–majority holding in Bank GiroCredit

40 Svenska Handelsbanken–Skopbank (Finland)

41 Bank America–Continental

42 Fleet Financial–Shawmut National

43 Wells Fargo–First Interstate

44 NationsBank–Barnett Banks

45 Cariplo–Banco Ambrovenuto

46 Bayerische Vereinsbank–Bayerische Hypobank

47 Bank Austria–Creditanstalt

48 Swiss Bank Corporation–Union Bank of Switzerland

3 Banking (II) –
The Role of the Central Bank

HISTORY OF THE MAJOR CENTRAL BANKS

We shall begin by looking briefly at the historic background of five major central banks – those of France, Germany, Japan, UK and US.

France

The Bank of France was founded by Napoleon in 1800 to restore stability, especially in banknotes, after the turbulent years of the French Revolution. It was set up as a joint stock company. Napoleon himself was a shareholder and the top 200 shareholders elected the 'Regents', the bank's principal officers.

It was brought more firmly under government control in 1808 and this process was completed in 1936 with the appointment of bank councillors by the government. A monopoly over banknote issue was given in 1848. During the difficult financial years of 1929–30 it intervened to rescue Banque de l'Union Parisienne but allowed Banque Nationale de Crédit to go under. It was nationalised in 1945 and an Act of 1973 redefined its powers and organisation.

The Governor of the bank and two deputy Governors are appointed by executive order of the President of the Republic for an indefinite term. These three head the General Council which consists of ten people appointed for 6 years. The bank was not originally independent of the government but was given independence in 1993 anticipating the proposed European Central Bank. It has about 200 branches.

Germany

The forerunner of the German Bundesbank was the Reichsbank, founded in 1876 to 'regulate the amount of money in circulation, facilitate settlements of payments and ensure that available capital is utilised'. It was a private bank but control was in the hands of the Reich Chancellor.

The terrible experience with inflation in the early 1920s led to a Banking Act of 1924 making the Reichsbank independent of the government.

Unfortunately, as Hitler acquired more power in the 1930s he was impatient with any idea of central bank independence; this was taken away in 1937 and the Bank nationalised in 1939.

After the Second World War, the old currency, the Reichsmark, was replaced by the deutschemark. A two-tier central banking system was set up. Each of the eleven Federal States had a Land Central Bank and between them they owned a central body, the Bank Deutsche Länder. It was responsible for note creation and policy coordination. In particular, it was independent of the government.

This system was abolished by the Act of July 1957 which set up the Deutsche Bundesbank – a unified central bank. The eleven Land Banks became part of it only as regional offices. They carry out the relevant regulations in their own area.

The Central Bank Council consisted of eleven representatives from the Federal States and a central directorate consisting of the President, Deputy President, and up to eight other people appointed by the President of the Republic and the Federal Government. The President is usually appointed for an 8 year term. Unification would have added 5 more Länder representatives to the Council. It was, therefore, decided that from 1 November 1992, the 16 Länder would have 9 representatives between them. There are about 200 branch offices run by the Länder.

The primary task of the Bundesbank in law is to protect the currency. It is independent of government instructions but must support the government's policy unless it conflicts with the primary task. It has clashed with various governments but usually wins. The current President, Hans Tietmayer, succeeded Helmut Schlesinger in 1993.

Japan

A central bank, modelled on the Bank of England, was set up in 1885 and by 1889 had become the sole issuer of banknotes. The Governor and assistant Governor are appointed by the Cabinet for a 5 year term. seven executive directors are appointed by the Ministry of Finance (MoF) on government recommendation. These nine form the Executive Board.

Technically, the Bank is independent of the government. This is prejudiced to some extent by the fact that the MoF appoints so many members of the Executive Board. Also the MoF still has the main responsibility for bank regulation and supervision. As a result, in April 1996, Mr Yasuo Matsushita, the Governor, urged a review of the central bank's legal status to grant it more independence.

The Zengin system for cheque clearing and electronic payments is run by the Tokyo Bankers Association.

UK

The world's first central bank is said to be the Swedish Riksbank in 1668. However, it was the formation of the Bank of England in 1694 that more clearly showed the potential for a state bank.

The bank was set up to help the government of William and Mary raise money for the wars against the French. Merchants of London and others raised £1.2m and the bank was granted a royal charter. It was the only joint stock bank allowed. From about 1715 onwards the bank was regularly raising money for the government by the sales of government bonds. By the 1826 Banking Act, joint stock banks other than the Bank of England were allowed, which led to a big increase in the numbers of banks. An Act of 1844 effectively gave the bank a monopoly of the note issue. Baring Bros hit trouble in 1890 (after unwise loans in S. America – yes, it's all happened before!) and the Bank of England rescued the bank, using a fund to which it and other banks subscribed.

The powers of the bank were exercised in fact rather than law and the bank was a private bank until 1946. In 1946 it was nationalised and banking legislation confirmed its powers in law in 1979 and 1987. In September 1984, it rescued the Johnson Matthey Bank, buying it for £1 and putting in its own managers to run it. Events during the First World War, rather than legislation, clearly established that the bank was an arm of the government and not independent.

The bank is run by a body quaintly called the 'Court'. It is headed by the Governor and Deputy Governor, four executive directors and twelve non-executive directors. The Governor is appointed by the Prime Minister for a term of 5 years and is usually re-appointed. The current Governor is Eddie George, formerly deputy Governor.

US

In the US, the constitution of 1789 put management of the currency firmly in the hands of the Treasury and the Bank of the United States was formed in 1791. As such it pre-dates the setting up of central banks in France and Germany, although its record is not continuous. The bank was responsible for the issue of dollar bills and control of government debt.

Due to opposition, the bank's charter was not renewed in 1811 but it was started again in 1816. Bearing in mind that the US is a federal republic, doubt about the constitutional legality behind the formation of the bank led to a withdrawal of privileges in 1836 and concessions were transferred to individual state banks. As a result, the Bank of the United States went bankrupt in 1841. An Act of 1863 distinguished between banks which were licensed and regulated by the federal government – 'National' banks – and those licensed and regulated by individual states. (This is why banks like Citibank are 'Citibank NA', that is, National Association.) State banks generally gave up their note issues or converted into National banks. By 1880, there were 2000 National banks all issuing banknotes.

It was only in 1913 that the Federal Reserve System was set up with a single central bank controlling note issue and operating it through twelve Federal Reserve Districts. The Board of Governors was appointed by the President, as today. Having been appointed, the central bank makes its own decisions on monetary policy without direction from the government. In March 1996, Alan Greenspan was appointed Chairman of the Federal Reserve for a third 4 year term.

Of the key central banks we discuss here, the Federal Reserve is the one whose authority as a central body is the least clear cut. As we noted earlier, the individual states can pass laws (and do), there is the role of the Federal Deposit Insurance Corporation (FDIC), as all deposits are insured up to $100 000, the Comptroller of the Currency supervises the national banks and the Federal Home Loan Bank System supervises the Savings and Loan Associations. Finally, credit unions are regulated by the National Credit Union Administrator.

CENTRAL BANK ACTIVITIES

We can summarise typical central bank activities as follows:

- ❑ Supervision of the banking system
- ❑ Advising the government on monetary policy
- ❑ Issue of banknotes
- ❑ Acting as banker to the other banks
- ❑ Acting as banker to the government
- ❑ Raising money for the government
- ❑ Controlling the nation's currency reserves
- ❑ Acting as 'lender of last resort'
- ❑ Liaison with international bodies.

Supervision of the Banking System

We saw in Chapter 2 that legally the central bank may not be responsible for banking supervision. There may be a separate supervisory body, like the Federal Banking Supervisory Office in Germany. Indeed, this is more often the case than not. Even in these cases, however, the practical day to day supervision and collection of information from the banks will be carried out by the central bank. The amount of information to be submitted (see Chapter 2) is considerable and may often involve several bank employees as a full time job.

Usually, the central bank will issue licences and may have to take decisions about rescues. In 1984, the Bank of England rescued the Johnson Matthey Bank. In the Autumn of 1991, the Bank of Finland had to step in and rescue the ailing Skopbank, the central bank of the savings banks. In March 1992, it was the Bank of Finland which announced a series of measures to bolster confidence in the bank sector, suffering due to the unprecedented recession. On the other hand, when Norway's banking sector was in trouble in 1991, it was the Bank Insurance Fund that set up a fund of state money to support the three major banks – Christiana, Den Norske Bank and Fokus Bank. In Sweden in 1992, the Ministry of Finance carried out rescues of Nordbanken and Forsta Sparbanken and later guaranteed all obligations of the Gota bank. When the Chicago bank, Continental Illinois, was in difficulty in 1984, it was the FDIC who moved in to help, not the Federal Reserve.

Special problems were created in the case of the infamous BCCI which collapsed in 1991. It was active in many countries but registered in Luxembourg, which may not have had the resources to monitor it properly. This problem is potentially more serious now as, in the EU, a 'single passport' policy applies. This says that an EU bank can set up a branch in any EU country with a license from its *home* bank and not its *host* bank, although supervision will be carried out by the *host* central bank. However, following the BCCI collapse the G10 banking supervision committee met at BIS in Basle and formed some new international rules. In particular, they say that a central bank may refuse a license if it believes that a bank is not properly supervised by its home authority.

The Bank of England, stung by criticism over its role in the BCCI affair, pointed out that in the 6 years prior to 1992 it had quietly revoked 16 banking licences and obliged 35 banks to recapitalise, change management or merge.

Monetary Policy

The decisions on monetary policy may be taken by the government, if the central bank is not independent, or by the central bank itself if it is. In any case, the central bank will cooperate with the government on economic policy generally and will produce advice on monetary policy and economic matters, including all the statistics.

'Monetary policy' refers to interest rates and money supply which we discussed in Chapter 2. We noted that central banks can use various weapons to control money supply – interest rates, open market operations and changes in banks' reserves held interest free at the central bank. The central bank's role as 'lender of last resort' means that it can control interest rates. The mechanics are discussed in Chapter 6.

The independence of central banks has become a topical issue. In part, this is because of the proposal that the EU might have a single currency and single central bank. It has already been decided at Maastricht that the EU bank will be independent. This implies that, gradually, the central banks of the twelve constituent countries will become independent too.

What is the argument about? It is whether the fight against inflation should be left to governments influenced by political motives and party political motives. On 11 September 1996, for example, the *London Evening Standard*, discussing a possible fall in interest rates, said 'A party conference cut remains more rather than less likely'. The decision whether to cut interest rates was evidently thought to be influenced by the timing of a political party conference. The Bundesbank would be horrified at any such possibility in its own market and, indeed, the new UK Labour government in May 1997 decided to give the Bank of England independence in setting interest rates within an inflation target set by government. However, there are, of course, *political* implications as high interest may mean low growth rates and high unemployment. As a result, although the Bundesbank's policies are admired by many, in August 1992, the head of the IG Metall trade union attacked the 'uncontrolled power' of the Bundesbank and said that it paid 'extensive and excessive' attention to inflation and ignored the need for economic growth and increasing employment.

Looking across Europe, we now only see a subservient central bank in Portugal. Of the more independent central banks, the Bundesbank comes first with the Netherlands, Denmark and Ireland following. There is always the question of independence *de jure* and *de facto*. The Bank of Italy, for example, has little independence in law but in practice is widely respected due to the weak influence at the bank of party politics in a country where party politics is all important.

In early 1993, Spain, Italy and France announced plans to make their central banks independent and later did so.

Banknotes

The central bank controls the issue of banknotes and possibly, but not necessarily, coins also. Most payments these days do not involve cash but cheques, standing orders, direct debits, credit cards and so on. Nevertheless, cash is important as banks' cash holdings are a constraint on creation of credit, as we have seen.

Generally, we can say that, if the economy grows at 2%, the central bank will be willing to issue 2% more new banknotes to oil the wheels. On the other hand, less stable central banks may print banknotes to help the government. At the time of writing, there is considerable concern at the huge volume of banknotes being printed in the Russian republic – the result is, naturally, rampant inflation. The commercial banks will buy new notes at face value. The cost of printing will, of course, be far less than the face value. This special profit may go straight to the Treasury and not appear in the bank's books. The central bank will also replace used banknotes with new ones. There are local variations here. The British seem to dislike old banknotes much more than, say, the Germans. As a result, the Bundesbank replaces far fewer notes than the Bank of England.

Banker to the Other Banks

The central bank will act as banker to the other banks in the economy, as well as holding accounts with international bodies like the IMF and the World Bank. It is a common habit for the central bank to insist that the other banks hold non-interest bearing *reserves* with it in proportion to their deposits. Apart from helping the bank to make a profit, these serve as an instrument of control over money supply, as we saw in Chapter 2.

In any case, major banks will have to hold *working balances* for day to day settlement for various activities. Cheque clearing will end each day with a net sum of money owed by one bank to another or due to it. Dealings in government Treasury bills and bonds will be settled through the central bank accounts, and also tax payments. The total of a bank's clients' payments of tax will result in a fall in that bank's balance at the central bank and a rise in the government's balance.

In Germany, the banks must keep non-interest bearing reserves at the Bundesbank as laid down by the rules which apply. Deposits are divided into sight deposits, time deposits and special savings deposits. For example, under the old rules, 4.95% of time deposits must be left at the central bank, and 4.15% of savings deposits. For ordinary sight deposits (=current accounts) the percentages vary according to the total amount on deposit. Reserves for residents' deposits are different from those for non-residents' deposits. These rates had been set in 1987 and remained unchanged until 4 February 1993. At the same time as the Bundesbank announced changes to the lombard and discount rates, they announced some relaxation in the rules for reserves. The savings and time deposit rates were cut to an average of 2% but left unchanged for sight deposits. This liberated DM32bn of reserves but, at the same time, the Bundesbank released DM25bn of new 'liquidity paper' in denominations of 3, 6 and 9 months. These securities can also be purchased by non-banks and marks the continuing build up of a money market in Frankfurt. A further relaxation of rules was allowed in March 1994 and August 1995.

(For simplicity, we have talked of 'deposits'. In fact, the reserves are based on 'liabilities' in a more general sense. A bond due to be repaid by the bank is not a deposit but counts as a liability for purposes of reserve requirements.)

The working balances which major domestic banks would need to keep at the Bundesbank are part of these reserves. The actual figures are averages of the balances held at the Bundesbank during the course of a particular month and the calculation is based on the daily average of the various types of liabilities held. The result is that, at the start of the month, the banks may hold reserves less than the required amount provided they catch up later, so that the overall average is the required figure. This leads to a lot of short-term lending and borrowing in the interbank market.

By contrast, the Bank of England abolished reserve requirements of this nature in 1979. The argument is that – as there are no exchange controls – sterling can be exchanged for foreign currencies and vice-versa without constraint. As London is a huge international banking centre, attempts to control money supply by sterling non-interest bearing reserves at the central bank would simply not be effective. The only reserve held is 0.35% of stipulated liabilities – not an instrument of monetary policy but a way of 'joining the UK bank club' and helping the Bank of England to make a profit!

The main domestic banks must still maintain working balances at the Bank of England but interest is paid on these, unlike the situation in Germany.

Banker to the Government

Normally, a central bank acts as the government's banker. It receives revenues for taxes or other income and pays out money for the government's expenditure. Usually, it will not lend to the government but will help the government to borrow money by the sales of its bills and bonds (see next section).

One exception here is Postipankki in Finland. Perhaps because it is owned by the government, it is this bank rather than the central bank which handles the government's money.

As citizens pay taxes, charges are made against their bank accounts and settled through their bank's own account at the central bank. The banks' balances fall and the government's rises. This is one reason why banks must keep working balances at the central bank. Of course, as tax rebates are made, the government's balance falls and the banks' balances rise.

As Treasury bills and bonds are paid for, money is passed to the government's account. As they are redeemed, money flows back to the banks' accounts. If the central bank discounts bills of exchange to help a commercial bank's liquidity, money moves into that bank's account. As the bill is presented for payment, money is credited to the central bank. As a result, there is a constant flow of money from the banks' accounts at the central bank to the government's accounts and vice-versa.

Raising Money for the Government

The government Treasury bill and bond markets are covered in detail in Chapter 6. While sometimes the Treasury or Ministry of Finance handles government issues, it is much more common for the central bank to control this and to settle payments through accounts that banks and financial institutions have with it. This is one of the reasons why these banks must keep working balances at the central bank.

We have seen that, in 1694, the Bank of England was formed specifically for the purpose of raising money for the government.

The cumulative sum of money owed by governments for all their borrowings is called the *national debt*. Over time, the debt grows and is not, in any real sense, ever 'paid off'. Does this matter?

The first point is that, for any individual, how serious debt is depends on their income. Governments are the same. Economists compare the national debt to the national income as a ratio to see if the situation is getting worse or better. For this purpose the figure for Gross Domestic Product (GDP) is used as equivalent to the national income.

In the US, due to heavy government borrowing in the 1980s, the ratio has risen from 33% to over 50%. In the UK, the figure, which was 100% at the end of the 1960s, has fallen to just over 40%.

This relationship of national debt to GDP has become an issue in the run up to a possible European single currency and economic union.

The meeting at Maastricht in Holland in December 1991 set out criteria which must be met before a nation could join in the single currency. (This will be examined in detail in Chapter 7.) One of the criteria is that the national debt/GDP ratio should not exceed 60%. Table 3.1 shows the position at the time of Maastricht.

Table 3.1   *National debt as % of GDP – end 1996 forecast*

	%
Luxembourg	12
Britain	52
Germany	54
France	57
Austria	58
Finland	65
Spain	67
Portugal	73
Holland	78
Ireland	79
Denmark	82
Sweden	108
Italy	123
Greece	125
Belgium	138

Source: European Commission.

Inflation is also a key factor. As time goes by, inflation simply erodes the value of the debt. A national debt of $100bn in 1960 looks a quite different figure today.

Finally, to whom is the money owed? Often the government bonds and bills are owned by financial institutions and individuals in the domestic market. There will be foreign holders but they will probably not account for more than, say, 20%. This is where the position of the LDC countries is so different – they largely owe the money to foreigners and it is denominated in a foreign currency (see Chapter 6).

Is there a level of national debt that is reasonable or safe? *The Economist* (27 February–4 March 1988) had an interesting article on this subject and this quotation provides a nice summary:

> Neither economic theory nor history gives any clue as to what is the critical level of public debt ... The crucial factor is the willingness of investors to hold public debt. If they lose their appetite then, either interest rates must rise sharply or the government has to finance its deficit by printing more money and hence stoking up inflation.

Controlling the Nation's Currency Reserves

Each nation has reserves of gold and foreign currencies held at the central bank. If the bank intervenes in the market to buy the domestic currency, it will do so using foreign currency reserves. If it intervenes to sell the local currency, it will acquire foreign currencies.

The foreign exchange markets are examined in Chapter 7. We shall see that the transactions in major currencies are considerable. The dealing in sterling, to take one example, is so great that the Bank of England alone can't control the exchange rate by its buying and selling. It can, however, influence the rate by careful timing and the knowledge by market operators that the central bank is acting in the market. Under the newer arrangements for European Cooperation, several EU central banks may act together. Equally, major countries' central banks may act together as part of the arrangements of the 'Group of seven' countries (G7, see below).

In the ERM crisis of September 1992, the Bank of France is thought to have spent about 40% of its reserves defending the franc – a sum perhaps as high as FFr150bn.

Where a currency is not widely traded, the central bank will have a much better chance of controlling the rate. The central bank of Finland can control the rate for the Finnish Markka much more easily than the Bank of England can control that for the pound.

The reserves will usually include gold as well as foreign currencies.

Acting as Lender of Last Resort

This does *not* refer to the role of the bank as a periodic rescuer of banks in trouble. It refers to the fact that the central bank will help the other banks temporarily when they meet problems with their liquidity. As we have just seen, tax transactions and settlements for government securities are causing a continuous ebb and flow of money out of and into the accounts of the banks at the central bank. In all cases, they are obliged to keep minimum working balances and in most cases they must keep reserves at the central bank also, although these working balances may be part of the reserves.

The central bank smooths out the peaks and troughs by being prepared to assist the other banks with short-term help. Since the banks are ultimately dependent on the central bank, the rate of interest charged governs other interest rates. How the bank carries out this role is discussed in detail in Chapter 6.

Liaison with International Bodies

Central banks will liaise with other international financial bodies like the International Monetary Fund (IMF) and the International Bank for Reconstruction and Development (IBRD) (see Chapter 7). They also liaise with and take part in discussions at the BIS in Basle. This bank was set up in 1930. By 1929 it was evident that for Germany to pay the massive reparations imposed on it after the First World War was an impossibility and some new arrangement had to be made. The new plan which was devised was called the 'Young Plan' and part of it involved setting up the BIS which would help to transfer reparation payments and other international debts. 84% of the shares are held by 33 central banks and the rest by private shareholders. However, on 9 September 1996, the BIS announced that it was offering membership to nine other central banks, including those in areas like the Far East and Latin America.

Today, the BIS is used by some 90 central banks and can be regarded as 'the central bankers' central bank'. It handles the payments made between world banks, sponsors cooperation, handles initiatives on key topics and hosts monthly meetings of the world's bankers at its headquarters near Basle's railway station. It also holds 10% of the reserves of major world central banks.

There is far more cooperation on economic matters by the world's major powers than there was 20 years ago. Of key importance here are the periodic meetings of the seven most advanced economic nations, called the 'Group of seven' or, simply, 'G7'. The seven are US, France, Germany, UK, Canada, Japan and Italy.

G7 members meet periodically to discuss world economic and financial affairs. Central bankers play a key role in preparing for these meetings and briefing the politicians. The world's top powers had realised by early 1985 that the foreign exchange markets were so big that only concerted intervention by all the major central banks could have any effect. Worried about the dollar's inexorable rise, key central bankers led by Paul Volcker, head of the US Federal Reserve, made a secret agreement. On Wednesday morning, 27 February 1985, they struck, selling dollars simultaneously. By the end of the day, the dollar had fallen from DM3.50 to DM3.30. In the process, the foreign exchange markets experienced what can only be called 'pandemonium'.

Later, in September 1985, the predecessor of G7 (G5) called a meeting at the Plaza Hotel in Washington (G5 is G7 minus Canada and Italy). Again the agreement was to force down the dollar, and again it worked. This first international agreement on currencies since Bretton Woods (see Chapter 7) is called the 'Plaza Agreement'. In later years there were other meetings (for example, the 'Louvre Accord' in February 1987). Usually, these were designed to push the dollar *up* and were not as successful.

A wider forum for international meetings is the so called 'Group of Ten' or 'G10'; (this is G7 with the addition of Sweden, Belgium, Holland and Switzerland). The reader will not need to be a mathematical genius to see that this is eleven countries, not 10. It's all to do with Swiss neutrality: the Swiss are always there, but officially they aren't there. It's called 'G10' but actually there are eleven countries participating.

SUMMARY

The Bank of France was founded in 1800; the Bundesbank in 1957; the Bank of Japan in 1885; the Bank of England in 1694 and the Federal Reserve in 1913.

Central bank activities are:

Supervision of the banking system Where it will play a key role even if legally there is a separate supervisory body.

Monetary policy Controlling interest rates and the money supply. However, some central banks are independent in this respect (the Bundesbank) and others are less so.

Printing of bank notes and minting of coins This must be linked to the growth in the economy or inflation will follow.

Banker to the other banks Domestic banks must leave sums of money with the central bank for various clearing and settlement systems. In some countries (for example, Germany) the central bank imposes minimum *reserves* as part of monetary policy.

Banker to the government In raising money for the government, it controls the account into which the money is paid. As taxes are paid, the government balance increases and the commercial banks' balances fall. When the government spends money, the opposite happens.

Raising money for the government This usually involves the sale of short-term treasury bills and medium- to long-term government bonds. The cumulative sum of money owed for all borrowing not yet repaid is the national debt. It is usually shown as a percentage of Gross Domestic Product to see if the situation is worsening or getting better. Over time, however, inflation erodes the burden of the debt.

Controlling the nation's reserves From time to time, central banks will buy or sell their country's currency to influence the rate. If they buy it, they will use the nation's reserves of gold and foreign currencies to do so.

Acting as lender of last resort Sometimes this refers to the rescue of banks in trouble but, more generally, it is the willingness of the central bank to assist banks with liquidity problems. Usually, this means their inability to meet the necessary balance levels at the central bank (as a direct result of central bank policy!). The rate of interest involved in the transaction gives the central bank control over interest rates.

International liaison This involves cooperation with bodies like the IMF, the World Bank and the BIS, It also involves supporting international meetings called G7 and G10.

4 Banking (III)
– Commercial Banking

INTRODUCTION

Commercial banks are essentially banks which are in the classic banking business of accepting deposits and making loans. Banks like Citibank, Chase Manhattan, Dai Ichi Kangyo, Barclays and National Westminster are all commercial banks. Other banks, like Deutsche and Union Bank of Switzerland, would say that they were 'universal' banks: that is, they cover all kinds of banking, including both commercial and investment banking. In the UK, if a commercial bank carries out investment banking, it will do so through a subsidiary, for example, National Westminster Bank – NatWest Markets. In Germany and Switzerland (and to a lesser extent France, the Netherlands and Spain) they will do so within the same legal entity. In the US and Japan, commercial banks are prevented from doing investment banking by regulation (see Chapter 5).

As we saw in Chapter 2, commercial banking may be *retail* or *wholesale*. Within their own country, the large commercial banks will carry out both retail and wholesale banking. Abroad, they will concentrate on the wholesale markets.

We shall cover retail banking in this chapter. We shall also explain some areas of wholesale banking, mainly the question of bank lending. Other aspects of wholesale banking will be treated in later chapters – money markets in Chapter 6, foreign exchange in Chapter 7 and finance for trade in Chapter 8.

RETAIL BANKING

Types of Service

Retail commercial banks offer an increasing range of services to their clients. Some relate to the handling of *money* – various forms of deposit accounts and loans. Others relate to *services* – advice, custody, purchase of stocks, shares, insurance and so on. The range of products is widening as the banks react to growing competition and falling profits by seeking to make money from a variety of offerings. We hear more and more of the phrase, the 'financial supermarket'.

Retail banking tends to be dominated by a handful of domestic banks. According to figures from Merrill Lynch, the top four banks in the economy control 75% of banking assets in Holland, 60% in France and 28% in the UK.

The one exception is the US where, due to the large number of banks (see

Chapter 2), the ten biggest banks only account for 20% of deposits. In Germany and Italy, savings banks are strong competitors for deposits and, in the UK, the building societies.

Money Banking – Deposits

Payments   The most important retail banking service (and the most expensive for the banks) is the provision of money transfers by way of cheques. The typical current account enables the client to pay money in and take money out by paying in a cheque or by writing a cheque in favour of a creditor. Alternatively, a bill may be paid by completing a giro form and sending the form to the client's own bank so that money can be transferred to the creditor's account (very common in the Netherlands, Germany, Austria and Switzerland). Cheque *clearing* needs to be organised and we shall discuss this later.

Another way to take money out is to use the ATM. The insertion of a plastic card with a magnetic strip enables the account holder to draw money up to a maximum sum. There are 300 000 ATMs worldwide with 85 000 in the US and 82 000 in Europe. The UK has 20 800 ATMs, the largest number in Europe and they are used for 60% of personal cash withdrawals. France and Spain also have large numbers of ATMs. The same card may serve as a 'cheque guarantee card'. A retailer will accept a cheque up to a given maximum if the card is produced. The advantage to the retailer is that the bank guarantees to pay even if the transaction is fraudulent. In the US, there is no such system and retailers are reluctant to accept cheques ('Don't you have a credit card?'). In France also there is no such system but retailers are happier to accept cheques, as writing a cheque when there are no funds to support it is a criminal offence.

The first ATM network in Eastern Europe was set up by the Czech Komercni Bank. There are problems, however, with poor communication links and currency convertibility in many countries, although not the Czech Republic whose currency became convertible in 1995.

An alternative to the cheque for payment in a retail shop is the *debit* card. This is simply a similar plastic card with magnetic strip. Machines at the point of sale extract the customer's account number electronically and pass the data down a telephone line so that the appropriate charge can be made to the customer's account and a credit to the retailer's account. If the customer wants to make a high value purchase, they can key in a special identification number on a pad attached to the retailer's machine and the bank account is accessed to authorise the purchase. In the UK, the growing use of debit cards means that, since 1991, the volume of cheques used (3.8bn) has actually fallen for the first time since the Second World War. 1 billion purchases by debit card were made in 1995 and the UK clearing organisation estimates that this figure will double by the year 2000 (Association for Payment Clearing Services, *Annual Review*, 1995).

There is a slight variation on the debit card idea in France where they have debit cards which charge transactions a month later. Unlike a credit card, however, this is charged to the current account and the holder is expected to have funds to meet the charge.

Some interesting figures from BIS on numbers of ATMs and Point of Sale terminals are shown in Table 4.1.

Table 4.1   *Number of cash dispensers, ATMs and EFT POS terminals, end 1991*

	Cash dispensers and ATMs		EFT POS terminals	
	No of machines installed	*No of inhabitants per machine*	*No of terminals installed*	*No of inhabitants per terminal*
Belgium	1 052	9 527	32 199	311
Canada	13 175	2 068	13 300	2 048
France	16 134	3 509	203 000	279
Germany	13 750	5 840	34 673	2 316
Italy	11 571	4 995	39 175	1 475
Japan	99 011	1 252	26 359	4 704
Netherlands	3 354	4 511	4 038	3 747
Sweden	2 221	3 891	8 878	973
Switzerland	2 371	2 882	5 183	1 319
UK	17 780	3 240	190 000	303
US	85 000	2 987	88 000	2 885

Source: BIS Statistics on Payment Systems in Eleven Developed Countries.

Current accounts   The position regarding the charge to the client for providing the current account facility varies. In the present competitive environment, banks either make charges but offset them with interest on credit balances or make no charges but have free use of the credit balances. French banks are not allowed in law to make charges but many vary the amount of time to clear cheques, which can be as much as 5 days. In the UK and Spain, competition has led to payment of interest on credit balances for the first time.

Other deposit accounts usually pay higher interest but do not allow cheque facilities. Some compromise by paying good rates of interest but allowing limited cheque facilities. Time deposit accounts are also common. This may be 7 days, 1 month or 3 months. The customer is paid interest on the understanding that the appropriate period of notice will be given before drawing out money. The bank has the advantage that it can rely on the money more than it can in accounts where money can be withdrawn without notice.

Money Banking – Bank Lending

Four types of loan are common:
- ❏ Overdraft
- ❏ Personal loan
- ❏ Mortgage
- ❏ Credit card.

The *overdraft* is a popular method of borrowing in some economies. The account holder is permitted to overdraw up to a maximum sum for a given period of time, perhaps 6 months. Interest is charged on a daily basis (and at a variable rate) on any overdrawn balance.

From the customer's point of view, the overdraft is informal and can be arranged quickly; it is flexible in that the amount 'lent' will vary and can be quite economical in that, when a monthly salary is paid in, the overdrawn balance will be reduced, or even eliminated, at least for a few days.

From the banks' point of view, the overdraft is informal; the facility is reviewed at the stated time interval and, if necessary, it is repayable on demand – an implication of which many borrowers are happily ignorant!

The overdraft is common in the UK and Germany, not particularly common in France and simply not allowed as a facility in the US.

The *personal loan* is an agreement to borrow an explicit amount for an explicit period of time with a set sum repaid monthly. $1000 might be borrowed for 2 years. The rate of interest is fixed and charged on the whole amount. If the rate on the above loan was 10%, then 10% p.a. on $1000 for 2 years is $200. This results in 24 monthly repayments of $50. As some of the principal is being repaid every month, the bank is not owed $1000 for 2 years but, on the average, a much smaller sum. The result is that the 10% rate is purely nominal, the actual rate will be nearly twice this.

Mortgages   Although there may be specialised mortgage lenders, the commercial banks may offer mortgages too. The loan is secured on the property and any loan which is secured will bear a much lower rate of interest as the bank is less at risk. In some economies, banks and other mortgage lenders will not lend more than, say, 50% or 60% of the value of the property. The easy lending from 1984 to 1988 led to a colossal rise in UK house prices, followed by a subsequent fall as recession struck. The Bank of England *Quarterly Bulletin* (August 1992) estimated that 1 million householders were living in houses whose value was actually less than the mortgage loan – a concept called 'negative equity'.

Another way of lending money is the *credit card*. The two major international brand names are Visa and MasterCard. They are offered by banks, retailers and others. The plastic card, with coded information on a magnetic strip, is offered at the point of sale and the purchase charged to the credit card account. A statement is sent monthly with a given time to pay. The consumer has the choice of paying the balance in full or paying only part and paying the rest later, incurring a substantial rate of interest for borrowing the money. It is very flexible in that the card holders can choose how much to borrow and how quickly to repay. They can, of course, choose not to borrow at all but repay in full each month, with perhaps 4/5 weeks to pay at no cost.

As a result, most issuing banks make an annual charge for the use of the card. It should be borne in mind that the bank also charges the retailer a percentage for the facility. Recent years have seen a large increase in card issuers and types of card. Among the issuers are retailers, bodies like AT & T, General Motors, General Electric (US) and mutual funds. In the UK, even the Trades Union Congress has issued a card!

(Notice that the American Express card and Diners Club card are not credit cards in that they do not offer *credit*. The consumer is expected to pay the balance in full every month. They are usually called 'travel and entertainment' cards.) American Express has a separate credit card called *Optima*.

In general, credit cards are now very widely used. The acceptability of Visa and MasterCard in other countries makes them a very useful way of solving foreign currency problems when on holiday. The one country where the use of credit cards is weak is Germany where, at the end of 1995, there were only 6m credit card holders as opposed to, for example, 29m in the UK. This is due to the opposition of the banks. However, things are now changing and we are seeing banks issue credit cards, and also retailers, like Hertie who have 62 stores and mail order houses, like Quelle who have 30m customers. In part, the move is a response to credit card initiatives in Germany from a foreign bank – Banco Santander, the biggest credit card issuer in Germany. Worldwide, Visa has 300m cards and Mastercard 190m.

Home Banking

Giving bank customers facilities which can be initiated from the home deserves a special mention. The older type of home banking involves either the use of a terminal linked to the television set or a special terminal. Enquiries can be made of account balances and bills can be paid by keying in account numbers. It has made the most progress in France with a service called 'Videotex'. This is because the government decided to give a boost to communication links by supplying free 'Minitel' terminals using the television set. One early use was to make telephone directory enquiries. There are 5m Minitel subscribers. The banks can supply software allowing balance reporting, enquiry of historical data and transfer of funds to creditors' accounts. More advanced software allows portfolio management and various financial calculations.

More recently, several banks have set up a branchless service using only the home telephone as a means of communication. The banks staff an answering service for, perhaps, 12 hours per day (or in the case of the Midland Bank's First Direct, 24 hours!). The names and bank account numbers for regular suppliers (gas, electricity, telephone and so on) are set up on file and, using special security passwords, a whole banking service can be initiated using only the telephone. Money can be drawn out by using plastic cards in the parent bank's ATMs. The bank has the advantage of not having the cost of a branch network and will pay a higher than normal rate of interest on credit balances.

Examples of such systems are:

- ❑ Germany   Bank 24 (Deutsche Bank)
- ❑ UK   First Direct (Midland Bank)
- ❑ Spain   Open Bank (Banco Santander)
- ❑ France   Banque Direct (Paribas).

The Midland Bank started its First Direct service in October 1989 and by 1995 had 400 000 customers. It expects to have one million by the year 2000.

The Electronic Purse

Another development which the banks are experimenting with what is called 'the electronic purse'. This is a so-called 'smart' card which has information stored on a microchip, including a balance of cash pre-loaded onto the card. The idea is that the card may be used for a wide range of retail transactions, many of which would be too trivial for a credit card.

Perhaps the most advanced development is in Portugal, where the card can be issued by any bank and used to pay for any service anywhere. There is, of course, no need for a continuous link to a central computer system and the card can be recharged using ATM machines.

In the UK, National Westminster Bank and Midland Bank have developed Mondex, an electronic purse undergoing trials in Swindon in 1995 and 1996. Standing by to take up this idea is the Midland's owner, HSBC Holdings, which will try it in Hong Kong and the Far East, and the Royal Bank of Canada and Canadian Imperial Bank of Commerce for trials in that country.

While there have been several trials of smart cards in the US (including one for the Olympic Games in Atlanta), the most ambitious involves cooperation between Citicorp, Chase Manhattan, Visa and MasterCard. A trial will be launched for New York's affluent Upper West Side late in 1996.

At the same time, Visa, MasterCard and Europay are cooperating on agreeing global standards for chip cards. This would enable retailers and banks to create products which can be used all over the world.

Other Services

There are a number of other services which are typically offered by banks.

Securities purchases   In some countries, like Germany and Switzerland, the 'universal' bank tradition has meant that the banks dominate stock markets and the commercial banking branches have been able to offer a full service to clients.

Elsewhere, brokers have traditionally had a monopoly of stock exchange transactions and banks would act as an agent for their customers, passing the order to the broker. Today, this might still be the case but all over Europe deregulation has been the rule, starting with the UK's 'Big Bang' in October 1986. As a result, banks have been allowed either to own brokers or set up their own operations and offer their branch customers a securities service.

Securities custody Often bonds and shares are in 'bearer' format and not registered. The share certificate will say that 'the bearer' owns, perhaps, 2000 shares in Daimler Benz. The problem is that, in the event of a burglary, the burglar is now 'the bearer'! Also, since there is no register, interest payments and dividends have to be claimed, voting rights followed up and so on. The banks will, therefore, often hold the certifications for safe-keeping, claim interest payments/dividends for clients, vote by proxy, notify them of AGMs, rights issues, scrip issues and other company events. Needless to say, a fee is charged for this service!

Mutual funds These are pools of shares run by investment managers and giving the small shareholder a spread of risk. The banks often own these and part of the securities service might be the advice that the client would be better off in a mutual fund than owning shares directly. It would be no surprise to find that the fund recommended is one the bank owns! These are sold in France as SICAVs and FCPs, in the UK as Investment Trusts and Unit Trusts and as Mutual Funds in the US. The idea has spread to Spain where 'Super Fondos' are now being offered by the banks. Following the European single market initiative, the term 'UCITs' may be encountered, and this is covered in Chapter 9.

Advice The bank manager is available for advice. This may be about investments, trust funds for children, wills and similar issues. Indeed, the manager may end up as the executor for a will and trustee for funds left for children. This position as adviser puts the bank manager in an ideal position to sell the bank's products. This has caused much anguish in the UK due to the operation of the 1986 Financial Services Act. The ruling now is that either the bank manager is an agent for the bank's products or an independent investment adviser. If the former, they must inform the client of this status and are not allowed to give wide ranging advice on a range of products. If an independent adviser, they must also make sure that the client is aware of this. If they recommend the bank's product it must be clear, beyond reasonable doubt, that this is best for the client or criminal prosecution may ensue. All the UK banks and the top ten building societies (except one) have decided that their managers will be agents for the bank's products.

Safe deposits Banks provide safe deposit boxes to house jewellery, other valuable items and cash. When there is a break in and the boxes are forced open, those clients with large sums, of which the tax authorities are unaware, face a problem when making a claim!

Foreign exchange Apart from the bank's wholesale foreign exchange operations, they will provide a service for their customers' holiday needs. This will involve travellers' cheques and cash. They may also be involved in requests to transfer sums of money to accounts abroad. This has become much easier in recent years with the *Eurocheque* system. A bank client in Germany can now write out a Eurocheque in French francs and send it to a hotel as a deposit or use it to pay the bill on the spot when actually there. Eurocheques are backed by Eurocard as a guarantee card. It can also be used to draw cash at ATMs. A new organisation called Europay International has been formed to unite Eurocheques and Eurocard with a standard European debit card under the MasterCard banner and as a check to the expansion of Visa in Europe. The big three German banks are in the forefront of the new development.

Insurance Most banks are now offering insurance policies either through an association with an insurance company or through their own subsidiary. This is discussed more fully below when we look at key current issues in retail banking.

Clearing Systems

Clearing payments between banks involves *paper* clearing (that is, cheques) and *electronic* clearing. Usually, the central bank is involved but the extent of the involvement differs greatly from country to country.

In the US, the Federal Reserve runs 48 cheque clearing centres. There are also private clearing centres and arrangements made mutually between groups of banks. 30% of cheques are cleared internally by the banks on whom they were drawn; 35% are cleared by private centres and mutual arrangements and 35% cleared by the Federal Reserve.

For salaries, standing orders, direct debits and supplier payments, data is encoded electronically and sent to an Automated Clearing House (ACH). For example, having processed salaries by computer and printed payslips for the employees, a corporate will send the data on magnetic media (or send it down a data communication network) to an ACH. Here, it will be sorted electronically and passed to the relevant employees' banks so that their salaries can be credited. There are 33 ACHs run by the Federal Reserve and a few are privately operated.

All Federal Reserve System Offices are linked for balance transfers between member banks by a system called *Fedwire*. The New York Clearing Houses Association runs CHIPS, an interbank funds transfer system in New York, and used for large international as opposed to domestic dollar payments.

In France, there are over 100 provincial clearing houses in towns where a branch of the Bank of France is located. If presented within the same catchment area as the bank on which it is drawn, the cheque will usually clear on the second working day after the presentation. Outside the catchment area, the bank will clear on the fifth working day after presentation.

Six banks have their own bilateral clearing arrangements.

Electronic clearing takes place through SIT (Système Interbancaire Télé-compensation). It is run by the Bank of France, which operates nine centres but policy is decided by the Bankers' Association.

In the UK, all clearing has been controlled since 1985 by a body called the 'Association for Payment Clearing Services' (APACS). The Bank of England is simply first amongst equals. APACS runs three main systems:

❑ General Cheque Clearing (usually 3 working days in total)
❑ CHAPS
❑ Bankers' Automated Clearing Services (BACS).

CHAPS is 'Clearing House Automated Payments Systems' and is a same day interbank clearing system for electronic entries.

BACS is for salaries, standing orders, direct debits and supplier payments just like the ACHs in the US. The Bank of England, on its own initiative, announced a same day Ecu clearing and settlement system in mid-1993. It is an electronic book-entry transfer system for banks involved in Ecu denominated payments.

Cross-border clearing is a subject attracting a lot of attention. In September 1990, the European Commission published a paper on cross-border cash and electronic payments. It acknowledged that the lack of a single compatible system would be a drawback in the age of the single market.

A group of European cooperative banks have set up a system called TIPA–NET (Transferts Interbancaires de Paiements Automatisés).

Giro clearing organisations in 14 countries have set up a cross-border transfer system called Eurogiro which started in November 1992. European savings banks have set up their own network called Eufiserv with links in ten countries.

Commerzbank, Société Générale, Credito Italiano and National Westminster have started their own cross-border transfer system called Relay.

The Royal Bank of Scotland and Banco Santander have started a joint system – IBOS. This would enable a Royal Bank customer who had pesetas to transfer them to a Spanish customer's account on the same day. The system is on offer to other banks and Crédit Commercial de France and Banco de Comercio e Industria have joined as well as ING Bank and the US merged bank First Union/First Fidelity.

Finally, it might be possible to link national ACH systems like CHAPS (UK), SIT (France), SIS (Switzerland), EAF (Germany), etc.

The plethora of independent and incompatible systems does not instil confidence for the future of an efficient system for cross-border payments.

Key Retail Banking Issues

Across all the western financial markets, the commercial banks face a series of key challenges. They are:

1. Growing competition
2. Cost control
3. Sales of non-banking products
4. Use of Information Technology.

Growing competition   Banks face growing competition from:

❑ Other financial institutions
❑ Retailers
❑ Insurance companies
❑ In-house corporate facilities.

Growing deregulation has meant an increase in competition from *other financial institutions* previously precluded from offering a total banking service. This includes the Savings and Loan Associations in the US; building societies in the UK; savings banks generally; post office banks in some sectors; and mutual funds which also offer savings accounts. The competition for deposits has intensified and we see the banks in Spain and the UK offering interest on credit balances for the first time.

Retailers are often increasingly active. Sears Roebuck in the US offer cheque book facilities and loans. In Germany, the huge mail order group, Quelle, is offering a range of financial services including credit cards. In the UK, Marks and Spencer offer unsecured loans, mutual funds, 'personal equity plans' (share purchase schemes with tax concessions) and life insurance. In Italy, Benetton are part of a major financial group, Euromobiliare. In Sweden, the furniture company, Ikea, began offering current account facilities in 1995.

Insurance companies are competing vigorously for savings with schemes which link life assurance with a savings product. These often involve the use of mutual funds to improve the return on the fund. While this is not new, pressure has intensified in recent years. Some are forming banks. The Swedish Trygg Hansa launched a bank in mid-October 1995 and the UK's largest life assurance and investment group, the Prudential Corporation, has announced plans to apply for a banking licence and start by the end of 1996.

In-house corporate 'banks' are now very common – Ford Motor Credit, Renault Crédit International, ICI Finance, Gemina (the Fiat financial services group), and General Electric Financial Services, to mention a few. While the largest effect here is usually on the banks' *wholesale* business, many are active in retail finance also. The General Electric subsidiary, for example, is into consumer loans and credit cards as well as leasing, real estate, corporate finance and has assets in excess of $100 billion. The UK retailer, Burton's, put its finance subsidiaries up for sale in 1990 and the buyer was General Electric Financial Services for a sum of £180m.

Cost Control   Growing competition together with bad debt reserves due to the LDC debt crisis (see Chapter 6) and recession in domestic markets has cut bank profits and made cost reduction essential. Increasingly, the banks' annual reports are referring to their success (or lack of it) in cutting the cost/income ratio.

In retail banking, a major cost is the branch network. What we are seeing is rationalisation and branch automation. 'Rationalisation' means dividing branches into those which only deal with corporates, full service branches (offering the complete range of products) and local sub-branches, which are largely points for paying in cash and withdrawing it. 'Branch automation' involves withdrawing paperwork to regional centres and making more of the branch 'front office' for dealing with customers. Midland Bank in the UK has settled on eight key centres which have cheque sorting machines which can handle 60 000 items per hour. The 1200 people in these centres have replaced 3000 who were in local branches. The UK's TSB has taken a slightly different approach, with 70 processing centres for branch paperwork. A general response to a fall in business has been a ruthless cutting of staff in those economies where labour laws permit this.

In the US, in-store branches now exist in more than 1400 supermarkets. The First National Bank of Chicago is putting ATMs into McDonalds hamburger stores and other outlets. In Finland, the Union Bank has developed a 'Customer Service Centre' which can handle standing orders, giro transfers and bank statements. These are not only being installed in branches but warehouses, supermarkets and kiosks. In Italy, the San Paolo Bank has designed a 'Bancomat' with the aid of Olivetti. This is the automated branch with ATMs and video disc machines selling insurance and giving share quotations. Banca Commerciale Italiana has a similar scheme, the Banca Non-Stop.

Since cheques are costly to process and staff in branches are expensive, the use of ATMs and debit cards help the banks to reduce costs. Increasingly, corporates are pressed to send computer data on salaries and supplier payments to the banks' automated clearing houses in order to reduce cheque volume. In London, same day cheque clearing of local cheques used to be possible for cheques down to as little as £10 000. The minimum was slowly lifted to £500 000 and then, in February 1995, the 200 year old system was terminated. The message is clear – cheques are going out and electronics is coming in. The projection from the UK clearing body, APACS, shown in Figure 4.1, is very indicative of current trends.

The Mori opinion poll company carried out a survey of 52 bank directors in 13 European countries in early 1991. The general opinion was that telephone banking, home banking and free standing teller machines would have a major impact on the number of bank branches in the following 5 year period. It was also believed that free standing ATMs would increase in places like shopping centres and airports.

(However, an interesting report from the Boston Consulting Group in the UK, in December 1992, suggests that the benefits of closing branches may well be exaggerated. Their report is called 'Retail Banking: will pruning branches kill the tree?')

Another way of cutting costs, or getting more sales for the same costs, lies in mergers or cooperation with other banks. The list in Appendix 2 to Chapter 2 (p.38) shows the large number of mergers in recent years. Some of these are very large – Midland and Hongkong and Shanghai; Chemical Bank and Chase Manhattan; Mitsui and Taiyo Kobe (now Sakura); Bank of Tokyo and Mitsubishi (now the world's largest in asset terms). As an example of possible savings in cost, Chase/

Chemical have set a target of $1.7 billion!

In addition to those mergers, we are seeing increasing cooperation. Cooperative banks are arranging for cooperative banks in other countries to offer services to their customer when abroad. A group called 'Unico' links cooperatives in the Netherlands, France, Germany, Finland and Austria. Between them, they have 37 000 branches in these six countries. In 1990, 15 European savings bank institutions jointly launched three mutual funds, covering money markets, bonds and equities.

Banco Santander and the Royal Bank of Scotland have taken a small shareholding in each other's company. They offer mutual services to their client base, have opened a bank in Gibraltar and have set up an electronic money transfer system. Other examples of cooperation include Lloyds Bank and Banco Bilbao–Vizcaya, TSB Group and Cariplo and Portugal's BCP and Spain's Banco Popular jointly setting up a bank in France (Banco Popular Comercial).

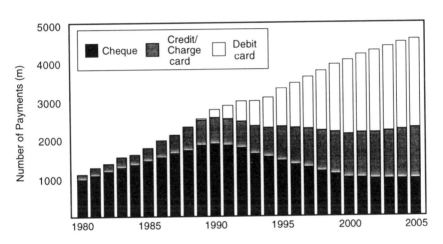

Figure 4.1 *Personal spontaneous payments*
Source: Association for Payment Clearing Services, UK.

Sales of non-banking products Another way to reduce the costs of branches is to make them more productive by selling more services. Some of these are products like insurance or mutual funds which might not have been regarded as classic banking products at one time. Other activities include acquisition of travel agencies and estate agencies.

If banking is less profitable and costs are rising, then the banks must increase their selling and marketing skills and promote a wider range of offerings than in the past. Part of the aim of branch automation is to use terminals to give access to all the information needed on the full range of the bank's services. For example, TSB have installed computer terminals with coloured screens which give the details and advantages of all the bank products and will even produce an application form.

Bank managers and staff have been sent on courses on marketing and selling. BBL (Banque Bruxelles Lambert), in Belgium, have brought in a former Unilever marketing man. In 1987, Kevin Gavaghan became Midland Bank's Marketing Director. His previous experience had been in Marks and Spencer and Thomas Cook. He quickly began to design different accounts to meet the needs of different customers. One essence of marketing is market segmentation – identifying different sectors and targeting accordingly.

Banks now look at their customer base as being divided into social sectors, each with their own needs:

- ❏ Pre-teens – can we get them used to the bank's brand with piggy bank money boxes?
- ❏ Teenagers – high spending. Banks offer savings accounts, ATM cards and merchandise discounts.
- ❏ Young marrieds – no children yet, high joint incomes but a change to come as children arrive.
- ❏ High net worth – young professionals with high incomes – worth a special approach.
- ❏ Over 50s – children have now grown up, wives are back at work, houses paid for – but retirement looms!
- ❏ Retired people – often with high incomes from personal pension plans and savings. This group has special needs.

The above breakdown has preoccupied banks in many countries, resulting in the design of new bank accounts and mail order marketing which was previously associated with consumer products.

Backing up this effort are large customer databases on computer containing not just accounting information but background details to enable the bank to sell new services, either now or later. In retail banking, 'cross-selling' has become the key phrase of the moment.

One product of obvious relevance is insurance – life assurance, endowment policies, assurance products backing mortgages, householder policies, building policies, sickness cover and so on. We are seeing three major trends here. One is full mergers with insurance companies; another is closer cooperation in cross-selling each other's products and a third is banks setting up full insurance subsidiaries.

One major merger is that of the Netherlands National Nederlanden group, the country's largest insurer, with the NMB–Postbank. The move would not have been possible but for deregulation, abolishing laws keeping banking and insurance separate. The bank is now called ING Bank. As an example of another arrangement, in the UK, Lloyds Bank bought 56% of Abbey Life, an insurance company. The Abbey National acquired Scottish Mutual. The Halifax Building Society has acquired Clerical and Medical.

Cooperation includes arrangements for cross-selling between the Swiss Bank Corporation and Zurich Insurance; Dresdner Bank and Allianz; Bancö Popular and Allianz; BNP and the French insurer UAP; Banco Santander and Metropolitan Life.

Banks who have set up full insurance subsidiaries include TSB, National Westminster, Deutsche, Barclays, Crédit Lyonnais, Banco Bilbao Vizcaya, Monte dei Paschi di Siena and Crédit Agricole. Crédit Agricole's subsidiary, Predica, has moved into France's top three insurance companies since its formation in 1987. Monte Paschi Vita, set up in mid-1991, collected L200 billion in premium income in the first 6 months. By the end of 1995, it was estimated that French banks had 56% of the life insurance market.

Regarding the cooperative ventures, one element of doubt may be creeping in. The evidence suggests that the banks are much more successful at selling insurance products than the insurance companies are at selling banking services! These links between banks and insurance have led to much use of the French phrase 'Bancassurance' and the German phrase 'Allfinanz'.

The growing effort to sell mutual funds, insurance, stocks, shares and other products has led to a rise in fee and commission income as opposed to interest. The desire to improve profits and control costs has also led to the banks increasingly charging fees for such things as arranging loans/overdrafts, an interview with the bank manager, sending an extra copy of a statement and so on.

Table 4.2 shows non-interest income as a percentage of total income and illustrates the trends dramatically. To be quite fair, however, this is not just due to *retail* trends. In the wholesale markets, banks have moved into securities trading, as deregulation has permitted it, and have increased activity in investment banking areas generally, including derivative products.

Use of Information Technology   Modern banking is unthinkable without the use of Information Technology (IT). Without it, the numbers needing to be employed in banking would have made the expansion of the last 30 years quite impossible. Many of the developments we have discussed above have IT at their heart. Branch automation, new account databases, telephone and home banking, EFT-POS, automated electronic clearing – all are essential to the banks' new strategies and all involve a large investment. Looking at the emerging markets in Central and Eastern Europe and the former Soviet Union, an enormous expenditure on computers and communications infrastructures is required as an essential first step in setting up modern banking systems. As John Reed, Chairman of Citicorp, has put it, 'money is information on the move'.

WHOLESALE BANKING

Wholesale banking includes a bank's wholesale lending, which will be discussed now, and other activities which will be covered in later chapters: money markets, Chapter 6; foreign exchange, Chapter 7; finance for trade, Chapter 8.

Table 4.2   *Non-interest earnings/Total income*

%	1980	1984	1988	1990	1991
Britain	25	33	36	40	43
Canada	25	23	30	31	31
France	19	26	35	45	n/a
Germany	31	30	39	41	39
Italy	27	35	34	30	n/a
Japan	24	18	27	46	n/a
Norway	28	33	33	26	n/a
Sweden	29	30	29	26	n/a
Switzerland	66	62	63	63	66
United States	27	31	42	47	47

Notes: Total income = net interest income + non-interest income, pre-tax.
n/a not available.

Source: Banks' annual accounts and OECD, published in the Bank of England *Quarterly Bulletin* (August 1992).

BANK LENDING

We can begin by breaking bank lending down into uncommitted facilities and committed facilities.

Uncommitted Facilities

Here there is little formal documentation and no network of various fees to be paid to the bank for setting up the facility. The bank agrees to lend money, usually on a short-term basis, but is not committed to renew the loan. The facilities are typically on a 'revolving' basis, that is, the client can repay the loan and then redraw money. There are three types:

Overdrafts   This is a great UK favourite with smaller firms. The client is allowed to overdraw up to a given maximum figure. Interest is charged daily on the overdrawn balance, most typically at bank base rates (not LIBOR) plus a given margin. The arrangement may be for, say, 6 months. The bank is not bound to renew the agreement but may well do so. There is no formal arrangement for 'paying back' as there would be with a normal loan. In addition, the overdraft is legally repayable on demand (if necessary).

Lines of credit Here the bank agrees to allow the client to borrow up to a maximum sum for periods such as a month, 3 months or 6 months. The rate of interest will be related to the interbank rate. The client can then repay and reborrow if required.

Bankers' acceptances Here the bank agrees to accept bills of exchange up to a maximum figure – 'acceptance credits'. The bank accepts a bill and may also discount it, or the client may discount it with another bank. If the bill is, say, 1 month, the client is expected to repay but may do so by means of discounting another bill. If the bank discounts the bill, it may keep it on its books or itself sell it in the discount market. The best bills are *bank* or *eligible* bills. These bills:

(a) Are recognised as top quality by the central bank.
(b) Must represent a genuine trade transaction and one of a type not excluded, for example, property and insurance.

Eligible bills are eligible for sale to the central bank in its role of 'lender of last resort'. As a result, they are highly liquid.

There are thus bills signed by a bank *not* on the central bank list and these are 'ineligible bank bills'. There are also bills signed by the trader and, therefore, 'trade bills'. However, the trader may be more creditworthy than some banks on the central bank's list! Nevertheless, the central bank still won't rediscount them.

The above three types of facility are not committed. They are also usually 'self-liquidating'. For example, a bill matures in 1 month and is repaid. The loan is often to support the working capital required for debtors and/or stocks. A swimsuit manufacturer begins producing well before the season – stocks are built up and wages must be paid. As the swimsuits are sold, cash flows in and loans can be repaid.

Committed Facilities

The loan facilities here are typically for 1 year or more. The bank is committed to lend, there are formal loan agreements and a structure of fees. There are three main types and one special case – Project Finance.

Term loans The term loan is typically up to 5 years but may be up to 7. The loan is amortised over the period, that is, the borrower pays back in stages, although there may be an initial 'grace' period. Sometimes the loan is payable in full at the end of the period – this is 'bullet' repayment. The interest is floating rate, linked to the interbank rate. The money borrowed cannot be relent when part is repaid.

Standby credit Here, the loan can be drawn down in stages or tranches without losing the availability of the undrawn section. Once repaid, however, the money cannot be reborrowed. It tends to be much shorter term than a term loan and may support other anticipated borrowings, for example, commercial paper. The standby credit may not even be drawn if the 'normal' borrowing method is successful. As an example of this type of arrangement, in 1990 Royal Insurance set up a 3 year £250m standby credit facility to replace another expiring 3 year deal. The credit was used to back the company's commercial paper programme.

The programme will be broken down into the total maximum commitment, the used amount and the unused. Thus, a $200m programme can be drawn down in tranches but repayments cannot be reborrowed. The banker's schedule as time goes by might be as shown in Table 4.3.

Table 4.3   *Drawing banker's commitment down in tranches*

		Total commitment $m	Used $m	Unused $m
1/1	Agreement	200	-	200
2/1	Borrows $75m	200	75	125
31/1	Borrows $25m	200	100	100
12/2	Repays $50m	200	100	100
1/5	Borrows $100m	200	200	-
1/7	Repays $100m	200	200	-
1/10	Repays $50m	200	200	-
1/1	Expiry	-	-	-

Note: Interest is floating rate linked to the interbank rate – LIBOR, PIBOR, FIBOR – or, in the US, 'Prime Rate'.

Revolving credit   Here, not only can the loan be drawn in tranches but, if repayments are made, the borrower can repay up to the limit: that is, the funds can be reused. Thus, the commitment is said to 'revolve' – the borrower can continue to request loans provided the committed total is not exceeded. The client gives the bank the appropriate notice and then reborrows within the terms of the agreement. If the amount were $200m, we can see the difference between this and the standby credit when we study a similar loan/repayment schedule in Table 4.4.

Generally these loans are unsecured. If bankers take security, it could well be one of the following: property, accounts receivable, plant/equipment, bonds/shares, bills of lading, inventories.

If the money is raised in the London market, the loans are floating rate 'linked to LIBOR' – but what is LIBOR? To begin with, LIBOR fluctuates throughout the day. For purposes of loan agreements, LIBOR is that stated by the reference bank(s) at 11.00 a.m. If the loan is bilateral, it may simply be the lending bank's own LIBOR at 11.00 a.m. on the quarterly or 6 monthly day on which the loan is 'rolled over' at a new rate of interest. If it is a syndicated loan, three 'reference' banks may be nominated and LIBOR is the average of the three. It may also be quoted as the 'BBA', or colloquially the 'screen rate'. The British Bankers' Association list 16 reference banks. Telerate omits the four highest and four lowest of the 16 quoted rates and averages the remaining eight. Telerate disseminates this on their dealing screens at 11.00 a.m. each day – hence the reference to the 'screen' rate. LIBOR, of course may be sterling, dollar, yen, or any other currency.

Table 4.4   *Loan/repayment schedule*

		Total commitment $m	Used $m	Unused $m
1/1	Agreement	200	—	200
2/1	Borrows $75m	200	75	125
31/1	Borrows $25m	200	100	100
12/2	Repays $50m	200	50	150
1/5	Borrows $100m	200	150	50
1/7	Repays $100m	200	50	150
1/9	Borrows $75m	200	125	75
1/10	Repays $100m	200	25	175

Note: Interest is floating rate linked to the interbank rate.

A term often used in the loan documentation for standby and revolving credit is 'swingline facility'. Sometimes the borrower is due to repay investors in, say, dollars on a particular day and discovers late in the day that they cannot. Swingline is a guarantee of same day dollars in New York to meet this emergency need. (It may not be dollars, but dollars seems to be common.) One banker has described this as 'belt and braces' and reassuring to credit ratings organisations looking at an issuer's loan facilities.

As the bank commits to lend, whether the user draws it all or not and as there is a formal agreement, there are *fees* involved.

There will be a *front end* or *facility fee* for setting up the arrangement. There will also be a *commitment* fee. For example, a bank supports a 3 year standby credit facility for $50m which is never used. The bank has committed some of its loan capacity and used up capital under capital ratio rules. As a result, commitment fees are often charged on the undrawn amount. They are typically 50% of the lending margin. The *margin* is the spread over LIBOR charged on the drawn amount itself, for example, LIBOR + 50 basis points, or bp. (A basis point = $\frac{1}{100}$ % or 0.01%.)

There are variations for commitment fees by which they may be charged on the whole facility or on the drawn amount *and* the undrawn amount (but at different rates). A recent loan to the Saudi European Petrochemicals Corporation referred to

25 basis points on drawn balances and 12.5 basis points on undrawn balances.

As we have seen in Chapter 3, the central bank may make all banks deposit some of their eligible liabilities with the Bank and pays them no interest. As bankers relend their deposits, they regard this as a cost of lending and will seek to recoup this.

Project finance   This is simply a special case of a term loan. It is 'special' in that the projects are typically of much longer duration than the conventional term loan, and usually much more complex to structure. They are large-scale exploration or construction projects (for example, Eurotunnel, the bridge over the Bosphorus and similar projects) and require complex and time consuming loan arrangements. In particular, a guarantee from a government or parent body may not be available (the banks' recourse is to the flow of funds from the project, called 'limited recourse financing') in which case the banks will want to see a full set of revenue projections to ensure that debt repayments can be met. They may also wish to see firm contracts for the construction project itself and (if possible) firm contracts for the sale of the completed service.

Recent projects include a 10 year $400m facility for Nesté Petroleum, a wholly owned subsidiary of a Finnish state-owned oil company; a $1.1bn facility for oil exploration for BP Norway; $600m for North Sea oil developments for Agip (UK), part of the Italian state-owned oil group and the Teeside Power Station project – £795 million with the loan to continue until 2008.

In the case of Nesté, while there is no explicit guarantee, there is a tacit understanding that the parent will support the subsidiary. The Agip loan will be supported by the parent for 2 years but revert to limited recourse thereafter.

Teeside Power is a huge gas power station to be constructed at Wilton, Teeside. The main equity sponsor is the Euron Power Corporation of the US. Finance was first secured from 14 underwriters and then went out to syndication. The margin over LIBOR is 125 bp up to completion of the station, 112.5 bp after that up to 8 years and 137 bp for the remaining years. However, these margins may be reduced, depending upon hitting performance targets. Semi-annual loan repayments began in April 1994. This is one of the largest and most involved limited recourse projects.

Syndicated Facilities

Syndicated loans arise because a bank does not wish to take on the whole amount of the loan. The task of syndication is also made easier by the fact that there are many banks who will be happy to take on some of the loan exposure at a second stage – banks that may not have a close relationship with major corporates or may not have the resources to compete at the primary stage.

Syndicated loans (sometimes involving as many as 100 banks) were common in the 1970s, when we saw 'petro-dollars' recycled in loans to sovereign borrowers and multinationals. This led to the LDC debt crisis, following Mexico's default in August 1982 (see Chapter 6). The volumes of large international syndicated loans fell somewhat for several years but recovered later. Many banks found that weakened balance sheets and capital ratio constraints made further loan expansion difficult. One result was the rise to popularity after 1982 of new types of syndicated facility – NIFs and RUFs.

NIFs and RUFs The 1980s became the era of the acronym – NIFs and RUFs, and later MOFs and many others. It was also a time of great competition, especially from Japanese banks. In 1986, the then chairman of Barclays accused the Japanese of 'dumping money', just as people had accused them of dumping goods in the 1920s and 1930s. NIF is 'Note Issuance Facility' and RUF is 'Revolving Underwriting Facility' (ask six bankers what the difference is and you will get six different answers!).

This was also a time in which we saw an increasing use of tender panels of banks, bidding competitively for loan business or bankers' acceptances. For example, a corporate which used bill finance frequently would periodically approach a tender panel to accept bills. This gave us yet another acronym – the RAFT, 'Revolving Acceptance Facility by Tender'.

NIFs and RUFs were facilities by which banks agreed to support note issues by corporates to raise money. The notes were usually called 'Euronotes' and were typically 1, 3 and 6 months. In effect, they were a sort of short-term Eurobond. On a revolving basis, the arranging bank would approach a tender panel to buy the client's notes. In the event that the notes could not be sold at or below a given lending rate, a further panel of underwriting banks stood by to lend the money. The facility was thus underwritten. It was, therefore, a mixture of commercial and investment banking techniques. Fees could be earned and US commercial banks could join in without contravening the 1933 Glass–Steagall Act. During the period 1982–1986, NIFs, RUFs and Euronotes were all the rage.

Today, the formal 1, 3 and 6 month Euronote has disappeared, its modern equivalent being either Eurocommercial paper or medium term notes. (The Bank of England uses Euronotes as a generic term for short-term Euro paper, whether ECDs or ECP.)

MOFs From 1986–7, a more flexible facility – the MOF – appeared. This is 'Multiple Option Facility'. Instead of committing the underwriting banks to support one type of borrowing only (for example, Euronotes), the banks' commitment is to a range of possibilities. The 'multiple options' might be:

❑ Bank loan (multi-currency)
❑ Acceptances
❑ Commercial paper – domestic
❑ Eurocommercial paper.

On a revolving basis, the arranging bank would approach a tender panel of banks for prices for either a bank loan or banker's acceptance to meet the client's need for, say, $10m for 3 months. At the same time, the arranging bank would contact commercial paper dealers to check rates for the same deal. The bank would then report back to the client and use the most attractive option. However, if the best option was above a given borrowing rate, a panel of underwriting banks would agree either to lend the money or sign acceptances at the agreed figure. At first this seemed to be the sort of flexible facility that the market needed and MOFs were all the rage for several years. Later, problems emerged.

To begin with, bank supervisors saw this as a clear off-balance sheet risk and demanded capital cover. Suppose, for example, that the rate at which the underwriting panel would guarantee to lend was LIBOR + 50 bp. The supervisors argued that if the market demanded a higher figure, this might suggest that the client was less creditworthy. The underwriting panel was forced to lend to a client whose credit quality was declining. The Bank of England decided that 50% of the unused capacity must be treated as if the money had actually been lent, for capital ratio purposes. The Bundesbank took a less harsh view. Later, the rules were harmonised through the Basle agreement. The first disadvantage, therefore, was that the banks had to provide capital to back MOFs, although initially they hadn't.

The recession produced other problems. To begin with, the credit quality of many clients did indeed deteriorate, leaving the underwriting banks 'holding the baby'. Secondly, due to poor trading, many clients broke the loan covenants (see later). If covenants are broken, the whole agreement can be renegotiated but *all* the banks must agree the revised terms. Sometimes, one or two banks with the smallest commitment might not agree. In a famous incident in 1989, Laura Ashley was nearly pushed into liquidation in these circumstances.

Finally, the market became less competitive – a lenders' not a borrowers' market. In part, this was due to the departure of the Japanese. The stock market in Tokyo collapsed in January 1990 and property values fell. The Japanese drew in their horns. In 1989, they accounted for 37% of all international bank lending in foreign currencies (BIS figures). In 1994, the figure was 25%. The departure of the Japanese, capital ratio constraints and the recession now put the banks into the driving seat. They were no longer willing to be pushed into tender panels and unattractive deals. In London, margins over LIBOR widened as a consequence. Corporates, too, saw the problems. Beating down the banks to tight margins was one thing. Expecting them to be sympathetic when the going got rough was quite another. There was much talk of 'relationship banking' – of this more later. The OECD, in its *Financial Market Trends* for June 1992, commented on the change in the syndicated credit market and the fall in the number of syndicated facilities: 'uncertainties about the creditworthiness of many potential borrowers added to the caution of financial institutions engaged in a process of profit enhancement and asset quality consolidation.'

With the end of the recession in the West, banks were flush with cash again in 1995 and, although the MOF concept has largely disappeared, margins on loans have fallen again.

Terminology   The facilities we mentioned earlier – term loans, standby credits and revolving credits – are usually syndicated. This leads to a variety of terms being used:

1. *Arranger/Lead manager* Initially, the 'arranging bank' or 'lead manager' deals with the client and discusses the probable terms on which a loan can be arranged. They advise the borrower on the loan structure, maturity and covenants. The arranger will coordinate the participation of other lenders. It may be, however, that a 'book-runner' is appointed. Their job is to do the 'leg work' of putting a syndicate together. Once the syndicate is together, the book-runner's role is finished. One way or another, once initial discussions with the client are concluded, an invitation is issued to co-managers to participate.

2. *Co-managers* Along with the arranging bank, they agree to underwrite the loan so that the client is now guaranteed the funds. Each co-manager takes a share – for example, $200m.

3. *Participating banks* They now join the syndicate. A co-manager will invite, perhaps, four participating banks to take, say, $25m of the loan each.

4. *The agent* The role of the bank acting as the agent bank is critically important and a special fee is earned. The agency is an administrative role. The agent collects the loan from each participant and passes it to the borrower. Equally, the borrower payments as made are passed to the syndicate in agreed shares. The agent notifies the borrower of the new interest rate related to the interbank rate every 3 or 6 months as agreed. The agent is responsible for the documentation and will notify both borrower and lender of all information relevant to the loan agreement. There is no credit risk but there is still risk. If the agent makes a mistake that loses the syndicate members money, they will be responsible for making this good.

As in the case of a bilateral loan, there will be various fees:

1. *Facility or front end fee* For agreeing to the arrangement, there will be a front end or facility fee for all involved. This may be a flat fee or a percentage of the money. The arranging bank will also take an extra fee for their special role. This is called a *praecipium*.

2. *Underwriting fees* These are paid to the group of underwriting banks which took on the initial commitment prior to extending the syndicate. There is a definite risk. In the case of the management buyout of Magnet Joinery, for example, a small group of lead banks led by Bankers Trust found themselves alone as the potential syndicate members withdrew their support, sensing that the risk was unacceptable – very wisely as it happened!

3. *Agent's fee* This is paid to the agent bank for the role they play, which was described earlier.

4. *Commitment fee* This was mentioned before in the case of bilateral loans. It is a payment measured in basis points for the commitment to lend which needs to be backed by capital. As we have seen, it may be based on the whole loan, the drawn section, or the undrawn section (or a mixture). Usually the fee is on the undrawn section and typically 50% of the margin (see 5 below).

5. *Loan margin* This is the actual margin over the interbank rate charged for the borrowed money, for example, LIBOR + 50 bp. It may not be a constant figure but related to loan tranches taken by the syndicate.

While commitment fees are usually 50% of the margin, any variation is possible. In mid-1995, for example, the German Thyssen Group arranged a $1.2 billion 7 year revolving credit facility. There was a front end fee of 8 basis points and the margin over LIBOR varied according to how much of the facility is used. For example, 10 basis points if less than 33% of the loan but 20 basis points if more than 66% is used.

The NIFs, RUFs and MOFs were all forms of revolving credit. In general, the term loan, standby credit, revolving credit and project finance are likely to involve syndicates, unless they are of modest size.

The fierce competitive battles of the 1980s, however, have led to much talk of 'relationship banking' and bilateral agreements.

Relationship banking The inference here is that the corporate encourages a close relationship with a small number of banks and may negotiate bilaterally. BAT, for example, in 1991 replaced a syndicated revolving credit facility with a series of some 20 bilateral agreements to a total of $2bn. Grand Metropolitan, requiring a $2.5bn 4 year revolving credit, talked separately to each of 30 banks, although the loan documentation was said to be standardised.

Usually, the number of banks will fall, too. BP, for example, in renewing standby credits reduced the number of banks from 67 to 27. Identical documentation was used but bilateral contracts were drawn up.

Bilateral agreements, however, can really only be used by corporates with skilled Treasury departments with large resources, unless the number of banks is very small. The work done by the agency bank in policing the loan should not be underestimated. A 30 bank syndicate means, for the corporate, one line of communication – the agent bank, which does the rest. 30 bilateral agreements means 30 lines of communication – one with each bank.

The emphasis in most of the comments above has been on *corporate* loans. Loans to governments have been seen in the light of the expansion in the 1970s and the subsequent LDC debt crisis. Loans to western governments and their subsidiaries continue as do loans to supranational organisations. For example, in August 1972, the EC was arranging an international syndicated loan for Ecu 500m with Crédit Lyonnais as lead manager. This loan was zero weighted for capital ratio purposes and the rate was only LIBOR + 3.125 bp with further fees of 10 bp. A loan, as opposed to a bond, has the flexibility for the EU that arrangements can be made to draw the money as required. The UK arranged a syndicated loan during the ERM crisis in September 1992. The loan was for Ecu 50 billion and raised by a syndicate of 18 banks. The rate was LIBOR + $\frac{3}{32}$. Spain arranged a 5 year Ecu 5 billion standby facility in mid-1995 paying a front end fee of four basis points and a margin of four basis points over LIBOR. Earlier in 1995, Italy borrowed Ecu 5 billion, also at a total cost of 8 basis points.

The Loan Agreement

If the loan is syndicated, there will be one loan agreement and one set of terms but the amount owed to each borrower is a separate debt.

The loan agreement will typically have four sections:

1. *Introduction* This will cover the amount of the loan and its purpose, conditions of drawdown and particulars of the participating banks.
2. *Facilities* The loan may be drawn down in separate tranches with different terms on interest and repayment. The procedures for drawing down will be covered.
3. *Payment* This covers the interest calculations, calculation of the interbank rate, repayment arrangements, fees, or any similar charges.
4. *Provisions* To protect the bank there will be covenants, events of default, procedures if basic circumstances change.

The final documentation is sent to the agent bank prior to drawing the money. The agent must ensure that the documentation embodies that which was agreed.

Covenants These are designed to protect the bank if the 'health' of the borrower changes. If covenants are breached, the banks' commitment will cease. The loan will have to be rescheduled. The usual covenants are:

❏ *Interest cover* This is the relationship between profit (before tax and interest) and interest. This is to ensure that there is a comfortable margin over the loan interest. If there is not, how can the borrower repay the principal? Sometimes cash flow may be used instead of profit. After all, profit is not cash!
❏ *Net worth* Suppose all assets were sold and liabilities paid, what is left? Normally, this should be the figure of share capital and reserves ± current profit/loss, minus goodwill, tax and dividends to be paid. The agreement stipulates a minimum net worth.
❏ *Total borrowing* This will be limited and must cover hire purchase, finance leases and 'puttable' capital instruments (see Chapter 6).
❏ *Gearing* Long-term debt to capital as defined in net worth above – a maximum ratio will be stated.
❏ *Current ratio* A minimum figure will be given for the ratio of current assets to current liabilities – a measure of liquidity.

Events of default This is a list of circumstances in which the loan will be regarded as being in default, for example, insolvency, change of ownership or similar circumstances. A cross-default clause is important. This means that defaults on other loans or bonds will cause this loan to be in default also.

Negative pledge Here the client undertakes not to offer security against a loan from any other party.

Assignment   One of the syndicate banks may assign part of its loan commitment to another bank. This cannot be done without the borrower's consent but the loan agreement usually says that 'such consent may not be unreasonably withheld'. However, there may be an initial delay in selling off any of the loan. For example, the $5.5bn Kuwait loan in the Autumn of 1991 had a clause forbidding reassignment to other banks for 180 days.

A *sub-participation* simply means that part of a syndicate bank's loan allotment will be lent to them by another bank and interest payments passed on to this bank. The loan agreement with the client is not affected.

With a *transfer* or *assignment*, the loan documentation changes, the borrower is aware of the change and the assignee is now legally the lender for this portion. Borrowers may worry here about not having a close relationship with the assignee if they hit trouble later.

Why sell part of the loan anyway? Capital ratio rules may make new lending difficult. A transfer would free part of the loan to be lent elsewhere, possibly more profitably. Alternatively, in order to improve capital ratio, the money may not be relent. If capital is no problem, the money may simply be released to take advantage of a more profitable opportunity. With a participation, we may be able to take, say, LIBOR + 22 bp from the client and pass on LIBOR + 20 bp, 'skimming' a little profit.

In the UK, sub-participation and assignment are subject to detailed regulations – BSD 1989/1, 'Loan Transfers and Documentation'.

Another interesting secondary market is that for the loans of corporates known to be in trouble. A bank, which recognises that it is not going to get all the principal back anyway, may sell some of the loan to another bank at a substantial discount. The second bank clearly hopes to improve on the situation.

As the boom years of the 1980s have been followed by a rise in companies finding difficulty in servicing the debt, a substantial market in 'value impaired' corporate loans has sprung up in the US. It follows a similar discounted market for LDC loans. Citibank has designed a US corporate loan index of 1000 loans to 600 companies. Some investment banks like Goldman Sachs or Bear Stearns are very active in the market as brokers. In the UK, a new brokerage, Klesch & Co, is broadcasting the price of more than 60 corporate loans via the Telerate service. EuroDisney debt was selling at 76% of list price in early 1996, Eurotunnel at 42% and Robert Maxwell (!) at 9.25%. To take one example, the UK advertising group WPP finally rescheduled its bank loan agreements in August 1992. However, during the process of renegotiation, one lender, the Bank of New York, sold off its $80m share of the loan at 65¢ in the dollar. Within days, one of the buyers had resold the loan at 68¢ in the dollar! The risky bank loan has become just another product!

SUMMARY

Commercial banks are in the classic business of accepting deposits and making loans. The business is both retail (the general public, shops, very small businesses) and wholesale (other banks, corporates and institutions).

Retail banking covers current accounts, cheque facilities, savings accounts, credit cards and loan facilities like overdrafts, personal loans and mortgages. Increasingly, communications developments are leading to the spread of home banking.

Clearing of payments may involve cheques or electronic payment systems. Cheques are expensive and banks are trying to reduce their use through home banking and the use of debit cards.

Key issues in retail banking today are the growing competition, control of costs, sales of non-banking products and the use of Information Technology. In particular, growing links between banks and insurance companies have led to the word *bancassurance*.

Wholesale banking covers bank lending to larger entities than those met in retail banking and activities described in other chapters – money markets, foreign exchange and finance for trade.

Loans may be uncommitted or committed.

Uncommitted facilities include term loans, standby credit, revolving credit and project finance.

Syndicated loans are common for large value domestic and cross-border business. There are arranging banks, co-managers, participating banks and agent banks.

Various fees are involved – facility or front-end fee, underwriting fees, agents fees and commitment fees. Finally, there is the loan *margin*.

The loan agreement covers the amount of the loan, its purpose, draw down facilities, interest calculations and provisions.

Among the provisions will be covenants. These are designed to protect the bank if the financial position of the borrower worsens. They include interest cover, net worth, total borrowing, gearing and current ratio.

Other provisions cover events of default. There will also be a negative pledge.

A bank may assign or transfer part of the loan to another bank or it may be a less formal sub-participation.

5 Banking (IV)
– Investment Banking

INTRODUCTION

We should, perhaps, recognise at the outset that 'commercial' and 'investment' banking do not exist in separate compartments. There are activities which overlap and are carried out by both types of bank, for example, accepting and discounting bills of exchange, foreign exchange and some aspects of trade finance. Nevertheless, there are certain activities which would be regarded as clear 'investment' banking (for example, underwriting share issues) and we shall discuss these in this chapter as well as those which involve a certain amount of overlap.

INVESTMENT BANKING

The range of activities of investment or merchant banks can be summarised as follows:

- ❑ Accepting
- ❑ Corporate finance
- ❑ Securities trading
- ❑ Investment management
- ❑ Loan arrangement
- ❑ Foreign exchange.

Accepting

Although commercial banks accept bills of exchange nowadays, it is a very historic activity for investment banks. Chapter 2 mentioned the Medici bankers helping a Venetian firm to trade with one in London using a bill of exchange in 1463. During the industrial revolution in the UK, enquiries were received from firms all over the world. The role of the British (and Dutch) merchant banks in backing this trade with bills of exchange was of crucial importance. Indeed, until December 1987, the club of top UK merchant banks was called 'The Accepting Houses Committee'.

While bills of exchange can be and are used in connection with inland business, their main use is for export/import business. An exporter sells goods for $100 000 to an importer. Their arrangement is that the goods will be paid for in 3 months, say, 2 February 1997. The exporter makes out the bill of exchange and sends it to the importer to sign. Its effective message is shown in Figure 5.1.

November 2 1996

You owe me $100 000 for goods received. Please pay on 2 February 1997

Signed: A. N. Exporter

Yes, I agree.

Signed: A. N. Importer

Figure 5.1   *Skeleton bill of exchange*

As you may well imagine, the actual document is rather more formal than this! Nevertheless, it expresses the basic idea. Notice that the *exporter* makes out the bill, that is, *draws* the bill. (There are similar documents used in international trade called *promissory notes*. Here, the *importer* makes out the document and the exporter has less control over the wording.)

The *importer* now has 3 months to put the goods to work before paying. The *exporter* has an internationally acceptable form of debt. True, he has allowed the importer 3 months to pay (not necessary but very common), but his alternative choice might have been to send an invoice, optimistically headed by the words 'Payment Terms – 30 days', with no real assurance that the money will be paid on time.

What if the exporter cannot wait 3 months but needs the money earlier to fund cash flow? The exporter can visit their bank for a loan, armed with a heap of bills proving that cash is on the way. Alternatively, the exporter can sell the bill to a bank (or, in the UK, a discount house). The bank is being asked to put up the money now and to collect it from the importer in 3 months. As the bank is lending $100 000 for 3 months, they are not going to give the exporter all $100 000 but some lower sum reflecting risk and the cost of money – say, $97 000. The bill is sold at a discount and this process is thus called *discounting the bill*.

Let's look at the process in diagrammatic form (Figure 5.2).

The problem is that the bank may be unsure of the credit status of the trader and unwilling to discount the bill. As a result, the practice grew of asking the trader to find a merchant bank to sign the bill in their place. If, in the 19th century, the bill was signed by Baring Bros, Rothschild's or Bank Mees, the bank would have no hesitation in discounting the bill. Naturally, a fee was charged for this service, which is *accepting* the bill. (Whoever signs the bill, promising to pay, is accepting the bill. When people talk of 'acceptances', however, they usually refer to a bank's signature.) In effect, the bank is giving the bill its own credit status and not that of the trader. Hence, its importance in the industrial revolution. (The large number of bills in existence in 1890 whose acceptor was Baring Bros led the Bank of England to rescue it that year after unwise investments in Latin America. In 1995, however, there was no second rescue!)

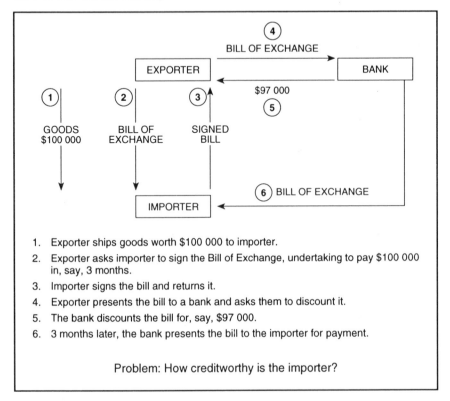

1. Exporter ships goods worth $100 000 to importer.
2. Exporter asks importer to sign the Bill of Exchange, undertaking to pay $100 000 in, say, 3 months.
3. Importer signs the bill and returns it.
4. Exporter presents the bill to a bank and asks them to discount it.
5. The bank discounts the bill for, say, $97 000.
6. 3 months later, the bank presents the bill to the importer for payment.

Problem: How creditworthy is the importer?

Figure 5.2 *The Bill of Exchange: I*

We can find Josiah Wedgewood writing to an Italian customer in 1769,
My foreign correspondents name me a good house, generally in London, to accept my draft for the amount of the goods
or Boulton and Watt in 1795,
We undertake no foreign orders without a guarantee being engineers not merchants.
(Quoted in Chapman *The Rise of Merchant Banking*, Allen & Unwin, 1984)
Our previous diagram is now altered a little (see Figure 5.3).

Today, the whole procedure for trade finance is tied up by arrangements between the importer's bank and the exporter's bank. Usually, a documentary letter of credit is involved. We shall discuss this in Chapter 8.

So far, we have discussed the bill in the context of an explicit trade transaction. The market in bankers' acceptances has reached a new level of sophistication today, especially in the London market. Major firms of good credit quality will ask their bank (whether investment or commercial) to accept a bill promising to pay a given sum at a future period of time. The corporate now discounts the bill in the local discount market as a way of borrowing money for trade in general rather than for an explicit transaction. Indeed, in London, firms like Harrods or Marks and Spencer will do this even though they are not selling on credit at all but retailers receiving cash!

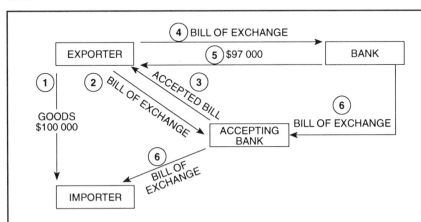

1. Exporter ships goods worth $100 000 to importer.
2. Exporter asks a bank to 'accept' the bill, undertaking to pay $100 000 in 3 months.
3. The bank accepts the bill and returns it.
4. Exporter presents the bill to a bank and asks them to discount it.
5. The bank discounts the bill for $97 000.
6. 3 months later, the bank presents the bill to the accepting bank for payment of $100 000. The latter will recoup this from the importer, or the importer's bank.

N.B. A bill signed by a trader is a *Trade Bill*.
A bill accepted by a bank recognised for this purpose by the Central Bank is a *Bank Bill* or *Eligible Bill*.
The Central Bank will itself discount the bill as part of its 'lender of last resort' role.

Figure 5.3 *The Bill of Exchange: II*

Commercial banks are very involved with accepting bills and this is one reason why the UK's 'Accepting Houses Committee' disbanded in 1987. The committee would not include either commercial banks or foreign banks. This was seen to be completely out of date. In any case, accepting had ceased to be a dominant role for UK merchant banks.

Bills of Exchange are used extensively in the UK, quite widely in the continent of Europe generally and very little in the US.

Corporate Finance

Corporate Finance is likely to be a department of major importance in any merchant bank. This department will manage:

❑   New issues – equities/bonds
❑   Rights issues
❑   Mergers and acquisitions
❑   Research.

New issues   New issues of either shares or bonds will involve pricing the securities, selling them to investors, underwriting and general advice regarding the regulations that must be followed. Close liaison with firms of lawyers and accountants will be necessary and their fees will be substantial, as well as those of the bankers!

Underwriting is an undertaking to buy any securities that the investors cannot be persuaded to buy. Fees will be charged (of course) and the risk will be spread amongst other merchant banks and investment institutions. One of the most dramatic incidents in modern times occurred when the UK government was selling off its remaining shares in BP. to the public. Unfortunately, the market crash of October 1987 occurred after the price was fixed but before the offer closed. The issue was a failure and the underwriters had to buy the shares at a substantial loss.

In the case of equities, the underwriters purchase the shares once it is clear that investors are not taking up their allocation. In the Eurobond market, on the other hand, the syndicate of underwriting banks buys the bonds from the issuer and then attempts to sell them to investors.

Rights issues (discussed in Chapter 9)   These also need to be priced and underwritten in case the market price falls below the offer price of the rights. Technically, BP was a rights issue as some shares were already quoted but new shares were being created. The government was allowing the public to buy these shares.

The many privatisations planned in the newly emerging free markets of central and eastern Europe and the former USSR are creating work for US and European investment bankers. Their advice and help is being sought for circumstances which have little precedent.

Mergers and acquisitions   Firms planning a takeover will turn to merchant banks for help and advice regarding price, timing, tactics and so on. Equally, the object of the takeover will turn to these bankers for help in fending off the predator. In the UK, Guinness took over the Scottish whisky company Distillers after a long and acrimonious battle. Unhappily, personnel in Guinness and their advisers, Morgan Grenfell, were brought to trial charged with various misdemeanours. In the course of this trial, it was revealed that Morgan Grenfell and associates had been paid £65m and lawyers, Freshfields, paid £2m. The fees involved can be substantial. In a large takeover, like this one, there may be three merchant bankers or more on each side.

Nowadays, takeover bids may be cross-border – for example, the Italian Pirelli tyre company bidding for the German Continental tyre company or the Swiss Nestlé buying the French Perrier or taking over a quintessentially British chocolate company, Rowntrees. This latter move caused much bitterness as Swiss restrictions on foreigners owning domestic shares made a similar bid in the other direction impossible. This is not unusual. In Germany, regulations make it very difficult for a hostile takeover to succeed.

Figures from KPMG, the consulting and accountancy firm, show cross-border mergers and acquisitions in Europe as totalling $23.1bn in 1991 but by the first half of 1995, deals for the top ten advisers totalled $21.6bn. A list of key advisers is shown in Table 5.1.

In the US, the notorious 'junk bond' era (Chapter 6) saw small companies raising huge sums with bonds to buy much bigger companies. (In the film 'Wall Street', the speech made by Gordon Gecko to shareholders in his planned victim company was said to be based on an actual speech made by Ivan Boesky. He is reported to have coined the infamous phrase, 'greed is good'.)

The fees earned by Drexel Burnham Lambert for bond issues and takeover bids during this era made them quickly one of the highest earning firms on Wall Street (as long as it lasted).

Certain jargon has come to be associated with takeover battles. If a takeover seems inevitable, the merchant bank may find a rival bidder who is preferable to the original predator. This more acceptable bidder is the 'White Knight'. Sometimes one or two people can be found who will take a substantial minority holding and block the takeover. These are the 'White Squires'. When Lloyds Bank tried to take over Standard Chartered in 1986, the bid was blocked by holdings taken (separately) by a few entrepreneurs in the Far East and Australia. As it happened, they did Lloyds a good turn as subsequent Standard Chartered problems would have severely weakened a bank with a high reputation for profitability.

Sometimes the 'White Squire' may become a 'Trojan Horse' (to mix our metaphors)! When Britannia Arrow faced a hostile bid in 1985, it found a White Squire in Robert Maxwell. Subsequently, he ousted the board and put in his own nominees.

Sometimes, the bidder may be persuaded to withdraw by the company buying back the shares at a higher price. This is called 'greenmail' (in contrast to blackmail)! In 1986, Sir James Goldsmith, the Anglo-French entrepreneur, made an unpopular bid for the US tyre company, Goodyear Tyre & Rubber Co. In the end, after an acrimonious fight, the firm bought Goldsmith and partners out. They made $93m in the space of a few weeks. However, the incident did damage his reputation in the US, although he always denied the 'greenmail' charge.

A popular defence against hostile takeover bids in the US is the so-called 'poison pill'. This was invented by a top takeover lawyer, Martin Lipton, in 1980 and has been adopted by two thirds of companies in the Standard & Poors 500 Index.

Once one shareholder's stake rises above a given percentage (usually 20%), the poison pill device is triggered. This allows the company to give all shareholders – apart from the 20% holder – the right to buy new shares at a large discount, often 50%. This makes the bid prohibitively expensive.

Table 5.1   *Financial advisers on European cross-border deals, leading advisers, 1995*

	Adviser	No. of deals	Value £m
1	Goldman Sachs (2*)	26	10 129
2	SBC Warburg (3**)	40	9 390
3	Morgan Stanley (1)	24	9 056
4	Schroders (17)	22	7 255
5	Credit Suisse First Boston (11)	25	7 102
6	Lazard Houses (5)	37	5 971
7	Rothschild Group (–)	25	5 969
8	Deutsche Morgan Grenfell (8)	34	5 456
9	Lehman Brothers (15)	15	5 381
10	Enskilda (–)	7	5 075
11	JP Morgan (16)	19	4 341
12	JO Hambro Magan (–)	8	4 053
13	Merrill Lynch (9)	14	3 142
14	Barclays de Zoete Wedd (–)	12	2 991
15	Hambros Bank(–)	8	2 472
16	Robert Fleming(–)	6	1 974
17	Kleinwort Benson (4)	10	1 749
18	UBS (6)	14	1 711
19	Baring Brothers (12)	10	1 636
20	Banque Indosuez (10)	9	1 587

Notes: The figures in brackets are the 1994 top 20 ranking
  * 1994 full-year ranking.
  ** Based on SG Warburg's 1994 full-year ranking.
Table 5.1 includes only those advisers acting on two or more transactions.
Source: Acquisitions Monthly/*Amdata III*

General advice This is always needed by the treasury departments of major firms. They will meet their merchant bankers regularly to discuss the outlook for exchange rates, interest rates, risk management and generally to help them to clarify their policies.

Sometimes the client may be a government or quasi-government authority. Baring Bros, the UK merchant bank, advises the Saudi Arabian Monetary Authority (SAMA). (It helped that, when the OPEC States earned huge revenues and needed advice, Baring Bros was not a Jewish house.)

Research capability This is clearly essential in the corporate finance department if the bank is to be able to give advice and play a major role in raising new capital. The firm may be innovative and invent new variations on standard techniques, for example, convertible capital bonds, perpetual variable rate notes, perpetual auction market preferred stock (AMPs) and similar instruments. Research may uncover potential victims for a takeover or give early identification of potential predators.

Securities Trading

In corporate finance we saw *primary* market activity – new issues and rights issues. Securities trading takes us into the *secondary* market dealing in the same equities and bonds.

The trading will take place in one of the modern dealing rooms with computer terminals and communications giving up to the minute prices and contact with other dealers and investors all over the world.

The dealings will cover domestic bonds and equities and international bonds and equities. International bonds are discussed in Chapter 6. International equities are those of companies outside the domestic market where the investment bank is situated.

The tradition in many countries (France, Belgium, the UK, Spain, Italy) has been to reserve domestic bond and equities to stock exchange members not allowed to be owned by banks. Change began with London's 'Big Bang' in October 1986 and spread to all the above markets. The result has been to allow banks access to these markets and break the previous monopolies. These banks are either pure investment banks as such, subsidiaries of commercial banks or 'universal' banks (see Chapter 2).

Alongside these traders will be the experts in the so called 'derivative' products – options, futures, FRAs and so on. We shall discuss these in later chapters, but they enable traders and their clients either to take a view on future price movements with less capital than actually buying/selling the underlying instruments or to hedge their risk. If a commercial bank has an investment bank subsidiary, then the expertise in derivative products will be found in that subsidiary.

The traders in this department carry out a twofold role. They act on behalf of clients (some of whom may be in-house departments) and they take positions of their own – usually called 'proprietary trading'.

Investment Management

The investment funds which these managers are controlling may be the bank's own funds or they may be, in effect, 'looking after other peoples' money'. These may be:

❑   High net worth individuals
❑   Corporates
❑   Pension funds
❑   Mutual funds.

High net worth individuals   They may approach a commercial bank to handle all their affairs, including investments. In Chapter 2 we called this 'private banking'. They could also approach an investment bank to handle their spare funds (but a minimum sum will be stated). This type of business is also handled by stockbrokers but with lower minimum sums than an investment bank would require.

Corporates   They may either have good cash flow and wish to pay someone else to handle their investments or may build up a large 'war chest', ready for some takeover activity later and, temporarily, pay an investment bank to handle this.

The entity need not be a conventional corporate as such. An excellent example is the SAMA.

Pension funds   Where economies have pension funds (for example the US, the UK, the Netherlands, Switzerland and Japan), then they may feel that they lack the skill to manage the funds and pay others to do so. In these economies, pension funds will usually be the biggest clients of the investment management department.

Mutual funds   These are discussed in Chapter 9. They are collective investments in money market instruments, bonds or equities. The bank may run its own fund and advertise its attractions to small investors. In addition, it will manage mutual funds for others. For example, several years ago the famous UK retailer, Marks and Spencer, launched a unit trust, a form of mutual fund. No doubt lacking in house skills in this area, they paid Mercury Asset Management (a subsidiary of S.G. Warburg) to manage the unit trust. Later, however, they replaced them with Robert Fleming. Fund Management these days is a very competitive business! Independent organisations provide regular statistics on fund performance and, if the manager has performed less well than comparable funds, they may find themselves being dismissed. This has led to charges of 'short-termism' in their investment decisions. However, as a director of one major fund commented to the author: 'The long run is the sum of the short runs. If we get them right, the long run will be right too.'

Typically, fund managers will charge a small percentage fee for handling the fund and the client will meet costs like broker's commission. Competition for the investment banks comes from firms of independent fund managers, who specialise totally in this business, or large pension funds who will look after the money of smaller funds as well as their own.

The role of fund managers as investment institutions who influence stock market activity will be discussed in Chapter 9.

Loan Arrangement

Where there are complex syndicated loans for special projects, we may often find that the arranger is an investment bank. The bank is using its special skills to decide on the terms of the loan and the cheapest way to find the money. It could involve using the 'swaps' market, for example, which we explain in Chapter 12. Often, several potential teams may be competing for these projects, for example, Eurotunnel, the new Hong Kong airport, the bridge over the Bosphorus. In the case of Teeside Power Station in the UK, a syndicate of banks is putting up the money but the loan arranger is the US investment bank, Goldman Sachs.

Outside of large, complex projects, investment bankers will help clients to raise finance for international trade. In this, there is an overlap with a major commercial bank activity. It may be a question of knowing sources of cheaper finance for exporter or importer (for example, a development bank) or even acting as an agent or middleman – an export house or confirming house. These activities are discussed under 'Finance for Trade' in Chapter 8.

Foreign Exchange

The foreign exchange markets are discussed in Chapter 6. Typically, we regard this as a commercial bank activity. However, investment banks who are permitted commercial bank functions will run a foreign exchange trading desk for their clients and their own proprietary trading and it may be an important source of profit. We make the above comment about being 'permitted commercial bank functions' because of the differing regulatory position in various countries, which we explain before the end of this chapter.

Typically, US and Japanese investment banks will have a modest foreign exchange section. UK merchant banks, however, fully licensed as banks, will often see foreign exchange dealing as a major activity and will, indeed, have a 'banking' department which will also offer deposit taking functions to clients.

Miscellaneous Activities

There are a range of miscellaneous activities which may be carried out by investment banks, possibly through separate legal subsidiaries. Commodity trading, for example, (including derivatives trading) is quite common and one thinks here, for example, of the links between the US Salomon Bros and Phibro. Bullion trading, too, is important for some UK merchant banks, like N.M. Rothschild and Samuel Montagu. Other activities include insurance broking, life assurance, leasing, factoring (see Chapter 8), property development and venture capital. This latter activity covers finance for new and growing companies which are not well enough established to attract money by equities, bonds or conventional bank loans. The venture capital company puts in a mixture of equity and loans and hopes to make large capital gains later when the firm obtains a flotation on the local Stock Exchange.

Many of these miscellaneous activities overlap with those of commercial banks – for example, leasing, factoring and venture capital.

REGULATION

We have seen that many commercial banks have investment bank subsidiaries and that universal banks do all kinds of banking anyway. We have also seen that many activities overlap commercial and investment banking and that it is not always possible to draw a clear distinction. As a result, one might conclude that the distinction between the two types of banking is not really significant. That is, until one realises that the two types are artificially separated by law in the two biggest markets of the world – the US and Japan!

When the Wall Street crash occurred in 1929, the US authorities concluded that, by engaging in stock market activities, commercial banks might be risking depositors' money. They decided to remove this risk by passing the Glass–Steagall Act of 1933 (named after the Chairmen of the relevant committees of the Senate and House of Representatives). This introduced a deposit protection scheme, gave the Federal Reserve Bank greater powers of supervision and separated commercial and investment banking. A commercial bank could take deposits but could not underwrite any securities. An investment bank could handle underwriting of securities but could not take deposits. As a result, we have US commercial banks on the one hand (Citibank, Chase Manhattan, Chemical, J.P. Morgan) and investment banks on the other (Salomon Bros, Goldman Sachs, Merrill Lynch). J.P. Morgan continued as a commercial bank but passed investment banking to Morgan Stanley, now a separate bank. In London, the already weak links with Morgan Grenfell were then broken.

The whole affair, however, may have been based on a misreading of the position. George Bentson, Professor of Finance at Emory University in Atlanta, has found that allegations that securities trading weakened banks had 'almost no basis in fact'.

As the Americans were in occupation of Japan after the Second World War, they passed the same restrictions into Article 65 of the Japanese Exchange and Securities Code. As a result, we have the commercial banks (Dai Ichi Kangyo, Mitsubishi, Sumitomo, Sakura) and, quite separate, the securities houses (Nomura, Daiwa, Nikko and Yamaichi).

A similar law was passed in Italy in the early 1930s leaving Italy with just one major investment bank, Mediobanca (partly state owned). In 1988, however, the law was repealed.

Two major attempts to repeal Glass–Steagall have been made in recent years. One was the Proxmire–Garn bill introduced in November 1987 and the other was a far-reaching reform bill, introduced by Nicholas Brady, Treasury Secretary, in February 1990, of which Glass–Steagall repeal was part. In the event, both bills failed to obtain the necessary support to pass into law. The new Congress in 1995 was also confidently expected to repeal Glass-Steagall but, once again, no action was taken.

Impatient with this, the Federal Reserve has acted on its own. In January 1989, it gave powers to underwrite issues of municipal bonds, mortgage bonds and commercial paper to five banks – J.P. Morgan, Citibank, Chase Manhattan, Security Pacific and Bankers Trust. However, the activities had to be handled by a separate subsidiary and not be more than 5% of the turnover of that subsidiary (later increased to 10%). In June 1989, J.P. Morgan were given permission to underwrite corporate bonds and, in September 1990, permission to underwrite equities (with the same limitations as before). Then, in January 1991, permission to underwrite equities in this limited way was also given to Bankers Trust, Royal Bank of Canada and Canadian Imperial Bank of Commerce. Later, in March 1997, the Fed lifted the 10% limit to 25% and, in April, Bankers Trust bought the investment bank, Alex Brown. The Glass–Steagall Act was crumbling!

In Japan, the Ministry of Finance circulated several papers outlining the possibility of similar deregulation in Japan. 1993 saw the first positive moves here. Some commercial banks were allowed limited operations in bonds and, in November 1994, the list of commercial banks allowed these dealings was widened. As a result, many major banks like Dai-Ichi Kangyo, Bank of Tokyo–Mitsubishi, Fuji, IBJ and LTCB have set up subsidiaries to deal in bonds. The 1993 move also allowed brokers to deal in investment trusts, land trusts and foreign exchange. Nomura, Daiwa, Nikko and Yamaichi all set up subsidiaries to be Trust Banks. Finally, in June 1997, the Ministry of Finance announced plans for complete deregulation by the year 2001.

One final point. In Europe, through separately capitalised subsidiaries, the American and Japanese banks can, at least to some extent, carry out activities proscribed at home by local regulations. For example, J.P. Morgan, a commercial bank, is a major underwriter of Eurobonds in London. Nomura Securities has a licence from the Bank of England to take deposits.

SUMMARY

Investment banking activities can be summarised as:

Accepting   This is putting the bank's signature on a bill of exchange to give it a better credit quality. The bill of exchange is a promise to pay a trade debt. If the bank is one on the central bank's list for this purpose, the bill is a *bank* bill. Others are *trade* bills. The bill is frequently sold at a discount. Commercial banks will accept bills, too, but it is an historic investment bank activity.

Corporate Finance   This covers new issues of equities and bonds, rights issues, mergers and acquisitions and research.

Securities Trading   The trading includes money market instruments, equities, bonds and derivative products.

Investment Management   The funds managed are those of high net worth individuals, corporates, mutual funds and (especially) pension funds.

Loan Arrangement   While the bank may not lend the money, it may help to assemble a syndicate for large-scale financial products.

Foreign Exchange   The large foreign exchange dealers are commercial banks but investment banks will still need to run a foreign exchange section.

In the United States, investment and commercial banks are separated by the Glass–Steagall Act. In Japan, they are separated by Article 65 of the Exchange and Securities Code.

Across Europe, banks which carry out both commercial and investment banking are called *universal* banks.

6 The Money and Bond Markets

THE RATE OF INTEREST

So far, we have taken the rate of interest involved in borrowing and lending rather for granted. The time has come, however, to look at it more clearly.

The rate of interest is the price of money. We talk casually of *the* rate of interest but, of course, there is no single rate. There are rates appropriate for different borrowers and rates appropriate for different time periods. A middle-sized company making machine tools will expect to pay a higher rate than a government does. A government pays a different rate for borrowing for 3 months than for 10 years.

What affects the rate of interest? We have just touched on two key factors – *risk* and *maturity*.

Risk

Let's take the risk first. Quite simply, a lender will expect a greater reward for lending to the company making machine tools than for lending to a government. After all, the company may go into liquidation and default. We do not expect our government to default, although Mexico's government and those of other Latin American countries caused panic in international markets when they defaulted in the 1980s (more on that later!).

So far as the governments of OECD countries are concerned, say, or the US government, the lowest rates of interest in their economies will apply to government transactions since they are regarded as the safest. The government rate thus becomes the benchmark for other rates. For example, an American corporate wishing to borrow for 3 months might be advised to expect to pay 'Treasuries plus 1%', that is, 1% more than the current rate for US government Treasury bills. It is more convenient to express it this way than as an absolute rate because rates vary in wholesale markets, even daily. For example, let's say 3 month Treasury bills pay $3\frac{7}{8}\%$. The rate for our US company is thus $4\frac{7}{8}\%$. However, tomorrow Treasury bills may be $3\frac{3}{4}\%$ and the corporate rate becomes $4\frac{3}{4}\%$. As a result, we find it easier to express the rate as 'Treasuries plus 1%'. Of course, the corporate may become more secure as profits increase and the balance sheet improves. Their investment bankers may express the view that they now see their appropriate rate as 'Treasuries plus 90 bp'. What does this mean? A basis point is very common terminology and is useful for expressing small differences in rates. It is $\frac{1}{100}$ of 1%. Thus, 50 bp is equal to $\frac{1}{2}\%$ and 100 bp is equal to 1%. The difference between any given rate and the benchmark US government rate will be called 'the spread over Treasuries'. In the above case, the corporate has found that its spread over US government Treasury bill rates has fallen from 1% to $\frac{9}{10}\%$.

Maturity

Maturity is another important aspect, and it doesn't always make sense in practice. Economic theory tells us that lenders will want a higher rate of interest for lending money for 5 years than for 3 months. This relationship between the rate of interest and time is called the 'yield curve'. If rates for longer-term lending are higher than for shorter-term lending, we would expect the yield curve to look like that in Figure 6.1.

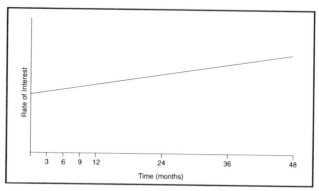

Figure 6.1   The yield curve

The yield curve is upward-sloping, or positive. Unfortunately, while this makes complete sense, it often doesn't work that way in real life at all. Sometimes short-term rates are higher than long-term ones and we talk of a 'negative' or downward-sloping yield curve. This may be due to government policy. They change short-term interest rates either to stimulate the economy or to slow it down. For example, from October 1989 to October 1990 in the UK, short-term rates were 15% while the government attempted to slow down a rate of inflation in excess of 10%. Investment in a 10 year government bond, however, only returned about 11%. Conversely, in mid-1992, the US government was desperately trying to 'kick-start' the economy. Short-term rates were only a little over 3%, while the price of a 30 year government bond was such that it yielded about 7½%.

Expectations

Markets are also affected by *expectations*. Suppose everyone believes firmly that the general level of interest rates is due to *fall*. Lots of people will want to lend money for long periods and benefit from higher interest rates. Not many people want to borrow long-term – they would rather wait until rates fall. As a result, long-term rates start to fall in relation to short-term rates. Conversely, if rates are expected to *rise*, then everyone wants to lend short-term, hoping to gain from higher rates later. Borrowers prefer to borrow long-term and lock in to lower rates while they can.

Long-term rates will now rise in order to attract funds to meet the demands of the borrowers.

Liquidity

Liquidity also affects the rate of interest – that is, how quickly can the lender get the money back? This is not quite the same as maturity. There may well be one rate for 3 month money and another for 5 year money but another consideration in the case of 5 year money is: can the lender change their mind and get the money back?

A savings bank will pay lower interest on a 'no notice' or 'sight' account than on a '3 months' notice' account. We have to pay (by way of a lower rate of interest) for the flexibility of being able to withdraw our money at any time.

In wholesale markets, if our lending of money is represented by a security, then one way of getting the money back prior to the normal repayment date is to sell the security to someone else.

Supply and Demand

Of course, we cannot ignore the whole question of supply and demand in different market sectors. For example, for over 2 years from 1988 to 1990, the UK government was in surplus and did not need to borrow by issuing bonds. The demand was still there, however, from UK and foreign pension funds, insurance companies and other investors. This contributed to a lowering of interest rates for government bonds. In Germany, however, the costs of unification have led to a large increase in government borrowing and a rise in interest rates on German government bonds. The supply/demand factor can be seen at its best perhaps when one looks at the yield curve for UK government bonds in mid-1992 and April 1996 and their most curious 'kinks' (see Figure 6.2). They also show how yields vary from year to year.

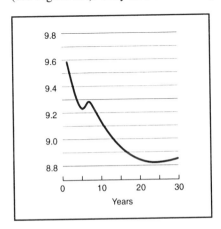
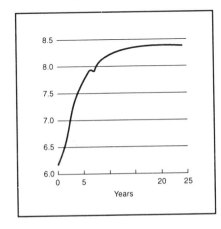

Figure 6.2 UK gilts yield, 1992 and 1996

Up to 5 years, there are plenty of lenders, for example banks and UK building societies. Over 10 years, there are plenty of lenders – pension funds and insurance companies. From 5 to 10 years there is a shortage and rates rise a little (if only 10 bp) to attract lenders.

Inflation

Finally, whether a given rate of interest represents good value or not may depend on the rate of inflation. Economists talk of the *real* rate of interest, that is, the nominal rate of interest minus the rate of inflation.

For example, in West Germany in 1986, short-term interest rates were about 4½%, while the rate of inflation was zero. In 1991, short-term rates were about 9% but the rate of inflation had risen to about 4%. Thus the *nominal* rates in 1986 and 1991 seemed very different – 4½% and 9%. Nominal rates had doubled. The *real* rate, however, was much the same – 4½% in 1986 and 5% in 1991. In the UK in 1989/90, interest rates reached 15% while the government desperately tried to curb inflation, which had reached 11%. In 1992, the rate of interest had fallen to 10% but inflation had fallen to less than 4%. Thus, although nominal rates had fallen from 15% to 10%, the *real* rate had risen from 4% to over 6%.

YIELD

Yield is arguably the most important term in the financial markets. 'Yield' is the return to the investor expressed as an annual percentage. As the markets are all about raising capital, the yield is crucially important. Unfortunately, it's not as easy as it seems!

Suppose we have a bond issued in 1996 and maturing in 25 years – 2021. The bond pays a rate of interest of 10% once per year. What is the yield? At first, the answer seems obvious – 10%. 'If I buy the bond', you argue, 'I get 10% – where's the problem?' The problem is that your answer is only true if you paid the full price for the bond.

Par Values

Bonds have a 'par' or 'nominal' value. This is usually taken to be $1000, £100, DM1000 and so on. This is the amount on which the rate of interest is based and the amount which will be repaid at maturity. You buy the 25 year 10% bond and pay the par value of $1000. Your yield is 10%. However, as secondary market trading begins, investors may pay either more or less than $1000 for the bond with a par value of $1000 – this affects the yield. The price of the bond is expressed as a percentage of the par value. For example, if the price is 90, then the price for $1000 par value is $900. In the UK, £100 is taken to be the par value. A price of 90 means that the price for £100 par value is £90.

Suppose the 25 year bond mentioned above is a UK government bond and you buy £5000 worth at issue: after all, government bonds are the safest, aren't they? 2 years later, you need the money and decide to sell. 2 years later, however, the level of interest rates has changed. The yield on long-dated government bonds is now 12½%. As you try to get full price for your 10% bond, no one is interested. Why should they pay you £100 to receive £10, when they could buy a new bond for £100 and get £12.50? They might pay you £80, because your bond pays £10 once per year and £10 for an investment of £80 is 12½%. Therefore, as interest rates went *up*, the price of your bond went *down*. The face rate of interest is 10% but by buying it more cheaply, the yield has increased to 12½% because £10 is 12½% of £80.

Let's say that you refuse to sell. 2 years later, you have lost your job and life is grim. You must sell your bonds, come what may. However, by now things have changed again. The yield on long-dated government bonds is now only 8%. When you attempt to sell your 10% bond you will find no shortage of buyers willing to pay you more than par, because 10% is very attractive if current rates are 8%. As a result, as interest rates went *down*, the price of your bond went *up*. In theory, buyers might pay £125, because the income of £10 returns 8% which is the market rate. That is to say, £10 is 8% of £125.

Interest Yield

Just to cover more market jargon, the face rate of interest on the bond is called the *coupon* (for reasons which will be explained later). The calculation we made above when arriving at the yield was:

$$\frac{\text{Coupon}}{\text{Price}} = \text{Yield}$$

for example

$$\frac{£10}{£80} = 12.5\%$$

or

$$\frac{£10}{£125} = 8\%$$

This calculation of yield is called the interest yield (the terms *simple, flat, running* and *annual* yield are also used). It's not difficult, but not really helpful either.

Gross Redemption Yield

Let's go back to the illustration above of the effect of yields rising to 12½%. We suggested that someone might buy your bond for £80. We argued:

1.   Buy the new 12½% bond for £100 – yield 12½%
2.   Buy the existing 10% bond for £80 – yield 12½%.

Unfortunately, we've omitted one crucial factor – redemption, When the bond is redeemed, the government will pay £100. In case 1 above, there is no capital gain. In case 2, there's a capital gain of £20. As a result, the yield is more than 12½% if we throw this factor in. Equally, if anyone paid £125, they would face a loss of £25 at redemption. The market does its calculations on the assumption that the bond is kept until redemption.

We need, therefore, an all-embracing calculation that includes the interest yield and modifies it by any gain or loss at redemption. The resultant figure is the *gross redemption yield* (or *yield to maturity*). ('Gross' means ignoring tax. As we don't know the investor's tax status, we ignore consideration of any tax that might be due on the interest or on any capital gain.) The formula itself is quite complicated, as it's based on discounted cash flow. We are taking the future stream of revenue – interest and redemption – and calculating the yield that would equate this to today's bond price. Alternatively, we could feed into the formula a desired yield and calculate the price to be paid that would achieve that yield. That's why it's so important – it's how bond dealers calculate bond prices.

Suppose, however, that a bond pays 10% and the market yield is 12½%, but redemption is not 2018 but 2 months away. Does this make any difference? Will the bond still only sell for about £80? Surely not – here is a piece of paper that, in 2 months, is worth £100. Why was the bond price so poor in our original example? It was because the bond offered 10% and the market wanted 12½% but, if there's only 2 months' interest payments left, this hardly matters. What matters is that redemption at £100 is quite near.

The result is that the nearer we get to redemption, the nearer the secondary market price moves to £100 and the less important interest rate changes are. Thus, long-dated bonds are highly sensitive to interest rate changes (interest rates *up*, bond prices *down* and vice-versa) but short dates are not.

Consider two 10% bonds. The ultimate reward for the buyer is the interest payments and the redemption value. Suppose one bond has 1 year to run and the other 20 years.

		Interest payments £	+	Redemption £	=	Reward £
1	1 year to go	10	+	100	=	110
2	20 years to go	200	+	100	=	300

In case 1, most of the reward is redemption, not affected by interest rate changes.

In case 2, most of the reward is interest payments. If these don't match the market yield, the effect on price will be very serious.

We could represent this diagrammatically, as shown in Figure 6.3.

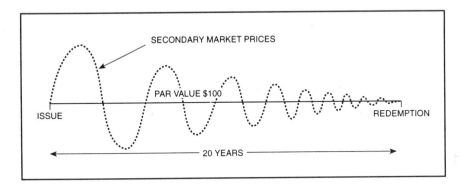

Figure 6.3 *Volatility of long-dated bonds*

Let's verify this against some real prices. These are prices for UK government bonds in April 1996:

	Bond		*Price*
1	15¼%	1996	100¹⁵⁄₁₆
	10%	1996	102¹⁵⁄₃₂
2	12%	2013/17	131²³⁄₃₂
	8%	2021	96⁷⁄₃₂

Notice that in case 1 we have two bonds, one paying 15¼% and one 10%. It might be thought that the 15¼% would be much more expensive, when in fact the prices are nearly identical – they are both near redemption.

In case 2, one bond pays 12% and the other 8%, and this is fully reflected in the two prices. Here, redemption is 20-30 years away.

(Incidentally, the redemption year shown above of 2013/17 means redemption between 2013 and 2017 at the government's decision. If, in 2013, rates are 10%, we can be quite sure that the government will redeem early and reborrow at 10%. If rates are 14%, however, what would be the point of stopping paying 12% in order to start paying 14%?)

You will also notice the habit in the UK and US bond markets of the use of fractions down to ⅓₂. Sensibly, continental Europe uses decimals. The smallest price movement, in one case ⅓₂ and the other 0.01, is called (curiously) a *tick*. Thus, a cry of 'Treasuries are up 5 ticks' in the US would mean ⁵⁄₃₂. A similar cry in Germany would mean 0.05.

You will gather from the above discussion that dealers holding an inventory of long-dated bonds are at risk to interest rate changes. They may seek to hedge this risk using a futures exchange, and we explain this later in Chapter 11. Equally, if you want to buy bonds as a short-term investment, it might be better to buy short-dated bonds, where the risk of market interest rate changes is less.

As an illustration of the dangers, you might like to read Michael Lewis's excellent *Liar's Poker* (Hodder & Stoughton, 1989). He tells the amusing story of how Merrill Lynch trader, Howie Rubin, lost $250m on long-dated bonds in 1987 in one fateful deal. (Well, it's amusing if you're not Howie Rubin!)

Accrued Interest

Unfortunately, there is one other factor to consider before we leave these somewhat technical questions. It is the question of the timing of the interest payments. Suppose the interest is paid twice per year on 16 January and 16 July. You buy a 10% bond in the secondary market on January 16 for £90. You have just missed the interest payment and will have to wait 6 months for the next one. Suppose that you have to sell after 3 months and that prices are unchanged. If you could only sell for £90, this would seem very unfair, as you've held the bond for 3 months and had no reward for your investment. Equally, the buyer would collect 5% although they had only held the bond for 3 months.

Naturally, it doesn't work like that. When you sell your bond you get the *accrued interest* to date. If you held £100 nominal value of the 10% bond for 3 months, you would get half the bi-annual interest, that is, £2.50. (The calculation is simply multiplying the yearly interest payments per £100 – £10 in this case – by the number of days the bond is held as a proportion of the days in the year.) The accrued interest is almost always quoted separately (there are some exceptions in some markets, such as convertible bonds). The price without the accrued interest is the *clean price*. The price you see on a computer screen or in the financial newspapers is always the clean price. If you sell, you will receive the accrued interest in addition. If you buy, you will have to pay it. One reason for accounting for the accrued interest separately is that in many countries any gain in this area is subject to income tax. Gains on the clean price are capital gains.

There is a complication. There must be a cut off point, at which time everyone on the register of holders gets the interest. After this the bond is marked XD (ex dividend). Suppose the half year payment is on 10 June. The bonds may go XD on 5 May. However, the interest accrues from 10 December to 10 June. Anyone selling on 5 May will get the half year interest to 10 June although they did not own the bond in the last 35 days. Anyone buying the bond on 5 May will not accrue any interest until 10 June, even though they have invested their capital 35 days earlier. As a result, when bonds are sold in the XD period, the seller (who gains) *pays* the accrued interest to the buyer (who loses). This is the exception to the way accrued interest is treated.

CREDIT RATINGS

We have seen that the higher the creditworthiness of the borrower, the lower the rate of interest. Some markets (for example, the US) want the credit rating of the borrower officially assessed so as to guide them as to the risk and the appropriate rate of interest. There are several companies in the credit rating business but the two most important are Standard and Poor's (McGraw Hill) and Moody's Investor Service (Dun and Bradstreet). For banks, there is a UK-based organisation called IBCA. This merged with the French Euronotation in October 1992. Some see this as the first move to a pan-European body to rival Standard and Poor's and Moody's.

These organisations look at bond issues and commercial paper issues (to be covered later) and rate them according to the risk. To quote Standard and Poor's themselves, the ratings are based, in varying degrees, on the following considerations:

1. *Likelihood of default* – capacity and willingness of the obligor as to the timely payment of interest and repayment of principal in accordance with the terms of the obligation
2. *Nature* and *provisions* of the obligation
3. Protection afforded to, and relative position of, the obligation in the event of bankruptcy, reorganisation, or other arrangement under the *laws of bankruptcy* and other laws affecting *creditors' rights.*

A bond which is the best risk is rated AAA by Standard and Poor's and Aaa by Moody's. The full list for Standard and Poor's is:

AAA
AA
A
BBB
BB
B
CCC
CC
C
C1
D

A bond rated 'D' is either in default or expected to default.

As a further refinement, the grade may be modified by plus (+) or minus (-), for example, AA+ or AA-. A bond may be issued as AAA but be reduced later to A if the position of the issuer deteriorates. This will increase their borrowing costs. Suppose the appropriate rate for an AAA bond is 10%. The rate for an A might be 10.75%.

Below the BBB rank there is a sort of invisible line. Bonds rated BBB and above are 'investment grade' – top quality if you like. Many investment funds will only invest if the grade is BBB or higher. Below BBB, to quote Standard and Poor's again:

> Debt rated 'BB', 'B', 'CCC', 'CC' and 'C' is regarded as having predominantly speculative characteristics with respect to capacity to pay interest and repay principal. 'BB' indicates the least degree of speculation and 'C' the highest degree of speculation. While such debt will likely have some quality and protective characteristics, these are outweighed by large uncertainties or major risk exposures to adverse conditions.

'Junk bonds' are simply bonds which are not investment grade. This quite a long story and we'll tackle it later.

Moody's have a similar system but use slightly different lettering.

The view of risk for a 3 month loan may be quite different from that for a 5 year loan. As a result, both organisations use a simpler system for the shorter-term commercial paper. For Standard and Poor's this is:

A1
A2
A3
B
C
D

As an example of the way organisations can lose ratings, we have only to look at the banks. In 1990, there were eight banks (not owned by the state) whose bonds were rated AAA by both organisations – Rabobank, Deutsche, Morgan Guaranty, Barclays, Swiss Bank Corporation, Union Bank of Switzerland, Crédit Suisse and Industrial Bank of Japan. Due to commercial bad debts following recession, by mid-1992 the proud band of eight had shrunk to four – Rabobank, Deutsche, Morgan Guaranty and Union Bank of Switzerland and, then, by January 1997 had shrunk to one – Rabobank!

Standard and Poor's and Moody's do not always move together. In 1992, for example, Moody's downgraded the Swiss Bank Corporation from AAA. Standard and Poor's did not follow suit until early 1995.

Credit ratings are used extensively in the domestic US market and the Euromarkets (to be explained later). It has not generally been a habit in Europe, but the default of Polly Peck's commercial paper issue in the UK has led to an increasing use of ratings in this market. It is likely, in fact, that ratings will be used increasingly in Europe. Ratings are not only applied to corporate issues but also to government issues ('sovereign issues'). In mid-1991, for example, a frisson spread through the market as bonds issued by the Italian government were downgraded from AAA to AA+.

Credit rating agencies, of course, exercise considerable power. Moody's habit of publishing unsolicited ratings has led to criticism. Since this rating will be based on imperfect information, it leads to pressure on the company to pay for a full rating in the hope of getting a better one. (The bond issuers pay, not the investors.) In March 1996, Moody's found itself the subject of an investigation by the US Justice Department into a breach of anti-trust rules.

Discussing the question 'who controls the raters?', the *Economist* in an article on April 6 1996 concluded that:

> In theory, the agencies have good reason to stick to the straight and narrow. Even more than accountants and lawyers, they must trade on their reputations. If bond investors lose faith in the integrity of the rating agencies' judgements, they will no longer pay attention to their ratings ... companies and governments will not pay their fees.

DOMESTIC MONEY MARKETS

We have previously mentioned that some markets are *domestic* (that is, transactions are in the local currency and under the control of the local central bank) and some are regarded as *international* (for example, a bond denominated in Japanese yen issued in London through a syndicate of international banks).

There are also *money* markets, which are short-term (that is, borrowing/lending of money which is 1 year or less), and *bond* markets, which are markets handling medium- to long-term borrowing/lending.

In this chapter we deal with domestic markets first, covering the various instruments and practices of the money markets, and follow this with bonds.

Then we will look at the international markets, both short and long-term.

When we look at domestic money markets, we find that there is no single marketplace here, like a stock exchange floor. All over the western financial markets there are large numbers of people who spend their day buying and selling money in one form and another. Huge sums of money are borrowed or lent, sometimes simply 'overnight'.

Transactions involving the general public and small businesses, like shops, are called the *retail* market.

Transactions between the big players are typically called the *wholesale* market. The players are central banks, other banks, financial institutions, corporates and specialists, like money brokers.

Most of this chapter will be concerned with the wholesale markets.

Call Money

There is a market in money which is borrowed/lent for a very short period of time and is not represented by a marketable instrument or security. Bankers talk of 'call' money and the 'call money market'. Money is lent by one bank to another and may be called back at any time. There is also money lent overnight by one bank to another. 'Overnight' usually means 12.00 p.m. one day to 12.00 p.m. the next day. Sometimes the money may be lent with a right to have the money back with, say, 3 or 7 days' notice. The result, on a bank's balance sheet, becomes 'money at call and short notice'. In the UK market, much of the money is lent to specialist operators called discount houses, and their role will be discussed later in this section.

The Interbank Market

Apart from the very short-term money mentioned before, there is generally a very strong interbank market in which the banks lend money one to another for periods ranging from several weeks to 1 year.

In our discussions on commercial banking, we concentrated on the idea of banks taking money from deposits and lending it to other people. The banks also top up their funds by borrowing from other banks which have spare liquidity. As this is the marginal cost to the banks for raising new money, their wholesale lending rates are based on the interbank lending rate.

The terms 'bid rate' and 'offer rate' are usually met in securities markets. The bid rate is the dealer's buying rate and the offer rate the dealer's selling rate. Obviously, the offer is higher than the bid, as the dealers will buy cheaper than they sell. The difference is called the 'spread'.

Curiously, when it comes to wholesale money, the deposit rate offered by a bank is called the bid rate and the lending rate is called the offer rate. Thus, the interbank rates in London are called LIBOR – London Interbank Offered Rate and LIBID – London Interbank Bid Rate. We therefore find PIBOR in Paris, FIBOR in Frankfurt, and EURIBOR when we have EC monetary union. One exception is the US, where the interbank rate is called the 'Federal Funds Rate'.

We have already seen that interest rates vary with time and so the interbank rates for 1 month, 3 months, 6 months and 12 months will probably be different. The most common maturity used in the market is 3 months. If someone asks 'What's the £ LIBOR rate today?' they will be referring to 3 month LIBOR. Of course, the interbank market in London deals in dollars, yen, deutschemarks and other currencies and so, although LIBOR is London, it doesn't necessarily mean sterling. Again, these wholesale rates vary all the time and each bank's rate could be different. If we say £ LIBOR is 10¹⁄₁₆% we mean the average of major banks in the market.

The spread between the bid and offer is surprisingly small. Let's look at rates quoted for 3 month money in major markets in the London *Financial Times* for 3 April 1996 (Table 6.1).

As London is a huge international market, the rate we hear of most commonly is LIBOR. We have seen that as LIBOR is the marginal cost of new money, then the lending rate in wholesale markets may be quoted as 'LIBOR +¼', 'LIBOR +35 basis points', 'LIBOR +½'. Equally, floating rate notes issued in London will have the rate reset periodically (typically every 3 or 6 months) as LIBOR plus a given margin. If the rate for a loan or floating rate note is reset every 3 months, but LIBOR is different at different times of the day, then we need to define this precisely. It is usually quoted as the average of the LIBOR rates given by nominated banks at 11.00 a.m. on the relevant day.

Table 6.1   *Interbank 3 month rates*

	Bid %	Offer %
Frankfurt	$3^5/_{32}$	$3^5/_{16}$
Paris	4	$4^5/_{32}$
Zurich	$1^5/_8$	$1^3/_4$
Amsterdam	$2^{31}/_{32}$	$3^1/_{16}$
Tokyo	$^{17}/_{32}$	$^{21}/_{32}$
London	6	$6^1/_8$
New York	$5^3/_{16}$	$5^3/_8$

Source: London *Financial Times.*

Money Market Securities

The markets we have described above – the call money market and the general interbank market – deal with wholesale borrowing and lending amongst banks and financial institutions. The transactions are not represented by any security that can be traded. We will now deal with money market transactions that do result in trading in securities.

Typical instruments are:

❏   Treasury bills
❏   Local authority/Public utility bills
❏   Certificates of deposit
❏   Commercial paper
❏   Bills of Exchange.

Treasury Bills

Governments find that their income from taxes does not come in at a steady rate, nor is their expenditure at a steady rate. Apart from raising money with medium- to long-term government bills, it's convenient and useful to be able to borrow for shorter periods and balance their cash flow. The chosen instrument is the Treasury bill (UK,

US); bon du trésor (France); Schatzwechsel (Germany, Austria) or similar terms.

The bills may or may not be offered to the same organisations who buy government bonds. In the US, the bills for 3 or 6 months or 1 year are sold by auction weekly to the same primary dealers who buy federal notes and bonds. In the UK, the 3 and 6 month bills are sold every Friday by auction to banks and discount houses. In France, anyone who has an account with the central bank can buy the 3 or 6 months or 1 year Treasury bill. They are sold weekly and money market dealers are usually called 'opérateurs principaux du marché' (OPMs). In Germany, by contrast, there is no regular timetable for selling bills and they are of widely varying maturities. They are sold to the same financial institutions who buy bonds.

The payment of interest on an instrument which only lasts 3 months is not necessarily convenient. Most typically, money market instruments are sold *at a discount*. For example, suppose we are talking about a 1 year US Treasury bill, value $100, sold by auction. A dealer may bid $94. If accepted, they pay $94 and 1 year later receive $100 from the government. They discounted the $100 by 6% but now earn $6 for investing $94, which is 6.38%. Thus, the market refers to the *discount rate* and the resulting *yield*.

We have mentioned the term 'sale by auction' (or 'tender'). There are two kinds. In one, everyone pays the price they bid ('bid price auction'). In the other, everyone pays the same price (often called the 'striking price)'. Anyone bidding at or above the striking price will receive an allocation, but not necessarily all they bid for.

Both types of auction are used in financial markets. For example, the Bank of England sells weekly Treasury bills by tender to the highest bidders – the bid/price technique. Government bonds may be sold on a striking price basis (and it's then called a tender) or on a bid price basis (and it's then called an auction)! If you're confused, don't worry – it's because it *is* confusing.

Just to make matters worse, a German publication I have in front of me says that the money market instruments are sold by auction on a bid price basis, which it calls 'US style', calling a striking price auction a 'Dutch auction'. A French publication says that money market instruments are sold on a bid price basis which it calls a 'Dutch auction'. For what it matters, I think that the Germans are right. Let's avoid all mention of Dutch auctions and simply say that if everyone pays the price they bid, it is a 'bid price' auction, and if everyone pays the same price, it is a 'striking price' auction. Both methods are used. On balance, the bid price method seems to be the most common.

Local Authority/Public Utility Bills

These may be offered by municipalities, geographic departments, federal states, or public bodies like railways, electricity, gas. There is a very strong market in public sector bills as well as bonds in France and Germany. There are issues by SNCF or Electricité de France, or by the railways and post offices in Germany (Bundesbahn and Bundespost), as well as by the individual federal states. The market in the UK for local authority/municipal bills is very weak but is quite strong in the US.

Certificates of Deposit (CDs)

These are receipts issued by banks when soliciting wholesale deposits. The lenders may be other banks or corporates or investment institutions. The advantage to the *borrower* is that the money is lent for a specific period of time, for example, 3 months. The advantage to the *lender* is that, if they need the money back earlier, the certificate can be sold to someone else quite easily. There is a very strong CD market in the US and the European economies, with the exception of Germany. There, banks must leave a percentage of their deposits as a reserve with the Bundesbank and this reserve earns no interest. Suppose the figure was 5%. Having taken a deposit of, say, DM500 000, only DM475 000 can actually be relent and the economics are spoiled. The lowering of some reserves, announced in February 1993, relieved but did not eliminate the problem. Elsewhere, CDs receive better treatment so far as reserves are concerned.

There is usually an active and efficient market in certificates of deposit. As a result, yield rates will be a little less than those for 'sight' deposits, as we must pay for the advantage of liquidity.

Commercial Paper (CP)

So far, we have looked at short-term borrowing by governments, municipalities, public sector bodies and banks. There remains the question of corporates. Commercial companies can borrow in the wholesale markets and offer a security called 'commercial paper' (CP). It's just another promise to pay back. Central banks have to agree, as this is a deposit taking activity and must be controlled. There will be rules on which companies can or cannot borrow using CP. For example, in the UK companies must have a balance sheet capital of £25m and be publicly quoted on a stock exchange (although not necessarily in the UK). The minimum denomination is £100 000.

Commercial paper is an older market in the US (where it is a huge market with outstanding money owed over $500bn). It has hit Europe in the last 10 years. Germany was the last major market to allow CP issues, in January 1991. Before that it was not practical due to a securities tax and the need for prior notification to the Treasury. Let's have a look at some figures on domestic commercial paper markets in key centres (from the BIS) in Table 6.2.

The market in Germany grew very fast, and the amount outstanding by mid-1992 had reached DM32bn (about $21bn), but later fell in popularity. CP has also reached some of the newer markets, too. In Czechoslovakia, Pilsen did an issue for 100m korunna in November 1991 and VW–Skoda for 300m korunna in January 1992.

CP issues are, of course, just another way of borrowing money and may provide an alternative to borrowing from the bank. In early 1990, the Bank of Spain was struggling to control the credit explosion and limiting banks' ability to lend. The result was a huge increase in CP ('pagares de empresa') issues, as companies borrowed by selling CP (in some cases to the same banks who couldn't lend them money!).

Table 6.2   *Domestic markets for commercial paper*

Market	Market opening	Amount outstanding April 1995 $ billion
US	pre 1960	677.7
Japan	end 1987	101.9
France	end 1985	29.5
Sweden	1983	20.2
Australia	mid 1970s	16.4
Canada	pre 1960	16.2
Spain	1982	10.0
UK	1986	9.9
Norway	end 1984	6.1
Belgium	1990	4.2
Germany	1991	4.0
Netherlands	1986	2.2
Finland	mid 1986	1.4
Total		899.70

Source: BIS Basle.

Deregulation applies here as in other markets. The French now allow non-French entities to issue domestic CP and Germany did so from August 1992. At the end of 1995, outstanding CP in Germany from foreign issuers was higher than that from domestic issuers.

How do the CP issuers find the lenders? They set up a programme (perhaps a 5 year programme) and announce a bank or banks as dealers. If the programme is $500m, then the issuer does not intend to raise $500m *now* (which would be the case if it were a bond issue) but will borrow money from time to time and repay it from time to time, up to the maximum figure. If they wish to borrow $50m for 2 months, they would notify the bank dealer(s), who ring round typical lenders (other corporates, banks and investment institutions) and tie up the deal, all for a small commission. The banks do not *guarantee* to find lenders but if lenders are scarce may buy the CP themselves as a matter of goodwill. The effect of borrowing from the lenders directly, instead of borrowing from the bank, means that the rate may be less than the interbank rate.

Bills of Exchange

Another way in which a corporate might raise money short-term is by selling on a short-term trade debt (we met this in Chapter 5). The seller draws up a bill promising to pay them for the goods supplied in, say, 3 months and asks the buyer to sign it. This is the bill of exchange. The seller of the goods can now sell this at a discount to the banks, general money market operators or specialists called 'discount houses'. We have seen that a bank's promise to pay may be better than a trader's and there is always a distinction between bills with the trader's signature (trade bills) and those with a bank's signature (bank or eligible bills). Bills may change hands several times in their short life. There are usually restrictions on the type of transaction that can be represented by a bill and so not all corporates can use bills of exchange. They are not especially popular in the US but widely used in Europe, especially in the UK. In France, the bill is 'lettre de change' and, in Germany, simply 'wechsel'.

We have now already met several ways in which a corporate might raise money short-term – bank overdraft, a general uncommitted bank line of credit, a revolving credit programme, a CP issue or using bill of exchange finance.

CENTRAL BANK ROLE

A key role is played in domestic money markets by central banks. They have a function as 'lender of the last resort', which we met in Chapter 3. They are prepared to help the other banks (especially commercial banks) with their liquidity problems.

Why would banks meet liquidity problems? In the first place, the key commercial banks must maintain working balances at the central bank. Where central banks insist on special reserves being left (Chapter 3), there will be times when the reserves look comfortable and times when they don't. The reserves are usually based on average balances over a month. Until the end of the month, the banks are not sure what the figure will be. Those banks in surplus will lend to other banks; those in deficit will borrow from other banks. At times, all the banks may have problems. This is when heavy tax payments are being made. The government's bank balance is going up; the banks' balances at the central bank are going down. The central bank will relend the money to keep everything on an even basis and to avoid wide fluctuations in money market rates. The rate set for the central bank's help gives it its control over interest rates. When interest rates change, it is because the central bank changes the rate for its help to other banks.

There are two ways usually in which a central bank will help: direct assistance at special rates such as the *discount rate* or *lombard rate*; or by what is called *open market operations*.

In late 1991, the Bundesbank dismayed other markets in Europe by putting up interest rates. It raised the discount rate to 8% and the lombard rate to 9¾%. Later, in July 1992, it raised the discount rate to 8¾% but left the lombard unchanged. Gradually, rates fell again and, in mid-April 1996, the discount rate and lombard rate were both lowered by ½% to 2½% and 4½% respectively.

What are these rates? The *discount rate* is the rate at which the bank will discount eligible bills of exchange (that is, top quality bills) for other banks. (The maturity of the bills must not exceed 3 months.) As this rate is below other rates, there is a quota for each bank, or life would be too easy. If we could discount a bill at 9½% and then refinance ourselves at 8¾% at the central bank we would soon make a lot of money.

The *lombard rate* is an emergency lending rate against top quality securities (eligible bills, bills of exchange or government/federal bonds). Usually, as it is higher than money market rates, no limit to the quantity need be set. At times, however, limits have had to be set for temporary periods (for example, September 1979, February 1981) because the lombard rate was lower than money market rates.

Open market operations means that the central bank may be prepared to buy bills of exchange, Treasury bills or similar securities to help the banks' liquidity or to sell bills to help drain excess liquidity.

A popular method nowadays is the 'sale and repurchase agreement' (commonly called the *repo*). The central bank will buy nominated securities from the other banks for a stated period, for example, 7 days, 14 days, 28 days. At the end of the period, the banks must be ready to buy them back at a rate which includes the rate of interest on the money. The banks sell the securities to the central bank but must repurchase later. This is a very common method all over Europe. In the UK, the more common method used to be that the Bank of England would simply buy eligible securities outright. Later, repos became much more common in the UK. In the quarter August/October 1988, for example, there were only eight repos but in the same quarter 1991, there were 63. On the other hand, by 1995 daily repos had died out in favour of outright purchase of eligible bills and treasury bills. However, on a fortnightly basis, repos still take place, using gilts this time. On 7 February 1996, for example, £3154m of gilts were purchased for re-sale on 22 February and £2046m of gilts were purchased for re-sale on 7 March.

These operations exist not only to help commercial banks with their liquidity but can also be used to influence money supply and market conditions. The central banks may keep the banks short of liquidity to keep credit scarce and stiffen interest rates.

For example, when a repo falls due, there will normally be another repo to keep the banks funded but the second repo may be for a smaller sum than the first. In Germany in 1992, two repos worth DM44.5bn expired on 4 March. Although it was a month for heavy tax payments, the new repo was only for DM42bn. This was interpreted as determination on the part of the Bundesbank to keep monetary policy tight. When the Bundesbank lowered the lombard and discount rates on 4 February

1993, they also pointed out that these rates only apply to about 17% of their transactions with the German banks. The repos are of key importance. This point was illustrated when the Bundesbank council meeting of 10 October 1997 did not change the formal lombard or discount rates but announced a rise in the repo rate from 3.0% to 3.3%. Several European central banks then lowered their interest rates.

One final point: these repos are done by tender so that the banks have to bid against each other for the money they require.

When central banks wish to formally raise or lower interest rates, they announce a change in these key rates. The Bundesbank may do so at its fortnightly council meeting. The Bank of England announces a new Minimum Lending Rate (MLR).

UK Discount Houses

A unique role has traditionally been played in the UK money markets by organisations called discount houses (see Figure 6.4). They get their name from their original role in discounting bills of exchange. Originally they acted as bill brokers, finding someone who would discount the bill. In 1830, however, they began to act as principals, discounting the bills themselves.

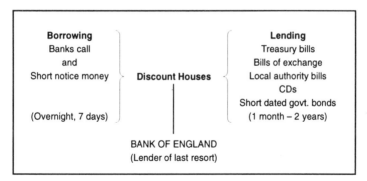

Figure 6.4 *The discount houses' role*

In the UK, the discount houses are the recipients of the banks' liquid funds – call and short notice money. They then put the money to longer-term use – buying Treasury bills, bills of exchange and CDs, all at a discount. They are borrowing short and lending long. Banks borrow short and lend long but not to the same extent as this.

For anyone else, this would be suicide but the system here is quite deliberate. The discount houses are funded daily by the Bank of England in its role of 'lender of last resort'. One has to bear in mind that the banks are not required to hold non-interest bearing reserves at the central bank (other than a trifling 0.35%). As a result, there are far more liquid funds outside the central bank than you might find elsewhere. The banks freely lend the funds (on a secured basis) to discount houses as well as other banks, and equally will take them away just as quickly. They may then ask the houses to discount bills of exchange held by banks to give them further assistance. They know the houses will always have the money. Why? Because the Bank of England will give it to them. Why doesn't the Bank of England provide help to the other banks directly? It's a good question and you may not be happy with the answer which is simply – tradition, that is, that's the way it's always been done. Part of this tradition is that the chairman of the Discount Houses Association visits the governor of the Bank of England wearing a silk top hat every Thursday. Also traditional is the fact that the houses guarantee the weekly Treasury bill tender: that is, if the banks don't want the bills, the houses will buy them (even if they have to borrow the money from the Bank of England!).

Bills of exchange have always played a major role in commercial life in the UK. The discount houses and banks deal in bills extensively and the Bank of England found it useful to have a controllable (but very skilful) body of people to deal with rather than the banks as a whole. It is also true that the bank is seeing overnight money put to good use by being lent longer in controlled circumstances. The UK money markets have a reputation for being extremely efficient.

The Bank of England thus deals with the discount houses at 12.00 p.m. and 2.00 p.m. each day, when they tender for assistance. 'Late assistance' may be provided at 2.45 and outright lending (if any) at 2.30. The rate involved is called Minimum Lending Rate (MLR) but the term MLR is only formally used when rates are being changed.

In 1993, with the large PSBR, the system was under strain and the Bank of England decided to supplement the help it gave the banks daily via the discount houses with fortnightly repos carried out directly with the banks and using gilts. This began in January 1994.

Later, came an even bigger change. In the spring of 1997, the Bank of England began a two year transitional period in which it will gradually phase out the exclusive daily dealing with the discount houses and deal directly with banks, using outright purchase of bills, repos with bills and repos with gilts. In return, the discount houses will no longer guarantee the weekly Treasury bill tender. It's all to do with "coming into line with Europe" and Eurosceptics may lament the death of one aspect of the City at its most traditional and esoteric.

DOMESTIC BOND MARKETS

Introduction

The term 'bond' applies to instruments which are medium to longer term. The term 'note' is also used in some markets. The US, for example, have 2, 3, 5, 7 and 10 year Treasury *notes* and a 30 year Treasury *bond*. In the UK, the same 5 year instrument would be called a bond.

Language here is a problem in that there is no consistency. The French, for example, call instruments up to 5 years (but prior to 1992, up to 7 years) 'bons du trésor' and from 7 years 'obligations du trésor'. The Spanish equally have 'bonos del estado' up to 5 years but after that they are 'obligaciones del estado'. On the other hand, the 10 year issue in Italy is 'buoni del tesoro'.

Let's look at some general characteristics of bonds. As we saw in Chapter 1, they are simply receipts or promises to pay back money lent. We are not, here, talking of short-term money, however, but medium- to long-term borrowings – in excess of 1 year and possibly for 30 or more years.

The general features are:

❑ The name of the bond
❑ The nominal or par value in the currency of denomination
❑ The redemption value – usually the nominal value, but there are other possibilities (index linking, for example)
❑ The rate of interest expressed as a % of nominal value; this is called the 'coupon': the frequency of payment is stated
❑ The redemption date.

The rate of interest is called the coupon because 'bearer' bonds have no register of holders. The bond states that the issuer owes the 'bearer', whoever that may be. The bond therefore has attachments called 'coupons' so that the bearer may detach these as required and claim the interest. Even where bonds are registered and the interest can be posted to the holder's home, the market still refers to the 'coupon' or 'coupon rate'.

The coupon could be variable in cases where the rate of interest is changed periodically in line with market rates. As the word 'bond' implies a fixed rate of interest, instruments like this are usually called *floating rate notes*. If issued in London, the coupon may be defined as 'LIBOR +45 basis points' and reviewed 6 monthly.

Some stocks have no redemption date and are called *undated* or *perpetual*. If the holder needs the capital, they must sell the bond to someone else in the secondary market.

Typically, bonds are classified by remaining maturity. The scale may well be:

❑ *Shorts* – life of up to 5 years
❑ *Mediums* – life of 5 to 15 years
❑ *Longs* – life of 15 years or over.

Notice that is the *remaining* maturity. A 20 year bond is a 'long' at first but 10 years later it's a 'medium' and 6 years later it's a 'short'.

At original issue, bonds may be sold as an open *offer for sale* or sold directly to a smaller number of professional investors and called a *private placing*.

In an offer for sale, a syndicate of banks with one bank as *lead manager* will buy the bonds en bloc from the issuer and resell them to investors. In this way, they underwrite the issue since, if the investors don't buy, the banks will be forced to keep them. Needless to say, they charge fees for this risk.

If the lead bank buys all the bonds and sells them to the syndicate, it's usually called the *bought deal*. The syndicate members may themselves then sell the bonds at varying prices. More commonly these days, the lead manager and syndicate buy the bonds simultaneously and agree to sell at the same price for a period – the *fixed price reoffering*. This is very common in the US and now in the so-called 'euromarkets'. Less frequently (apart from government bonds) there may not be a syndicate but the bonds are sold by competitive *auction*.

There are several types of bond according to the issuer:

- ❑ Government bonds
- ❑ Local authority/Public utility bonds
- ❑ Mortgage and other asset backed bonds
- ❑ Corporate bonds
- ❑ Foreign bonds
- ❑ Junk bonds.

Corporate bonds may also be:

- ❑ Debentures, or
- ❑ Convertibles

and there is a hybrid type of instrument, the preference share or participation stock.

Government Bonds

Almost always, these seem to dominate the bond markets. Most modern governments are running a budget deficit and this leads to large-scale issues of bonds. Sometimes the secondary market is run on stock exchanges (France, Germany, UK) and sometimes outside stock exchanges (US).

As regards the types of bonds and method of issue, there are many variations:

- ❑ The bonds may be issued by the central bank (US, UK, Germany, France) or by the Ministry of Finance (Netherlands, Japan).
- ❑ They may be sold on a regular day per month (US, UK, France, Italy, Spain) or ad hoc (Germany).
- ❑ The issue may be to specialist dealers (US, UK, France, Italy) or to a syndicate of banks in agreed proportions (Germany, Switzerland).
- ❑ Bonds may be 'bearer' status or registered. For example, in the UK, government bonds are registered and the registrar's department handles 5m interest payments per year and 1m changes of ownership. In Germany, the

most important government bonds for the wholesale markets are bearer bonds. There are no certificates and buying/selling is entered on the computerised Bundeschuldenbuch.

❑ Some markets pay interest twice per year (US, UK, Italy, Japan), others only once per year (France, Germany, Netherlands, Spain, Belgium).

❑ UK and US government bonds are priced in fractions (down to $^1/_{32}$). Elsewhere bonds are priced in decimals.

Let's look at some examples:

In the *US*, 2 and 5 year Treasury notes are sold every month, while 3, 7 and 10 year Treasury notes and 30 year Treasury bonds are sold every quarter. They are sold by auction, on regular dates, to some 40 primary dealers.

In *France*, government bonds are called OATS (Obligations Assimilable de Trésor) and are sold on a regular monthly auction basis (on the first Thursday in each month). They are sold to primary dealers who have an obligation to support the auction. They must take up 3% of annual bond issuance and trade 3% of secondary market turnover. The primary dealers are called 'spécialistes en valeurs du trésor' (SVTs). However, at each auction the offerings are usually more of existing bonds rather than offering new ones each time. Some bonds are variable rate (TME, TMB, TRA or TRB) and some are issued in Ecus. A point to note is that there are 2 and 5 year issues called Treasury bills rather than bonds. These are known as BTAN (Bons du Trésor à Interêt Annuel). (Short term Treasury bills are BTF – Bons du Trésor à Taux Fixe.)

In the past, some fixed rate bonds have been issued which are convertible later into floating rate and floating rates convertible into fixed. Also in the past, some zero-coupon bonds (to be explained later) called 'Felins' have been issued (but none in recent years).

After not issuing bonds at floating rate for several years, the Bank of France announced proposals in 1996 to issue new floating rate bonds with the interest paid quarterly and linked to a new benchmark for the yield of 10 year OATS called TEC10 (Taux de l'Echéance Constante).

In *Germany*, there were 2 and 4 year medium-term notes – Bundesschatzanweisungen, but these maturities were lowered in mid-1996 to 6 months to 2 years and referred to as Bubills. There are also 5 year government bonds – Bundesobligationen and 10–30 year bonds – Bundesanleihen. The 10 year issues are the popular ones (rather than of longer duration) and most are fixed rate, although there is the occasional Floating Rate Bond. There are 1 and 2 year issues also of Treasury Financing Notes.

In Germany, there are bond issues from the Federal States (Länder), the railways and the post office. There are also issues from the German Unity Fund (Fonds Deutsche Einheit). All are issued for them by the Bundesbank.

German government Bundesanleihen issues used to be shared out amongst a syndicate of banks with 20% only reserved for foreign banks. In July 1990, however, part of an issue was sold by auction to the highest bidder. In October 1991, the 20%

rule was abolished and, in late 1997, it was announced that the syndicate would be scrapped and replaced by a 'Federal Loan Bidding Group' in 1998. The new Bundesschatzanweisungen are sold totally by auction but there have been no new issues since mid-1995. They were replaced in late 1996 by a new 2 year Treasury Note.

Bundesobligationen are issued in series. A series is offered continuously for 4–6 weeks 'on tap'. They are aimed at retail buyers, as are the Treasury Financing Notes (Finanzierungschätze). At the end of the period, the unsold bonds are offered for sale by auction. The main retail bond for savers, however, is the Bundesschatzbriefe. These are sold continuously by all banks and financial institutions and are for 6 or 7 years. The bonds can be sold back at par at any time but the longer the holder keeps them, the greater the rate of interest.

In *Japan*, government bonds are sold by auction by the Ministry of Finance. 4% are sold to a bank syndicate in agreed proportions; 60% are sold by the auction method. 2, 5 and 10 year bonds are sold monthly and 20 year bonds are sold quarterly. Interest payments are semi-annual.

In the *UK*, government bonds are called 'gilts' or 'gilt-edged', meaning a very secure investment (the term came into widespread use in the 1930s). The bonds are issued on regular dates and sold to specialist dealers called 'gilt-edged market makers'. Bonds not taken up at an auction are bought by the Bank of England and sold whenever the dealers want them as 'tap stock'. Maturities range typically from 5 to 25 years.

Gilts are divided into three main classes:
1. Dated
2. Undated
3. Index linked.

New undated gilts are no longer issued but there are eight still in existence. There is no redemption date. In bond markets, bonds with no redemption date may be called undated, perpetual or irredeemable. There is very little trading of undated gilts by the wholesale markets.

Index-linked gilts pay a rate of interest and a redemption value based on the change in the Retail Price Index in the same period. Other governments which offer index-linked bonds are Australia, Canada, Iceland, Israel, New Zealand and Sweden. The UK index-linked sector is much the biggest of these. Issue began in 1981. In May 1996, the US Treasury Secretary announced that they would issue index-linked Treasury Notes and Bonds for the first time.

(In 1973, the French government issued bonds – Giscard bonds – linked to the change in the price of gold between then and 1988. As the price of gold rose, this caused great embarrassment!)

Spanish government bonds are called 'bonos del estado' with maturities of 3 and 5 years but the 10 year maturity is called 'obligaciones del estado'. The central bank sells these on a regular date each month.

Italian government bonds are called BTP (Buoni del Tesoro Poliennali) if fixed rate. These are 2–10 years in maturity. However, there are floating rate bonds of similar maturity called CCT (Certificati Credito del Tesoro). Both are sold by the central bank to 20 primary dealers on fixed dates every month. There are also 6 year bonds which buyers can sell back after 3 years called CTO (Certificati del Tesoro con Opzione).

Local Authority/Public Sector Bonds

We have already mentioned issues in Germany by the railways, post offices, Federal states and the German Unity Fund. Public sector issues are also very common in France. There are the utilities like SNCF, Electricité de France and Gaz de France. There are also public sector bodies like Crédit Foncier (housing credits) and Crédit Local de France (local authority financing). There bonds are so important that at the end of 1991 a new set of primary dealers was set up to handle the issues and to quote bid and offer prices. They are called 'spécialistes en valeurs du secteur public'.

Local authority and public sector issues are very rare in the UK, although some long-dated bonds issued in the 1970s are still traded. Municipal bonds are a big market in the US.

Mortgage and Asset Backed Bonds

In some markets, there is a big market in mortgage bonds. In the US, for example, it has been the custom for many years to bundle up mortgages and use them as the backing security for mortgage bonds. The mortgages may be guaranteed by bodies with names like Ginnie Mae, Fannie Mae and Sallie Mae. (They, naturally, stand for something much more formal and boring, for example, Government National Mortgage Association – GNMA and hence Ginnie Mae.) The US mortgage bond market is huge – about $1000bn outstanding, compared with £9bn in the UK, Europe's biggest mortgage-backed market.

In Germany some 40 banks, including eight public mortgage banks, have the right to issue mortgage bonds called Pfandbriefe. The maturity is 3–10 years and they are sold on stock exchanges. There are also mortgage bonds with similar maturities issued by mortgage banks in Finland.

The mortgage bond is just one example (although the most important one) of taking the stream of principal and interest payments from an asset and converting it into a security – hence the phrase 'securitisation of assets'. It was mentioned in Chapter 2, when capital ratio was discussed, as a way of getting an asset off the balance sheet. We mentioned, in that context, car loans, credit card receivables and loan portfolios. In early 1996, for example, Volkswagen did a DM500m issue in Germany backed by car lease receivables. It was only the second asset-backed deal issued in Germany and the first backed by car leases. We have had several examples from Latin America. One interesting case was Telmex, the Mexican telecommunications company, which raised $280m secured against telephone receivables – payments owed to it for long distance calls between Mexico and the US. As a result, the issue received an A rating from Duff and Phelps and Baa1 from Moody's. Similar deals in Latin America raised $2.8bn in 1995.

In 1995, Standard & Poors rated $94bn of asset-backed issues in the US and $9.9bn in Europe.

Corporate Bonds

There are, of course, bonds issued by corporates and there is a very strong market in the US. In Europe, as a generalisation, the corporate bond market is weaker, being overshadowed by the government and public sector bond market. In Germany there is, anyway, a big tradition of reliance on bank finance as opposed to either bonds or equities. Very large European corporates may, in any case, find it easier to issue the bond in London as a *Eurobond* than as a domestic bond (see later in this chapter).

Corporate bonds can, however, be quite long dated. In the UK, a property company (MEPC) issued a bond in 1988 that will redeem in 2032 – 44 years. Also, British Land did a 40 year issue in September 1995. Property companies look far ahead to long-term leases and commitments. Who among the investors looks so far ahead? The answer is pension funds and life assurance companies who have to meet long-term liabilities.

There are a number of variations on the theme:

Debentures are corporate bonds which are backed by security, for example, land and buildings. If the issuer goes into liquidation, these assets must be sold to pay the bondholders. Because they are more secure, however, the rate of interest is less. Some investment funds will only invest in corporate bonds which are debentures. Again, language is a problem. The definition given is the UK usage of the term. In the US and Canada, 'debenture' may be used to describe any bond. Just bear in mind that corporate bonds may be unsecured (the majority) or secured on specific assets. Whilst securing a bond gives a corporate cheaper finance, it's also inconvenient to tie up assets in this way. Lengthy and tedious legal procedures must be gone through before these assets can be disposed of and replaced by others. MEPC and British Land (mentioned above) have both unsecured bonds and debentures on the market. The unsecured bonds pay 1.1% more than the debentures in the case of MEPC and 70 basis points in the case of British Land.

A *convertible* is a bond which can be converted later, either into another type of bond (for example, convertible gilts) or into equity. The difference between the implied conversion price of the equity and the market price is called the 'premium'. For example, the bond may confer the right, after 3 years, to convert $100 of bond into 50 shares. The conversion price is $2 per share; if the market price is $1.60 at the time, then the initial premium is 25%. If the conversion price remains above the market price, then the bond will redeem in the normal way.

The attraction to the *investor* is the mix of risk and return – the steady income we associate with a bond with the possible capital gain we associate with a share. For the *issuer*, the finance is cheaper as the interest rate will be less due to its attraction. (In April 1991, Hanson Group issued a convertible at 9½%. As an ordinary bond, the coupon would probably have been 12%.) What if investors wish to convert, where do the shares come from? The issuer creates *new* shares. Suppose the bond is $500m. The issuer hopes that instead of having to find $500m to redeem the bond, they will issue $500m of new shares instead. True, the equity will be diluted but it probably won't be by a large margin. In Europe (but not as clearly in the US), shareholders must give approval for the issue of convertibles because, generally, any new shares issued for cash must be offered to the existing shareholders.

An alternative to a convertible bond is to issue a bond in which the right to buy shares later at a certain price is contained in a separate *warrant*. This is more flexible than the convertible, in that the warrant can be used later to buy shares more cheaply while still keeping the bond. The warrants are often detached from the bonds and sold separately.

Sometimes, an entity which is not the company may issue warrants on the company's shares, for example, Salomon Bros offering warrants on Eurotunnel shares. This is often called the *covered warrants market* because Salomon must cover the risk by owning the shares. If Eurotunnel issued a bond with warrants, it has the right to issue new shares if need be. Naturally, Salomon Bros do not have that right and must obtain the shares conventionally. Warrants may (and frequently are) offered on a 'basket' of different shares. These covered warrants (very popular these days) are really simply part of the traded options market and priced accordingly (see Chapter 10). For example, in February 1996, James Capel issued a series of basket warrants linking shares tipped as potential takeover victims in 1996 in five different markets – insurance, banking, general finance, utilities and mixed.

Preference shares usually pay dividend as a fixed percentage rate. If there is any shortage of money, their dividends must be paid out before other dividends. In the event of liquidation, preference shareholders have priority over ordinary shareholders. They normally have no voting rights. If the dividend cannot be paid, it is legally owed to them. Hence they are 'cumulative' (normally). On the continent of Europe, these are typically called participation certificates or, in Germany and Switzerland, genusscheine. While preference shares may be redeemable or irredeemable, genusscheine are usually dated, for example, Dresdner Bank issue in March 1991 of DM500m with 9% coupon and maturing in 2002.

The Americans use the term 'preferred stock' and the French have several variations on this theme:

❑ Certificats d'investissement
❑ Titres participatifs – public sector only and the dividend may be partly fixed and partly linked to profit
❑ Actions à dividende prioritaire (ADP) – the dividend is the ordinary dividend plus a given percentage.

The general features of all the above are non-voting, preference in the event of liquidation and cumulative. They are hybrid instruments with some characteristics of a bond and some of an equity. Banks have done many issues to raise capital to count as Tier 1 Capital (National Westminster Bank, September 1991) or Tier 2. To count as Tier 1 they must be undated and non-cumulative. In April 1996, TB Finance did an issue of ¥100bn preference shares, convertible into common shares of Tokai Bank. As conversion at some point is mandatory, the issue counts as Tier 1 capital.

Foreign Bonds

Foreign bonds are domestic issues by non-residents – 'bulldogs' in the UK, 'yankees' in the US, 'matadors' in Spain and 'samurai' in Tokyo.

Notice that the bonds are domestic bonds in the local currency, it's only the *issuer* who is foreign. They should not be confused with *international* bonds (also called *Eurobonds*), which are bonds issued outside their natural market.

Non-US firms seeking dollar funding, for example, have a choice. The bonds may be issued in London as 'Eurobonds' or in the US as 'yankee' bonds. The investment community is different in both markets. While the ultimate investors in the US might have a slightly parochial attitude to European firms, the investment institutions themselves have sophisticated credit assessment teams. In the absence of formal credit ratings, they will make up their own minds. The Eurobond market might be guided by credit ratings (or their absence) rather more slavishly. In any case, market conditions change from time to time. Sometimes it's easier to raise dollars in New York, sometimes in London. There have been major issues in New York, for example, by well known British corporates such as ICI and Grand Metropolitan.

In Japan, Asian issues are often better received than in London although the market is not as liquid. In August 1992, the Ministry of Finance relaxed the rules for sovereign borrowers to allow issues rated BBB (previously, they had to be at least A). This proved very attractive to BBB issuers like Hungary, Turkey and Greece as London Eurobond issues rated BBB need to carry a higher coupon than Samurai. On the other hand, costs are higher than in London. Banks (they must be Japanese) act as custodians and paying/fiscal agents in Europe. As a result, commission fees must be paid. Then, early in 1996, the Ministry of Finance decided to allow non-investment grade issues. This was followed by a spate of samurai issues – ¥2200bn in the first 7 months of 1996 as opposed to ¥1700bn in the whole of 1995.

Foreign bonds may be subject to a different tax regime.

Junk Bonds

This was a phenomenon which occurred in the US domestic markets in the 1970s and 1980s. We mentioned earlier, under 'credit ratings' that bonds rated below BBB grade were essentially speculative. As a result, they offered a much higher rate of interest.

A clever researcher at Drexel Burnham Lambert, one Michael Milken, did a study of the behaviour of such bonds in the early 1970s. He proved that an investment in these bonds would return a better yield than investment grade bonds, even deducting the loss due to greater defaults. He was not the first to discover this – other academic studies had come to the same conclusion – but he was the first to do anything about it. At first, his firm dealt in underpriced bonds in this category in the secondary markets. They then began to look at the potential for new issues. The bonds of 90% of US corporates would, if issued, not be investment grade. Drexels (and Michael Milken) began to do primary issues too, arguing that the judgement of the rating agencies was too harsh.

Then the bonds were used to raise large sums of money for takeover bids. The market began to refer to them as 'junk bonds' (Drexels called them 'high yield bonds', a more respectable title!).

Junk bonds slowly became notorious because huge sums of money were raised with these bonds by entrepreneurs who bought companies much bigger than they were – the 'leveraged' takeover – for example, Nelson Peltz/National Can; Ronald Perelman/Revlon; Carl Icahn/TWA.

Each year at Beverley Hills, Drexels would hold a 'High Yield Bond Conference' at which the wheeler-dealers and the potential investors would sit at the feet of the 'junk bond king' Michael Milken and be entertained in lavish style. The rather less formal name for the conference was the 'Predators' Ball'. (The whole amazing story is told in Connie Bruch, *The Predators' Ball*, Simon & Schuster, 1988.)

Later, the US Securities and Exchange Commission decided that Drexels and Michael Milken had broken the law in various ways during the course of their activities. In addition, banks and other investors realised that they had gone too far, especially with the arrival of the recession. The bubble eventually burst. The firm of Drexel Burnham Lambert collapsed in early 1990 and the 'junk bond king' Michael Milken was jailed for 10 years for infringing various laws, although the sentence was reduced later.

Opinion is still divided between those who believe that Milken revitalised corporate America and those who think that his sentence wasn't nearly long enough!

INTERNATIONAL MARKETS

Background: Eurocurrencies

Some markets are called *international* markets or, misleadingly, *Euromarkets*.

We are talking here of dealing outside of the natural market of the transaction. For example, in 1992, General Motors (a US company) made an 'international' offering of new shares – shares offered in Canada, Europe, Japan and other major markets. End 1996 should see the second biggest privatisation of all time – Deutsche Telekom (the Japanese NTT being the biggest). Shares will be offered in tranches to Germany,

UK, the rest of Europe, the Americas and Asia.

In late 1991, Kuwait raised a huge dollar loan, $5.5bn, from a syndicate of banks in London to repair the damage caused during the Gulf War. It's an 'international loan'.

Bonds are frequently raised in London by syndicates of banks of all nationalities and in dollars, yen, deutschemarks and other major currencies. We call them 'Eurobonds' or, more correctly, 'international bonds'. For example, SNCF (the French railways) may decide to issue a bond in London and in dollars, instead of in Paris and in French francs.

How did all this begin? Its origins lie in the period after the Second World War. Russia and so-called 'Iron Curtain' countries which held dollars were worried that the US authorities might seize them for political reasons. The Russians owned a bank in France, Banque Commercial pour l'Europe du Nord, and concentrated their holdings there. This bank lent the dollars to other non-US banks in Europe. Some say that the term *Eurodollars* was used because the telex code of the bank was Eurobank. Others believe that it was a natural name for dollar dealings outside the US.

In the post-war years there were plenty of dollars in the hands of non-Americans. American spending in Europe through the Marshall Plan was one source. 1957 saw the Treaty of Rome and the arrival in Europe of American multinational firms – earning dollars and spending them. A European firm might earn, say, $20m for sales to US firms. The dollars were credited to its account with, perhaps, Banque Nationale de Paris. These were now Eurodollars and could be lent to other entities in Europe. They were dollars outside the control of the US authorities. For years, for example, there was a strict control on interest rates called 'Regulation Q'. It put an upper level on interest rates offered to depositors. If our mythical European firm above chose not to convert the dollars into francs but lend them to BNP on deposit, BNP's interest rate was not constrained by Regulation Q – hence an increase in dealings in dollars held by non-US residents.

(The *Oxford English Dictionary* in 1972 suggested that the first recorded reference to the phrase 'Eurodollar' was in the financial review of *The Times*, 24 October 1960.)

In July 1963, President Kennedy decided to tax 'yankee bonds'. Remember yankees? They are dollar bonds issued in the US by non-residents. The perception was that perhaps these bonds could be issued in Europe, finding the investors amongst those non-US residents who held dollar balances. In 1963, Warburgs lead managed a bond issue in London worth $15m for the Italian motorway authority, Autostrade – generally believe to be the first *Eurobond* – a dollar bond issued in Europe and not the US. London, with its non-protectionist policies and its long traditions, became the natural market for this new business. To quote Al Alletzhauser in his interesting history *The House of Nomura* (Bloomsbury, 1990):

Almost overnight the world's financial centre shifted to London. The big four Japanese stockbrokers wasted no time in setting up offices there. If they could not sell Japanese stock to the Americans, they would sell them to the Europeans. Over the years, it proved to be one of the most profitable moves Japan's brokers ever made abroad.

In 1950, there were 140 foreign banks in London; by 1973 the number had risen to 340 and today there are 541. It was a vital shot in the arm for the London financial market which had suffered from the post-war decline of the UK as a major economic power.

We said earlier that the term 'Euro' is misleading. For example, dealings might take place in Tokyo, relending dollars held by Asian organisations. The terms 'Euromarkets' and 'Eurobonds' are well established, however, although 'international markets' is a more correct term for dealings in a currency outside its natural domestic market (and, thus, outside the *control* of its domestic market). Eurocurrencies is a wider term, reminding us that the currency might not be dollars but yen, deutschemarks, French francs.

For reasons we shall see below, Eurocurrency dealings have grown enormously from an estimated $1bn in 1959 to an estimated $6bn by 1992 (BIS figures).

The irony is that while these markets grew as a result of restrictions in the US, they did not disappear when the restrictions were later abolished.

The Syndicated Loan Market

In 1973–4 came events that led to a large increase in dollars held by non-US residents – the OPEC countries' oil price increases. Oil, which was $3 per barrel in October 1973, was $10.5 per barrel by January 1974. This led to a huge rise in dollar balances held by OPEC countries and a huge reduction in the dollar balances of many sovereign states. The services of international banks were required to recycle these dollars from those with the surpluses to those in deficit, many of whom were underdeveloped countries – largely in Africa and South America.

The original use of the Eurodollars was for the short-term interbank market. Then we saw syndicates of banks getting together to lend the dollar balances as part of, say, a 7 year loan to Mexico. As the source was dependent on what might be short-term balances, the loans were all at floating rate, so that rates could be adjusted according to the new LIBOR rates in London. The banks might argue (as we look back on this period) that they were encouraged to lend by the world's financial and political authorities, worried about a bottleneck in the world's financial system.

To share the risk, the banks spread each loan across a syndicate of banks, perhaps with as many as 100 banks in a syndicate. Notices of these loans would appear in the London *Financial Times* and other relevant publications – 'as a matter of record only'. What was the notice for then? It was an advertisement for the banks concerned – a *tombstone* notice, in the jargon of the trade (some say because financial notices in the last century were placed next to those for births and deaths!).

Whether the banks were encouraged to lend or not, they did so and on a large scale – plenty of dollars, plenty of borrowers and nice rates of interest. To be fair, they must have looked at some borrowers, for example, Mexico or Nigeria and thought 'How can we go wrong, when they have this precious commodity, oil?'

The biggest lender was Citibank, whose chairman, Walter Wriston, encouraged the others with the famous words 'Sovereign borrowers do not go bust.' He meant that governments come and go but countries would always survive and they had assets which could, if necessary, be seized.

The International Debt Crisis

Walter Wriston couldn't have been more wrong. For a time, indeed, 'all went merry as a marriage bell' as the poet Byron says. However, his next line is: 'But hush! hark! a deep sound strikes like a rising knell!'

The deep sound in this case was the voice of the Mexican finance minister telling an audience of bankers in New York, on 20 August 1982, that repayment of principal on bank loans was to be deferred for 3 months. Brazil, Argentina and others quickly followed suit.

Falling oil prices, falling commodity prices generally and a large rise in dollar interest rates (remember, the loans are floating rate) had done the damage. Mexico followed its announcement by imposing total exchange controls and nationalising all the banks.

To understand the banks' reaction to this, we must realise that the three largest South American debtor nations owed commercial banks $150bn, and that Mexican debt alone accounted for 44% of the capital of the nine largest US banks. The very survival of some of the world's largest banks was in question, and that meant that the whole international financial system was in jeopardy.

The banks met in fear and panic at the IMF in Toronto in September 1982. A wit described the meeting as 'rearranging the deckchairs on the Titanic'. The key figures – Jacques de Larosière, IMF managing director, Paul Volcker, chairman of the Federal Reserve Board, Gordon Richardson, governor of the Bank of England and Fritz Leutwiler, chairman of BIS – mapped out a strategy. The essence was to buy time – to ask the debtors to implement economic policies to reduce the deficits that had led to the initial problems and to ask the banks to give the new policies time to work. The loans were to be rescheduled and repayments of interest deferred.

In a sense, it was a cat and mouse game. J.M. Keynes once said 'if you owe the bank £1000 you may be in trouble; if it's £1 million, maybe the bank's in trouble'.

The banks were as much at risk as the debtors. Cut them off from new supplies of money and they can no longer buy Western goods. Drive them into the ground with austere economic programmes and you may provoke a coup d'état and a communist government. America hardly wants a communist government in Mexico, on its doorstep.

Things were not easy. In 1985, the IMF suspended loans to Brazil and Argentina as economic targets were missed. Peru announced a limit on debt repayments. In December, oil halved in price from $30 per barrel to $15 – Mexico's situation worsened.

Everyone called it the 'LDC debt crisis' (LDC, Less Developed Countries). 1987 was a crisis year, as Brazil suspended interest payments and spent all year arguing with the banks.

Up to 1987, banks had had bad debt reserves of only about 5%. Walter Wriston's successor at Citibank, John Reed, decided in May 1987 to grasp the nettle and increased the bad debt charge against profit to $3bn (30%), plunging them into loss. Other banks followed suit. Of the UK's big four banks, Midland and Lloyds, the two smallest, had the largest exposures and declared in 1987 their first losses this century. This was followed by their second losses this century in 1989, as all the banks added to these bad debt reserves, which now ranged in total from 40% at Citibank to 100% in the case of J.P. Morgan's medium- to long-term LDC debt.

The LDC debt crisis was sad news for the ordinary citizens of these countries. It would be nice to think that the money (about $300bn in total) had been spent strengthening the infrastructure of the countries but a great deal was wasted on grandiose prestige projects. Even worse, much has found its way into bank accounts abroad. Meanwhile, at home, the poorer citizen took the consequences – *sunt lacrimae rerum.*

Several attempts to solve the LDC problem have been tried:

(a) Banks sold LDC debt at a large discount to other banks, simply spreading the risk.

(b) Debt for equity swaps – some LDC debt was exchanged (at a discount) for equity in the country concerned. For example, the American Express Bank swapped $100m of its Mexican debt at a discount for equity in Mexican hotels. In a bizarre incident, some Brazilian debt was used to buy a Brazilian centre forward for Eindhoven, the Dutch football team! Other Brazilian debt was purchased at a discount and invested to protect rainforests.

(c) In 1985, US Treasury secretary, James Baker, unveiled the 'Baker Plan' – economic reform to promote growth in LDC countries combined with increased lending by commercial banks.

(d) In 1989, the new US Treasury secretary, Nicholas Brady, launched the 'Brady Plan'. Building on experience gained with the Baker Plan, this envisaged encouraging the creditor banks to allow debt reduction. For example, LDC debt would be exchanged at a heavy discount for 30 year LDC government bonds backed by 30 year zero-coupon US Treasury bonds, thus guaranteeing eventual repayment of principal. Alternatively, banks prepared to lend new money would be rewarded by no write down on the existing debt. The first case was Mexico in 1989–90. Of the creditor banks, 90% swapped $42bn of debts for bonds on terms implying a discount of 35%. 10% of the banks lent new money. Later, 'Brady Plan' type deals were struck with the Philippines, Uruguay, Venezuela, Costa Rica, Peru, Brazil and Argentina.

Today, Latin America has reappeared in the world's financial markets and new capital inflows are increasing rapidly. Where there are problems, like Brazil, they are more *political* than *economic,* although Brazil returned in May 1995 with its first Eurobond issue since 1980.

Whatever the eventual outcome, for the banks concerned the LDC crisis was a disaster. Standard and Poor's and Moody's didn't like what they saw and reduced credit ratings. Not only did this mean that the cost of new money for the banks went up, but often their best customers had a better credit rating than they did. In 1982, banks like Chase, Bank America and Manufacturers Hanover were all of AAA status. By 1990, they were hanging on to single A if they were lucky. Manny Hanny was BBB – almost a junk bond! Yet in June 1986, Marks and Spencer, the famous UK retailer, issued a $150m Eurobond rated AAA by both the main organisations. Why should M and S borrow from Lloyds or Midland Bank in 1986? Its credit rating was better than either.

Capital, too, was hit by bad debt reserves and the changed situation. Due to capital ratio constraints, banks found it difficult to expand their lending but still needed to earn money. In Chapter 4, we saw how new techniques were tried – the NIFs, RUFs and RAFTs followed by the MOF. Unfortunately, however, many corporates could avoid the banks by borrowing from other lenders, using the securities market. For example, top quality borrowers could raise money by selling commercial paper to lenders, with the bank role limited to taking a commission. The classic role of the bank is that of intermediary. It takes money from depositors and lends it to borrowers. Cutting out the bank, borrowers meeting lenders directly, is often called *disintermediation.* Another term is *securitisation*, that is borrowers borrow by selling a security to lenders rather than borrowing from the bank. The biggest illustration of this process of either disintermediation or securitisation was the rise in the issue of Eurobonds from 1982 onwards.

The Eurobond Market

From 1982, we see a fall in the size of the international syndicated loan market and a rise in the issue of Eurobonds. Banks which could not expand their lending due to capital ratio constraints could make some money by underwriting bond issues. Borrowers found that the holders of Eurocurrencies, which provided a short-term deposit market, could now be persuaded to buy bonds denominated in the same currencies and create a longer-term market. As before, London became the major market for these bond issues.

Typical terms for Eurobonds were in the range of 5–25 years (the longest so far – 31 years – was issued by SNCF in 1992). A syndicate of banks with a *lead manager* underwrote the issue, sold the bonds to investors and ran secondary markets.

Settlement between the professionals (in the secondary market) is 3 working days: that is, buy the bond on Monday, pay on Thursday; buy the bond Tuesday, pay on Friday and so on. There are two settlement and clearing organisations – Cedel and

Euroclear. They are both owned by banks, and the first is in Luxembourg and the second in Brussels. What they do is to ensure that bonds are transferred to the ownership of the buyer and that money is taken from the buyer's account to pay for them. Using another technique, which always seems curious to an outsider, they can arrange to lend bonds to sellers who have sold bonds they don't actually own. The sellers can use these bonds to settle the deal and buy them later in the market in order to return them to the lender. This is *stock lending* and is very common in bond markets everywhere. The lender earns a small fee for their trouble and it makes life easier for the seller.

There is an International Primary Markets Association (IPMA) and an International Securities Markets Association (ISMA) to coordinate issues in the secondary market. (The latter used to be called the Association of International Bond Dealers.)

The techniques for selling these bonds are investment banking techniques, as opposed to the commercial banking techniques used for syndicated loans. The rise in Eurobond market activities after 1982 led to a big increase internationally in investment banking at the expense of commercial banking.

The *borrowers* in this market are governments, quasi-governments (for example, EU), international financial organisations (for example, the World Bank), banks and large corporates. As the bonds are not secured, a good credit rating is essential.

The *lenders* are retail investors (that is well-off private individuals), banks and investment institutions.

The interest on the bond is paid gross and, therefore, the onus is on the retail investor to declare this to the local tax authority. On the other hand, the bonds are *bearer* bonds (that is, no one knows who owns them). While it is, of course, wrong to think evil of people it is, unhappily, seldom incorrect. As a result, there is a strong incentive for the retail buyer to indulge in sheer tax evasion and enhance the yield on the bond by not paying any tax. The cliché in the market for the retail buyer is the 'Belgian dentist'. The idea is that they cross the border into Luxembourg (where the paying bank often is), present the coupons and pay the money into a local bank account. (Luxembourg banks have a great tradition of secrecy, like the Swiss.)

For professional investors, who will not indulge in tax evasion, there is still a *cash flow* advantage because the interest is paid gross. By the time they come to year end and the auditors agree the tax figures with the authorities, it may be 18 months before the tax is actually paid.

As a result of the tax situation, Eurobonds may offer a yield that seems less than general market rates.

An early variation on the theme was the *floating rate note* (FRN). This pays a variable and not a fixed rate of interest. This appeals to financial institutions, which *lend* at floating rate and therefore find it easier to *borrow* at floating rate. If rates fall, their income falls, but so do their costs. Assets and liabilities are nicely matched.

Let's look at some Eurobond issues to get the flavour of the market, both for types of issue and types of currency (see Table 6.3).

Table 6.3   *A selection of Eurobond issues*

Issuer	Maturity years	Currency
Republic of Austria	12	Yen
National Bank of Hungary	6	Pesetas
Basque Country	10	Swiss Francs
Republic of Argentina	10	Dollars
Thomson–Brandt Int.	3	French Francs
World Bank	5	Pesetas
Republic of South Africa	5	Deutschemarks
Nestlé Australia	4	Swiss Francs
World Bank	10	Dutch Guilders
Skandia Insurance Co.	10	Dollars
Halifax Building Society	5	Yen

You may wonder why some of these issuers want a particular currency and why, for example, a financial institution like the UK's Halifax Building Society is borrowing at fixed rate. The curious answer is that perhaps they don't want the currency at all, nor does the Halifax want a fixed rate commitment. It's all to do with the world of *swaps*, which we discuss fully in Chapter 12. The investment bankers advise you in which currency in the prevailing market conditions it will be easier to raise the money. They then swap it for the currency you really want. They advise you whether a fixed rate bond or FRN will be best received by the market, and then swap the interest rate obligation with you.

Let's take the Halifax case. First we have the *currency swap*:

They arrange at the same time to swap back at maturity so that the Halifax can redeem the bond.

Then we have an interest rate swap for the interest element:

The swap bank passes the Halifax a stream of money in yen to pay the interest. The Halifax passes them a stream of money in sterling at floating rate. The obligations of the Halifax to the bond holders are unaltered.

Notice that in the above case, we have not only swapped a fixed commitment for a floating one but the fixed is in sterling and the floating is in yen, that is we have arrived at the CIRCUS (Combined Interest Rate and Currency Swap).

The result is that issuers raise money where it is easiest and cheapest to do so and then the investment banks swap it into the arrangement they really want.

Our real discussion on swaps is in Chapter 12 but it's impossible not to mention them here, as it is estimated that 70% of Eurobond issues are swapped one way or another.

The market is very innovative and ingenious. It was noted at an early stage that some professional investors were stripping off all the coupons separately, leaving behind a bond paying no interest. Perhaps they wanted a capital gain rather than income from a tax point of view. As a result, the market invented the *zero coupon bond* in the primary market.

If the bond pays no interest, why buy it? The answer is that the investor buys it at a substantial discount. Suppose market yields for 5 year bonds are 10%. An investor could buy a 10% bond at par. Alternatively, they could buy a zero coupon bond for $62.09 for each $100 nominal. They invest $62.09 and in 5 years receive $100 – also a yield of 10%.

For example, the World Bank offered a zero coupon 5 year bond in 1987 in Australian dollars. The bonds were sold at A$53 for each A$100 nominal value.

From a tax point of view, it may suit the investor to receive capital gain and not income. In Japan and Italy, for example, the increase in the bond price is taxed as a capital gain, not as income (but this is not the case in the UK). In addition, if the bond is in a foreign currency, the exchange rate risk is limited to the principal not the coupons. These bonds are also even more sensitive to interest rate changes then a normal bond. This might suit a speculator who was convinced that interest rates would fall. Remember – interest rates *down*, bond prices *up*.

Take a conventional 10 year bond paying 10%. The market yield falls to 9% and the price goes up to $106.4 (a rise of 6.4%). Suppose an investor had bought a 10 year zero coupon bond instead. A price of $38.55 per $100 nominal would give a yield of 10%. However, when yields fall to 9%, the price goes up to $42.24 (a rise of 9.6%). This is due to the *gearing* effect. In taking a position on a 10 year bond for $38.55 instead of $100, the investor has increased their exposure to the market. This is another aspect of the term 'gearing', which we met in Chapter 1.

Of course, if bond yields go up and not down, then the loss on the zero coupon bond is even greater. (The unfortunate Merrill Lynch dealer mentioned earlier was not only holding zero coupon bonds but had made them zero coupon by selling the coupons separately!)

In early 1992, the perception was that yields in European bond markets (especially

Spain, Portugal and Italy) would slowly fall to those on DM bonds. As a result, there were several zero coupon issues to take advantage of later price increases as interest rates fell.

Coupon Stripping

We mentioned earlier that it is not uncommon for innovative investment banks to take an ordinary bond and remove the coupons, making it a zero coupon bond. This is called 'stripping' the bond and is very common with US Treasury issues. The Bank of England will allow this for UK gilts in 1997 and Italy and Germany have also announced plans to allow this in 1997.

For example, take a $100m 5 year 10% bond and assume that the market yield is 10%, the bond selling for 100.0. The interest payments are stripped to form five zero coupon bonds of $10m each, maturing one per year in years 1–5. The principal of $100m is itself now a zero coupon bond. Someone needing $10m in 3 years can buy the 3 year zero coupon bond for $7.51m in 3 years. This enables investment institutions to match future assets and liabilities more closely.

| | *Normal Bond* | *Stripped Bond* | | | | | | |
| | | *Coupons* | | | | | *Principal* | *Total* |
		1	*2*	*3*	*4*	*5*		
Payment now	100	9.09	8.26	7.51	6.83	6.21	62.1	100
Receipt:								
Year 1	10	10						10
Year 2	10		10					10
Year 3	10			10				10
Year 4	10				10			10
Year 5	10					10		10
Year 5	100						100	100
TOTAL	150	10	10	10	10	10	100	150

Figure 6.4   *Coupon stripping*

The first US government bond was stripped in 1982 and there were some $225bn of US treasury bonds in stripped form by the end of 1995. Strips began in Canada in 1987 and in France in 1991. Strips will begin in UK gilts before the end of 1997 and later in Germany, Spain and Italy.

Other Variations

There are many, many variations on the theme in the Eurobond market – far too many to cover them all here. Let's just look at a few to get some idea of the possibilities:

Callable/Puttable bonds   If *callable*, the issuer can redeem the bond at a stated earlier date if they choose to. The investor is compensated for this disadvantage by a higher coupon. If *puttable*, the investor can sell the bond back at a stated earlier date. The investor has an advantage now and pays for it by receiving a lower coupon. The UK government's huge $4bn FRN issued in 1986 was *both* callable and puttable.

Convertibles   Corporate bonds which can be converted into equity are common, as in domestic markets. However, conversion could be from fixed into floating or floating into fixed.

Warrants   Again, as an alternative to a convertible, separate warrants entitling the investor to buy equity later may be attached. When the Nikkei index in Japan rose strongly up to 1990, Japanese convertibles and bonds with warrants were so popular they accounted for 20% of the market. When the bubble burst as the Nikkei fell, Eurobond issues in 1990 fell as a result. Some Yen 10 trillion of warrant bond issues in the 1980s matured in 1993.

Dual currency   These are bonds which pay interest in one currency but redeem in another.

Rising/Falling coupon   A 10 year bond might be 3% for 5 years and 10% for the last 5 (or some other variation).

Both the above variations were combined in one with an issue by Banca Nationale del Lavoro. The issue was in yen with 60% of the redemption in yen and 40% in dollars at a fixed rate of ¥163. In addition, the coupon was 4.7% for the first 5 years and 7.5% thereafter!

Collars   In mid-1992, several banks led by Kidder Peabody, issued FRNs with both a lower and upper limit to the interest paid. This idea had been used in 1985 and called 'mini-max'. The revival was due to the unprecedentedly low US interest rates in mid-1992. A *floor* giving a lower limit was attractive, even if there was a maximum upper level to the interest paid.

Reverse FRNs   As the interest rates go *up*, the interest on the FRN goes *down* and vice-versa. In January 1993, the Republic of Austria issued a DM500m reverse FRN with 10 year maturity. It appealed to investors who believed that German interest rates were bound to fall from the high levels at the time. It could either be speculation or a hedge of risk. As a further variation on the FRN theme, Aegon, the Dutch insurance company, did a 12 year issue in 1992 which was an FRN for the first 2 years and fixed 8¼ for the remaining 10!

Global bonds   Pioneered by the World Bank in 1989, global bonds are designed to be sold in the eurobond market and the US at the same time, thus increasing liquidity for the bond. The two markets have different conventions – eurobonds are bearer, pay interest gross and annually; US bonds are registered, and pay interest net semi-annually. However, the eurobond issues are registered with the Securities and Exchange Commission (SEC) in the US and can be sold to all classes of US investors. Eurobonds cannot be sold into the US initially unless registered under SEC rule 144a, when they can only be sold to qualified institutional investors anyway.

Dragon bonds A dragon bond is similar to a eurobond but is listed in Asia (typically Singapore or Hong Kong), aimed at investors in the region and launched in the Asian time zone. The first issue was made by the Asian Development Bank at the end of 1991. Other issues were made by the General Electric Capital Corporation and the European Investment Bank, but the really interesting one was the 10 year issue for the People's Republic of China in late 1993. All the issues have been in dollars.

The market is very competitive and each investment bank is seeking ways to score over its rivals with some new innovation. The cliché here is the *rocket scientist* – the highly numerate trader who invents more and more complex instruments.

Medium-Term Notes (MTNs)

These became very popular in the period 1991–2. They are very flexible programmes. Within the same programme and legal documentation, the issuer can issue bonds in various quantities, maturities and currencies and either fixed or floating. MTNs were designed in part to meet investor driven transactions. In other words, an investor might request, say, $10m more of a previously issued bond and the issuer will release more to meet this demand. The issuer can thus issue a new bond, more of an existing bond, or create a bond to a specification suggested by the investor. The structure is particularly useful for issuing small tranches of notes/bonds. Indeed, one investment banker has suggested that issues down to as little as $500 000 are now practical.

According to OECD figures, MTN programmes grew from $16bn in 1990 to $97.9bn in 1992 and $263.4bn in the first 9 months of 1995.

Amongst those with programmes are IBM International, Abbey National, the European Bank for Reconstruction and Development, GMAC Europe (the finance arm of General Motors), Monte dei Paschi di Siena, Finnish Export Credit and GE Capital, the market's most frequent issuer.

As an example of the flexibility of issue within a single programme, we can look at GE Capital's $4bn facility. Under this, it issued a 2 year Ecu75m tranche in February 1992, a 5 year £70m tranche in March 1992 and a 5 year C$150m tranche in June 1992.

Sometimes the programmes are underwritten, like bond issues, sometimes not.

The Money Markets

We have been looking at syndicated loans and Eurobonds. Short-term transactions in Eurocurrencies which are not simply deposits/loans but are represented by securities result in *Eurocertificates of deposit* (ECDs) and *Eurocommercial paper* (ECP). The generic term for these short-term transactions is usually *Euronotes*. The *committed* loan facilities which we mentioned in Chapter 4, like NIFs/RUFs and MOFs, have largely died. OECD gives the figures for the first 9 months of 1995 for underwritten facilities as $3.1bn as opposed to $25.4bn of simple non-underwritten ECP programmes and $263.4bn of non-underwritten MTN programmes.

(There used to be explicit 1, 3 and 6 month Euronotes in the period up to 1985–6. These were underwritten facilities and often part of the NIFs and RUFs. This explicit short-term note seems to have disappeared and been replaced by ECP.)

The strong interbank market in London in the Eurocurrencies gives rise to references to Eurodollar LIBOR, Euroyen LIBOR and similar expressions for other currencies.

Repos

Earlier in this chapter, we mentioned that a central bank may use a 'repo' to help out other banks in its role as lender of last resort. A repo is a sale and repurchase agreement. Party *A* may sell stock to *B* and receive a collateral payment. At a later point in time (which may be fixed or variable), Party *A* must buy the stock back and return the collateral plus interest to Party *B* (see Figure 6.5).

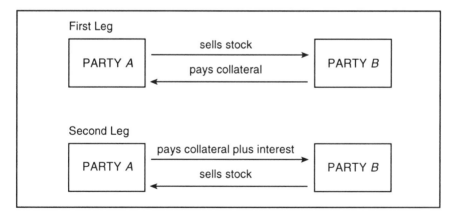

Figure 6.5   The Repo

The repo technique is used very widely outside of the use by central banks. Any dealer may find that they have a short position in stock, that is they have sold stock but not yet purchased it. As an alternative to buying the stock, the dealer can get hold of the stock on a temporary basis using the repo technique. The stock is used to settle the deal and purchased later for its return in the second leg of the repo. Why bother? Maybe the dealer found some difficulty in buying the stock at an attractive price. Perhaps the dealer believed that stock would be cheaper in a few days time. Sometimes the dealer has actually bought and sold stock but the buy side of the deal fails settlement, and it is the settlement department that uses the repo to fulfil the bank's obligation to deliver. This, of course, gives the market more flexibility and encourages liquidity. For this reason, the technique is often referred to as 'stock lending and borrowing'. (The classic repo is not quite the same as stock borrowing and lending, but let's not get too complicated!)

Often the repo is used for the opposite reason – that is not to get hold of the stock but to get hold of the collateral. A dealer must fund their position. If the bonds which have been purchased are not needed at once, they can be sold via the repo to obtain the cash to fund the purchase. As the borrowing is secured, it will be a cheaper rate than unsecured borrowing.

The repo thus suits everyone. The bond dealer can use it either to run a short position or to borrow money at the best rates. An institution which chooses to lend stock earns a small percentage to enhance yield on the portfolio and the deal is secure as collateral has been received.

Repos are widely used in the US treasury markets; the Bank of England allowed repos in UK gilts in 1996 and the market began properly in Japan in April 1996 after new regulations solved problems with the previous rather weak repo technique (collateral surrender could not be enforced).

Statistics

Table 6.5 shows the statistics for issues in 1994 and 1995. Syndicated loans are continuing to grow and, in many cases, help to finance large international takeover deals, for example, AT&T buying NCR.

Table 6.5   *Announced Euromarket new issues and syndicated credits*

	1994 $bn	1995 $bn
Syndicated Credits	250	272
Eurobonds	329	361
FRNs	93	70
Euronotes	193	272

Source: *Bank of England Quarterly Bulletins (November 1995, February 1996).*

As we have seen, these are large wholesale markets and the transactions involve:

❑ Governments
❑ Municipalities
❑ Public sector bodies
❑ International financial institutions
❑ Commercial banks
❑ Investment banks
❑ Investment institutions:
  1. Pension funds
  2. Insurance companies
  3. Mutual funds
❑ Large corporates.

There are also brokers who act as intermediaries, displaying anonymously on computer the best prices in the market and putting principals in touch with one another for a small commission (as little as 2 bp).

In the syndicated loan market, Euromoney Loanware gives the top ten banks in 1995, as shown in Table 6.6.

Table 6.6   *Top ten banks in syndicated loans*

Rank 1995	Arranger	Amount ($m)	No. of issues
1	Citicorp	36 212	180
2	J.P. Morgan	33 361	89
3	Deutsche Morgan Grenfell	25 308	141
4	NatWest Markets	25 140	157
5	BZW Syndications	23 844	136
6	Union Bank of Switzerland	19 068	117
7	Chemical Bank	15 006	101
8	ABN–Amro	13 624	149
9	Bank of America	12 630	120
10	HSBC Group	11 907	113

Source: Euromoney Loanware.

For Eurobond issues, Euromoney Bondware gives the top ten lead managers in Table 6.7.

Table 6.7   *Top Eurobond lead managers, 1995*

Rank	Manager	$m	Issues	%
1	Merrill Lynch	30 207	187	6.51
2	SBC Warburg	25 990	147	5.60
3	CSFB/Credit Suisse	25 884	147	5.58
4	Nomura Securities	23 915	194	5.16
5	Morgan Stanley	23 107	152	4.98
6	Deutsche Morgan Grenfell	19 391	81	4.18
7	Daiwa Securities	17 998	119	3.88
8	JP Morgan	17 599	115	3.80
9	Lehman Brothers	17 532	82	3.78
10	Union Bank of Switzerland	15 747	113	3.40

Source: Euromoney Bondware.

The same source breaks down the issues by currency in Table 6.8.

The Euromarkets are the most important financial development of the last 30 years. They have created a vast pool of international money seeking investment in the best place it can, with no especial loyalty to any particular market.

It seems appropriate to close this chapter with a quotation from Citicorp's chairman from 1970–84, Walter Wriston (quoted in Adrian Hamilton, *The Financial Revolution*, Penguin, 1986):

The information standard has replaced the gold standard as the basis of world finance. In place of systems, like the gold standard, based on government established rules, communications now enable and ensure that money moves anywhere around the globe in answer to the latest information or disinformation. Governments can no longer get away with debasing the coinage or controlling the flow of capital. There now exists a new order, a global marketplace for ideas, money, goods and services that knows no national boundaries.

Table 6.8   *Eurobond Issues by Currency, First Quarter 1996*

Rank	Currency	Total raised ($bn)	No. of issues
1	US$	65.64	279
2	D-Mark	42.07	139
3	Sterling	14.31	62
4	Yen	13.89	290
5	FFr	11.47	29
6	SFr	8.66	94
7	Guilder	7.68	27
8	Lira	4.92	29
9	C$	3.59	14
10	A$	3.18	11

Source: Euromoney Bondware.

SUMMARY

The rate of interest is the price of money. It varies with risk, maturity and liquidity. There is, finally, supply and demand.

Bonds have a par or nominal value. They may sell at below or above par value and the resulting return to the investor is *yield*. If we ignore the profit or loss at redemption, it is interest yield. If we do not, it is gross redemption yield. As interest rates go up, bond prices go down and vice-versa. This volatility is most marked for long dated bonds. If the bond is sold before going ex dividend, the buyer pays *accrued interest*.

Credit ratings (such as AAA or BB) are assigned to bonds to guide investors as to the risk and, hence, the necessary yield.

Money markets cover transactions whose maturity is 1 year or less. They include:

Money at call and short notice   Liquid funds lent for very short periods.

Interbank market   The rate at which one bank will lend money to another is the offer rate for money, hence London Interbank Offered Rate (LIBOR) or Paris Interbank Offered Rate (PIBOR).

Treasury bills, local authority and public sector bills   These represent the short-term borrowing of these entities, say, 3, 6 and 12 months.

Certificates of Deposit   Short-term borrowings by banks.

Commercial paper   Short-term borrowing of corporates, very big in the US.
Bills of Exchange   Discussed in Chapter 5.

Central banks control short-term interest rates using key rates such as lombard rate, discount rate, minimum lending rate and similar terms. In the UK, the discount houses play a key role here.

Bonds are transactions in excess of 1 year. The face rate of interest is called the coupon and they may be short, medium or long dated. They may be sold through an offer for sale or a private placing.

Government and public sector bonds are usually the most important. Frequently, they are sold at monthly auctions on set dates to specialist dealers. Exceptions are Germany and Switzerland, where there are no set dates and no specialist dealers.

Mortgage and other asset-backed bonds use the flows of interest and capital to back bond issues.

Debentures (in the UK) are corporate bonds backed by fixed rates.

Convertibles are bonds that may be converted to another bond or equity. The right to buy equity later at a set price may be contained in an attached *warrant*.

Preference shares usually pay the dividend as a fixed rate of interest. They are preferred to other shareholders for dividends and in the event of liquidation and are non-voting.

Foreign bonds are those issued in the domestic market by non-residents.

Junk bonds are bonds below investment grade, offering high yields.

International or Euromarkets refers to primary market activity (loans, bonds or money market instruments) outside the domestic market of that currency, for example, a dollar loan raised in London or a dollar bond issued in Singapore. London is the major centre for these activities.

Coupon stripping refers to detaching the coupons from a bond and selling the principal and the coupons all separately. They are all now zero-coupon bonds.

Medium-term notes are flexible programmes for issuing paper in any currency, any maturity, any quantity and fixed or floating.

Repos stands for Sale and Repurchase Agreements. These are used either to borrow bonds for short positions or finance long positions.

7 Foreign Exchange

INTRODUCTION

The Market

Foreign exchange dealing rooms at times of peak activity resemble bedlam. Shirt-sleeved dealers look at computer screens, talk into several phones at once and yell to colleagues. They talk in the space of minutes to key centres – London, New York, Paris, Zurich, Frankfurt. The phrases are terse and mysterious – 'What's cable?'; '50/60'; 'Mine!'; 'Yours!'; 'Cable 70/80 – give five, take three'; 'Get me dollarmark, Chemical Hong Kong'; 'tomnext'; 'What's Paris?'

The foreign exchange market is international, open 24 hours a day, adjusts prices constantly and deals in huge sums. 'Five' always means 5m whether of dollars, yen or deutschemarks. 'Yards' is a billion. Central bankers have now fallen into a pattern of doing a full survey of the size of the market every 3 years. 1986 showed a total world market which traded over $300bn every *day*. The 1989 survey doubled this to $650bn. The 1995 results from key centres suggest a figure nearer $1200bn. London is the biggest centre in the world, trading $464bn daily with New York at $244bn and Tokyo $161bn.

Buyers and Sellers

Who is buying and selling all this foreign exchange? One's first thought is of importers and exporters. When the 1989 survey was done, BIS added up the figures to a net $650bn foreign exchange trading daily. They also calculated the daily value of imports and exports. The latter were $\frac{1}{32}$ of the value of daily foreign exchange dealing! What drives the market these days is huge capital transactions. Looking at buyers/sellers of foreign currencies we see:

- ❏ Importers/Exporters
- ❏ Tourists
- ❏ Government spending (for example, for troops abroad)
- ❏ Speculators
- ❏ Banks and institutions.

We've mentioned importers/exporters and the role of tourism and government spending is easy to understand and not crucial.

As exchange controls have been abandoned by major centres, pension fund managers, investment fund managers and insurance companies can invest in foreign equities and bonds. They then need the foreign currencies to pay for them.

Investors with spare funds will move money around freely. Convinced that Spain, Italy and the UK offered high interest rates together with low exchange rate risk due to the Exchange Rate Mechanism (ERM), they put their funds into these currencies. The head of research at Mitsubishi Bank in London, for example, estimated that free funds of some £40/£50bn flowed into the UK during 1985–92 attracted by high interest rates. As the ERM all but collapsed in the dramatic days of September 1992, the funds flowed out of the high yielding currencies as exchange rate risk became a reality once more. Amongst these investors could be corporate treasurers at multinationals trying to protect their overall position. Those with heavy dollar earnings might worry if the dollar weakened and move spare funds into deutschemarks.

The banks not only deal on behalf of their customers but do proprietary deals of their own. They will 'take a position': that is, what anyone else would call 'speculate'. If dollars seem to be falling they will sell dollars and expect to buy them back more cheaply 30 minutes later. In September 1992, as the lira fell below its official floor in the ERM, dealers would buy knowing that the central banks would have to support the lira. As it rose to its official floor of L765.4 to the deutschemark, they would sell it again at a guaranteed profit. As they all sold, the lira would fall again and the process would restart.

During this period of turbulence, banks selling sterling and lira (which both eventually left the ERM) made tens of millions of dollars profit. One dealer at Bank of America who casually revealed his huge profits to a television reporter was later said to have been disciplined! The Bank of England's London survey in 1995 showed interbank business at 75% of the market.

Bank Profits

Foreign exchange profits are important for the major banks. Citibank's forex profits in 1995 were $1053m and HSBC made $572m in the same year. The US comptroller of the currency calculates that forex dealing accounts for half the profits made by the big commercial banks.

The risks have grown, too. Big corporate customers have become more sophisticated, some with their own dealing rooms; new capital ratio rules have increased the cost of forex exposures; counterparty risk has become a major worry; dollar volatility in recent years has become more unpredictable. As a result, the business is increasingly concentrated in a handful of major banks. The ten most active banks accounted for 44% of the market according to the Bank of England's 1995 survey as opposed to 35% in 1989. Top traders according to *Euromoney* magazine are shown in Table 7.1.

Table 7.1 *Top 30 interbank traders by % share of forex market*

1996	1995	Bank	Estimated share (%)
1	1	Citibank	9.10
2		Chase *	9.04
3	3	HSBC/Midland	6.50
4	7	NatWest	4.90
5	8	JP Morgan	4.22
6	5	UBS	3.53
7	11	Barclays Bank	2.98
8	6	Bank of America	2.81
9	22	Deutsche Morgan Grenfell	2.78
10	9	SBC	2.59
11	18	ABN Amro	2.28
12	16	Credit Suisse	2.02
13	10	Standard Chartered	1.83
14	27	Goldman Sachs	1.79
15	15	Indosuez	1.74
16	14	SE Banken	1.71
17	19	Royal Bank of Canada	1.66
18	—	National Australia Bank	1.58
19		Tokyo–Mitsubishi Bank **	1.44
20	13	BNP	1.37
21	—	Bank of Montreal	1.20
22=	17	Bankers Trust	1.19
22=	21	Lloyds Bank	1.19
24	—	Merrill Lynch	1.16
25	12	First Chicago	0.91
26	—	Société Générale	0.88
27	25	Fuji Bank	0.77
28	29	Commerzbank	0.76
29	—	Royal Bank of Scotland	0.74
30	—	Bank of Scotland	0.72

Notes: * 1995 Positions: Chase 2, Chemical 4.
** 1995 Positions: Bank of Tokyo 28, Mitsubishi 24.
— Not in top 20 in 1995.

Source: *Euromoney* (May 1996).

WHAT DETERMINES EXCHANGE RATES?

Amongst economists, the most popular theory for explaining exchange rates is that of *purchasing power parity* (PPP). At its simplest, if a given basket of goods is priced at $10 in the UK and DM20 in Germany, then this suggests the exchange rate should be $1 = DM2. If the exchange rate is actually $1 = DM1, then the Germans can buy a basket of goods in the US at half the price it costs them at home and dollar imports will rise heavily, causing the deutschemark to weaken. As time goes by, one factor causing US goods to become either more or less expensive than German goods is inflation. If US inflation is worse than Germany, then they might sell less goods to Germany. However, if the dollar exchange rate weakens, the cost to the Germans is the same.

At least, that's the theory. Like most economic theories, it raises serious problems in practice. To begin with, what should go in the basket of goods, since nations' purchasing habits are different? Again, many of the prices in the basket will be for goods and services not traded internationally anyway. Even if they are traded, trade-based purchases are only a small part of the market as we have seen.

(The *Economist* has some fun periodically with its McDonald PPP: it compares the price of a hamburger in key world capitals and arrives at an exchange rate which it compares with the real one!)

If inflation in one country is consistently higher than in another, then the expectation is that the exchange rate will deteriorate in the country with the higher inflation. How do we persuade foreigners to hold this currency? Answer – by offering them higher interest rates than they can get at home. The higher interest rates compensate for the anticipated higher inflation rate. Thus interest rates enter the equation along with inflation and balance of payments figures.

The relationship between inflation and the exchange rate is nicely shown by a graph prepared by Samuel Brittan of the *Financial Times* in an article in the issue of 9 October 1992 (using original figures from Datastream). Brittan plotted the declining purchasing power of the pound against the declining deutschemark/sterling exchange rate from 1964 to 1992. The correlation is striking. We show this as Figure 7.1.

The balance of payments is the difference between what a country buys and what it sells. It buys and sells physical goods and services. There are also the financial items called 'invisibles'. A French investment bank holds US government bonds and earns interest on these bonds. A German firm pays Lloyd's of London premiums for insurance. The balance between all the above items is the *current account*. Then there is the holding of assets – foreign securities, factories, land and so on, called the *capital account*. The balance of payments is said to always balance because any deficit on current account will be offset by a surplus on the capital account. Unfortunately, the figures don't always balance and so we have 'balancing items' to account for errors and transactions which cannot be traced. Sometimes, the balancing items are huge, reducing confidence in the figures.

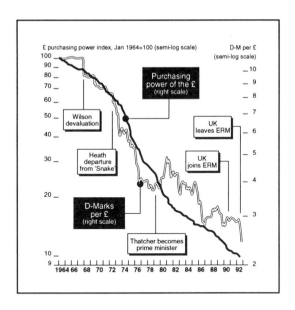

£ purchasing power index, Jan 1964=100 (semi-log scale)

D-M per £ (semi-log scale)

Purchasing power of the £ (right scale)

Wilson devaluation

UK leaves ERM

Heath departure from 'Snake'

UK joins ERM

D-Marks per £ (right scale)

Thatcher becomes prime minister

1964 66 68 70 72 74 76 78 80 82 84 86 88 90 92

Figure 7.1   *Domestic and external purchasing power of the pound, 1964–92*
Source: Datastream: *Financial Times,* 8 October 1992

If a country has a consistent deficit on the current account, the inference is that the country is not competitive and the expectation is that the exchange rate will weaken in the future.

Since trade sales/purchases only account for a small amount of forex daily dealing as opposed to capital movements, attention has switched away from PPP to the question of investments. Investors are looking for high real interest rates, that is, the return after taking account of inflation and currency risk. The theory is that investors will shift assets from one country to another according to the relative prices of international assets, expectations of inflation, expectations of exchange rate stability or volatility and actual exchange rates. This is the *portfolio balance model.*

In a way this is more attractive than PPP if we look at the sheer volatility of exchange rates. In January 1991, for example, the dollar had weakened dramatically – it was virtually $2 = £1. Within weeks, however, the dollar strengthened to $1.70 = £1. Had the price of a basket of goods changed in this period? Surely not.

The problem with all these theories is when artificial systems, like the ERM, interfere with market forces. For example, in October 1990, the UK joined the ERM with a target rate of DM2.95 = £1. Although UK inflation rates fell over the next 2 years and German rates increased, the UK had on average higher inflation in the period and lower productivity in manufacturing. In the middle of a severe recession, it was running an extraordinary deficit on current account suggesting structural problems and severe difficulties to come as the economy came out of recession. In addition, UK interest rates were barely higher than Germany in September 1992. While inflation then, on a like for like basis, was much the same as Germany's, investors' *expectations* were different. They were far more confident that Germany would get inflation lower than they were that the UK would stop it rising further. They also had greater confidence in the Bundesbank holding interest rates high (unpopular politically but the Bundesbank is independent) than in the Bank of England (not independent) keeping interest rates high in the middle of a severe recession.

In spite of this, sterling moved over the 23 months within its ±6% band compared to the deutschemark. However, sentiment that the pound was overvalued and would have to devalue grew stronger. Financial institutions and corporates holding pounds sold them. Speculators joined in. Finally, the leak that the Bundesbank thought that sterling should seek a new parity was all that was needed for the dam to burst. On Wednesday, 17 September, the UK government withdrew sterling from the ERM and saw the rate fall in 2 weeks from a level of about DM2.80 to DM2.50 causing the experts to produce their favourite quotation, 'you can't buck the market'. The Italian lira had a similar experience.

Finally, what we can't ignore in looking at exchange rate determinants is the sheer psychology of the markets – the 'herd' instinct, for example, which causes dealers to act in concert and for the market to frequently 'overshoot' when new data is released. Paul de Grauwe and Danny Decupere of the Catholic University of Leuven in Belgium produced a study of 'Psychological Barriers in the Market' in 1992. They found, for instance, that traders tended to avoid certain exchange rates, especially those ending in round numbers!

Perhaps because of psychology, there are forecasters of movements called *chartists* who plot historic price data and look for patterns and trends. They talk of upper (resistance) levels and lower (support) levels. If a level is broken, the chartists believe that the break will be decisive. Those who look at the underlying economic factors – interest rates, inflation, productivity, balance of payments – are the *fundamentalists*. The same two approaches are used in equity and bond markets. The chartists and fundamentalists often clash in battle, like Guelphs and Ghibellines in mediaeval Italy or Catholics and Protestants. In fact, all banks use a blend of both techniques.

BRETTON WOODS

In the post-war period up to the early 1970s, currencies did not fluctuate as they do today but operated on a fixed basis. The system was set up at a conference in Bretton Woods (New Hampshire, US) in 1944. The conference was attended by world finance ministers and major economists, like J.M. Keynes, from 44 countries. It was called to discuss the international financial arrangements that would apply after the Second World War. In particular, it set up:

❑ A system of exchange rate stability
❑ The International Monetary Fund
❑ The World Bank.

Exchange Rate Stability

Exchange rate stability was achieved by members adopting an external or *par value* for their currency, expressed in terms either of gold or of the US dollar. America had no choice but to adopt a par value for the dollar expressed in gold; the dollar was convertible to gold on demand at $35 per oz but all other members pegged to the dollar. This Bretton Woods System was, therefore, termed the *Gold Exchange Standard*, with the dollar being linked directly to gold and other currencies indirectly linked to gold via the dollar. Having adopted a par value, the central banks of member countries had to routinely intervene in the foreign exchange markets to keep their exchange rate against the dollar within 1% on either side of the par value: selling their currency (and buying the dollar) when it threatened to rise above 1%; doing the opposite when it fell 1% below the par value. The central banks efforts to keep their currency at the agreed rate could be supported by the International Monetary Fund (IMF) – hence its relevance to these arrangements.

International Monetary Fund

The decision to set up the IMF was taken at the Bretton Woods Conference in 1944 but the Fund did not come into operation until 1946. Its headquarters are in Washington, DC. The prime object in setting up the Fund was to prevent any return to the restrictive international trade environment and erratic exchange rate fluctuations of the inter-war period. The Fund's main task was to preside over a system of fixed exchange rates. Ancillary to this, it provided borrowing facilities for its members, these also allowing trade deficit nations to embark upon more gradual corrective policies that would be less disruptive for trading partners.

When a member country had a balance of payments deficit, it borrowed from the IMF to finance it, as well as to obtain supplies of foreign currency with which to buy up its weak currency in the foreign exchange markets, in order to prevent it falling more than 1% below its par value. Thus, in this way the *borrowing facilities* function was ancillary to the stable exchange rate goal. When members exhausted their borrowing entitlement, they had perforce to adopt a new, and lower, par value. *Devaluation* (and revaluation) was possible but had to be carried out in discussion with the IMF, the latter having to be satisfied that a state of 'fundamental disequilibrium' in the member country's balance of payments did exist. Thus, although under the Bretton Woods system exchange rates were fixed, they were not immutably fixed.

For example, the UK, having sold every foreign asset to pay for the war, was in a weak position.

After the war it adopted (possibly foolishly) an exchange rate of $4 = £1. In 1949, however, it devalued to $2.80 = £1. Devaluation is always difficult. Governments cannot announce devaluations in advance as everyone will immediately sell their currency. As a result, they always deny any intention to devalue in the strongest terms. Then, they suddenly devalue. The result is that protestations about a determination not to devalue may, in the end, simply be disbelieved. When enough people disbelieve it, devaluation is inevitable due to the massive selling of the currency. The chaos in the ERM in September 1992 illustrates these forces at work.

Member countries had to pay a subscription to the IMF, related originally to their pre-war value of trade. This subscription had originally (but no longer) to be one quarter in gold, with the remainder in the member's own currency. In this way the IMF acquired a vast pool of gold and members' currencies, giving it resources to lend. *Borrowing entitlements* were basically 125% of subscription, although the needs of small-subscription countries, as well as the oil price rise of the 1970s, called for additional categories of borrowing facilities to be brought into being. IMF loans are conditional upon the borrowing country agreeing to adopt certain corrective economic policies, generally of an unpopular, restrictive nature.

In the late 1960s, there had been concern that *international liquidity* (the means of payment for international trade) would not keep pace with the volume growth in trade, thus exerting a deflationary pressure. A new function for the IMF was therefore brought into being, that of creating man-made international liquidity in the form of *Special Drawing Rights* (SDRs). These were credits created in the books of the IMF and allocated to members to pay for their balance of payments deficits (surplus countries accumulating SDRs). SDRs were first issued in 1971 but thereafter, with the fear now being one of inflation rather than deflation, further subsequent issues of SDRs have been limited. The value of an SDR is calculated daily, based on an average of the exchange rates of the world's major five currencies, that is dollars, deutschemarks, yen, French francs and sterling. As Switzerland did not join the IMF formally until 1992, Swiss francs were not used.

The World Bank

The official title is the *International Bank for Reconstruction and Development* (IBRD). The IBRD began operations in 1945 and was initially concerned with the 'reconstruction' of war-devastated Europe. Nowadays, it is primarily concerned with helping LDCs to develop their economies. It makes loans for up to 20 years at rates of interest slightly below the commercial level, with repayment being guaranteed by the government of the borrowing country. The majority of these loans are for specific projects in the areas of agriculture, energy and transport. Recently, more generalised 'programme' and 'structural adjustment' loans have also been extended to aid less developed economies. The IBRD obtains its funds from members (the same 100 or so countries that are members of the IMF) as well as by the issuance of international bonds. The IBRD is a major borrower in the Eurobond market. Under the umbrella title of the World Bank are two other institutions.

The *International Finance Corporation* (IFC) was set up in 1956 as a multilateral investment bank to provide risk capital (without government guarantee) to private sector enterprises in LDCs, as well as being a catalyst in encouraging loans from other sources. In the latter respect, the IFC is also concerned to stimulate multinational corporations' direct investment in LDCs, this being further encouraged by the Multilateral Investment Guarantee Agency to provide insurance against non-commercial risks.

The *International Development Association* (IDA) (1960) is the soft-loan arm of the World Bank. It gives interest-free loans for up to 50 years to the poorest of the developing countries. The IDA's resources come from donations from the rich members of the World Bank, with the US usually contributing not less than 25% of funds.

FLOATING RATES

By August 1972, there were huge pressures on the dollar, partly due to the cost of the Vietnam War. In August, the US authorities abandoned any guaranteed convertibility of the dollar into gold. An international meeting took place in Washington and attempted to hold the fixed exchange rate system together but the effort failed. The European Common Market was concerned that freely floating rates would upset the operation of the Common Agricultural Policy (CAP) and set up an arrangement known as the *snake*, designed to keep currencies within a band of $\pm 2\frac{1}{4}\%$. The oil price rises of the 1970s put the arrangements under pressure and membership gradually dwindled.

The arrival of floating rates meant that central banks didn't have to intervene to the same extent and didn't need the IMF to help with intervention. However, nations still needed to finance their balance of payments deficits. The fact that these were often less developed countries (LDCs) with large international debts and seeking World Bank assistance has led some observers to comment on a confusion between the roles of the IMF and the World Bank and indeed, a certain amount of rivalry.

In this period of floating exchange rates, the dollar has proved to be a very volatile currency. Foreign trade as a proportion of GDP is much less for the US than for many countries and they seem to be able to live with wild fluctuations that would cause havoc elsewhere. It has implications for world trade that may cause international central banks to wish to intervene, and we shall examine this later in the chapter.

Sterling has not exactly been a stable currency either. Table 7.2 is an extract of dollar/sterling rates over the years 1972–92.

Table 7.2   *Sterling/Dollar exchange rates, 1972–93*

	Year	Dollar/Sterling rate $	
	1972	2.50	(year of floating)
	1977	1.75	
	1980	2.32	
Jan	1985	1.03	
Late	1985	1.40	
Jan	1991	1.98	
Mar	1991	1.70	
Aug	1992	1.98	
Jun	1993	1.55	

Our previous comments about the effect on an exchange rate of one country's higher inflation and lower productivity is dramatically illustrated by looking at the list of sterling/deutschemark exchange rates shown in Table 7.3.

We can see the efforts of the UK government in the 1980s to reduce inflation and increase productivity culminating in accepting the ERM 'straitjacket' in October 1990.

Table 7.3   *Sterling/Deutschemark exchange rates*

	Year	Sterling/Deutschemark rate DM	
	1960	11.71	
	1970	8.67	
	1980	4.23	
Feb	1987	2.85	
July	1989	2.76	
Oct	1990	2.95	(ERM Target)
Sep	1992	2.51	(Sterling leaves ERM)
Apr	1996	2.27	

THE EUROPEAN MONETARY SYSTEM (EMS)

The mixed fortunes of the *snake* led the EC to look for a better exchange rate system and the framework for the EMS was agreed in December 1978. The system commenced in March 1979. Many features had their origins in the Werner Report of 1970 which discussed 'the establishment by stages of economic and monetary union in the Community'.

The legal and institutional basis of the EMS is quite complex but, in essence, it set up three systems:

❑ The Exchange Rate Mechanism (ERM)
❑ The European Currency Unit (Ecu)
❑ The European Monetary Cooperation Fund (EMCF).

The Exchange Rate Mechanism

Under this arrangement, member currencies agreed to keep their rates within an agreed band against other currencies. There was the *narrow* band of ± 2¼ % and the *wide* band of ± 6%. Prior to the upheavals of September 1992, the position was as follows:

❑ Greece was not a member of the ERM
❑ Spain, Portugal and the UK were members operating the wide band
❑ The remaining eight members of the community operated the narrow band.

The central banks of each pair of currencies would intervene to keep rates within the agreed band and might get assistance from other central banks in this process.

The *Parity Grid* is the table of currencies showing their central rate and the limits shown by the narrow or wide band.

Thus, Germany and Italy were allowed a fluctuation of ±2¼%. The upper, central and lower rates expressed as lira per 1 deutschemark in mid-1992 were:

Upper	765.40	± 2¼%
Central	748.22	—
Lower	731.57	– 2¼%

Sterling, however, was in the wide band in mid-1992 and the similar rates in deutschemarks against sterling were:

Upper	3.132	± 6%
Central	2.950	—
Lower	2.778	± 6%

In mid-1992, 11 countries were members of the system. As the Belgian and Luxembourg franc are tied together, however, the parity grid would show ten currencies in a grid with their central rates and upper and lower limits.

There is also the *Divergence Indicator*. Each currency is given a target rate against the Ecu itself. When the actual rate reaches 75% of the maximum deviation of each currency against the Ecu, the 'divergence threshold' has been passed and participants are expected to take action. Unfortunately, the calculation of the divergence indicator is complicated since each currency is also part of the Ecu. Suppose the deutschemark is seen to be weak compared with its target Ecu rate. The Bundesbank takes steps to buy deutschemarks and, say, raise interest rates. Now the deutschemark strengthens against other currencies making up the Ecu and also the dollar. However, the deutschemark has a weighting in the Ecu calculation of some 30% and as it strengthens, *so does the Ecu!* As the deutschemark seeks to strengthen itself against the Ecu, it's a case of 'three steps forward and one step back'. The effect of this has to be calculated, as does the absence of the currencies from the ERM but their presence in the Ecu.

The system is not set in stone and, with the permission of all members, realignments may take place. Between the start of the system and end of 1982, there were seven realignments. Between 1983 and end of 1986 there were four. A major realignment in January 1987 was followed by a long period of stability with only minor adjustments to accommodate the lira moving from the wide to the narrow band and the peseta, sterling and the escudo joining the system.

By January 1992, it had been 5 years since a major change and participants began to regard a further adjustment as some kind of defeat. In retrospect, we can see this as a mistake. As economies diverge in inflation rate, productivity and government deficits these periodic realignments are necessary to adjust the currency rates to the new circumstances. In the UK, in particular it became a matter of pride, of 'machismo', that the target rate for the pound against the deutschemark was DM2.95. As a result, interest rates were set at a rate wholly inappropriate to a nation in the midst of a severe recession.

The pressures for change building up in August and September of 1992 reflected:

❑ Weakness in the dollar due to low US interest rates leading to 'hot' money flowing into the deutschemark
❑ High German interest rates due to excess inflation following unification
❑ A growing belief that the parities for the lira and the pound sterling could not be maintained
❑ The rejection of the Maastricht Treaty by Denmark and nervousness that, perhaps, France, too, would reject it. This might lead to the collapse of the ERM.

The mark grew stronger and pressure on weaker ERM currencies increased. On Sunday 13 September came the dramatic announcement that the lira was to devalue by 7% and Germany would lower interest rates. The lowering announced on the Monday was only ¼% off the lombard rate (see Chapter 6). The Italian devaluation was seen as evidence that the principle of change was now accepted. On Wednesday, 16 September, the UK withdrew from the ERM, followed later by Italy. A wild burst of speculation against the French franc followed in July 1995 countered by heavy central bank intervention. The European Union members called a meeting for the weekend of 31 July/1 August 1993. The general view was that the ERM was finished as it could not face such pressures. The tension can be seen from the fact that the results of the meeting were announced as late as 2.00 a.m. Monday morning! The announcement said that the ERM would continue but with a single band of ±15% (except for the Dutch guilder which would remain in a ±2¼% band against the deutschemark). Austria joined the ERM on joining the EU in January 1995, followed later by Finland, and Italy rejoined, and that is the position at present.

The Ecu

The Ecu is an average of all EU currencies put together. It is a composite or basket currency. The average is a weighted average. The deutschemark has more influence on the average than the drachma. The weights are based on a mixture of relative trade and the GDP. There is provision for changing the weights every 5 years.

Thus, an amount of each currency is put into the 'basket'. These amounts multiplied by their dollar exchange rate at that moment give a dollar equivalent. Adding these up gives the Ecu value against the dollar at that moment.

The weights were last fixed in September 1989 when the peseta and the escudo joined the system. The whole basket, the dollar values and weighting are shown in Table 7.4.

Table 7.4 *The Ecu's composition, 1989*

Currency	Amount	$	%
Mark	0.624	0.321	30.10
Fr. Franc	1.332	0.203	19.00
Sterling	0.0878	0.139	13.00
It. Lira	151.8000	0.108	10.15
Dutch Gdr.	0.219	0.100	9.40
Bel. Fr.	3.301	0.081	7.60
Peseta	6.885	0.056	5.30
Danish Kr.	0.197	0.026	2.45
Irish Punt	0.0087	0.012	1.10
Escudo	1.394	0.008	0.80
Greek Drachma	1.44	0.008	0.80
Lux. Fr.	0.13	0.003	0.30
At 20.9.89	1 Ecu =	$1.065	100.00

Note that the amounts are fixed, not the weightings. If the French franc, for example, were to strengthen against the dollar more than the other currencies, the dollar equivalent would grow bigger than that for the other currencies and the weighting would change.

From Table 7.4 we have a dollar/Ecu rate. We also have a dollar/deutschemark rate, a dollar/French franc rate and so on. One multiplication in each case gives us an Ecu/deutschemark rate, an Ecu/French franc rate and an Ecu rate for all the other currencies.

Having arrived at a value for the Ecu, what is it for? It is a *unit of account* for the EU. All statistics are produced in it, all national contributions and EU fines on members. Any tender for the supply of goods and services to the Community will be in Ecus.

We have already seen its use as the basis for the *divergence indicator*. It is also used as an official currency as part of the EMCF (see below).

The belief that the Ecu might form the basis of a genuine single European currency and the general usefulness of this average of EU currencies has led to extensive *private* use of the Ecu. Many Eurobonds have been denominated in it and also government bonds issued by France, Spain, Belgium, Italy, UK and Spain. The UK and Italy have issued Treasury Bills denominated in the Ecu and, in 1992, the UK government introduced an entirely new instrument – the 3 year Treasury Note – in Ecus (see Figure 7.2)

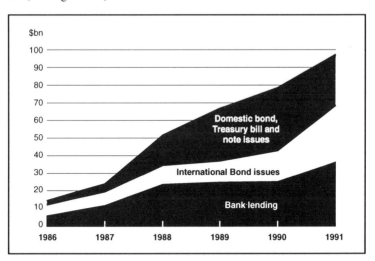

Figure 7.2   *Growth of Ecu financial markets, 1986–91*
Source: BIS, Basle.

In addition to the bonds and bills, there were also syndicated loans in Ecus. As a composite of various currencies, it was seen to have greater stability than any single currency on its own.

The UK government, perhaps aware of criticism that it is not sufficiently 'pro-Europe', has been particularly active. In August 1992, for example, the Bank of England announced that it was setting up a same day Ecu clearing and settlement system for banks operating in the City in Ecu markets.

Not to be outdone, the Bank of France, in October, announced a new same day Ecu clearing system in Paris, to commence in early 1993.

The effect on this use of the Ecu of the collapse of confidence in the Maastricht ideal is discussed later.

THE EUROPEAN MONETARY COOPERATION FUND

This fund was actually set up in 1973 following the Werner Report of 1970 and the formation of the 'snake' in 1972. It was effectively dormant until the EMS and, even now, has not played the major role originally envisaged.

Under EMCF arrangements, each of the Community countries deposits centrally 20% of their gold and foreign exchange reserves and receives Ecus in exchange. (Control of this is handled by the BIS.) This is what is called the *official* Ecu. The fund can only be used for transactions between EMS central banks and named monetary institutions.

The EMCF also keeps track of usage of *very short-term financing facilities*. Central banks obliged to intervene in the markets because of ERM rules can draw on unlimited credit within the system. There are provisions for repayment within a stated period and the official Ecu may be used to settle these debts.

As a result of these arrangements, a central bank may hold these *official* Ecus (whose use is restricted) and *private* Ecus obtained from the sale of government Treasury bills and bonds.

EUROPEAN MONETARY UNION (EMU)

The Werner Report of 1970 envisaged an ultimate economic and monetary union. The EMS was a major step on the way.

The apparent success of the ERM in promoting exchange rate stability and the signing of the single European Act in 1986 led to a revival of interest in EMU. In June 1988, the EC set up a committee, including all twelve central bank governors, and chaired by Jacques Delors (then European Commission President) to examine how economic and monetary union could be achieved.

The Delors Committee reported in April 1989. It suggested that EMU could be achieved in three stages. The European Council set up an Inter-Governmental Conference in 1990 to detail the stages needed for EMU and the necessary changes to the Treaty of Rome. The conference drew up a treaty which was signed at a European Council summit meeting in December 1991 at Maastricht.

The Maastricht summit laid down a time-table for European Monetary Union as follows:

1. *End 1996*, a decision on a possible EMU in 1997 *if* seven nations minimum can meet the convergence conditions (described later).
2. By *1999*, there would be EMU in any case if two nations are able to meet the convergence conditions.
3. A European Central Bank (ECB) will be set up 6 months prior to EMU but a body called the 'European Monetary Institute' (EMI) will coordinate policies prior to setting up the Central Bank, and be set up in *1994*.
4. Amounts of each currency in the Ecu basket will be fixed at the next recalculation of weights in *1994*.
5. Special protocols allowed the UK to opt out of a final move to a single currency and Denmark to hold a referendum in *June 1992*.
6. The convergence conditions are:
   (a) Inflation rate within 1½% of the best three
   (b) Long-term interest rates within 2% of the average of the lowest three
   (c) Currency within the 2¼% ERM band and no devaluation in the previous 2 years
   (d) Budget deficit to GDP ratio not exceeding 3% and national debt not exceeding 60% of GDP.

The German experience with unification showed the dangers when a weak economy merges with the currency of a strong economy. Inefficiencies are exposed, factories close and unemployment rises. That is why we have these convergence conditions.

The belief that EMU was actually going to be achieved led to increased use of the Ecu and heavy dealings in Spanish, Italian and Portuguese bonds. The purchasers could enjoy high interest rates, limited currency risk and capital gain as interest rates gradually fell to the average level in the EU.

However, *Dis aliter visum* – the gods willed otherwise.

The Danish referendum in June 1992 rejected the Maastricht Treaty by a narrow majority. The French referendum in December accepted the treaty, but by a tiny majority. The withdrawal of Italy and the UK from the ERM and its turbulence in September 1992 shook confidence. Opinion polls in Germany showed strong opposition to the idea that the Bundesbank would be replaced by a European Central Bank in which all twelve nations would be allowed a say. In parliament, Chancellor Kohl talked of calling the new currency the 'Euromark'!

There was talk (denied officially) of a dash to a form of monetary union by a small nucleus of states – Germany, France and Benelux.

The effect of these doubts on the private Ecu market was disastrous. By July, well before the later crises, liquidity in Ecu bond trading had begun to dry up. Institutions were selling heavily and market makers sitting on large stocks of bonds with no investors to be seen.

The Ecu bond has a theoretical yield – the summation of the yields on constituent bonds factored by their weighting. For example, an investor could sell Ecu bonds. With the Ecus, constituent currencies could be purchased and used to buy the government bonds denominated in those currencies. Arbitrage suggests a theoretical yield for the Ecu bond. In 1991, a year of optimism for EMU, the actual yield fell to less than the theoretical yield as investors saw yields on constituent bonds fall due to convergence. By September 1992, the actual yield was 50 bp higher than the theoretical yield.

The European Monetary Institute was set up in Frankfurt on 1 January 1994 and began planning for monetary union. It produced a timetable for introducing a Single European Currency in November 1995. By that time it was accepted that the 1997 date could not be met. The four steps were:

1. A decision in early 1998 on which countries will take part in economic and monetary union (EMU).
2. On 1 January 1999, the exchange rates of countries participating in EMU would be locked together. The European Central Bank would conduct monetary and foreign exchange policy in the new currency. Public debt would also be issued in the new currency and banks would change over to it for wholesale operations.
3. On 1 January 2002 'at the latest' the banks would begin issuing the new European coins and banknotes.
4. By 1 July 2002, Stage three should be complete, local currencies withdrawn, and the new currency would become the single legal tender.

The Madrid Summit in December 1995 decided that the new currency would be called the 'euro' (a classic committee decision which pleased almost no one!).

By the spring of 1995, there were widespread doubts about the 1999 date. In particular, budget deficits, due to widespread recession, were well above the Maastricht targets. There were doubts especially about France and a view that, if France could not join, then EMU would not start in 1999. If it did not start at that point, would so much momentum be lost that it would never start? The French Prime Minister, Alain Juppé, introduced measures to cut social security costs and increase taxes. These were met by widespread strikes and some of the measures were withdrawn. The problem can be seen when we look at Table 7.5. Belgium is well off target on both budget deficit and gross debt percentage and France is in trouble on the budget deficit figure. Many other countries seemed a long way from meeting the targets. It seemed that less than a handful of countries would qualify. A European Monetary Union consisting of Luxembourg and Germany only was not exactly what people had in mind!

At the time of writing this, in the autumn of 1996, the position was not clear. With high unemployment, could countries raise taxes and cut government spending sufficiently to meet the Maastricht targets? It seemed doubtful, although several are trying.

Table 7.5   *Countries' performance on three EMU criteria, spring 1995*

	Inflation %	Budget deficit (or surplus) as % of GDP	Gross debt as % of GDP
Belgium	1.4	-4.5	134.4
Denmark	2.3	-2.0*	73.6
Germany	1.6	-2.9*	58.8*
Greece	9.0	-9.3	114.4
Spain	4.7	-5.9	64.8
France	1.7	-5.0	51.5*
Ireland	2.4	-2.7*	85.9
Italy	5.4	-7.4	124.9
Luxembourg	1.9	0.4*	6.3*
Netherlands	1.1	-3.1	78.4
Austria	2.0	-5.5	68.0
Portugal	3.8	-5.4	70.5
Finland	1.0	-5.4	63.2
Sweden	2.9	-7.0	81.4
United Kingdom	3.0	-5.1	52.5*
Total EU	3.0	-4.7	71.0

TARGETS
Inflation: No more than 1.5 percentage points above the average of the best three countries.
Deficit: No more than 3 per cent of GDP.
Total debt: No more than 60 per cent of GDP.
Note: * Meets criteria.
Based on European Commission forecasts in autumn 1995.
Estimates from national authorities suggest higher deficit to GDP ratios in the case of countries such as Germany, the Netherlands, Finland and Sweden. They also suggest lower deficit ratios for Denmark, Ireland, Portugal, Spain, Italy and Greece.

Source: European Commission.

FOREIGN EXCHANGE RISK FOR CORPORATES

Types of Risk

Companies which compete in an international market place are at risk to changes in foreign exchange rates. These risks are of three types:
1. Transaction risk
2. Translation risk
3. Economic risk.

Transaction risk   This is the most obvious and common risk. A German importer needs to pay for dollar imports in 6 months which are ordered today. If the deutschemark weakens against the dollar, the imports will cost more. A German exporter has sold goods to someone in the US to be paid for in dollars. By the time the goods are shipped and paid for, say in 9 months, the deutschemark may have strengthened against the dollar, making the dollar earnings worth less money.

Most corporates will decide to reduce this risk by the technique called hedging. Our concentration in this chapter will be on this type of risk.

Translation risk   A French firm has overseas subsidiaries reporting profits in Italian lira. It also owns land and property in Italy. If the lira weakens against the franc, the profits are worth less in francs when included in the annual report. The value of the land and property may be unchanged but, translated in francs, the assets seem to have lost value.

Should these exposures be hedged? This is a subject of huge controversy. Not hedging may distort asset values and earnings per share. On the other hand, hedging means spending real money to protect accountancy figures. In any case, sophisticated investors will take the exposure into account. Knowing that our French firm has a heavy exposure to Italy, they will adjust their view of the firm's prospects. If, however, the risk has already been hedged away, their view will be incorrect. It may be complicated by the fact that the French firm makes extensive purchases in lira, thus giving a natural offset of risk.

We can sum this up with the totally opposite views of two firms in not dissimilar businesses.

SmithKline Beecham, the UK-listed pharmaceuticals group, makes 90% of its profits outside the UK. The treasurer (in the *Financial Times,* 27 November 1991) argued in favour of producing less volatile earnings by hedging: 'stable and predictable earnings are more valuable to investors'.

The UK chemicals and pharmaceutical group, ICI, makes 55% of its earnings overseas but does not hedge. Their treasurer (1991 *Financial Times* article) argues: 'Translation exposures do not have any immediate cash flow consequences yet any hedging activity will involve cash expenditure.'

Economic risk   This is by no means as obvious as the other two. Suppose a Dutch firm is selling goods into Germany and its main competitor is a British firm. If sterling weakens against the deutschemark, the Dutch firm has lost competitive advantage. The UK left the ERM in September 1992. Sterling fell 15% against the deutschemark in a matter of weeks but the Dutch guilder did not. Obviously this is serious for the Dutch firm but it may not be easy to hedge such a risk. It does need to be considered as part of marketing and competitive strategy.

Transaction Risk – Forward Rates

Let's take a German computer software company which imports computers from the US, paid for in dollars. It resells them with its added-value services – software, installation and so on. A contract has just been signed with a German customer and two computers ordered from the US in order to fulfil the contract. The computers cost $100 000 and the exchange rate is $1 = DM1.50. The cost is, therefore, DM150 000. By the time the computers arrive and the German firm is due to pay for them (say, in 3 months' time), the dollar may have strengthened and the exchange rate changed to $1 = DM1.65. The cost in deutschemarks is now DM165 000. If the German firm costed the computers at DM150 000 when making the sale, then DM15 000 has just been lost from its profit. How can it prevent this happening?

This is, of course, the standard problem facing all importers and exporters. Importers pay later but don't know what the exchange rate will be. Exporters earn foreign currencies at a later date but equally don't know how rates will move.

One simple solution for the importer is to buy the dollars today at $1 = DM1.50. The dollars are not needed for 3 months, so the $100 000 is put on deposit to earn interest. In 3 months' time, they are taken out of deposit and used to pay for the machine.

In principle, there's nothing wrong with this solution apart from the assumption that the importer has the DM150 000 now to do this as opposed to having to find it in 3 months when, perhaps, his own customer has paid. However, there is another solution which is so common that this is probably the one that would be used. The importer buys the dollars from the bank *3 months forward* – the *forward* deal.

The bank is requested to provide $100 000 in 3 months in exchange for deutschemarks. Today's rate (called *spot*) is DM1.50. The bank may quote, say, DM1.5225 for the 3 month deal. The importer now has certainty. The rate could depreciate later to DM1.65 but the purchase of dollars will be made at DM1.5225. It's a little bit worse than the spot rate but it has bought peace of mind.

The question is, how did the bank decide that DM1.5225 was the correct rate? Does the bank have analysts studying key exchange rate trends and making a forecast? Do they have, in a discreet corner of the dealing room, a gypsy and crystal ball?

The bank is, of course, now at risk instead of the importer. If they do nothing, then in 3 months they face buying dollars at, say, a rate of DM1.65 and only getting $1.5225 from their customer. Before, we suggested that the firm could buy the dollars today and put them on deposit. The bank can do the same. It can buy the dollars today at DM1.50 and simply lend them in the interbank market for 3 months until their client needs them. The question is – what is the cost to the bank?

The consequence of their action is that money which had been in deutschemarks and earning interest (or borrowed – the argument is much the same) is now in dollars and earning interest. But suppose dollar rates for 3 months' money are 4% p.a. and deutschemark rates are 10% p.a.? The bank has lost 6% p.a. (that is, 1½% in 3 months) through being in dollars. It is what economists call the 'opportunity cost'. It has lost the opportunity to earn interest on deutschemarks and the cost is 1½%. This will be charged to the client as a worsening of the spot rate from DM1.5 to DM1.5225. Thus forward rates arise *from the difference in interest rates in the two currencies concerned.*

We can try this argument from another angle. A rich American, with $1 million on deposit in the US earning 4%, sees that German interest rates are 10% and moves into deutschemarks for 1 year to earn an easy extra 6%. The snag, of course, is that, if deutschemarks depreciate by 10% against the dollar, then the original $1 million will later only be worth $900 000 and this loss has wiped out the interest rate gain. To prevent this, the American sells the deutschemarks (and buys back the dollars) 1 year *forward.* If the charge for this is any less than 6%, then our American has a locked in profit and no risk. This will apply to dozens of other Americans with spare funds. The result is that billions of dollars will flow into deutschemarks until the laws of supply and demand put up the cost of the forward rate to 6% and make the whole exercise no longer worthwhile.

As dollar interest rates are less than deutschemark interest rates, we say the dollar is at a *premium* (and the deutschemark at a *discount*). Notice, however, the effect of this on an *exporter* in Germany. This firm will, say, earn $100 000 in 3 months and asks the bank to quote a forward rate for buying the dollars from them and providing deutschemarks instead. What steps can the bank now take to avoid risk? As it's a little more complicated than our previous example, let's lay out the steps the bank can take:

Today	1.	Borrow $100 000 for 3 months
	2.	Buy DM150 000 with the dollars at today's rate of DM1.50
	3.	Put the DM150 000 on deposit for 3 months.
3 months later	1.	The DM150 000 comes off deposit and is sold to the bank's client for dollars
	2.	The client gives the bank the $100 000 earned from exports
	3.	The dollar loan is repaid with the $100 000.

The effect of this is that the bank has paid 4% p.a. interest on the dollars and earned 10% p.a. interest on the deutschemarks for 3 months (that is, gained 1½). The bank has now made money from the interest rate difference and the forward rate is *more favourable* than the spot rate.

(In all these examples, the question of bid/offer spreads has been ignored in the interests of simplicity.)

Where the dollar is at a *premium* to the deutschemark this means that:

❏ For the *importer* the forward rate is *less* favourable
❏ For the *exporter* the forward rate is *more* favourable.

(The importer may not be quite sure when they will pay for the dollars and ask for a forward purchase of dollars, for example, 'between 1 and 28 February'. This is a *forward dated option contract* and not to be confused with 'options' as such.)

Transaction Risk – Options

Let's go back to the case of our German importer. The $100 000 needed for imports are bought forward at a rate of DM1.5225. However, in 3 months, the rate is actually DM1.40 and has improved from the deutschemark point of view. The $100 000 could be bought spot for only DM140 000. However, they can't be bought spot as the importer has already committed to buy forward at DM1.5225. This illustrates a most important point about forward purchases:

> *The forward purchase protects against a deterioration in the rate but the forward buyer cannot now gain should the rate improve.*

The importer will probably not worry about this, being happy to have protected the profit in the computer deal. Others may not take this view and argue as follows:

> *Today's spot rate is DM1.50. I want protection if the rate worsens in 3 months to DM1.65 – I still want to buy dollars at DM1.50. On the other hand, if the rate improves to DM1.40, I want to forget the above protection and buy spot at DM1.40.*

In other words, there are those who wish to have their cake and also eat it. The markets being advanced and ingenious, provide a means by which this can be done called *options*.

Options can become quite complicated when considered in detail. Happily, the principle is very easy. The importer does not commit to buy the dollars forward at DM1.50 but pays for an *option* to do so. If, later, the rate has worsened, the importer takes up the option at DM1.50. If, however, the rate has improved to, say, DM1.40, the importer abandons what was only an option and buys dollars spot at the better rate.

This is clearly more flexible and advantageous than buying forward and naturally costs more (or who would buy forward?). The cost is called the *premium* and usually paid in advance. We can, therefore, say of options:

The option purchase protects against a deterioration in the rate but the option buyer can still benefit from an improvement in the rate. There is a cost – the premium.

Where would the importer (or exporter) go to buy this option? There are two possibilities:

❑ Deal through a Traded Options Exchange, or
❑ Deal through a bank – called OTC ('Over the Counter').

There are very few currency options contracts available in Europe. This is largely due to the strength of the OTC market there. The biggest currency option deals are handled in the US at either the Chicago Mercantile Exchange (CME), also called the International Monetary Market (IMM) or the Philadelphia Stock Exchange (PHLX).

The characteristics of an exchange is that there are standard contract sizes and standard expiry months. If we take our German importer, he could go to either the CME or PHLX for dollar/deutschemark options and would find the terms shown in Table 7.6.

Table 7.6   Dollar Deutschemark options terms

US EXCHANGE	*$/DM*	*OPTIONS*
Exchange	*Contract size (Deutschemarks)*	*Contract months*
CME	125 000	Jan/Mar/Apr/Jun Jul/Sep/Oct/Dec and spot month
PHLX	62 500	Mar/Jun/Sep/Dec plus 2 near months

The first problem for the importer is that DM150 000 needs to be covered and the contract size is DM125 000 (or 2 × DM62 500). The next problem may be that the expiry in 3 months is 18 February and neither exchange handles this expiry date.

The advantage of the standard contracts is that, being standard, there is plenty of competition for the business. In particular, the contracts can be sold back later, called '*trading the option*'.

Finally, the exchange protects contracts from default by the use of a body called a 'Clearing House', and we shall explain this further in Chapter 10.

Going to the bank, the terms can be tailored to the needs of the option buyer, for example, DM150 000, expiring 18 February. The bank may also offer a number of variations on the deal (see below). However, the options cannot normally be traded and, if the bank is BCCI and crashes into liquidation, the contract is not guaranteed. In currencies the OTC market with the banks is huge. Perhaps this is because the bank may be helping the importer/exporter with general finance for trade anyway and it seems natural to ask them to handle the options business. In addition, the banks may construct attractive variations on the options theme, some of which have proved very popular. Here are three examples:

Breakforward   This was invented by Midland Bank. Here the client is offered a forward rate (at a rate not quite as good as the normal forward) but, at a predetermined rate, the contract can be unwound, leaving the client to benefit from a future favourable rate.

For example, a British firm needs to import dollar goods and buy dollars in 3 months. The forward rate is £1 = $1.89. The firm wants downside protection but feels that it is just as likely that sterling will improve.

The bank offers a 'floor' rate of $1.88 and a 'break' rate of $1.91. The effect is that, up to a rate of $1.91, the client will buy dollars at $1.88. Above $1.91, the client is freed from this obligation and can buy dollars at the spot rate less 3¢ (that is, the difference between the 'floor' and the 'break' rate which the bank is cleverly using to buy an option!).

Thus:

❏   Future spot rate $1.80, client buys at $1.88
❏   Future spot rate $1.91, client buys at $1.88
❏   Future spot rate $1.98, client buys at $1.95.

The firm thus gets almost complete downside protection but can benefit from a forward rate to a large extent. This leads naturally to participating forward.

Participating forward   Again, a 'floor' rate is agreed as is a participation level in future favourable rates. Let us say that the normal forward rate is $1.89, the 'floor' is $1.86 and the agreed participation in improvement above $1.86 is 80%. If the spot rate later is worse than $1.86, the client buys dollars at $1.86. If the rate is, say, $1.96, the client rate is based on 80% of this improvement. The spot rate is 10 points better than $1.86 so the client can have a rate 8 points better, that is $1.94.

Thus:

❏   Future spot rate $1.80, client buys at $1.86
❏   Future spot rate $1.91, client buys at $1.90
❏   Future spot rate $1.96, client buys at $1.94.

Again, the client has substantial downside protection but can also benefit to a large extent from an improvement in the rate. The client can discuss the desired participation level with the bank – the higher the level, the lower the floor rate!

Cylinder or Collar   This technique is identical to the 'collar' technique used in interest rate futures.

Again, a UK importer needs to buy dollars in 3 months. Let us say that today's spot rate is $1.90. The importer can come to an arrangement with the bank that the future dollars will be bought within a range of, say, $1.85–$1.95. (As a result, the technique is also called 'range forward'.)

❑   If the future spot rate is worse than $1.85, the client buys at $1.85
❑   If the future spot rate is better than $1.95, the client buys at $1.95
❑   If the future spot rate is between $1.85 and $1.95, the client buys at that rate.

The client now gets some downside protection and also some upside gain. Depending on the rates chosen, the cost may be small or even none at all.

How does the bank achieve the above end objectives for the client? The answer lies in very ingenious use of option techniques.

The whole question of option trading is treated in detail in Chapter 10.

FOREIGN EXCHANGE DEALING

Quotations

The forex dealer is surrounded by computer terminals giving exchange rates quoted by banks all over the world. The main information provider is Reuters but Telerate and Quotron are both very active. The rates quoted are 'indicative' only. For a firm rate the dealer must telephone and ask for a quotation for a given currency pair. The dealer merely asks for a quote and does not say if this is a sale or purchase.

The market has its own curious jargon for exchange rates, for example:

Cable	Dollar/Sterling
Swissy	Dollar/Swiss franc
Paris	Dollar/French franc
Stocky	Dollar/Swedish Kroner (from Stockholm)
Copey	Dollar/Danish Kroner (from Copenhagen)
Dollarmark	Dollar/Deutschemark.

In London, even cockney rhyming slang is used. The Japanese yen rate is the 'Bill and Ben'!

As elsewhere in financial markets, rates are given as 'bid and offer', that is, buying/selling. For example, asked for a 'dollarmark' quote, the reply might be DM1.4250/DM1.4260 or more likely '50/60' as the dealers are following rates every second of the day. If in any doubt, the enquirer will ask, 'What's the big figure?' and the reply is, '1.42'.

This means that the fellow dealer will *buy* dollars at DM1.4250 or *sell* dollars at DM1.4260. The 10 bp in the rate is the profit margin or 'spread'.

We can see this by following it through slowly. Suppose the dealer begins with DM1.4250 and buys $1. Now the dealer owns $1 (they would say, 'is *long* of dollars'). On a second enquiry, the dealer sells the dollar at the selling rate of DM1.4260. Now the dealer, having started out with DM1.4250, has ended with DM1.4260 after buying and selling dollars.

If this all seems terribly obvious, we apologise. The problem is that foreign exchange can be very confusing for the newcomer. For example, two currencies are involved not one (as when buying bonds or equities in the domestic currency). Thus, if the dealer buys dollars at DM1.4250 that is also the rate at which he *sells* deutschemarks. If the dealer sells dollars at DM1.4260, that is also the rate at which he *buys* deutschemarks. So bid/offer is buy/sell for dollars. For deutschemarks it is best viewed as sell/buy.

It gets more confusing if we consider sterling. Here the convention is to quote a rate of *dollars for the pound sterling*, for example, the rate is given as $1.70. Everywhere else, we give a rate for each currency against the dollar. Asked to quote for 'cable' (sterling/dollar), the dealer quotes '60/70' or, in full, $1.7360/$1.7370. This time the buy/sell rate is in terms of *sterling*, that is, the dealer buys sterling at $1.7360 and sells it at $1.7370. In dollars, it's the sell/buy rate.

The result of this way of quoting sterling can be seen when we consider an importer who wishes to buy dollars. One importer is in Germany and the other in the UK. The quotes are (mid-point rates):

Dollar/Deutschemark   DM1.50
Dollar/Sterling $1.73

Later, the rates change to DM1.55 and $1.78 respectively. For the German, the increase gives a *worse* rate as they must give up DM1.55 to buy $1 instead of DM1.50. For the UK importer, the increase has given a *better* rate. For each £1 they obtain $1.78 instead of $1.73. (Notice that, for an exporter, the results would be exactly the opposite.)

Foreign exchange rates can be very confusing for the newcomer, unless these basic points are borne in mind from the outset:

The market is oriented to the dollar. The dealers quotes are normally given as an amount of the currency to the dollar and the bid/offer is buy/sell from a dollar point of view.
Sterling is the exception, typically quoted as an amount of dollars for the pound sterling. From the dollar point of view, the bid/offer is now sell/buy.

Cross-rates

When a French firm telephones their bank to buy Canadian dollars, the bank will buy US dollars with the French francs and with the US dollars buy Canadian dollars. The market is wedded to the dollar and finds organisation easier and simpler if dealers go in and out of the dollar, even if some 'double counting' is involved. To attempt to deal directly between any pair of currencies would be too complex. The Bank of England survey of the London market (the world's biggest), in April 1995, found that over 80% of deals involved the dollar.

An exchange rate between two currencies, neither of them the dollar, is a *cross-rate*. If a dealer goes directly from French francs to deutschemarks, it would be called a direct cross-rate deal or *cross*. Due to the arrival of the ERM and the wild fluctuations of the dollar, crosses are now much more common. We can see this when we look at the figures for crosses as a percentage of the total business in London as given by the Bank of England's surveys in 1989, 1992 and 1995 (see Table 7.7).

Table 7.7   *Cross-rates as % of total deals, by value*

1995 %	1992 %	1989 %
16	17	11

Source: Bank of England, *Quarterly Bulletin* (November 1995).

The growth in the popularity of cross-rate deals can be seen from the development of cross-rate option contracts on the CME and PHLX in 1991.

Foreign Exchange Swaps

When we discussed the problem of the mythical German importer, we suggested that the bank, requested to *sell* dollars to its client in 3 months, might buy the dollars today and put them on deposit. For a client wanting the bank to *buy* dollars in 3 months, the procedure was more complex but involved borrowing dollars for 3 months, buying deutschemarks and putting them on deposit.

Whilst both techniques are quite feasible, they tie up balance sheet assets and liabilities. They impact on the banks' credit limits, involve counterparty risk and use up capital under capital ratio rules.

As a result, the problem is usually solved instead by the *foreign exchange swap*. Before going any further, these swaps have nothing to do with the swaps market for interest rate and currency swaps. The use of the same term can cause confusion. Many forex dealers simple call them 'forward' deals because that's how they handle forward requirements.

The swap is *one* transaction which combines *two* deals, one spot and one forward. In the first deal a bank buys a currency spot and in the second simultaneously sells it forward for delivery at a later date. The bank will, therefore, return to the original position at the future date. Thus, bank *A* may have £10m and enters into a swap with bank *B* for dollars:

1. Bank *A* sells £10m *spot* for, say, $20m to Bank *B*
2. Bank *A* sells the $20m *forward* for £10m in 3 months.

At the moment, then, bank *A* has $20m. In 3 months, bank *A* will exchange the $20m for £10m returning to the original position.

Thus, the foreign exchange swap is a combined spot and forward deal.

When a bank commits to sell a customer a currency at a future date, there may be others wanting to buy the currency for the same date. However, while some deals will offset in this fashion, in most cases the dealer won't be so fortunate. If he has sold $2m for delivery on 20 March, he may find that he is due to buy $2m for £ on 30 March – leaving an exposure 'gap'. Alternatively, he is due to buy $ for £ on 20 March, but only $1m, leaving the dealer 'short' of $1m for 20 March delivery.

One way of handling the problem is to buy $2m today and put it on deposit until 20 March. This may mean having to borrow the £ to do it. This involves finding suitable lenders and borrowers and ties up lines of credit with other banks.

Instead it will be easier to buy $2m spot. The $, however, are not required until 20 March, so the dealer now enters the *swap:*

1. The dealer sells the $2m spot for £, returning back to a £ position
2. At the same time, the dealer sells the £ forward for $2m to be delivered on 20 March.

The counterparty to the swap who had £ originally is now sitting on $ until 20 March. Since $ interest rates are lower than £ the swap rate will reflect the difference in interest rates. Thus if UK interest rates were 6% higher than the US, then a 6 month forward deal would involve a *premium* of 3% (ignoring yield curve variations). If spot were, say, $1.80, then the 6 month forward premium would be about 5.40¢. The spot rate might thus be quoted as $1.8000/$1.8010 with a forward margin or spread of, say, 5.40¢/5.30¢ (or quoted as basis points 540/530). As the $ is at a premium, these rates will be *subtracted* from the spot rates (if at a discount, the rates would be added to the spot rates).

Thus, an *importer* wanting to buy $ for £ in 6 months will be quoted as follows:

Spot $ 1.8000
Premium   540   –
                 _____
Forward rate $1.7460

An *exporter* wanting to sell $ for £ in 6 months will be quoted as follows:

Spot $ 1.8010
Premium   530   –
                 _____
Forward rate $ 1.7480

The *importer* has a *worse* rate than spot as he only gets $1.7460 for £1 rather than $1.80.

The *exporter* has a *better* rate than spot as he only gives up $1.7480 to obtain £1 rather than $1.8010.

Thus the swap handles the request from a customer for a forward deal. It would also handle a situation where the dealer was 'long' in spot $ (and thus at risk) but 'short' of the same quantity for delivery in 3 months. He sells the $ spot for £ (and is no longer 'long' of spot $) and sells the £ back for the $ in 3 months.

(Those which have very quick minds will see that, while the dealer is no longer at risk to changes in currency rates, he may be at risk to changes in interest rates. The cost of the swap is based on an interest rate difference between dollar/sterling of 6% p.a. But what if this changes to 4% p.a. or 7%? There is, indeed, a potential problem here but the solutions are outside the scope of an introductory book of this nature!)

Brokers

In these markets, extensive use is made of brokers. In fact, the 1995 Bank of England survey showed that brokers were used in 35% of deals by value.

A dealer who is long on dollars and anxious to sell may not wish to reveal their position to others. The desire to sell, say, $50m for sterling at a given rate can be passed to a broker who will disseminate this information anonymously using computer screens or voice boxes. Another dealer, who finds this rate acceptable, may close the deal via the broker. The broker takes no risk. The clients settle directly and the broker takes a small commission.

A broker may quote 'Cable 70/80 – give five, take three'. Cable is sterling dollar and the broker has a client who will buy £3m at, say, $1.7370 and sell £5m at $1.7380.

The new Reuters system, Dealing 2000/2, was released in mid-1992. This enables the computer system itself to match deals automatically and anonymously. Its progress is being watched closely. If successful, it could have an impact on the use of brokers and cut costs. Fearful of Reuters acquiring a potential monopoly position, eleven banks funded a rival development via Quotron called EBS which was released in 1993. A third, similar, system is MINEX which was developed by Telerate and KDD of Japan.

By April 1995, there was very little doubt that the new electronic broking systems were having an impact. The EBS group bought out MINEX, which resulted in just two competitors. It is clear that conventional brokers were losing business. The Bank of England 1995 Survey showed, as we have said, that 35% of business was placed via brokers but, of this, 5% was already handled by electronic broking. One unusual side effect was the fact that small banks began to use the broking systems, to some extent, instead of placing orders with larger banks.

Settlement

Getting paid is, naturally, crucially important. Doing the deal on the telephone is called 'front office'. Getting paid, reconciling accounts and so on is 'back office'.

In some systems, the dealer writes the details of the deal on a slip of paper. These are later encoded into the computerised back office system. In other cases, the dealer enters the deal into the computer system used for front office which prints a deal slip and holds the data electronically for transfer to the back office system.

A domestic bank thinks of its account with a foreign bank in the foreign currency as its 'nostro' account. For example, BNP thinks of its dollar account with Citibank in New York as its 'nostro' or *our* account with you. Equally, it regards Citibank's account with BNP in French francs as the 'vostro' or 'loro' account, that is, '*your* account with us'. This all goes back to those clever Italian bankers years ago.

The department dealing with settlement and reconciliation is thus the 'nostro department'. Agreeing our calculation of the value of the foreign currency account with the foreign bank's statement for the same account is 'nostro reconciliation', an important but tedious chore for which computer systems are used to speed up the process.

Banks today are most concerned about counterparty risk (even before BCCI!). For example, all spot deals are settled in two working days. What if we settle the foreign currency deal but the counterparty doesn't? The bankers call this Herstatt risk, following the failure, on 26 June 1974, of ID Herstatt, a German bank, to settle the dollar side of its transactions (6 hours behind) although the deutschemarks had been paid to it. This risk has led to the use of techniques called *netting*.

A system of bilateral netting of foreign exchange deals has operated in London for several years. The system is known as FX Net and involves about 16 banks.

Netting no longer requires the exchange of two payments for each pair of currencies dealt with. The two parties make or receive one net payment for each currency deal for each settlement date.

For example, suppose counterparty A and counterparty B enter into the four transactions for the same settlement date, as shown in Figure 7.3.

In the conventional way, each counterparty would process eight transactions each, paying away four and receiving four.

In the FX Net system, running accounts are maintained for each currency and settlement date and at settlement each counterparty would process three *net* deals, one for each currency. The running accounts would appear as shown in Figure 7.4.

Settlement of the net amounts occurs as each settlement date is reached.

Using conventional settlement methods, if we take the $ account, A will pay B $40m and B will pay A $20m. Taking the £ account, A will pay B £10m and B will pay A £5m. Suppose A defaults and does not settle? B will lose $40m and £10m. Under the netting, B would lose $20m and £5m. In other words, a key reason for net settlement is to reduce substantially the underlying risk of foreign exchange dealing.

The influential bank 'think tank', G30, produced an important report on settlement. Amongst other things, it recommended netting arrangements to reduce risk.

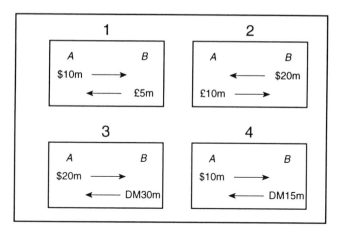

Figure 7.3 *Netting by counterparties*

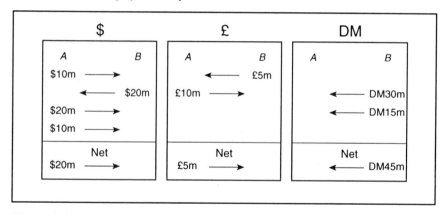

Figure 7.4 *Running accounts*

Up to now FX Net has been run by Quotron, which receives the counterparties' SWIFT messages (MT300) and at cut off time notifies the counterparties of the net amounts due with SWIFT payment instructions (MT202/MT210) and a SWIFT statement (MT950). The fact that gross details of transactions are sent as well as net details allows full nostro reconciliation to take place as required. (The SWIFT system is explained in Chapter 8.)

A multilateral netting system called Echo began operations in 1995, as did a similar system in the US. Then, in March 1996, came the announcement that 20 major banks, 'the group of 20', were preparing to set up a global clearing system to handle foreign exchange settlement. The aim is to produce an instantaneous settlement system in which a payment by one bank is immediately offset by a payment by another. This would eliminate Herstatt risk. The development timescale is 3 years.

ARBITRAGE

'Arbitrage' is a term that was first used in the foreign exchange markets. In the days when communications were not as good as today, one might find a disparity in rates quoted for the same pair of currencies. Perhaps the offer price for dollar/sterling in Paris is less than the bid price for dollar/sterling in London or any similar disparity in rates quoted by various banks. A currency could be bought in Paris and resold in London for an easy profit.

In general, arbitrage is taking advantage of any pricing anomaly. More arbitrage opportunities and more sophisticated arbitrage opportunities than ever before are being spotted due to the use of computers, often linked to constant feeds of live prices and using 'expert systems' techniques. At the same time, the paradox is that a dealer has to be quicker than ever to take advantage of an arbitrage opportunity, because everyone else is using computers too!

For example, a dealer may spot that another dealer's forward rate does *not* eliminate the difference in interest rates. As a result, perhaps the low interest rate currency is borrowed, sold for the high interest rate currency and this put on deposit for, say, 6 months. At the same time, to avoid currency risk, the low interest rate currency is bought back forward in 6 months' time so that the original loan can be repaid. The forward rate cost, however, is less than the interest rate difference leaving a risk free profit. This is called *covered interest rate arbitrage*.

Arbitrage can be found in any market these days, not just foreign exchange. As it is essentially risk free, it's good business if you can find it. All the banks employ arbitrage specialists who look for these opportunities, especially in the derivative products market place. The argument in its favour is that it keeps pricing efficient. In spite of this, arbitrage between equities and futures markets *(stock index arbitrage)* rouses great suspicions and is a subject of considerable controversy.

(One of the earliest records of telegraphic links was that between Rothschild's of London and Behrens of Hamburg in 1843 to exchange prices of securities, currencies and bills of exchange. Rich arbitrage opportunities for those quick off the mark!)

CENTRAL BANK SURVEYS

At the start of this chapter, we explained that the central banks of the US, UK and Japan carried out a simultaneous survey of their markets in 1986, 1989, 1992 and 1995.

Recent results in the three major centres can be seen in Table 7.8.

The first point to note is the huge size of the figures. London trades 464 000 m dollars worth of business each day and every day! The BIS, in Basle, collects all the figures and eliminates double counting (a deal done in London with a New York bank will be reported in both centres). The total figure in 1986 was just in excess of $300bn daily but rose to $650bn in 1989. The 1992 figures released in April 1993 showed a further rise to $880bn and the 1995 figure was $1230bn.

The second point is the rate of growth. In London and New York, the 1986 figure has grown to between five and 6 times as big by 1995. Tokyo doubled between 1986 and 1989 but then the growth rate slowed.

Tokyo is a special case. We saw in Chapter 4, on Commercial Banking, that the Japanese have withdrawn a little from the international markets. Cross-border capital flows have slowed down. Trust banks in Japan, major players at one time, have been hit by the decline in Trust Fund Investment. The fall in the Nikkei index after January 1990 and the collapse of property values has hit the market generally. Bank mergers have reduced the number of players and the coming BIS capital ratio rules in 1993 have made the banks more cautious.

Table 7.8   *Central bank Forex surveys – daily Forex dealing*

	1995 $bn	1992 $bn
London	464	290
New York	244	167
Tokyo	161	120

Source   Bank of England, *Quarterly Bulletin* (November 1995).

One problem for central banks, intervening from time to time to support their currencies, is that the forces that can be marshalled against them are much bigger. If we look at the ERM crisis as it unfolded in August/September 1992, we see the Bank of England sitting on reserves of gold and foreign currencies of about $44bn. The trading in deals involving sterling, including cross-rate, amount to some $79bn every single day (see Appendix to this chapter, p.173). Even with the assistance of the Bundesbank, the resistance was simply swept away.

What we have seen in recent years is concerted action by major central banks acting in tandem and usually agreed at G7 meetings.

It all began at the beginning of 1985. The rise of the dollar was making USA exports uncompetitive and the pound/dollar rate was nearing parity. After a series of secret telephone calls, the world's major central banks hit the dollar simultaneously on Wednesday morning, 27 February. There was near pandemonium on the forex markets and within an hour the dollar had fallen 6% against the mark, from DM3.50 to DM3.30.

Intervention came again in September that year. The Group of Five (G5) major economies (later to expand to G7 and include Canada and Italy) met at the Plaza Hotel, New York on 22 September. A statement was issued that the dollar was overvalued, but although that seemed to be words only, it did the trick. On Monday

23 September, the dollar fell 3.5% without the central banks spending anything. The dollarmark rate was then DM2.70. Later, the central banks did intervene to reinforce their wishes and, by November, the dollarmark was DM2.50. This has become known as the 'Plaza Agreement' and was, perhaps, the first international agreement on currencies since Bretton Woods.

If the Plaza Agreement seemed to mark a new milestone, this has not really proved to be the case. The central bankers met again at the Louvre in Paris (February 1987) and this time declared the dollar undervalued. It also announced a resolve to hold major world interest rates within narrow bands. This became known as the 'Louvre Accord'. However, this and several concerted attempts later to boost the dollar were not nearly as successful as attempts earlier to halt its runaway success.

WHY LONDON?

The figures shown in the last section reveal London not only as the biggest forex market in the world, but by a considerable margin. In view of the decline of the UK as an economic power and the weakness of the pound as a major currency, one may well ask why it is the major forex market.

There are, perhaps, four factors:

- ❏ *Time-zone*   London is well placed here. It can talk to Tokyo for an hour in the morning; the Middle East at about 11.30; New York/Chicago at 1.30 and Los Angeles/San Francisco at 4.30. New York and Tokyo are in non-overlapping time zones.
- ❏ *Tradition*   London has a historical and traditional role as a major financial centre. There are over 500 foreign banks trading there and it has the infrastructure needed – accountants, lawyers, speciality printers.
- ❏ *Euromarkets*   The Euromarkets have large implications for foreign exchange. London's traditional role and its lack of protectionism led to the Euromarket business emanating from London and the huge population of foreign banks to which we have just referred.
- ❏ *English language*   English is the major language in international finance. The use of English as a first or second language is actually growing. This certainly helps London to score over Paris or Frankfurt. Indeed, the French insistence (at the highest official level) on the use of French militates against their desire to promote Paris further as an international centre.

The Appendix to this chapter shows the breakdown of London dealing as shown by the Bank of England surveys in 1989, 1992 and 1995. The current strength of the deutschemark can be seen by the fact that the biggest trading currency in London, after the dollar, is no longer sterling but deutschemarks – $/DM deals are 21.1% and cross-rate deals involving deutschemarks a further 11.5%. Indeed, the BIS paper in 1995 showed that the deutschemark is involved in 37% of foreign currency deals worldwide, second only to the dollar.

SUMMARY

The foreign exchange market is huge, trading a net £1200bn a day in 1995 with London the biggest market.

The demand for foreign exchange arises from trade, tourism, government spending, international security trading and speculation.

Interbank business in London is 75% of the market by value and the top ten banks accounted for 44% of the market. Foreign exchange dealing accounts for half the profits of the big US commercial banks.

One economic theory for explaining exchange rates is *purchasing power parity* (PPP). Pricing the same basket of goods in two countries should result in the exchange rate. If a country consistently has higher inflation than another, its currency will tend to weaken compared with that of the country with lower inflation. The high inflation country will have to offer higher interest rates to persuade non-nationals to hold its currency. The theory that investors will shift assets according to factors like these is the *portfolio balance model*.

The post-war period of fixed exchange rates was agreed at a meeting in Bretton Woods in 1944. This also set up the IMF and the World Bank.

The *European Monetary System* (1979) created the *Exchange Rate Mechanism* and the use for official purposes of a unit of accounting called the Ecu. The Maastricht Treaty of 1991 determined conditions for *European Monetary Union* (EMU). A European Monetary Institute was set up in 1994 to prepare for EMU. Later meetings decided on 1999 as the first possible date.

Foreign exchange risk for corporates has three elements – *transaction* risk, *translation* risk and *economic* risk.

Spot rates are today's exchange rates with settlement in 2 days. *Forward* rates are fixed rates for a transaction at a later date. They are determined by the difference in interest rates in the two currencies concerned.

The forward rate, being fixed, protects against the currency moving to the buyer's/seller's disadvantage, but they cannot benefit if it moves in their favour. This can be achieved by *currency options*. Options can be dealt on an exchange or over the counter (OTC).

Foreign exchange quotations are shown as a bid/offer rate. The dollar lies at the heart of foreign exchange dealing, as most transactions involve moving in and out of the dollar. Sterling and currencies which were linked to sterling quote so many dollars to the domestic currency. Other currencies quote a quantity of that currency to the dollar. A rate between two currencies, neither of them the dollar, is called a *cross-rate*.

The purchase of a currency spot accompanied by its simultaneous sale forward is the foreign exchange *swap*.

Brokers are active and link buyers and sellers on an anonymous basis. Electronic broking systems like Reuters 2000/2 and EBS are now being used.

A bank's foreign currency holdings with banks abroad are its *nostro* accounts. The foreign banks' balances with it in the domestic currency are *vostro* accounts. Bilateral *netting* of foreign exchange settlement is now common to reduce settlement risk. Multilateral netting is on the way.

Arbitrage is taking advantage of an anomaly in rates to make risk-free profit.

Central banks carry out a foreign exchange survey every 3 years (1995 was the last occasion) with the results coordinated by the BIS.

Appendix

Table *7.A1   Bank of England Forex surveys, 1989–95, % of daily dealing values*

	1995 %	1992 %	1989 %
$–DM	21	24	22
$–£	13	17	27
$–Yen	17	12	15
$–SF	5	6	10
$–FF	5	3	2
$–C$	2	2	2
$–A$	2	1	2
$–Lira	3 ⎫	⎫	
$–Peseta	2 ⎬	9 ⎬	7
$–other EMS	6 ⎭		
$–Other	4	3 ⎭	
Ecu	4	5	2
Cross Rates:			
£ –DM	4	5	3
£ –Other	1	1	1
DM–Yen	2	2	2
DM–EMS	5	4	—
Other Crosses	3	4	3

(Figures may not add up to 100 due to rounding errors)

Source: Bank of England, *Quarterly Bulletin* (November 1995).

8 Finance for Trade

GENERAL PROBLEMS

If we consider the various problems which will arise in the export/import business, there are many ways in which banks can provide assistance:

1. *Payment services*   The basic question of money transfers
2. *Collection of debts*   The heart of the matter – how to ensure that we get paid
3. *Extension of credit*   This involves ensuring that we get paid and the question of extending credit using, say, the bill of exchange
4. *Finance* This may be for the exporter to fund completion of the contract or for the importer to help pay for goods
5. *Foreign exchange*   Sales/purchases of foreign currency spot, forward and by way of options, which are discussed in Chapter 7
6. *Trading guarantees*   This covers many questions – quality of goods already paid for (importer), failure of chosen supplier to perform on award of a tender (importer), insurance against political risk, sudden withdrawal of export licences (exporter)
7. *Miscellaneous*   This involves market intelligence, letters of introduction, correspondent banking facilities and similar services.

PAYMENT SERVICES

There are various ways in which the banks may arrange to remit funds:

❏ *Mail Transfer* (MT) – instruction by letter
❏ *Telegraphic Transfer* (TT)
❏ *SWIFT* – Society for Worldwide Interbank Financial Telecommunication. A cooperative of 2900 banks running an international message transfer system on computers. For example, a payment would be made by an instruction to pay. The message is not in itself a payment, as in, for example, an ACH. SWIFT became operational in 1977 and handles 2.7m messages per day. It employs standardised message formats suitable for automated data handling and eliminating language and interpretation problems (Figure 8.1). In 1996, the number of users had risen to 5300, most of them banks.

There are seven message categories. The categories and the percentage of the traffic represented by each is shown in Table 8.1.

Table 8.1   *SWIFT message categories and share of business, 1995*

	Category	%
1	Customer payments and cheques	25.6
2	Financial institution transfers	29.6
3	Foreign exchange	14.0
4	Collections and cash letters	2.1
5	Securities	8.1
6	Documentary credits	4.0
7	Cash management and customer status	16.6

Source: SWIFT.

Although Category 500, Securities, is only 8% of the traffic, it is the fastest growing section, increasing by 45% in 1995.

SWIFT Message	
Explanation	**Format**
Sending institution	GEBABEBB
Message type	100
Receiving institution	RABONL2U
Sender's transaction ref. nr.	:20: CT0987A101
Value/date/currency/amount	:32A: 940811NLG374,76
Ordering customer	:50: MR ET MME KLEIN
	RUE DE BRUXELLES 7
	HALLE
Beneficiary	:59:/432 04546
	TULIP EXPORTS NV
	KAASSTRAAT 52
	AMSTERDAM
Details of payment	:70:/RFB/INV 10435 - 30 MAY 96
Authentication result	MAC/ES78B741

Figure 8.1   *MT100 customer transfer*
Source: SWIFT.

The geographic spread of messages in 1995 was:

		%
❏	Europe/Middle East	62.0
❏	The Americas	20.0
❏	Asia/Pacific	17.0

We show in Figure 8.1 an example of Category 1, Message Type 100.

Mr and Mme Klein order Générale de Banque, Brussels to pay Dutch Guilders 374,76 to the Rabobank, Utrecht for the account of Tulip Exports NV in payment of invoice number 10435 of 30 May 1996.

Générale de Banque specifies that the account number for Tulip Exports is 432–04546.

❏ *International Money Transfer* (IMT) or *Express* IMT – modern terms for the mail transfer and telegraphic transfer
❏ *International Money Order* (IMO) – A UK bank, for example, may issue a cheque drawn on their New York office
❏ *Bank Draft* – This will be drawn on a bank's home account or on their nostro account at a correspondent bank.

The last two documents are usually sent by the customer and not their bank.

COLLECTION OF DEBTS

There are methods which may not involve extension of credit:

❏ *Advance payment*   This seems ideal but there are still problems. Suppose the advance payment is not received? What if the order is cancelled *prior* to sending the payment? Time must be allowed to clear the cheque/draft anyway. From the *importer's* point of view, the goods may not be shipped, or the wrong goods may be shipped, or the shipping documents may be wrong.
❏ *Payment on shipment*   The exporter telexes notice of shipment and awaits payment. The exporter could find themselves having shipped goods and yet the payment does not arrive. The bill of lading may give the importer title to the goods. From the *importer's* point of view, the goods may be found to be faulty or the wrong goods.
❏ *Open account trading*   We despatch the goods and send an invoice marked 'payment within 7 days' (for example). Full of risk but quite suitable for circumstances where a valuable trading relationship has been set up and trust exists. This is very common in the US.

EXTENSION OF CREDIT

We now consider methods which involve extension of credit or cash on delivery but where we ask for a bank's help in collecting the money and guaranteeing arrangements to a certain extent.

Bill of Exchange

This is drawn by the exporter on the importer, with the latter agreeing to pay on demand or at a determinable future time the value of the goods to a specified person or bearer of the bill. This is explained fully in Chapter 5.

Sight bill or Demand draft   Immediate payment upon presentation of the bill and documents, with no required acceptance of the bill by the importer, as part of a documentary credit.

Usance, tenor or term bill   Payable in a number of days or months, usually 'accepted' by a bank, the exporter then sells to a bill broker who holds to maturity or trades.

Documentary bill   With documents (bill of lading, invoice, insurance cover and similar documents) attached.

Clean bill   Without documents.

Documentary Letter of Credit

A bill of exchange is drawn by the exporter. A documentary letter of credit is opened by the *importer*.

There is an international code of practice for documentary credits set out in the International Chamber of Commerce's *Uniform Customs & Practices for Documentary Credits.*

(The International Chamber of Commerce was set up in 1919 to define the rules and norms by which trade is carried out. 60 national commissions make up its federal structure.)

The importer opens a documentary credit with his bank (*Issuing Bank*). This arranges for the Issuing Bank, upon instructions from the importer, to:

(a) make payment to the exporter (the *Beneficiary*) (see Figure 8.2); or

(b) pay on or accept a bill of exchange drawn by the exporter; or

(c) authorise another bank (probably its correspondent bank in the exporter's country) to be the *advising bank*, which makes payment to the exporter or accepts his bill of exchange (thus becoming a 'documentary acceptance credit'). The advising bank may also be asked to be the *confirming bank*, to add its guarantee that the exporter will get paid if the issuing bank does not.

(However, some countries, for example Iran, prohibit banks from opening credits on terms that require an advising bank to add its confirmation.)

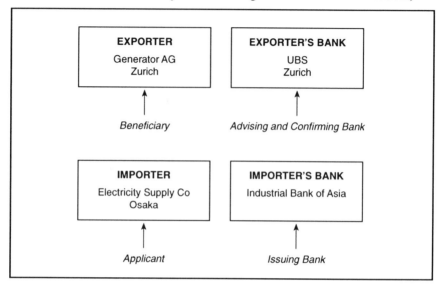

Figure 8.2   *Documentary credit*

All the above have to be backed by *stipulated documents*.
These *documents* include:

❏ *Transport documents*   Usually by sea under a *bill of lading*, which gives evidence that the goods have been dispatched, purport to be of the type and quality ordered and be properly transported. A copy of the bill of lading is the buyer's claim to possession of the goods when they arrive.
With container traffic these days there may be a *forwarder's bill of lading* – not necessarily a document of title.
If by air there is an *air waybill*, not however a document of title, merely acknowledgement of acceptance for delivery.
If by road or rail there is a *carrier's receipt* or *railway receipt* and this is also not a document of title.
❏ *Commercial invoice*   Specifying quality, quantity and unit and total price.
❏ *Insurance documents*
❏ *SAD document*   Simplified customs form for the EU.
❏ *Other documents*   Certificate of origin; certificate of quality; health certificate; veterinary certificate; weight note.

There are potential problems with documents – documents missing, incorrectly completed or showing an invoice value different from that on the documentary letter of credit. The bank's staff check these and should see, for example, 'freight paid' on the bill of lading and insurance certificate if goods are sent CIF. Incorrect documents can cause delays at the port on landing and incur costs such as local storage.

Types of Documentary Credit

- ❏ *Confirmed credit* – when the advising bank also guarantees payment.
- ❏ *Revocable/Irrevocable credit* – *Revocable* may be amended/cancelled by the issuing bank if the importer is not satisfied. This is obviously not usually acceptable to the exporter but may be suitable for selling to overseas subsidiaries where letters of credit must be used by local regulation. *Irrevocable* can only be amended/cancelled with agreement of the confirming bank and the beneficiary.
- ❏ *Sight credit, term* or *acceptance credit.*
  Sight – the exporter draws a demand draft (bill) and presents it to the correspondent bank for payment.
  Term/acceptance – the exporter draws a draft for a period of time (30, 60, 90 days) on the issuing or confirming bank.
- ❏ *Negotiation credit* – the confirming bank is instructed by the advising bank (if they are not one and the same) to negotiate the bill which is drawn on the advising bank. *Or* the bill may be drawn on the confirming bank who will accept it, making it a bank bill and therefore 'discountable'.
- ❏ *Standby credit* – to fall back upon if payment has not been made to the beneficiary by the other arranged methods.
- ❏ *Deferred payment credit* – payment made later.

An example of a Documentary Credit covering the example in Figure 8.2, reproduced from Union Bank of Switzerland *Guide to Documentary Transactions in Foreign Trade*, is shown in Figure 8.3.

Comments:

- ❏ Irrevocable, sight credit.
- ❏ *Issuing bank* – Industrial Bank of Asia.
- ❏ Importer – Electricity Supply Ltd, Osaka, Japan – opener of documentary credit with Industrial Bank of Asia.
- ❏ Exporter – Generator AG, Zurich (the *Beneficiary*).
- ❏ *Advising bank* – Union Bank of Switzerland – also acting as *Confirming bank.*
- ❏ The consignment is a generator to be shipped from Rotterdam to Osaka, Japan.
- ❏ Documents: Invoice, marine bill of lading, certificate of origin, work certificate, weight list. *Insurance documents* are listed at a later stage.

Industrial Bank of Asia
Tokyo

Lieu d'émission et date
Ort und Datum der Ausstellung
Place and date of issue

Tokyo, 8th March 19..

Except so far as otherwise expressly stated, this documentary credit is subject to the Uniform Customs and Practice for Documentary Credit of the International Chamber of Commerce issued for the first time in 1933 and including subsequent amendments.

Crédit documentaire irrévocable
Unwiderrufliches Dokumentar-Akkreditiv
Irrevocable documentary credit

L/C No de la banque émettrice/ der eröffnenden Bank/of issuing bank	L/C No de la banque notificatrice/ der avisierenden Bank/of advising bank
999'999	

Banque notificatrice/Avisierende Bank/Advising bank

Union Bank of Switzerland
Bahnhofstrasse 45

CH-8021 Zurich

Bénéficiaire/Begünstigter/Beneficiary

Generator AG
Postfach 642

CH-8045 Zurich

Montant/Betrag/Amount
max. SFr. 378'000.—

☐ Notre préavis du / Unsere Voranzeige vom / Our preadvice dated

☐ Confirmation de notre câble/télex du / Bestätigung unseres Kabels/FS vom / Confirmation of our cable/telex dated:

Nous émettons en votre faveur ce crédit documentaire qui est utilisable contre remise des documents suivants

Wir eröffnen hiermit dieses Dokumentar-Akkreditiv zu Ihren Gunsten, benutzbar gegen Einreichung folgender Dokumente

We hereby issue in your favor this documentary credit which is available against presentation of the following documents

valable jusqu'au / gültig bis / Expiry date   *15th June 19..*

chez/en / bei/in / with/in   *Zurich at sight*

Donneur d'ordre/Auftraggeber/Applicant

Electricity Supply Ltd.
P.O. Box 1593

Osaka/Japan

Sofern nicht ausdrücklich etwas anderes bestimmt ist, gelten für dieses Dokumentar-Akkreditiv die «Einheitlichen Richtlinien und Gebräuche für Dokumentar-Akkreditive» der Internationalen Handelskammer, erstmals veröffentlicht 1933 und ihre seitherigen Änderungen.

1. *Signed commercial invoice in triplicate*
2. *Full set of marine bill of lading, issued to order, blank endorsed,*
   notify: Electricity Supply Ltd., P.O. Box 1593, Osaka
   and marked "freight prepaid"
3. *Certificate of origin in duplicate, evidencing Swiss Origin and legalized*
   by the Chamber of Commerce.
4. *Work certificate*
5. *Weight list*

concernant / deckend / covering

1 complete generator unit as per order No. 6348 of 4th March 19..
C & F Osaka
Latest shipment 31st May 19..

Sauf stipulations particulières expressément définies, ce crédit documentaire est soumis aux «Règles et Usances uniformes relatives aux Crédits Documentaires» de la Chambre de Commerce Internationale établies pour la première fois en 1933 et tenant compte des modifications intervenues.

Expédition, Embarquement/Versand, Verschiffung/Despatch, Shipment de/von/from	a/nach/to	Expéditions partielles/Teilverladungen/ Partial shipments	Transbordements/Umladungen/ Transhipments
Rotterdam	*Osaka*	*prohibited*	*prohibited*

Conditions spéciales/Besondere Bedingungen/Special conditions

The advising bank is requested to add its confirmation to this credit. Payment to be
effected to the debit of our account with Union Bank of Switzerland, Zurich.

Nous garantissons que le paiement sera dûment effectué contre les documents présentés en conformité avec les termes de ce crédit.

Wir verpflichten uns hiermit, dass Zahlung geleistet wird gegen Einreichung von Dokumenten in Übereinstimmung mit den Bedingungen dieses Akkreditivs.

We hereby engage that payment will be duly made against documents presented in conformity with the terms of this credit

Indications de la banque notificatrice/Mitteilungen der avisierenden Bank/ Advising bank's notification

Industrial Bank of Asia

B. ....

Lieu, date, nom et signature de la banque notificatrice
Ort, Datum, Name und Unterschrift der avisierenden Bank
Place, date, name and signature of the advising bank

Figure 8.3   *A documentary letter of credit*
Source: Specimen from the UBS booklet, *Guide to Documentary Transactions in Foreign Trade.*

When Generator AG despatch the generator, they will send the stipulated documents to the Union Bank of Switzerland. If the documents are in order, UBS will pay Generator AG for the goods, debiting the vostro account of the Industrial Bank of Asia. The documents will then be sent to this bank so that they can make the necessary arrangements with their client, the Electricity Supply Co., for the latter to collect the goods.

Typically, in the western world, all questions of import licences, exchange controls, insurance and documentation have been settled prior to issuing the letter of credit.

From the point of view of the *exporter* he has these advantages:

❑ Assurance of a payment or acceptance on shipping the goods.
❑ If an acceptance, then it will be a banker's acceptance and at best discount rates. Who pays the discount is a matter for negotiation!
❑ Generally, the reassurance of a bank (or banks) rather than just the importer's promises.

The *importer*, too, has advantages:

❑ No money will be paid until the goods are shipped and the required documents lodged.
❑ There may be time to pay, if a bill of exchange is involved. Again, acceptance will not be made until the goods are shipped.
❑ All formalities are complete before authorising the letter of credit.

There is, finally, the question of the relationship of the *bank* and the *bank's client* wanting to issue a letter of credit. The request to the bank for a letter of credit must be signed by someone in authority as it incurs obligations for the client (the 'accountee'). Links with the bank in this day and age may be *electronic*. The whole trade deal must conform with local import regulations and EU rules if the client is a member of that community.

From the *bank's* point of view, this is a contingent liability and affects existing credit agreements and limits. It is also an off-balance sheet transaction which needs capital under BIS capital ratio rules. The bank will probably charge the client a deposit and needs authority to debit expenses and charges. If a bill of lading is not used, the bank may require the goods to be at the disposal of the bank or consigned to the bank.

If the bank is the *advising* bank, it is responsible for seeing that the proposed credit is authentic.

Documentary Collection

The exporter ships the goods and presents the documents through a bank. The bank may be requested either to collect the payment in return for the documents or to see that a bill of exchange is accepted in return for handing over the documents.

The bank, however, is only using its 'best efforts' to collect the money or acceptance. The importer may still refuse the documents. If the goods have been shipped and the documents are *not* documents of title, the importer might even be able to collect the goods anyway. We may request the collecting bank to protect our interest in the event of default. If the importer doesn't pay or refuses the transaction, the goods (having been despatched) may have to be stored locally.

FINANCE FOR THE EXPORTER

The exporter may need finance while waiting to be paid other than that provided by, say, discounting the bill of exchange. two possibilities are Forfaiting and Factoring.

Forfaiting   This is traditionally associated with longer-term high value capital goods and construction projects. In the UK, London Forfaiting has a high concentration of deals in excess of £50m in value. However, others – Midland Bank Aval and Morgan Grenfell Trade Finance – have also done a lot of 60 day business with £250 000 probably a minimum figure.

A Bill of Exchange or Promissory Note is bought 'à forfait', meaning *without recourse* to the exporter: that is, the purchaser forfaits all recourse to other parties. They look to the importer's bank to sign the bill or promissory note to guarantee payment and the bill/note will be unconditional. They can then sell the note/bill in an active secondary market. The major currencies are dollars, Swiss francs and deutschemarks.

For the exporter, forfaiting has the advantage that the finance is without recourse and has no effect on credit limits with their bank or any other. It is useful where export credit guarantees (or private insurance) are not available and, where it is available, avoids cash flow problems while waiting for a claim to be met. However, the forfaiter needs to be satisfied about client, country and political risk and the discount may be expensive. Also, they may not finance 100% of the value.

Factoring   Factoring companies purchase trade debts of clients and usually pay 80% of the full value of debts due to be paid in less than 6 months. Normally, this is used for continuous rather than ad hoc business. The remaining 20% is passed to the client after all the debt has been collected. The factor runs the sales ledger and collects the money. Factoring can be with or without recourse. The latter can be very convenient, especially for export business, but is, naturally, more expensive. Frequently 'open account' terms are used. As well as a charge for providing finance, there is also a service fee for running the sales ledger and collecting the debt. This service fee varies from ½% to 2%. A variation on the theme is *invoice discounting*, in which the factor provides finance against invoices as before but the client runs the sales ledger and collects the debt.

The overseas agent of a factor will investigate credit status so that a quick report can be made to the factor, and the agent will usually underwrite the debt and deal with any queries locally. Factors may have their own offices abroad or be part of a network of independent factoring organisations. The largest such network is Factors Chain International (FCI), founded in 1968. It has 90 member companies in 35 of the world's main commercial centres. Factoring companies are often subsidiaries of banks – for example, in the UK, Midland Bank–Griffin Factors, National Westminster–Credit Factoring International. The exporter has the advantage of dealing with a bank subsidiary, funding working capital on normal finance terms, not having to run the sales ledger and collect the debt and (in the case of non-recourse) peace of mind.

As stated, factoring is only provided for short-term debts and continuous sales of consumer items. In principle, it is similar to an overdraft.

While most factoring is *domestic*, international factoring is on the increase. The UK-based International Factors reported a 34% increase in export-related clients in the first 3 months of 1996. The biggest markets using international factoring are the Netherlands, Germany, Italy, the UK, France, Belgium and the US.

Other finance   The exporter may require more general financial help than that merely required to bridge the gap while waiting to be paid – finance to produce capital goods, for example, that may take up to a year to deliver. Most large banks have departments which specialise in export finance and have 'packaged' schemes available. Sometimes some form of government aid or support may be available and the most important of these is insurance from a government export credit guarantee body (discussed later). If it is a large international project, then the term used may be 'project finance' with a syndicate of banks involved, and recourse is available only to the stream of funds from the project. The exporter, in some cases, may be interested in the question of aid to the *importer* to help purchase the goods. In a small number of cases, where factors are involved, the factor's overseas agent may get involved with providing finance to the importer also. On many occasions, however, a key component will be official sources of finance.

There are programmes from donors such as the World Bank, the EU and the African Development Bank. It is estimated that more than one third of sub-Saharan African imports are aid financed. Assistance is focused on countries implementing the economic reform programmes of the IMF and the World Bank. The paperwork and bureaucracy are formidable but payments are guaranteed and there is no currency risk.

In other cases, banks provide 'buyer credits' in conjunction with export credit guarantee insurance.

FOREIGN EXCHANGE (This subject was dealt with in Chapter 7)

TRADING GUARANTEES

The question of guarantees has been mentioned and the concerns of both exporters (political and currency risk) and importers (faulty goods or general non-performance of contracts). There is a series of schemes for trading guarantees other than export credit guarantees. These refer to guarantees backed by banks:

Bid or tender bond   This is required to support an exporter's offer to supply goods or a contractor's offer to carry out a service.

The bond safeguards a buyer against loss if the tender is awarded but the seller fails to proceed by signing the contract or submitting a performance bond.

A bid bond is guaranteed by the seller's bank and is usually 2%–5% of the value of the contract.

Performance bond   When the seller's bid accepted, the bid bond is replaced by a performance bond, usually 10% of value of the contract.

It is issued by the seller's bank, guaranteeing that he will supply goods (to the standard required by the buyer) or perform a service. If the buyer does not accept that goods are up to standard then they can claim under the performance bond.

Advance payment guarantee   The buyer pays the seller an agreed percentage of the contract price as an advance payment, which can be claimed back if goods/ services provided are not satisfactory.

Retention monies guarantees / progress payment bonds   Part of the contract price (usually 5%) which the buyer can hold back for a certain period to give time to assure himself that the goods or services supplied are satisfactory, or stage payments may be made on a similar basis.

These may be conditional or unconditional – for example, conditional on the seller admitting the fault or having won an arbitration proceeding or legal case. The bank must have a counter indemnity with their client, authorising debit of the said sum if money is paid under the guarantee. 'Unconditional' means that the bank will pay up simply on the signed statement by the buyer that the seller has failed in their obligation.

The bank guarantee may have to be paid *even if the bank's client goes into liquidation.*

An example of an unconditional performance bond (supplied by UBS) is shown as Figure 8.4.

Export credit guarantees   Government departments often provide exporters with facilities for insuring their shipments of goods against default by foreign importers and most other risks, except for normal marine insurance. Premiums are charged but the service is generally provided on a non-profit making basis. Such government departments do not themselves extend export finance but in providing insurance against risk encourage the banks to do so.

There are, however, also private insurers that will quote premiums for trade risk; for example, in the UK, Trade Indemnity. The UK's Export Credit Guarantee Department was founded in 1919. There is a distinction drawn between short-term projects, up to 2 years, and longer-term risks. The short-term end was located in Cardiff and called the Insurance Services Group (ISG). However, the government sold this in December 1991 to the Dutch insurer NCM. The new name is 'NCM Credit Insurance'. NCM also took control of the short-term export insurance in Sweden following the collapse of Svenska Credit.

PERFORMANCE BOND

Dear Sirs,

We have been informed that you have concluded on ....with Messrs
.... contract No ....for the delivery of
.... For the due performance of the terms of
the contract it was agreed to furnish a security in form of an indemnity.

At the request of Messrs .... waiving all rights of objection and defence arising from the principal debit, we, the Union Bank of Switzerland, London, herewith irrevocably undertake to pay you on first demand any amount up to

GBP .... (in words ....)

against and upon receipt of your written statement confirming that Messrs ....
have not complied with the terms and conditions of the contract.

For the purpose of identification, any claim hereunder has to be presented through the intermediary of a first rate bank confirming that the signatures on such claim are binding for your firm.

Our indemnity is valid until

....(Ninety-...................................)

and expires in full and automatically should your written statement confirming such claims not be in our possession by that date.

This indemnity is governed by English law and we hereby submit to the jurisdiction of the English Courts.

Yours faithfully

A.N. Other Bank

Figure 8.4 *Specimen unconditional performance bond*
Source: UBS, *Guide to Documentary Transactions in Foreign Trade.*

The insurance protection is against non-payment, insolvency, withdrawal of import licences, problems due to foreign government decree and war and earthquake. Cover is typically up to 90%.

Given export credit guarantees, the banks are obviously happier to provide export finance and may arrange and administer the policy as part of the deal.

Other export credit guarantee organisations are:

- ❏ Hermes   Germany   (private sector)
- ❏ NCM   Holland   (private sector)
- ❏ COFACE   France   (state majority holding)
- ❏ SACE   Italy   (state majority holding).

An example of international cooperation here is seen in the case of the financing of the new international airport in the Portuguese colony of Macao. Export Credits will be supported by ECGD (UK), Hermes (Germany), Eximbank (US), EFIC (Australia) and COSEC (Portugal).

MISCELLANEOUS SERVICES

Export Houses   These are market experts who know about shipping, insurance, quotas, licences, exchange terms and local conditions. They may:

- ❏ Handle all the paperwork and even promote sales abroad but the exporter is still the principal although the export house carries the risk
- ❏ Act for an overseas buyer – find a supplier, arrange shipment and insurance and confirm the contract on the buyer's behalf
- ❏ Act as an agent and buy goods and resell them but only against firm orders.

Confirming Houses   Similar to export houses but will place an order for a buyer as a *principal* and will pay the exporter when the goods are despatched. May arrange credit for the buyer.

International Credit Unions   Finance houses and some banks have entered into reciprocal arrangements to arrange local finance to help an importer to import goods from a fellow member. An exporter, for example, may be asked by the importer of capital goods for instalment terms of payment. The bank may be able to arrange this through the partner in the Credit Union in the foreign company. The local bank/finance house will investigate and arrange finance – typically for machinery and capital goods generally. Examples are European Credit Union, Amstel Club, Export Finance International.

Barter/Countertrade   These arrangements are common where currencies are not convertible or subject to any restrictions preventing normal issue of export licences. Barter is a simple exchange of goods; countertrade is a wider term including things like counterpurchase and buy-back. Under these arrangements, exporters may agree to buy back goods from the importing companies, for example, the exporter of textile machinery must agree to buy back textiles. Alternatively, the exporter agrees to buy back goods in a more general way to a given percentage value of the exports.

For many years, Russia dealt with Finland on the basis that Russian oil purchased by Finland accumulated credits that could only be used to buy Russian goods. Other examples: car imports into Tunisia (Peugeot, VW) were only permitted on the basis that spare parts were purchased from Tunisian companies to a value of 50% of the cost of the car; Balfour Beatty in the UK won a contract for £2m in Malaysia on the basis that Balfour Beatty had to find buyers for tin, palm oil and rubber goods.

General   Banks also provide a host of other services in connection with export/import business – market intelligence, credit status enquiries, letters of introduction, correspondent banking, translation, legal and accountancy facilities.

SUMMARY

Banks facilitate international trade with cross-border payment systems. The *SWIFT* system is the most important.

Simply sending an invoice to the importer and awaiting payment is *open account trading*.

Credit may be extended by the use of a *bill of exchange* which may be a *sight*, *tenor*, *documentary* or *clean* bill.

A promise by the importer's bank either to pay for the goods or to sign a bill of exchange on despatch is a *documentary letter of credit*, which may be *revocable* or *irrevocable*. The importer's bank is the *issuing* bank in this connection and the exporter's bank is the *advising* bank.

The exporter is the *beneficiary*. If the exporter's bank agrees to pay for the goods, even if the importer or the importer's bank doesn't, it is a *confirmed* letter of credit.

With *documentary collection*, the exporter's bank attempts to obtain payment by offering the shipping documents to the importer's bank.

Finance for export might be based on *forfaiting* or *factoring*. There may also be official help from development banks. Export credit guarantees, offered by governments or the private sector, insure against non-payment. The banks offer other guarantees such as *bid* or *tender bonds*, *performance bonds*, *advance payment guarantees* and *progress payment bonds*.

Miscellaneous services offered by banks include acting as *export* and *confirming houses* and assisting with *barter* and *countertrade*.

9 Stock Exchanges

HISTORY OF ASSOCIATIONS FOR TRADING

The early associations for trading were either sole owners or partnerships. The first modern shareholding enterprise is generally recognised as the proposal by Sebastian Cabot, the British explorer, to set up an enterprise to find a North East trade route to China and the Orient.

In 1553, 250 merchants put up £25 each to equip three ships for the voyage. They thus shared the cost and any eventual profit. two ships foundered but one reached the port of Archangel and the crew were taken to the court of the so-called Ivan the Terrible. Trade was started between England and Russia and the company's short name was the 'Muscovy Company'. As the shares were held jointly, they were 'joint stock companies'. The famous East India company was formed in 1600 and was dominant in trading up to about 1850. Of these early trading companies, several are still in existence, the most famous being the Hudson's Bay Company (1668). With the importance of the Dutch Empire, we also see the formation of the United East India Company of the Netherlands in 1602 and the Dutch West India Company in 1621.

Trading began in the shares of these companies. Amsterdam opened a stock exchange in 1611, Europe's oldest. The Austrian Bourse opened in Vienna in 1771, largely to trade government bonds to finance war. By the end of the 19th century it had 2500 equities listed and was one of Europe's most important financial centres. In London, brokers and jobbers (as they were called) met in coffee houses. To regulate the market, New Jonathan's Coffee House was converted into the 'Stock Exchange' in 1773. Curiously, there seems to be some doubt about the formal start of securities trading in New York. A newspaper, called 'The Diary', indicated in an issue of March 1792 that dealers in stock met each noon at 22 Wall Street (so called because of the building of a wall to keep livestock in and Indians out by early Dutch traders who founded New York). Most trading was in government bonds and bank shares. Inspired by the success of an organisation set up by brokers in Philadelphia, a 'New York Stock Exchange and Board' was set up in 1817 (quoted in F.L. Eames and Thomas G. Hall, *The New York Stock Exchange*, 5th edition, John Wiley, 1987).

In France, we can trace an early shareholding company, the 'Société Des Moulins Du Bazacle' in Toulouse with 96 lots or shares which could be bought and sold. Quite logically, this became the local electricity company in the 19th century and was quoted on the Toulouse Stock Exchange until 1946. This was, of course, an earlier example than the Muscovy Company but more of an isolated instance. A form of stock exchange, a 'Bourse', appears in Lyons in 1540 with dealers called, in a decree of 1639, 'agents de change'. A bourse was established in Paris in 1724 but does not seem to have been particularly active. With the revolution, agents de change were abolished in 1791 and the exchange closed in 1793. Under Napoleon, the bourse was officially opened again in 1801 with the agents de change given a monopoly of trading but not allowed the privilege of limited liability.

only in the UK (shares or bonds)

STOCKS AND SHARES

We refer to 'stocks and shares' as though there is a clear difference. Strictly speaking, shares are equities in companies, paying (typically) a variable dividend. Stocks are instruments where the payment is by way of interest, such as bonds and similar instruments. Unfortunately, while 'shares' is only used to refer to shares in companies, 'stocks' is a much vaguer term in everyday parlance. In the US, shares are 'common stock' and the shareholders are the stockholders. In the UK, the term 'stocks' is frequently used to mean either shares or bonds, and we shall follow this practice.

Generally, however, exchanges always split turnover between the fixed interest element and equities. Whilst most transactions in number are usually equities, the bond values are high because of the importance here of the professional investors with high value deals. In the UK, for instance, the average domestic equity deal is about £60 000 and the average government bond deal about £3m. In general, bonds are about 55% of turnover in London, 75% in the German exchanges and 80% in Paris. In New York however, almost all turnover is in equities as few bonds are traded on the exchange.

Figures for the world's largest exchanges are shown in Table 9.1 (the figures have been compiled by the London Stock Exchange and are in sterling). The initials NASDAQ stand for 'National Association of Securities Dealers' Automated Quotations'. They have never had an exchange as such and deal on computer screens. The shares are, therefore, technically OTC but the companies are much larger than one usually finds with OTC trading and include many technology stocks such as Microsoft, Intel and Apple.

Table 9.1 has a note that the turnover has been halved in certain cases. Some exchanges report a deal twice, that is, when bought and when sold. Others record it only once.

Looking at Table 9.1, one can see that there is no simple answer to the question: which are the world's biggest stock exchanges? What does 'biggest' mean? It could be market value, total turnover or just equity turnover.

The market value is the number of shares in existence multiplied by the share price. It's also called 'capitalisation' (but beware – it's nothing to do with capital on the balance sheet). Share prices go up and down and the capitalisation is only that at the moment the calculation is done. That's part of the problem. In this case, the valuation is that at the end of 1995. Had one taken Tokyo at the end of 1989, before their market crashed, Tokyo would have appeared as the world's biggest exchange. The other problem is whether we take an exchange or a country. The German

Federation of Stock Exchanges adds the figures for all the eight German exchanges. Frankfurt is perhaps 65%/70% of the value. If we add all Germany's exchanges, should we not also add all those in the US, Japan and Switzerland?

Table 9.1   *International stock market comparisons, turnover, year ended 31.12.95; market value at year end*

Exchange	Fixed Interest £bn	Equity £bn	Total £bn	Market Value £bn
New York	4	1985	1989	5643
NASDAQ	n/a	1501	1501	793
London*	830	718	1548	3900
Germany*	1406	384	1790	1783
Paris	722	135	857	865
Switzerland	107	202	309	256
Tokyo	142	522	664	2283
Osaka	24	152	176	3031
Taiwan	n/a	240	240	141

Notes: * Turnover has been halved for comparison purposes.
n/a = not available

Source: London Stock Exchange, *Quality of Markets Service*.

Of the London equity turnover figure of £718 billion, the claimed foreign equity content is £395 billion, the highest in the world.

Taking capitalisation at the end of 1995 our sequence is:

❏   New York
❏   London
❏   Osaka
❏   Tokyo
❏   Germany
❏   Paris.

Taking turnover, the next question is whether we take equities only or total turnover including bonds. If we do the latter, it may not seem fair for exchanges where bonds are traded outside the exchange.

On *total* turnover, the top six are:

- ❑ New York
- ❑ Germany
- ❑ London
- ❑ NASDAQ
- ❑ Paris
- ❑ Tokyo.

If we take *equity turnover* only, however, our top six become:

- ❑ New York
- ❑ NASDAQ
- ❑ London
- ❑ Tokyo
- ❑ Germany
- ❑ Taiwan.

We have included NASDAQ, although this is not an exchange and OTC dealings have not been included in other exchanges' figures.

From the above you will see that the question, 'which are the world's biggest stock exchanges?' elicits a somewhat complicated response! The very statistics are themselves controversial. Some exchanges insist that trades handled by local brokers are recorded locally for regulatory reasons even if the trade is actually passed to a foreign exchange. For this reason, London's claim for its foreign equity share has been attacked by many as an exaggeration. A French academic study published in February 1996, for example, says that London's claim to handle 52% of French equity turnover is wrong and that the true figure is only 8%.

INTERNATIONAL EQUITY

In the 1980s, it became common for multinational companies to seek a listing on several foreign stock exchanges. This may be to attract a wider investor market or because the local exchange is a little small for the ambitions of the company (for example, Stockholm and Electrolux). The result has been a large expansion in primary market issues and secondary market trading in non-domestic equities.

For example, although German accounting rules are not as tight as those in the United States, Daimler-Benz has listed in New York and accepted the implications for greater transparency. The French insurance group, Axa, became the first French financial services company to secure a US stock exchange listing in mid-1996.

Large new equities are now offered on an international basis and there have been many involving national telephone companies. The second biggest privatisation of all time will be Deutsche Telekom, which will be offered to markets all over the world at the end of 1996.

One key factor here is that US mutual funds and pension funds have gradually become less parochial and are investing more abroad. Greenwich Associates estimate that the overseas content of corporate US pension funds will grow from 5.9% in 1991 to 10.6% in 1997 and that of public pension funds from 2.9% in 1991 to 11.9% in 1997.

INDICES

Share indices are usually based on market capitalisation. If the index is of, say, the top 50 companies, then 'top' means biggest by market capitalisation. Sometimes, the index is described as 'weighted'. This simply means that a 1% change in the price of the largest company in the index will have more impact than a 1% change in the price of the smallest. Since the share price is always changing, it follows that the 'top' shares are not always the same. There is provision for removing some shares and adding others, say, every quarter. For example, in March 1996, Adidas was included in the DAX 30 and Asko excluded. From December 11 1995, Inchcape was dropped from the UK FT–SE 100 and Pilkington included.

In the modern age, the desire to use an index for purposes of options and futures transactions (see Chapters 10 and 11) has led to the creation of several new indices, which are recalculated every minute of the day.

Strictly speaking, we should distinguish between *averages* and *indices*, although the terms are used as if they were the same. In 1884, for example, Charles Dow (publisher of the *Wall Street Journal*) began publishing share *averages* beginning with an average of eleven railway stocks. The modern Dow Jones industrial average began in 1896 with twelve shares, and was increased to the present 30 in 1928.

As an average, the Dow simply averages the share prices and (but for stock splits, which we explain later) would divide the total of all 30 prices by 30. If, however, a stock split causes a price to fall from $100 to $50, this must be taken into account. The method used is called 'constant divisor'. The Dow used to be calculated hourly but is now done every minute.

In London, the *Financial Times* Ordinary Share Index began in 1935. Its average is even more complicated. The 30 share prices are multiplied together and a thirtieth root of the answer taken.

Modern *indices* are based on taking the number of shares and multiplying by the price. This gives proper weight to the companies worth the largest capitalisation. In 1957, for example, Standard and Poor's introduced the S&P 500. In 1983, the Chicago Board Options Exchange began trading options on its 100 share index, changing its name to the S&P 100 in July of that year. Both these indices are based on market capitalisation.

Also based on market capitalisation was the New York Stock Exchange index, introduced in 1966 and now consisting of some 1500 stocks. The American Stock Exchange introduced its American Stock Exchange Index in 1973. It is another capitalisation index and is based on about 800 stocks. One interesting and unusual feature is the inclusion of dividends as additions to the index. Thus, the index measures a *total* return (as does the German DAX – see later).

As a competitor to the Dow Jones index, the American Stock Exchange introduced its 'Major Market Index' (MMI) of 20 top stocks in 1980. Its composition and calculation make it similar to the Dow Jones and it has a 90% correlation.

Other important US indices are: the NASDAQ Composite Index (1984); the NASDAQ Industrial Index (1984); the NASDAQ 100 (1985); the Philadelphia Stock Exchange Value Line (1700 stocks – 1985).

In Japan, the main index is the Nikkei Dow 225, an index of 225 shares. It is, however, based on average prices, not capitalisation. As a result, a Nikkei 300 was introduced in 1984. There is another index based on capitalisation, the Tokyo Stock Exchange Price Index (TOPIX), an index of all shares listed in the first section of the TSE.

In London, the need for a more satisfactory measure than the 30 ordinary share index led to the *Financial Times*–Stock Exchange 100 index in January 1984. This is the FT–SE index and, thus, known locally as the 'Footsie'. It is also based on capitalisation, is calculated every minute of the day from 8.30 a.m. to 4.30 p.m. (with a pre-index level calculated from 8.00 a.m.). The index began at the level of 1000. It represents 72% of the capitalisation of the whole market.

In October 1992, it was decided to broaden the indices and two new ones were added. The FT–SE 250 is the 250 shares after the FT–SE 100 and the FT–SE Actuaries 350 is the addition of the FT–SE 100 and 250. It is calculated every minute and includes figures for market sectors. An older, larger index, is the *Financial Times* Actuaries Indices, started in 1962 and widened to include some 800 stocks in December 1992. It covers 98% of the market's capitalisation.

In France, the CAC 40 was started in 1987. It is based on capitalisation and is calculated every 30 seconds. It is 60% of the capitalisation of the whole bourse but the top seven stocks account for 43% of the CAC 40. One interesting point is that the CAC 40 is chosen to represent *all* major market sectors. The FT–SE 100 is the top 100 regardless of sector. The older index in Paris is the SBF 240 which is based on opening prices and only calculated once per day. In September 1993 this was replaced by the SBF 250 index which is calculated every minute and integrates dividends as well. At the same time, a new index – the SBF 120 – was introduced. This is based on the 40 shares in the CAC 40 and 80 others. It is calculated every minute. In May 1995, an additional index of middle capitalisation stocks – the MIDCAC – was launched.

The older German indices are the FAZ 100 (from the business newspaper *Frankfurter Allgemeine Zeitung*) and the Commerzbank index of 60 shares on the Dusseldorf exchange. Both these were started in the 1950s and are calculated once per day. The popular new index, however, is the DAX (Deutscher Aktienindex) index of 30 shares introduced in December 1987. This is not only a modern index, calculated continuously, but includes dividends and thus calculates a total return. This makes it especially attractive for some 'swap' transactions of a kind we shall discuss in Chapter 12. It represents 80% of stock market capitalisation and covers all the country's exchanges.

Other prominent indices are:

Amsterdam	CBS Tendency
	EOE 25
Brussels	General Return Index
	BEL 20
Copenhagen	SE All Share
	KFX 25
Hong Kong	Hang Seng
Madrid	Madrid SE
	IBEX 35
Milan	Comit All Share
	BCI
	MIB 30
Singapore	Straits Times
Stockholm	Affärsvärlden General
	OMX
Vienna	WBK-Index
	ATX
Zurich	Swiss Market Index
	Swiss Performance Index

With the growth of international equities in investor portfolios, we also have the use of international indices. There are *world* indices, such as the Morgan Stanley World Index, that run by Salomon Bros and Russell and the *Financial Times* Actuaries World Indices.

For *Europe*, there is the Eurotop 100 from the European Options Exchange in Amsterdam, the FT–SE Eurotrack 100 (not including UK shares) and the FT–SE Eurotrack 200 (including the UK) – both from the London Stock Exchange.

WHO OWNS SHARES?

Small Investors vs Institutions

The pattern of ownership varies in different world markets. In the US, there is still a strong tradition of equity ownership by private investors who own 50%. In Germany, however, the equivalent figure is only 6%. In between comes France, with 31% and the UK, with 19%.

Germany has lagged behind other markets in the past. It is the largest economy in Europe but only the third by stock exchange capitalisation. The German Share Institute, DAI, published figures for the value of new equity issues in Germany in the period 1991–3. The figure was $3.2bn compared with $115bn in the US and $23bn in the UK in the same period. However, perhaps things are beginning to change, with issues in 1995 totalling $5.4bn, spread over 20 new issues including Adidas sports goods and Merck pharmaceuticals.

Private share ownership is usually contrasted with that of the 'institutions', by which we mean pension funds, insurance funds and mutual funds. In some markets, private pension funds look after the pensions of individuals whether collected by their firms or contributed individually. Life assurance companies collect premiums for years in order to provide a pay out at death. General insurance companies also invest premiums paid in advance but face greater uncertainty with regard to payouts. Storms, hurricane or oil disasters like the Exxon Valdez, lead to unexpectedly large payouts. Mutual funds are explained below.

Pension Funds: Funding vs Unfunding

How active the equity market is will usually depend on the activity of the institutions and, especially, pension funds. The precise effect may depend on the asset allocation policy of the pension fund as between equities and bonds.

This brings us to the fundamental question: how are pensions funded? The first point is whether pensions are largely provided by private funds or the state. The second is whether there *is* a fund or whether the pensions are paid out of current taxation and contributions.

Where money contributed by private individuals is invested in funds to provide pensions, the biggest markets are the US, UK, Netherlands, Japan and Switzerland.

Figures for the size of assets at end 1993 are in Table 9.2 and provided by PDFM Ltd. In some of these cases, the funds are handled by the state.

In Germany, the employees' pension contributions are handled by the company and held in a *book reserve* in the accounts of the company. The amounts are available for the general purposes of the company and the payments are made from corporate funds. It's interesting that events which caused horror in the UK – Robert Maxwell having access to the pension funds – is the routine in Germany. There are some invested funds but the total is relatively modest, as can be seen from Table 9.2.

Table 9.2 *Pension funds, size of assets, end 1993*

Country	Size £bn
US	2908
Japan	1753
UK	726
Germany	254
Netherlands	216
France	200
Switzerland	195
Canada	162
Australia	122
Sweden	62
Singapore	33
Norway	31
Denmark	14
Ireland	14
Spain	13
New Zealand	8
Hong Kong	7
Belgium	6
Total	6724

Source: PDFM Ltd (May 1996).

In Sweden, pension provision is largely by the State, but the money is invested and the system can be regarded as funded. In France, on the other hand, whilst the state also handles most pension payments through the Caisse de Retraite, they are not funded but paid for out of current taxation. Private pension provision is largely confined to schemes for senior executives.

This 'unfunding' is likely to change due to demographic factors. Right across Europe (and Japan), populations are ageing. With six or seven employees funding each pensioner the older systems may have been satisfactory. The future is likely to see two or three workers for every pensioner. Figure 9.1 shows the incidence of ageing populations.

The World Bank estimates that, by the year 2030, the number of people over 60 will triple to 1.4 billion. A British think tank, Federal Trust, published a report in early 1996, *The Pensions Time Bomb in Europe*. They calculated a dependency ratio, that is the ratio of people aged 65 and over to the 15 to 64 age group. Over the twelve countries of the EU (prior to 1995), this ratio is expected to increase from 21% in 1990 to 43% in 2040 and 48% in Italy and the Netherlands (see Table 9.3). The Netherlands, at least, have funded pensions; Italy does not. In Germany, by 2030, pension contributions could be 30% of gross income with one worker for every pensioner.

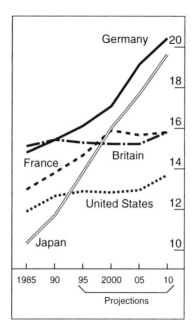

Figure 9.1 *Ageing populations, % of population aged 65 and over*
Source: *UN.*

Countries are slow to make progress on this issue. How can we persuade people to pay tax now to fund today's pensioners and put aside extra money for their own retirement at the same time? The French have increased the number of years private sector personnel must work for a full pension from 37.5 to 40. An attempt to do the same for the public sector met with strikes and was withdrawn! The Germans passed a law in 1992 making it less worthwhile to retire before 65. All this, however, is really only tinkering with the problem, although the announcement by Deutsche Bank, in April 1996, that it would set up its own funded pension scheme was seen as significant.

In Japan, pension funds are big but past protectionist rules have curtailed competition and performance has been poor. However, deregulation from April 1996 will open the markets to foreign investment advisers on a wide scale.

The coming of the single market should have resulted in abolition of many restrictions on pension fund investment. For example, Italian funds cannot hold more than 20% in private company equities; Portuguese and Danish funds cannot invest in other countries' securities; German funds cannot hold more than 5% in foreign bonds and, in Belgium, 15% of the fund must be held in domestic government bonds.

Work was done on a pensions directive which sought to abolish these restrictions or at least modify them. After fierce argument, however, it was withdrawn in 1995. The Commission says that it will pursue liberalisation by other means, for example, the Capital Liberation Directive. There is little real hope of this. It is demographic pressures which will force change in the end.

Table 9.3   *Age dependence ratio, persons over 65 as a % of persons aged 15–64*

Country	1990	2040
Belgium	21.9	41.5
Denmark	22.2	43.4
Germany	23.7	47.1
Greece	20.5	41.7
Spain	17.0	41.7
France	21.9	39.2
Ireland	18.4	27.2
Italy	20.4	48.4
Luxembourg	20.4	41.2
Netherlands	17.4	48.5
Portugal	16.4	38.9
UK	23.5	39.1
All EC	21.4	42.8

Source: Federal Trust Report, *The Pensions Time Bomb in Europe.*

Equity Investment

The effect of pension fund activity depends, of course, on their attitude to asset allocation. The key choice is between equities and bonds with a further sub-division between domestic and international. Property is a popular investment in some markets and, clearly, there will also be liquid funds on deposit and invested in money market instruments, like certificates of deposit.

Table 9.4 shows the asset allocation in the five major countries where pensions are funded.

With pension funds usually the major operators in stock exchanges, their importance for the equity and bond markets can readily be seen. For equities alone, however, the US and UK lead the way with 57% and 77% in equities respectively. Elsewhere, bonds are the predominant investment and also 32% in the US. The UK's 77% equity asset allocation stands out as the exception. It reflects the poor UK record so far as inflation is concerned. The general belief is that equities give better inflation protection than bonds – that is, firms will put their prices up and make more money in nominal if not in real terms. (Having said that, the high UK figure of 77% is a modern phenomenon. The equities content in the 1960s and 1970s was typically about 50%.) As a contrast to the UK, such funded pensions as Germany has invested 75% in domestic bonds.

Table 9.4 *International asset allocation, end 1994*

	US %	UK %	Netherlands %	Japan %	Switzerland %
Domestic Equities	47	54	9	22	8
International Equities	10	23	20	4	5
Property	5	5	13	3	19
Cash	6	4	2	8	9
Domestic Bonds	30	10	49	57	54
International Bonds	2	4	7	6	5
	100	100	100	100	100

Source: PDFM Ltd (May 1996).

Looking at portfolio management generally and not just that of pension funds, Table 9.5 shows the top centres for equity portfolio management.

Table 9.5   *Top centres of portfolio management, December 1995, ranked by institutional equity holdings*

City	Equities ($bn)
Tokyo	1524
London	1016
New York	896
Boston	604
Zurich	411
San Francisco	289
Geneva	264
Paris	261
Los Angeles	243
Chicago	179

Source: Technimetrics Inc.

Mutual Funds

If a small investor has, say, $3000 to spend on equities, there are two choices. The money can be spent on just one or two companies' shares or spread widely over ten companies' shares. In the first case, the risk is great if one company performs badly. In the second case, with $300 spent on each share, the dealing costs are discouragingly high. The answer may be to put the money into *mutual funds*. These are collective investments, run by fund managers. They may be investments in money market instruments, equities or bonds. Indeed, nowadays, there are funds whose investments are in financial futures (see Chapter 11).

In the case of equities, the fund will invest in a wide range of equities; the $3000 is thus spread over a range of shares but without excessive risk. The fund is run by skilled managers and fees must be paid. There are two kinds of fund.

The open-ended fund (Unit Trusts in the UK)   Here the fund raises, say, $50m and spends it on a wide range of shares. Simplifying, the fund is divided into 50m units at $1 each. Later investors can buy units from the managers or sell them back to the managers. If investors with $5m to spend *buy* units, the managers buy more shares and the fund is now $55m. If investors with holdings worth $10m now *sell* the units back to the managers, shares will have to be sold to raise the money and the fund is now only $45m. Hence, we have the term 'open-ended fund'. As the shares grow in value, so do the units and this is how investors make their money. In practice, there are fees to pay and also the basic costs. Units thus have a bid/offer price like an ordinary share.

The closed-ended fund (Investment Trusts in the UK)   Here the fund is a shareholding company, much like any other. It raises $50m and, instead of being in engineering or groceries, invests the money in a portfolio of equities. If, later, investors with $5m to spend want to join in, they buy the shares of the fund on the open market *from someone else who sells them*: that is, the fund doesn't get the money but remains at $50m – hence, 'closed-ended fund'. The idea is that if, in 3 years, the shares double in value, so should the market share of the fund itself. The investors can now sell and take their profit this way. The extent to which the share price may not double but remain at a discount to the asset value per share attracts a lot of attention from analysts and needs to be studied by potential investors. This is because the share price of the closed-ended fund will reflect supply and demand as well as the underlying asset value.

These mutual funds are well established in the US, UK, Netherlands, France, Germany and Italy. In Spain, the banks are now beginning to sell the open-ended fund concept. In France, they are very popular, partly due to tax concessions. The open-ended fund is the SICAV (Société d'Investissement à Capital Variable) and the closed-ended fund, the FCP (Fonds Communs de Placement). As well as equity funds, SICAVs and FCPs for money market instruments are very popular.

As one might expect, the concentration in the UK is on equity investments and in Germany, bonds. Of the UK's £100bn invested in unit trusts, less than £2bn is invested in bonds. Mutual funds were allowed in Italy in 1983 but the equity funds lost popularity after the October 1987 crash. Today, some 55% of the money is invested in Treasury bills.

The US is a huge market for mutual fund investment. By end 1995, $2.6 trillion was invested in some 5600 mutual funds and one third of US households were fund holders. The country's biggest fund group is Fidelity with $288bn of assets under management. This alone is more than the total UK market! Investment is about 40% equities and 60% bonds and fixed interest.

UCITs is a term which has arrived due to an EC directive in October 1989. These are 'Undertakings for Collective Investment in Transferable Securities'. The directive sets minimum standards for open-ended funds (not closed-ended). For example, no more than 10% of the investment can be in one security. Investment in commodities, property and money market instruments is excluded. The UCITs managers can take a fund which has domestic authorisation and offer it anywhere within the Community. It must be recognised by regulators in the country where the fund is to be marketed. However, while the marketing regulations are those which are in use locally, investor compensation is from the home country of the fund.

Luxembourg has become a popular centre for UCITs to be sold across Europe. This is because the dividends can be paid gross. A UK UCIT, for example, will deduct tax on dividends at source. While foreigners can reclaim tax, French and German investors, for example, will be reluctant to fill in the forms of the UK Inland Revenue!

Active vs Passive Management

It is beyond the scope of an introductory book of this nature to explain the various theories which exist on asset allocation and pricing of securities. One issue, however, should be mentioned and that is the question of active vs passive management of the funds. Active management can be summarised as 'picking winners', that is, active selection of specific securities with frequent reorganisation of the portfolio. This is often driven by sophisticated computer models and called 'programme trading'. (The same term, however, is used to cover stock index arbitrage and dynamic portfolio insurance strategies.) Passive management, on the other hand, makes an investment in all the stocks in a well known index, such as the S&P 100, and leaves the fund to perform as the S&P 100. The argument for this is that statistics show that less than 50% of funds beat the index anyway and also that 'indexing' (as it is called) incurs fewer dealing costs. The subject is, naturally, controversial. It appears that in the US, some 50% of pension funds are indexed and in the UK, perhaps 15%–20%.

East Europe

The emerging markets of Central and Eastern Europe and the former USSR faced considerable problems in privatising large sectors of their industry. In Poland and Czech Republic, the use of the closed-ended fund has been seen as a partial solution. Citizens have been allowed to purchase vouchers giving them a holding in a closed-ended fund which holds shares in a range of firms which were formerly state owned. The funds are often run by Western fund managers. Foreign subscriptions have been allowed in the case of the Czech Republic and there has also been participation from the European Bank for Reconstruction and Development. The first such Czech fund has Robert Fleming as the manager of the fund.

DEALING SYSTEMS

Systems in Stock Exchanges for buying and selling stock usually follow one of three patterns:

❑   Order driven systems
❑   Quote driven systems
❑   A mixture of the two.

Order Driven Systems

Most systems on the continent of Europe are order driven. That is to say, an intermediary (usually a broker) matches buy and sell orders at a given price. The broker takes no risk in that shares will not be bought or sold unless there is a counterparty with the equivalent deal on the other side. The broker makes a living by charging commission. The systems in France, Germany, Belgium, Italy. Spain and Switzerland are of this type.

The older type of system saw activity on a physical floor with the broker for a given share surrounded by others calling out buy and sell orders. The broker then matched the orders and declared an official price, which might last until the next session. Today, computer systems are usually used, at least for the major shares. A popular system in Europe is the one taken from the Toronto Exchange, called CATS (Computer Assisted Trading System). Sometimes it is given a different name locally, such as CAC in Paris (Cotation Assistée en Continu).

As CATS is used in Belgium, France, Spain and Italy it may be worth examining how it works.

(The French have rewritten the system as Nouveau Système de Cotation (NSC) or Supercac and sold it back to Toronto but the principles are the same.)

Let's take Paris as our example. Orders may be keyed into the system directly, fed to member firms, or fed to the CAC system from member firms.

Orders are entered with a price limit, for example, a buyer is prepared to buy 500 shares up to a limit of FFr154 or a seller will sell 400 shares but at a price no lower than FFr151. Some enter an order to be filled at the 'market price'. From 9.00 a.m. to 10.00 a.m., these orders are fed into the system. At 10.00 a.m. the market opens. The computer then calculates the opening price at which the largest number of bids and offers can be matched (see Table 9.6).

Table 9.6   *Opening prices*

Stock XYZ			
Buyers		*Sellers*	
Quantity	*Price limits*	*Price limits*	*Quantity*
500	Market price	Market price	400
200	156	150	250
250	155	151	400
500	154	152	500
750	153	153	600
1000	152	154	1250
3000	151	155	1700

Source: SBF – Paris Bourse.

In this example, the market reaches equilibrium at FFr153 with 1700 shares at the offer rate (that is, 200 + 250 + 500 + 750 – all these are prepared to pay at least FFr153) and 1750 shares at the bid rate (that is, 250 + 400 + 500 + 600 – all these are prepared to accept FFr153).

All the orders at the market price are now filled in so far as it is possible. Unfilled orders at the market price are carried forward with FFr153 as the limit price.

From 10.00 a.m. to 5.00 p.m., trading takes place on a continuous basis and the arrival of a new order will trigger a match if matching orders exist on the centralised book. An in depth display of data on a given security is given at the same time (Table 9.7).

Very large orders present a problem. They may wait quite a long time until they can be matched and their very presence will tend either to raise or lower the price. Block trades between institutions can be matched by brokers if there is a matching price but stamp duty (amongst other things) prevent a *market maker* (*teneur du marché*) either buying a large block (not knowing to whom they will sell them) or selling a large block they will now have to buy. The liquidity in trading for large orders attracts business to London from Paris, Frankfurt, Milan, Brussels and Madrid. We shall discuss the *market maker* system shortly.

The use of computer systems potentially poses a threat to brokers. As a result, we have seen strikes by floor traders (Procuratori) in Milan and resistance to new systems from independent brokers in Germany (Freimakler).

In Germany, on the official market there are official price fixers – (Amtliche Kursmakler), on the second market there are independent brokers (Freimakler). The whole system is dominated by the banks handling their own and client orders. As a result of conflicts of interest, there have been three rival computer systems – the banks with IBIS, the Kursmakler with MATIS and the Freimakler with MIDAS. However, IBIS eventually became the sole system for top shares and was itself replaced by Xetra in December 1997.

In Japan, there are eight stock exchanges: Tokyo, Osaka and six others. The Tokyo exchange trades the shares of about 1600 companies. Investors place their orders with stock exchange members. Specialists – *saitori* – match orders through an open outcry system. The details are circulated on computer screens.

Quote Driven Systems

In quote driven systems there is someone called a *market maker*. They quote continuously bid and offer prices at which they will buy or sell shares. The difference is the *spread*, that is their profit margin.

As a result, they will buy shares at the bid price, not knowing to whom these shares (or bonds) will be sold. They also agree from time to time to sell *short*, that is, to sell stock that they don't actually own but will now have to go out and buy. This clearly involves risk and needs capital (not to mention strong nerves!).

Table 9.7 *Data on a given security*

A			B			C					
XYZ			106 500			+ 0.80					
7	3 800	114.0	114.10	500	1	37	03	500	114.10	11:19	
1	500	113.9	114.30	3 000	2	35	07	900	114.10	11:17	
2	5 500	113.8	114.40	11 000	4	43	21	1 200	114.20	11:16	
2	6 000	113.7	114.50	5 500	3	15	15	3 500	114.00	11:15	
2	5 500	113.6	114.60	7 000	3	41	37	500	114.30	11:07	
D	E	F	G	H	I	J	K	L	M	N	
Buy orders			Sell orders			Last trades					

A	Security symbol
B	Number of shares traded since opening
C	Change between price at last trade and previous day's close
D	Number of buy orders placed
E	Total volume asked
F	Price limit of buy orders
G	Price limit of sell orders
H	Total volume bid
I	Number of sell orders placed
J	Buyer's code
K	Seller's code
L	Number of shares traded
M	Price of the trade
N	Time of the trade

Source: SBF – Paris Bourse.

The systems, therefore, tend to be driven by the quotations. The prices, especially first thing in the morning, do not necessarily reflect the prices at which deals have taken place, as the market makers can change the quotations whenever they wish. Usually these prices are firm for a given quantity of shares and may be shown thus:

Share XYZ	Bid	Offer	Bid quantity	Offer quantity
	100	102	50	50

Seen on a computer screen in the UK, this would indicate that the market maker will buy shares at say £1.00 or sell them at £1.02 for any quantity up to 50 000 shares. For higher quantities, brokers will then negotiate on behalf of clients.

The main quotation driven systems are NASDAQ (in the US) and London's SEAQ (Stock Exchange Automated Quotations), which was heavily modelled on NASDAQ. Please note, however, that London is considering a move to a hybrid system in late 1997. Where there are such systems, there are now two types of trader – the *broker* and the *market maker*.

The broker approaches market makers on behalf of clients and buys shares from them for the clients or sells the clients' shares to them. They make a living by charging a commission and do not take risk. In London, a broker may match buy/sell orders from a client providing the price is better than that available from a market maker. This is a slight complication and leads to the term *broker dealer*. Generally, however, the role of the broker is that of an agent, especially for smaller clients.

Large clients, like the investment institutions, don't have to use a broker but may approach a market maker directly. If they do use a broker, it will be on a *quid pro quo* basis – that is, the broker in return for the business will make available equity research reports free of charge. As a result, providing top quality equity research is essential to attract business.

The key European economic analysts are Goldman Sachs, UBS, Deutsche Bank, J.P. Morgan, Enskilda Securities, SBC Warburg, Morgan Stanley, BZW, Nomura and Midland Montagu (HSBC).

The market is very competitive and there may be 15–20 market makers competing in a particular share with the prices freely available to all. This ability to take risk is useful for large deals as the market maker will buy and sell and keep liquidity going. Very large deals hit problems with order driven systems. On the other hand, market makers are reluctant to handle small company shares in which there is little trading. The spreads are very wide and this further discourages trading!

To combat this, the London Stock Exchange launched a 'bulletin board' for lesser traded shares in 1992. This was an electronic notice board onto which orders to buy and sell could be logged. As this was not particularly successful, they launched a new system in October 1992 called SEATS – Stock Exchange Alternative Trading System. This is a hybrid system, similar to those in New York which we discuss below. A single market maker is appointed for illiquid stocks and will be obliged to make continuous two way prices. At the same time investors will be able to post buy and sell orders at limit prices. When market makers trade they must fulfil orders that are posted first if they are at the same price or better than a proposed trade. In addition, any orders to be matched in brokers' offices must first be offered to the official market maker who may trade at a better price on their own account or by matching the posted orders.

The NASDAQ and SEAQ systems are very similar. Let's examine the SEAQ type of display for a major share, such as Allied Lyons (now Allied Domecq), in Figure 9.2.

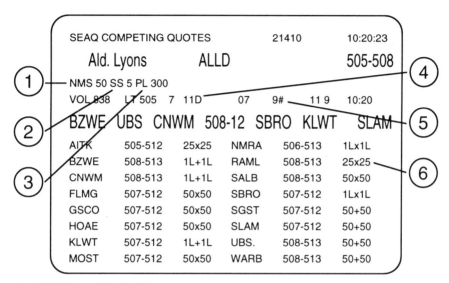

1. NMS: Normal Market Size.
2. SS: SAEF Size.
3. PL: Publication Level.
4. D: Delayed Trade. This marker indicates that trade publication has been delayed.
5. #: Agency Cross. This marker denotes an immediate publication of an agency cros- trade.
6. Reduced Size Market Maker (example only). A market maker concerned primarily with retail business who has permission to display prices in reduced sizes on SEAQ.

Figure 9.2 *SEAQ screen layout*
Source: London Stock Exchange.

First, we must explain some terms:

Normal market size (NMS)   This is the minimum quantity of shares for which a firm quotation is given. (Smaller market makers can register as 'reduced size market makers' and post half this figure.)

SAEF   This is SEAQ Automated Execution Facility. Orders can be entered at a computer terminal, matched with the best price, allocated to a market maker and taken through to settlement automatically. This is similar to New York's 'SuperDOT' system. However, there is a limit to the size of orders that can be handled this way – it is defined as 10% of NMS.

Publication level   The prices of the latest orders are shown on the line above the best prices. However, publication of the price of large orders is delayed 60 minutes to allow the market maker to unwind the position. 'Large' for this purpose is defined as six times NMS.

As a result, in Figure 9.2, the NMS is 50 000 shares, the SAEF size is 5000 shares and the publication level is 300 000 shares.

We can see that for Allied Lyons, there are 16 market makers competing for the business. The main display shows the market makers' initials, the bid/offer price and the bid/offer quantity. For example, on the bottom right we see that Warburg's are quoting a price of £5.08 bid and £5.13 offered for quantities of 50 000 shares bid and offered.

We don't even need to search for the best prices as the panel at the top shows us the best bid and offer – 508-12. These are called the 'touch prices'. The spread at the touch is usually measured and a record kept as an indication of the market's efficiency. Above these figures are shown the cumulative volume of shares traded so far and the latest prices. All prices must be entered within 3 minutes of the conclusion of the deal.

Note that the trading itself is not automated. If the broker wishes to deal, the arrangement is concluded on the telephone. Only the SAEF system is automated. It only applies to smaller deals and is not widely used anyway.

Hybrid Systems

Hybrid systems, with both order driven and quote driven characteristics, are found in New York and Amsterdam (and London's new SEATS system, to which we referred above).

In New York, each share is allocated to a *specialist*. The specialist acts as a broker, executing orders for other brokers on a commission basis. However, they may act for their own account (like a market maker) by buying from the public when there are no other buyers and selling to the public when there are no other sellers, all at or near the price of the last transaction. In other words, they match buyers and sellers when there are plenty of them but will keep the market going, by buying on their own account, when there is a shortage. There are about 60 specialists on the New York exchange and the system dates from before the First World War.

In a given stock, a specialist may have buyers at $45¼ and sellers at $45½ – these are the best prices, that is, highest bid and lowest offer. A broker approaches and is quoted '$45¼/$45½'. The broker's client wants to buy 100 shares. He tries '$45⅜' in case anyone in the crowd surrounding the specialist wishes to match this. If this fails, he raises the bid to $45½ and the specialist calls out 'sold' and gives the broker the name of the first order on his book at that price.

At the start of the day, the specialist is faced with many orders – some at the closing market price, some at limit prices. His duty is to set a price as near as possibly to the close (to maintain an orderly market) and yet also match as many orders as possible. Sometimes the system works well in a crisis, sometimes not. On Monday, 26 September 1955, following President Eisenhower's heart attack the previous day, there was frenzied trading. Specialists, holding stocks worth $50m, bought almost another $50m to help stabilise the market. However, on 'Black Monday', 19 October 1987, the specialists were overwhelmed and for hours there was no trading in two key stocks, IBM and General Motors. In London, the market makers kept going but there were frequent accusations of not answering the telephone!

There is an important automatic electronic order execution service in New York, DOT (Designated Order Turnaround), which was introduced in 1976 to transmit to the trading posts orders of up to a given maximum size and to send back confirmation of completed orders. In 1984, this was replaced by SuperDOT, able to handle bigger volumes. This itself was integrated with OARS (Opening Order Automated Report Service) which collected and stored the opening orders each day. The system pairs buy and sell orders and specialists can quickly see imbalances and determine the day's opening prices.

In Amsterdam, the market is split between retail and wholesale. Retail orders go via the 'hoekman' who may match orders or take a position like a market maker. Wholesale orders go through an order matching system called AIDA. Banks and brokers can also advertise their desire to buy and sell via a system called ASSET.

Inter Dealer Brokers

In some markets (for example, London), transactions between market dealers are facilitated by *inter dealer brokers*. Their function is like brokers in money markets or foreign exchange. They publish (on computer screens) large potential deals at bid and offer prices, but anonymously. Another dealer may see the quotation and decide to make a trade. The transaction is carried out by the broker and the two counterparties never learn of the other's identity. The dealer who identifies a trade and indicates a willingness to conclude it, pays the commission and is called (curiously) the 'aggressor'.

Stock Borrowing and Lending

A dealer may sell shares or bonds they don't have, going 'short'. An alternative to buying the stock prior to statement is to borrow it from institutions who will lend stock for a commission. Typically, the stock is paid for and the money returned when the dealer actually buys the stock and returns it. This facility greatly assists the liquidity of the market and was identified by the G30 report on settlement as an area to be developed (see Chapter 14).

On the other hand, dealers have to fund their 'long' positions. One way to fund them is to lend stock not needed and take the money to help fund other positions.

Thus stock lending may be done by institutions merely to enhance income, or may be done by dealers as a means of financing their position.

To complicate matters, although everyone calls it stock *lending*, in fact, the Stock is *sold*, albeit on a temporary basis. In other words, the whole arrangement is the sale and repurchase agreement, or *repo*, which we met in Chapter 6. There it was a means of banks funding their liquidity by selling stock (temporarily) to the central bank.

This market is particularly large for bonds, although there is some lending of equities.

The language, as usual, is used loosely. Generally 'stock lending' is used where dealers want to cover short positions and is driven by borrower demand. 'Repo' is used where the transaction is to meet funding needs. However, there are no hard and fast rules.

Bought Deals/Block Trades

Occasionally, very large share deals are executed called bought deals or block trades. The investment bank involved buys the shares using its own capital and hopes to sell them to investors at a profit. It can be very lucrative but also involves great risk.

In August 1990, ICI wanted to sell its 24.9% stake in Enterprise Oil. The shares were sold to SG Warburg and Cazenoves at £6.00 and resold for £6.07 in 30 minutes for a combined profit of £7.92m. The proceeds added up to £680 million.

In November 1994, UBS placed 72 million Guinness shares at £4.57 in 20 minutes to domestic and international institutions for £329m.

It is usually a competitive process. In December 1995, for example, NM Rothschild held an auction for the sale of the UK government's remaining stake in BP. SBC Warburg won the business by offering £5.08 per share and later sold them for £5.13m making about £5m. The sales total was £500m.

Perhaps encouraged by this, the French government also selected NM Rothschild to hold an auction to sell the government's remaining stake in Total. The auction was held one Tuesday evening in March 1996. Crédit Lyonnais and Lehman Bros won by bidding to sell the stock at FFr326 each, a 2.4% discount to the market price. The shares were placed by 9.00 am on Wednesday morning and a commission of between 0.5% and 0.7% was believed to have been earned. The total proceeds were FFr3.1bn.

It's not always easy, of course. Kleinwort Benson once attempted to sell a block representing Burmah Castrol's 29.7% holding in Premier Consolidated. They lost £34m!

Share Buy-Backs

An interesting issue is that of companies buying back their own shares. This is very common in the UK and the US. For example, in July 1996, National Westminster Bank bought back shares worth £450m and Barclays Bank bought back shares worth £470m. The idea is to cancel the shares so that profit and dividend per remaining share are then enhanced. In France, however, it is common to buy shares back as a defensive move, either to support price or prevent a takeover.

In Germany and Scandinavia it is illegal, but has recently been allowed in Switzerland and Ireland. In April 1996, however, it was revealed that the German justice ministry had discussed legalising buy-backs but doubted if it would be law before 1997. BASF, with liquid funds of DM3.4bn, announced that it would mount a buy-back as soon as the law allowed it.

In Japan, share repurchases have not been as common and have traditionally been frowned upon as a way of manipulating share prices. They became more attractive, however, in 1995, when a tax provision which acted as a disadvantage was waived until 1999. With economic recovery, many companies believe that their capital will be better spent on research and development. In spite of this, Toyota Motors bought back 1.2% of its shares, Komatsu 2% and Asahi Breweries 1.9%.

SETTLEMENT

Settlement is the basic question of paying money and receiving stock or receiving money and delivering the stock. If the stock cannot be delivered without money being credited to pay for it, this is called 'Delivery Versus Payment' (DVP) and is the ideal. It is another recommendation of the G30 report on settlement.

Sometimes settlement systems are 'rolling settlement', for example, rolling 5 working day settlement. This means that a deal on Tuesday must be settled on the next Tuesday, a deal on Wednesday must be settled on the next Wednesday and so on. This is called 'T+5', that is, 'Trade Date +5'. The G30 report recommends rolling settlement systems and 'T+3' if possible. The US is T+3, Germany T+2 and France T+3 under their new 'RELIT' system (Reglément Livraison de Titres).

The alternative is the system of an 'account period'. For example, Paris has its *Règlement Mensuel*, which can still be used to settle if requested. The 'month' is the 5 last working days of the month plus the next month up to 5 working days from the end. All deals within this month are settled on the last trading day of the month. There is, however, also a cash market *(marché au comptant)*. This is used for less actively traded stocks, all the second market, OTC and all bonds.

The UK had a fortnightly account system. In the UK, settlement day was a week on Monday, following the end of the two weekly account ending on the Friday. All member firms' deals were then settled as one net figure. The system was handled at the Stock Exchange and was called Talisman. It was to be replaced by a new system called Taurus, which would have involved rolling settlement and abolition of share certificates. However, after three separate start dates for the new system were announced and cancelled, the whole project was abandoned in March 1993. Its successor abolishes the use of share certificates, but only for professionals. The private investor is still able to use share certificates if they wish. The system is called CREST and is run by a new company – CREST CO – with the Stock Exchange as one shareholder amongst many. It started operation in the second half of 1996. Where paper certificates no longer exist and transfer of ownership is on computer register only, this is called *'dematerialisation'*. The French *RELIT* system is of this type.

Italy dropped its monthly settlement system and moved to T+5 rolling settlement in February, 1996.

In general the trend is towards new rolling settlement systems and dematerialisation.

NEW ISSUES

Handling issues of shares of new companies coming to the market is very much the essence of a stock exchange.

In general, there are two systems – the public offer for sale and the placing, or private placement.

In the case of a *public offer for sale* (an *initial public offering* in the US) the offer receives wide publicity and investors are invited to submit applications for the shares. If oversubscribed, some form of rationing or allocation must take place.

Usually, a detailed prospectus giving details of the firm's history and accounts must be produced. The issue is brought to market by a bank or stockbroker. They will advise on the pricing of the issue, will attempt to persuade the market of its merits and arrange *underwriting*. This means that, in so far as the investing public does not buy the shares, the group of underwriters undertake to purchase them. For this they receive a fee, perhaps 1½% to 2% of the value underwritten. The risk is spread widely and investment institutions will often participate, hoping to keep the fee and sleep well at night. 'Black Monday' in 1989 occurred in the middle of the UK government's privatisation of further shares in British Petroleum. The underwriters had to purchase the shares at the offer price and incur a considerable loss. Sometimes, if the market is seen to be weak, a planned issue is withdrawn. In September 1992, Commerzbank withdrew a planned offering of more shares worth DM600m due to the weak state of the market.

In the *placing*, the broker concerned contacts investment clients with the details of the offer and sells the shares without any public offering. The number of shareholders for a given sum raised is usually set at a minimum by local stock exchange rules.

The placing is much easier and cheaper from the administrative point of view and also saves underwriting fees. Other things being equal, firms may prefer a placing. However, there are usually local Stock Exchange rules on this subject. For example, in the UK, if the sum of money raised was more than £3m, a placing was not allowed. In 1986, this limit was raised to £15m and in 1991 more complex rules were introduced. These envisage the possibility of a new issue which is part placing and part offer for sale, a 100% placing being ruled out if the amount raised exceeds £50m. In 1992, there were several new issues which were 50% offer for sale and 50% placing. However, from 1 January 1996, these rules were abolished and there is now no limitation on the amount that can be raised by a placing.

Another possibility is for a company to be admitted to the list of shares which are being traded on an exchange by an *introduction*. This is typically a firm quoted on a foreign stock exchange which seeks an admission to the list of firms traded on a domestic exchange. Normally, no new money is being raised at that time. This became very common in the 1980s as part of the 'international equity' idea which we discussed earlier. The Japanese firm Toshiba, for example, is listed on nine European Stock Exchanges. Daiwa began to trade on 7 European Stock Exchanges simultaneously in April 1990. Volkswagen was listed on all four Spanish stock exchanges in June 1990 and Volkswagen and Bayer Chemicals became the first foreign companies to be listed on the Milan Stock Exchange in the same year. Daimler Benz became the first German company to list on the New York Stock Exchange in 1993.

Foreign shares listed in the US would have a disadvantage if quoted and dealt in their own currency. There are also higher costs for investors in buying foreign shares and worries (in some cases) about receiving share certificates. As a result, many foreign companies' shares trade in the US as *American Depositary Receipts* (ADRs). The receipt for one or more of a foreign company's shares is held by a trustee (often Morgan Guaranty Trust) and the receipt is traded rather than the shares themselves. For example, a BP ADR is worth twelve ordinary shares. The US investor avoids the inconvenience of collecting dividends and converting them to dollars. The sponsor bank takes care of this. The first ADR was issued in 1927 for the British–American Tobacco Company.

A more general theme is Global Depositary Receipt (GDR) which refers to using the same technique as ADRs for listing shares on exchanges outside the US. The first of these was issued in 1990 and they have proved very useful for emerging markets. For example, there were 23 GDR listings on the London Stock Exchange in 1995. South Korea accounted for eight, India four, Taiwan and South Africa three, Indonesia two and Poland, the Czech Republic and Cayman Islands one each.

RIGHTS ISSUES

Later, a firm may decide to offer the existing shareholders the right to buy some new shares in proportion to the shares they already hold. This is why they are typically called 'rights issues'. Across most of Europe, the law requires that existing shareholders have pre-emptive rights to any new shares issued for cash. (New shares may not necessarily be issued for cash – they may be issued in order to fund a takeover bid by offering them to the shareholders of the company to be taken over.)

In the US, shareholders' rights to new shares are not so firmly established. The whole question of these pre-emptive rights is controversial. Periodically, articles appear arguing that firms should be able to issue a block of new shares by auction without offering them first to the existing shareholders.

Of course, the shareholders may be approached to waive their rights. When Midland Bank sold 14.9% of its shares by way of new shares to the Hongkong and Shanghai Bank in 1987, they approached the existing shareholders for their permission.

The new shares will be offered at a discount to the existing shares, for example, an offer of one new share at $90 may be made for every three existing shares whose market price is $110. The discount is more apparent than real. The firm is regarded as having diluted the value of the issue by this offer of extra shares at a discount. An averaging or pro-rating now takes place as follows:

			$
3 existing shares	@ $110	=	330
1 new share	@ $90	=	90
Therefore each block of four shares		=	420
So 1 new share		=	105

When the shares are declared *ex-rights* (XR), the price will be $105 if the market price remains at $110. 'XR' means that anyone buying the shares does not enjoy the rights to the new shares. It now seems that the shareholder will not gain from taking up the rights in any explicit sense but will lose if they do not. They may have 100 shares at $110 per share and soon will have 100 shares at $105 per share!

They may not have the money to buy the new shares. Some shareholders sell some of their existing shares to buy new ones or the rights may be sold to someone else for a quoted premium. In the above case, the premium would be $15. The purchaser of the rights will pay the shareholder $15 and later pay the company $90, paying $105. The shareholder has shares at present for which each set of three are valued at $330 and will soon be valued at $315 – however, they sold the rights for $15.

The market price does not obligingly remain stable while the shareholders make up their minds. The premium for buying the rights thus goes up and down. What is particularly serious is if the rights price ends up above the market price. Suppose the market price in the case above falls to $80. How many people will wish to buy shares at $90 if the existing shares can be purchased for $80? This reminds us that a rights issue must be underwritten just like a new issue.

In 1991, in the UK, British Aerospace announced a rights issue at £3.80 at a time when the market price was £5.00. The announcement of poor profit prospects, however, saw the market price plunge to £3.60 as the market lost faith in British Aerospace. The underwriters took up 95% of the offering.

Rights issues are examined carefully by the market. The new money needs to be used wisely if profit per share and dividend per share are not to suffer. Sometimes, the rights issue is seen as positive and well received, sometimes as negative, the sign of a firm in trouble and the share price suffers. In the UK, the largest rights issue so far was Barclays Bank raising £921m in 1988. As more than this sum has now been written off as provisions for bad debts, the shareholders can be forgiven for feeling a little annoyed!

SCRIP ISSUES AND SPLITS

Sometimes firms offer shareholders free shares in proportion to the shares they own. For example, they may be offered one free share for every share owned. This is the *scrip* issue. Alternatively, the shares are *split*. For example, every share, 'par' or 'nominal' value $1, is replaced by two shares, 'par' or 'nominal' value 50¢.

In each case, the market value of the share will fall to half of the previous figure. The idea is that markets recognise a broad range of trading prices for shares. With growing profits and dividends over the years, the share price increases. Sometimes, the market feels that the new price is inconvenient and deters small shareholders from buying. The theory is that shareholders are happier with 100 shares at $50 than ten shares at $500. If this doesn't seem logical it is because it is, in fact, quite illogical – it's pure investor psychology.

For example, the UK market likes share prices in a range, say £1 – £5, whereas the average share price of the Dow Jones in early 1996 was $63. Above this level, companies frequently do scrips or splits to bring the price down to a 'better' trading price, one which is thought to lead to a more widespread holding and more liquidity. Thus, in 1991, Mercury Asset Management did a 3 for 2 scrip issue to lower the price from £9 to £3.60. Guinness did a 1 for 1 scrip issue to bring the price from £10 to £5.

In the US, the same idea prevails, but at much higher share price levels. On the Continent of Europe, too, shares trade typically at far higher prices than in the UK. When Paribas was privatised, for example, 3.8m applied for the shares and received just four each – but the price each was about FFr450. Switzerland is a place when, traditionally, the shares of the banks, pharmaceutical companies and Nestlé have traded at a price equivalent to several thousand dollars. However, the law, which required a minimum legal value of SFr100 per share has been altered to lower this to SFr10 per share. In May 1992, Nestlé took advantage of this to replace each share, legal value SFr100, by 10, with legal value of SFr10 each. The effect was to lower the price each from SFr9,600 to SFr960. Other large Swiss companies have followed suit.

In 1979, IBM shares hit $350 each. They did a four for 1 split to bring the price down to a level at which people could trade more easily in lots of 100 shares, New York's normal standard for trading.

When BNP, the French Bank, was to be privatised in 1993, the government did a split to halve the price from the equivalent of £56 a share to £28. Rhône-Poulenc did a 4 for 1 split in preparation for privatisation.

We have seen from the above that shares typically have a 'par' or legal value which may not bear any relationship to the market price – IBM at $1¼, for example, or AT & T at $1. There is no minimum for the legal value either in the US or the UK. In Germany, however, there was a minimum legal value of DM50, but this has been lowered to DM5, which may be part of a move to a lower average price. A low par or legal value enables the company to issue more shares when it is first formed and gives it greater flexibility later.

The scrip issue does not change the par value but gives, say, one additional share free. This doubles the par value on the balance sheet and the money is taken from reserves. A split does not alter the *total* par value owned as, say, one share at FFr75 is replaced by three at FFr25 – the total par value on the balance sheet is unchanged.

Finally, let's note that a *reverse split* or *consolidation* is possible. Here, say, five existing shares are replaced by one new one whose par value is five times as high. This is for situations where the share price is so low that it suggests a firm in serious trouble. Again, it's simply psychology. For example, in June 1992, the British advertising group Saatchi and Saatchi carried out a 1 for 10 consolidation when the share price touched a low of 15p each.

SCRIP DIVIDENDS

A common practice in many markets is to offer a choice of cash dividends or more shares – the scrip dividend. From the firm's point of view, it saves cash as it's easier to create new shares than pay dividends. From the investor's point of view, if dividends are not needed as income, it's a way of getting new shares without paying share tax or broker's commission.

The reaction to the scrip dividend will depend on the tax position. In the UK, shareholders who are not taxpayers can reclaim the tax on dividends. Shares offered for the net value of the dividend are not attractive and acceptances probably only average – about 15%. In France, the tax situation is different, and acceptances a higher percentage. On 29 May 1996, for example, Rhône-Poulenc advertised an option to have scrip dividends of ordinary A shares payable in the second half of the year.

SECOND MARKETS

It is quite common to have a 'second market' for shares who do not fulfil all the requirements for a full official listing. Both France and Belgium have 'second markets'; the UK has the 'Alternative Investment Market' (AIM); Germany has the 'Geregelter Markt' and a third market the 'Freiverkehr'; Amsterdam has its 'parallel' market.

In addition to this, there may be an active 'Over the Counter Market'. Paris has its 'Hors Cote', the US the huge NASDAQ market, and the UK a market called 'OFEX'.

Usually, the key requirements that the second or third market firm may not fulfil are the number of years' trading record and the percentage of shares in outside hands. The general European rule, under the 'Mutual Recognition of Listing Particulars', is that 3 years' trading is needed for a full listing and for recognition of a firm already listed on another EU exchange.

In both Paris and London, for the official list, 25% of shares must be in outside hands. The rule for the Paris Second Market is that only 10% need be in outside hands. There are 272 firms on the Second Market in Paris and 136 on the AIM in London.

A consortium of US and European Banks have formed a new pan-European market called EASDAQ, modelled on the US NASDAQ market. It expects to open before the end of 1996 with 20 companies and grow to 500 companies in 5 years.

ANALYSTS' RATIOS

When a firm makes an initial public offering of its shares, how does it decide what price to ask for the shares? A simple answer seems to be 'divide the value of the company by the number of the shares'. The problem is that the value of the company is the share price!

Sometimes people suggest 'asset values' as a possible guide. However, on 1 October 1987 companies' share prices were a great deal higher than at 31 October 1987 and yet the assets were the same. In any case, some firms are quite valuable but have few assets. 'People' companies like computer software houses or stockbrokers are like this.

The fact is that price is simply what the market will pay. We must, therefore, look at what the market does pay for similar companies. Their share prices will all be different, which doesn't immediately help. There are two rewards for buying a share – dividends and an increase in the share price. Both of these depend on *profits*, so what we need to do is see how the price per share of comparable companies compares to the profit per share. We might find an overall relationship of, say, 10. That is, if the profit is $4 per share, the share price is typically $40. If our profit per share is $3, this suggests a price of $30. Let's make it $28 and persuade everyone that it's a bargain!

This relationship of share price to profit is the *P/E* – the Price/Earnings Ratio and the most famous ratio of them all. We've seen one of its key uses, to help us set a price initially. Each time new profits are announced, a new P/E is calculated and the share may seem cheap or dear now compared to its peers in the market sector.

Sometimes analysts look at the P/E for the whole stock market, and compare this with historic values to see if the market is overpriced or not.

Sometimes it is not easy to find the market sector. When the composer, Andrew Lloyd Webber, went public as the 'Really Useful Group', it was difficult to find anything comparable! In that case, what took place was the *offer for sale by tender*. Investors put in their various bids and the share allocation is decided accordingly. In that case, it was a 'striking price' tender, that is, everyone paid the same price.

As dividends are part of the reward for holding shares, the market looks at dividend income as a percentage of the share price. To avoid complications, the dividend is grossed up if it is normally paid net, for example:

$$\frac{\text{Gross dividend}}{\text{Share price}} = \frac{\$2.5}{\$50} = 5\%$$

This ratio is the *gross dividend yield* or, simply, the *yield*. It will be compared with the yield on other shares and with the yield on bonds in particular. Analysts talk of the *yield ratio* – the ratio between the yield on government bonds and the yields on shares. As shares may have capital gain, the yield is usually less than that on medium maturity bonds (although this has not always been the case). Typical P/E ratios and yields for key exchanges in April 1996 are shown in Table 9.8.

Table 9.8   *P/E ratios and yields, April 1996*

Exchange	P/E	Yield
US	18.5	2.1
Germany	16.0	1.7
UK	16.6	3.7
France	15.8	3.1
Japan	66.2	0.7

Source: Various.

Looking at the dividend paid, we may want to see how comfortable the firm was when paying the dividend out of profit. Was all the profit used? How much profit is retained for growth? We compare the profit per share with the *net* dividend per share, for example:

$$\frac{\text{Profit per share}}{\text{Net dividend}} = \frac{\$5}{\$2} = 2.5$$

This ratio is the *cover*. If the profit is small but the firm feels it must maintain the dividend, the net dividend paid may exceed the profit per share. We say the dividend is *uncovered*. Clearly, it is being financed out of the reserves (that is, previous years' profits) and the firm's capital is being weakened.

At a time of recession, there is fierce argument about the extent to which firms should try to maintain dividends even if they are not justified by profits. Pension funds or insurance companies who need income to meet commitments are concerned when dividends are cut or not paid. Trustees of some investment funds will not allow investment in any firm which has passed a dividend in a given previous time period.

Finally, analysts look at *earnings per share* and use this as a record of the firm's performance. Problems arise when accounting conventions may allow (legitimate) massaging of the profit figure. Should extraordinary items for unprecedented events (for example, acquisition costs) be charged against profit for this purpose? This is just one of many controversial issues in this area. For the EU, trying to impose common national standards is a veritable minefield. A new British accountancy standard is about to be enforced but has already incurred criticism from some quarters. At the same time, a book by a former UBS Phillips & Drew analyst on how firms legitimately 'massage' their accounts went into the bestseller list! (Terry Smith, *Accounting for Growth*, Century Business, 1991).

DEREGULATION

In the second half of the 1980s, deregulation spread across Western Stockmarkets at a rapid pace. It was preceded on 1 May 1975 by the abolition of fixed commissions on the New York Stock Exchange by order of the SEC. This led to a wave of takeovers and mergers in the early 1980s, following the expansion of the market in the late 1970s. American Express bought Shearson Loeb Rhodes and also Lehman Bros Kuhn Loeb; Phibro Corporation bought Salomon Bros; Sears Roebuck bought Dean Witter; Bank America bought Charles Schwab; Prudential Insurance bought Bache Halsey Stuart Shields, and so on.

In Europe, the big event was London's 'Big Bang' of 27 October 1986. Prior to this the market had various restrictions:

❑ Jobbers (nowadays 'market makers') would only deal with brokers
❑ Brokers' commissions were on fixed scales
❑ No firm could be broker *and* jobber ('single capacity')
❑ No outside firm could own more than 29.9% of a stock exchange member (it had been limited to 10% up to 1982)
❑ No foreign firm was allowed to be a Stock Exchange member.

The whole system was clearly anti-competitive. With the growth of technology and communications, however, large institutions could buy shares like ICI, Shell, BP, Reuters and others in New York and did so. They found it quicker and cheaper. These same institutions were also unhappy as the shortage of capital meant that the 17 firms of jobbers were too small to take the risk of handling large deals on their own. The bigger deals had to be spread over several jobbers.

The stock exchange was complacent but the government and the Bank of England were worried. A threatened court case in the Restrictive Practices Court set in motion the train of events that led to the so-called 'Big Bang' in October 1986:

❑ Fixed brokers' commissions were abolished
❑ The market was no longer forced to route orders through brokers
❑ 'Single capacity' was abandoned
❑ Outside ownership of stock exchange members was allowed
❑ Foreign firms could be stock exchange members.

Whereas jobbers had handled both equities and gilts, we now saw Equity Market

Makers (33 set up to handle domestic and foreign equities) and Gilt-Edged Market Makers (27 were formed).

For 200 years, the Bank of England had sold gilts through one firm of brokers (Mullens) and an official called the 'Government Broker'. They now decided to follow the US route and have dedicated primary dealers. They admitted, however, that 27 was too many (today there are 19).

The stock exchange could see that the floor would be crowded with all these new firms and set up the computer system, SEAQ, to supplement floor trading. In March 1986, a magazine asked Stock Exchange members their opinion on the effect of the new system on floor trading. 65% said that it would have no effect whatsoever. Inside 4 months, the floor was deserted (except for option traders) – technology had won!

While individual members remained members, they lost their voting rights which were now given to member firms. (Individual membership was finally abolished in 1992.)

Foreign firms flocked to join – Nomura Securities and Merrill Lynch were the first two. UBS bought Phillips & Drew; Hongkong and Shanghai Bank bought James Capel; BNP bought Quilter Goodison; Citibank bought Scrimgeour Kemp Gee and Vickers da Costa, and so on.

British banks moved as well. Barclays bought the biggest jobber (Wedd Durlacher Mordaunt) and Warburgs bought the second biggest jobber (Ackroyd and Smithers).

While business boomed at first, the crash of October 1987 saw a big shake out in the number of firms trading. Commission levels were forced down. The institutions would regard the changes as a big success – dealing is cheaper and liquidity is better; deals for the small investor are more expensive and trading in the shares of small firms seems to have suffered.

A wave of similar changes swept across Europe. Paris reorganised its government bond market, appointing primary dealers and reorganising the government bonds as the new OATS (Obligations Assimilables De Trésor). The brokers' monopoly, given to them at the time of Napoleon, was swept away; commissions were opened to competition; the Bourse hours changed from the sleepy 12.30–2.30 to 10.00–5.00; outside ownership was permitted; Paris and the provincial exchanges were formed into one legal exchange; the CATS computer system was installed. A symbolic moment came on 14 July 1987 during the national holiday. The inner area for the brokers, called 'La Corbeille' (basket), was dismantled.

Germany has followed somewhat more slowly, partly due to the existence of eight exchanges. One legal stock exchange has been formed – the Deutsche Börse – and this includes the DTB, the derivatives exchange. The computer system, IBIS, will continue for major shares but the floor will be used for the rest. A new supervisory authority has been set up and new laws on insider dealing and takeovers have been passed. The government bond market has also been opened to competition.

The Bundesanleihen are sold partly by auction (instead of to a syndicate in set proportions) and the 2 and 4 year Bundesschatzanweisungen are sold totally by auction.

In Belgium, Spain and Italy there have been similar changes. Commission has been opened to competition; new computerised trading has commenced; outside ownership of brokers has been permitted; brokers have had to form into companies; bond markets have been reorganised; the power of provincial exchanges is likely to weaken (Barcelona retains a strong independence from Madrid, although there has been surprising cooperation in the areas of options and futures trading).

In Switzerland, the market is still dominated by the banks but fixed commissions have been abolished. The banks effectively closed four provincial exchanges by concentrating on Zurich, Basle and Geneva. With the arrival of computerised trading in mid-1996, the three separate exchange floors are in the process of closing. As with Germany, one new exchange has been set up – EBS – and this includes the SOFFEX derivatives exchange. Supervision of the markets has been transferred from Cantonal control to the Federal Banking Commission.

Amsterdam has set up a new computerised system for bonds and equities; the AIM was established for large block trades between the institutions, minimum commissions have been abolished and the market reorganised on retail/wholesale lines as described earlier.

The changes saw domestic and foreign banks taking over stockbrokers or making an alliance as we saw in the US and the UK. Here are some examples:

❏ France

Crédit Lyonnais	Cholet Dupont
James Capel	DLP
Warburg	Bacot Allain
J.P. Morgan	Gwenael Gautier

❏ Italy

Société Générale	Studio Albertini
BHF Bank	Pastorini
Warburgs	Giubergia
Crédit Lyonnais	Mortari
Friends Provident	Gamba Azzoni

❏ Spain

ABN–AMRO	Capital Markets Equities
Kidder Peabody	Benito y Monjardin
Barclays	Pizarro y Recoder.

Further changes took place in the UK in 1995 with the feeling that UK merchant/ investment banks needed to be bigger to survive. SG Warburg were taken over by Swiss Bank Corporation, Baring Bros by ING from Holland (for a different reason!), Kleinwort Benson by Dresdner Bank and Smith New Court by Merrill Lynch.

EU RULES

The EU single market which commenced in January 1993, has relevance for stock exchange trading. Attempts to set up any kind of 'Pan-European Stock Exchange' have so far foundered. A common quotation system – Euroquote – was agreed in principle but no money was voted for it! Attempts are now concentrating on the idea of top firms being able to list on all twelve community exchanges – Eurolist.

Investment Services Directive

At the end of June 1992, EU finance ministers reached agreement on the final shape of the Investment Services Directive (ISD). This extends the 'single passport' idea seen in the Second Banking Directive. Stockbrokers in one country have the right to deal in the shares of any other EU country, without having to set up a local office or buy a local stockbroker. (At the moment Italy's new laws are in conflict with this. They demand that anyone dealing on Italy's exchanges must incorporate locally as a SIM – Societa di Intermediazione Mobiliare.)

One problem holding up agreement was that of transparency of dealing. London's market makers wanted to keep the 90 minute delay on publishing large deals to give them time to unwind a position. Continental markets, like Paris, used to immediate publication, wished to continue with this.

An inevitable compromise was reached:

❏   The highest and lowest prices over a rolling 2 hours will be published every 20 minutes but with 1 hour delay
❏   A weighted average of prices and volumes in transactions over a 6 hour period will be published 2 hours later
❏   These rules may be suspended for very large transactions or transactions in illiquid stocks; the definition of 'large' will be made locally.

Looking at the above rules, one is reminded of the saying that 'a camel is a horse designed by a committee'!

The ISD took effect from January 1 1996. (However, at that date only seven of the 15 member states had passed the legislation.) From this date, firms are able to operate in any EU member state provided they are regulated in one of them. This operation is subject to local rules on conduct of business.

In addition, all exchanges and futures and options markets can trade throughout the EU. The effect of all this is to increase competition between the Union's 32 stock exchanges and 24 derivatives exchanges. Thus, from January 1 1996, NatWest Markets began trading on the Swedish stock exchange but from their office in London. There was no longer any need to pay a local Swedish broker. Equally, the German DTB, the derivatives exchange, opened an access point in London for local members to do business directly with Frankfurt.

Capital Adequacy Directive

Alongside the ISD is the Capital Adequacy Directive (CAD). This has also provoked fierce debate. Where there is a universal bank tradition, like Germany, the banks were happy to cover the investment banking activity under commercial bank capital ratio rules. US and UK operators, however, not owned by banks, were strongly opposed to this. The rules require dealers to have a minimum amount of capital to back their transactions but taking into account the precise nature of the risk and allowing for hedging of transactions.

The EU is, naturally, not the whole world. The so-called Basle Committee has been studying capital adequacy for investment banking and so has the International Organisation of Securities Commissions (IOSCO). The hope was that the two might be able to agree, thus leading to two main standards – those of the EU and those of IOSCO/ Basle. In fact, the IOSCO meeting in October 1992 was totally unable to agree with a draft Basle proposal and unable to agree amongst themselves. To some people's surprise, Richard Breeden, Chairman of the US SEC, attacked the agreed Basle rules on capital ratio for commercial banks. He argued that, because government bonds are zero-weighted, US banks were already cutting loans to companies and investing in the bonds instead.

The SEC current rules require investment banks to cover their position with 15% equivalent capital. The proposed IOSCO rules suggest 2% of gross holdings plus 8% of net long and short positions and will make full allowance for hedging.

It now looks as if the SEC, governing the world's most important market, will end up with quite different capital adequacy rules from those in force elsewhere. In particular, IOSCO, at its Trinidad meeting in February 1993, decided to abandon efforts to reach common international capital adequacy rules, although meetings with the BIS in May 1996 suggested a fresh attempt to harmonise rules.

From 1 January 1996, the European CAD came into operation. Investment banks must allocate capital to cover the risks of losses through changes in market prices. The BIS ratios, as we have seen, only covered default risks for lending. Large banks were covering this risk anyway but have had to cover the costs of rewriting IT systems to follow the new rules and monitor exposures constantly. Since most countries had local rules to cover capital adequacy, the effect has not been too serious in terms of banks having to provide extra capital.

Mergers and Acquisitions

The EU agreed a Merger Regulation in 1989. This defined circumstances in which a merger would have a 'European dimension' and come under the rules of the EU, and when a merger would be decided by national bodies. In one case, in particular, the Commission vetoed the takeover of De Havilland, the Canadian aircraft maker, by Aérospatiale of France and Alenia from Italy (to the fury of all concerned). On the other hand, objections to the Nestlé takeover of Perrier had little effect and Nestlé and BSN of France now control 75% of the French mineral water market.

The EU has abandoned the idea of a detailed takeover bid directive in favour of one which outlines principles with which local legislation must comply – for example, equal treatment of all shareholders. It hopes to get this directive adopted by the end of 1996.

Eurolist

Eurolist is a project managed by the European Federation of Stock Exchanges. It gives Europe's major listed companies simplified access to listing on European stock exchanges outside their home market, offering them standardised multi-listing procedures.

The project was launched on 9 October 1995 and began with 59 large European Corporates in nine countries. Companies must have a capitalisation of 1 billion ecu and a turnover of 250 million ecu.

SUMMARY

Strictly speaking, stocks are fixed interest securities and shares are equities.

Share indices are usually based on market capitalisation and calculated every minute.

In most economies, the major shareholders are investment institutions (pension funds, insurance companies and mutual funds) rather than private shareholders. The world's ageing populations will lead to a growth in funded pensions.

Mixed pools of shares are popular investments. They may be *closed-ended* (for example, UK investment trusts) or *open-ended* (for example, US mutual funds).

Order-driven dealing systems are those where orders of buyers and sellers are matched. Quote-driven systems are those where *market makers* quote firm bid and offer prices. Hybrid systems, like New York, involve elements of both types.

Dealers with *long* positions can lend stock to get collateral to fund their position and those with *short* positions can borrow stock (offering collateral) to match their sales. This is *stock borrowing and lending*. Very large deals are *bought deals* or *block trades*.

Sometimes firms buy their own shares back in order to cancel them and enhance dividends and earnings per share.

Settlement systems are usually *rolling settlement*, although settlement of all deals in a given trading period still exists (for example, France).

With new issues, shares may be a *public offer for sale* (or *initial public offering*). The alternative is the *private placing*, although sometimes a mixture of both is used.

An offer of more shares to existing shareholders is a *rights issue*.

A *scrip* issue offers shareholders free shares and a *split* divides the par value of the existing shares. The objective in both cases is to lower the price to improve liquidity. A *consolidation* replaces a number of existing shares by one new one to enhance the price. A *scrip dividend* is an offer of shares instead of cash dividends (optional).

As well as the normal market for shares, there may be a secondary market for newer companies who do not meet the requirements for a full listing. There may also be dealing outside the exchange – *over the counter* (OTC).

When a firm goes public, we look at the relationship between the price of similar shares and the profit per share to guide us as to the correct offer price of the new share. This is the *price/earnings ratio* (P/E). We also look at the likely dividend as a percentage of the share price to calculate the *gross dividend yield*. To check if the latter is achieved by giving away all the profit, we compare the profit per share to the net dividend to calculate the *cover ratio*. Finally, analysts look at the *earnings per share*.

Deregulation over the last 20 years has led to an opening of stock markets to greater competition, more cross-border trades and the use of computer systems for trading, sometimes leading to the closure of trading floors.

From 1 January 1996, the EU *Investment Services Directive* took effect. This enables member firms to trade across all 15 markets.

Also taking effect from 1 January 1996 was the EU's *Capital Adequacy Directive*, which links capital to market risk.

Some 60 large European corporates have simplified access to listings on all 15 EU exchanges through *Eurolist*.

10 Traded Options

Probably the fastest growing sector of the financial markets today is that of what are called *derivative products*. They are so called because they derive from another product. The buying of $1m for sterling is the product. The option to buy $1m for sterling later at a price we agree today is the derived product. Borrowing $1m at floating rate for 5 years is the product. A bank offering (for a fee) to compensate the borrower should rates rise above a given level in the next 5 years is the derived product – and so on.

In currency rates, interest rates, bonds, equities and equity indices there is volatility. Where there is volatility, there are those who believe they know what the next price movement is and back their judgement with money. We call them *speculators*. There are those who will lose money from a given price movement and seek to protect themselves from this. We call them *hedgers*. Both will use the derivative markets for this purpose. The interesting paradox is that one is using them to take risks and the other to reduce risks. Finally, there are those who perceive pricing anomalies and seek to exploit this. They are the *arbitrageurs*.

Thus, the three types of users of derivative products are:

❏ Speculators
❏ Hedgers
❏ Arbitrageurs.

Speculators are easy enough to understand but, before we look at hedgers and arbitrageurs, it will be as well to explain one of the derivative products first.

The two key products are *Options* and *Futures*. If the reader can obtain a good working knowledge of these products, they are well placed to understand others (FRAs, Swaps, Caps) since they are simply variations on the options and futures themes.

This chapter will discuss options, Chapter 11 covers futures and Chapter 12 the remaining derivative products.

One last point. In Chapter 7, we mentioned that currency options could be purchased on a trading exchange or OTC, that is, direct with a bank or trader. While this was mentioned in the context of currency options, it is generally true that there are exchanges for traded options and financial futures but that these products can also be purchased OTC.

The advantage of a trading exchange is that there is plenty of trading liquidity, there are competing traders to ensure good prices, and there is the implicit protection against default provided by a body called the *Clearing House*. The disadvantage is that the products are standardised and may not suit the user's exact requirements. To take an example that we've already met, the cable contract on the Chicago Mercantile Exchange is based on multiples of £62 500. This means that if the amount required to be bought or sold for dollars is £75 000, then the product offered is not an exact fit.

The big advantage of OTC dealing is its flexibility. The product offered to the users can be tailored to their exact needs. On an exchange, however, it may be possible to 'trade' the product later – that is, sell it back to the exchange. Sometimes OTC products cannot be traded or, if they can, the user is very much in the hands of the seller for a price. This market is often accused of a lack of liquidity when it comes to trading even standardised products at a later stage. Finally, the user must consider the risk of default. If the seller is Deutsche Bank or the Union Bank of Switzerland, we can be quite happy, but the US house Drexel Burnham Lambert crashed in February 1990 and defaulted on any OTC products outstanding.

Let us turn now to the subject of options.

TRADED OPTIONS: EQUITIES

Calls and Puts

Traded options are standardised options which grant the buyer the right (but *not* the obligation) to buy or sell financial instruments at standard prices and dates in the future. A premium is charged for this right, and is usually paid when the option is bought.

Let us take a simple example. Suppose we look at the UK Company, General Electric, and the share price is £1.86. We may be optimistic and believe that the price may well rise to, say, £2.10 in the next 3 months. The option to *buy* a given quantity of GEC shares at £1.86 in the next 3 months is very attractive. If we are right and the price goes to £2.10, we can use the option to buy the given quantity of shares at £1.86 and sell them again in the conventional way at £2.10. If we are wrong and the price falls or remains constant, we don't have to do anything as it was only an option, not an obligation. This is clearly a privileged position, and we must pay for it. The price we pay is the *premium* for the option. This right to *buy* a financial product later is the *call* option. We buy a call when we wish to gain from an increase in price later.

We may, alternatively, be pessimistic about GEC and believe that the price of £1.86 will probably fall to £1.60 in the next 3 months. The option to *sell* a given quantity of GEC shares at £1.86 in the next 3 months is very attractive. If we are correct, we can buy them later for £1.60 and use the option to sell them at £1.86. If we are wrong and the price rises or remains constant, we don't have to do anything as it was only an option, not an obligation. Again, we pay a premium for this privilege. The right to *sell* a financial product later is the *put* option. We buy a put when we wish to gain from a fall in price later.

Let's look at some figures. Suppose the call or put contract is for 1000 shares and that the premium in each case is 10p per share. We'll look at the call and the put in turn.

Call option   We have the right to buy 1000 GEC shares within the next 3 months at £1.86 and pay a premium of 10p per share (= £100) up front.

GEC Share Price Later:

£1.60?   ← ———— £1.86 ————→   £2.10?

Suppose the price falls to £1.60 and we have come to the end of the 3 months. The right to buy at £1.86 is of no value as we can buy them at the market price of £1.60. The option will expire. There is no action to take – we just abandon our option. Our loss is the premium of £100 (which we've already paid). Notice that whatever happens, we *can't lose more than the premium.*

Suppose the price rises later to £2.10? Now, we can contact our broker, advise them that we are exercising our option to buy 1000 shares at £1.86 and ask them to sell them in the usual way for £2.10 (no further capital needs to be paid). We have made 1000 × (£2.10 - £1.86) = 1000 × 24p = £240. We paid a premium of £100 so the net gain is £140 or 140% (for convenience, dealing costs have been ignored).

The share price rose 24p from £1.86, a rise of about 13%. This rise of 13% generated us a profit of 140%. This effect is called *gearing*, which we met in Chapter 1 (the Americans call it *leverage*). In general, it's making a given sum of money go further. In Chapter 1, we looked at balance sheet gearing – making money go further by borrowing other people's money. This is another example. If we had bought 1000 GEC shares, we would have paid £1860. We backed our view on £1860 of shares with just £100 premium. In addition (at least in theory) the remaining £1760 can be in the bank earning interest. The result, as in the above case, is that a small change in the price of the underlying asset (13%) may lead to a large percentage profit gain (140%). However, gearing cuts both ways. A small fall in price of just, say, 4% could result in 100% loss of our premium! Nevertheless, gearing is a big attraction in derivative products.

Put option   We now have paid for the right to sell 1000 GEC shares within the next 3 months at £1.86 and pay a premium of 10p per share (= £100) up front.

GEC Share Price Later:

£1.60?   ← ———— £1.86 ————→   £2.10?

At this point the reader might wonder how we can buy the right to sell shares that we don't even own. We shall find that not only is this not a problem, it is part of the beauty of the put option!

Suppose the price rises to £2.10 and we have come to the end of th
We have the right to sell 1000 shares at £1.86. If we had the shares (whic..
we could sell them on the market for £2.10. Our right is of no value and will expi..
losing the premium of £100.

Suppose the price falls later to £1.60. We have the right to sell 1000 shares at £1.86 but don't actually own any. What we do, of course, is buy 1000 shares in the conventional way at £1.60 and use the option to sell them at £1.86, making 26p per share or a net 16p after deducting our cost of 10p per share. Our profit is £160 or 160% although the change in share price was only about 14%.

Option Writers

Who, in the first instance, sells us the GEC shares at £1.86 when the market price is £2.10? Who, in the second instance, buys our shares from us at £1.86 when the market price is £1.60? The answer is the person who sold us the option in the first place, called the *writer* of the option. They took our premium and believed that it was a good price for the risk.

There are, thus, four possibilities in the option game. One can buy calls or puts and one can write calls or puts. The risk profile is quite different for buyers and writers:

	Maximum Loss	Maximum Gain
Buyers of Options	The premium	Unlimited
Writers of Options	Unlimited	The premium

Because the writers of options face unlimited risk, they pay a deposit, called *margin*, to the clearing house. When the deal is opened they pay *initial margin*. If the price moves against them they must pay more margin – *variation margin* – to cover their losses. If they go into liquidation, the deal is honoured by the clearing house.

Trading Options

In the above cases, we either abandoned our option or exercised it. On a trading exchange, there is the further choice of *trading the option*.

Let's illustrate this, and some of the real life complications, by looking at the prices that were quoted for GEC shares at one time on the London International Financial Futures Exchange (LIFFE). The exchange deals in the shares of about 70 UK companies and also offers options on the main share index, the FT–SE 100 (to be explained later).

The position is more complicated than in our previous example:

❏   There is a choice of share prices at which calls/puts can be bought/written. They are called *exercise* or *strike* prices. There is a choice of dates for expiry of the contract. three dates are offered to a maximum of 9 months ahead.
❏   The options must be dealt in multiples of 1000 shares (that is, standardised contract sizes, as we saw when looking at currency options).
❏   Options can be traded – that is, sold back to the market for a later premium.
❏   Having bought an option, it can be exercised at any time prior to the expiry date. This is called an *American* option. (It's nothing to do with America! Most options on European exchanges are American options.)

Let's first look at the matrix of choice and assume that we came to the market on 27 March and looked at options for GEC (Table 10.1).

Table 10.1   *GEC, call options, 27 March*

Market price	Exercise price	Exercise expiry dates		
		April	July	October
	180			
186	200			
	220			

Notice that we have standardised exercise prices of £1.80, £2.00 and £2.20. None of them is the market price (£1.86) except by coincidence. We have a further choice of expiry in April, July or October – a maximum of 7 months. Had we come to the market on 1 February, we would still have seen April, July and October and hence, our maximum time horizon of 9 months.

There are thus nine choices and for each there is a quoted premium in pence per share. Suppose the premiums for all three exercise prices were the same? Naturally, we would pick the exercise price of £1.80 since we all like to be able to buy at the cheapest price. It will be no surprise to find that the premium for £1.80 is more expensive than that for £2.00 and much more expensive than that for £2.20. Again, suppose the premiums for all the three expiry dates were the same? Naturally, we would pick October to give GEC the maximum time to go up in price. For the same reason, the writer of the option (who is not stupid!) wants a higher premium for October than April.

Let's look now at the full list of prices in Table 10.2.

On 27 March, the right to buy GEC shares at £1.80 before an expiry in April costs 16p per share. For the minimum contract of 1000 shares this is £160. On 27 March, the right to buy GEC shares at £2.00 before an expiry in October costs 21p per share. For the minimum contract, this is £210. Notice the gearing. To *buy* 1000 GEC shares today would cost £1860.

Table 10.2   *GEC, call options, 27 March*

Market price	Exercise price	April	July calls	October
	180	16	24	32
186	200	7	14	21
	220	3	7	12

Which of these nine options do we choose? There is no magic answer. It depends how strongly you feel GEC is undervalued, how soon you think the price will rise, and how risk averse you are.

You could choose £1.80, already cheaper than the stock market price and October expiry, giving the largest time for GEC to go up in price. It looks attractive but at £320 per 1000 shares is the most expensive.

At the other extreme, you could choose £2.20 and expiry in April. This is 34p dearer than the stock market price and perhaps only 4 weeks to the expiry date. It doesn't look attractive but its cheap at £30 per 1000 shares.

Intrinsic Value and Time Value

The £1.80 option is already 6p cheaper than the market price of £1.86. We can argue, therefore, that the premium must be at least 6p. Suppose the premium was 4p? You would buy as many options as you could possibly afford and immediately exercise, buying the shares for £1.80 and selling for £1.86. An obvious profit of 6p for a cost of 4p. No chance! The market has a piece of jargon for this 6p – it's called *intrinsic value*. This occurs when the call exercise price is cheaper than the market price or a put exercise price is dearer than the market price.

The option premium for the April expiry is 16p. We know that it must be at least 6p and can see that 10p has been added to cover the possibility of GEC going up in price prior to expiry. We call this the *time value* in the option. The exercise price of £2 is dearer than the market price and it has no intrinsic value (we don't use negative intrinsic value).

Breaking the premium down like this, into intrinsic value and time value, let's look at the £1.80 calls for April, July and October and the £200 calls for the same expiry dates in Table 10.3.

Table 10.3   *£1.80 and £2.00 calls for April, July and October*

Exercise price	Expiry	Intrinsic value		Time value		Premium
180	April	6	+	10	=	16
	July	6	+	18	=	24
	October	6	+	26	=	32
200	April	0	+	7	=	7
	July	0	+	14	=	14
	October	0	+	21	=	21

We can see how time value goes up steadily for later expiry dates.

Calculation of the Premium

Where does this time value come from? How are the premiums calculated?

Usually, in human activity, if we want to forecast the future, we start with the past: as T.S. Eliot tells us, 'In my beginning, is my end'. We look at the previous behaviour of the share price, say over the last 6 months, and project this forward using statistical techniques and laws of probability. These may suggest that there is a given probability that the GEC share price in October will be within a given range. We look at the exercise price, the current market price, one or two other factors we don't need to go into, and the statistical calculations use the past behaviour to produce a theoretical or *fair value* for the premium. There may then be a question of whether the option writer believes that future price behaviour will be different, and also sheer demand and supply. If there are more option buyers than sellers, premiums will rise, and vice-versa. Experts will compare the market premiums with the fair value premiums and decide if the premiums look cheap or expensive.

These statistical techniques were developed in May 1973 when Fischer Black and Myron Scholes wrote a paper on the pricing of options in the *Journal of Political Economy*. The Black–Scholes formula, with one or two possible modifications, is still widely used to calculate premiums. Black and Scholes were professors at the University of Chicago and the timing was apt as the Chicago Board Options Exchange had started trading options in April 1973. A few years later, more professors appeared – Messrs Cox, Ross and Rubenstein. They produced a similar formula (one based on a binomial progression for those who understand such things). The experts argue about the merits of one formula as opposed to another; for the lay person, the results are very similar.

In looking at the past behaviour of two shares, one may be much more volatile than another although the average price may be similar in each case. The more volatile share may produce higher or lower share prices later than the less volatile one and thus the premium will be higher.

Look at Figure 10.1

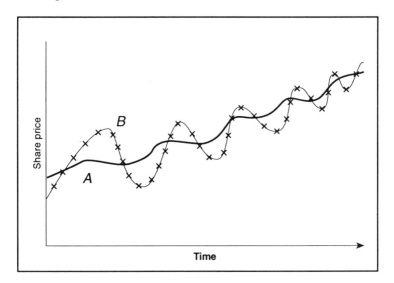

Figure 10.1 *Price behaviour of two shares, A and B*

For the writer of the option, share *B* is clearly more dangerous and risky than share *A*, even though the average price over time is much the same. Without knowing anything about statistics, we can accept that the option premiums quoted for share *B* will be higher than for share *A*. Those who understand statistics will be aware that this volatility is the standard deviation and a key element in the pricing formula. Experts will analyse market premiums to see the *implied volatility*. They will then decide if they agree with this figure, bearing in mind that future volatility may not be the same as past or *historic volatility*. These are advanced considerations that need not concern us in an introductory text. Be aware, however, that volatility is a big word in the options game.

Volatility is usually quoted as a percentage figure, for example, 20%. This would mean that, over 1 year, there is a 68% chance in laws of probability that a share price will be either 20% higher or lower than the starting price.

Suppose a share price is £1.00 and the volatility is 20% The premium for a 1 year call option, the right to buy the share at 1.00 within the next year, would be 9.9p per share. If the volatility were 40%, the premium would be 17.1p.

(The above assumes 10% interest rates and 5% dividend yield, factors that are also taken into account.)

Exercise or Trade?

Going back to the GEC prices on 27 March, let's assume that we bought a call option with exercise price £1.80 and expiry in July. Let's also assume that it's the minimum of one contract, that is, 1000 shares. The premium is quoted as 24 and so we will pay £240 plus broker's commission and a small charge for the costs of the clearing house.

(The premiums are actually quoted with a bid/offer spread so that 24 may be a mid-point representing a quote of 22/24. We will ignore this in the interests of simplicity.)

Let's move on now to 6 June in the same year. We can look at the current call option premiums in Table 10.4.

Table 10.4   6 June

Market price	Exercise price	July	October	January
	180	36	44	52
206	200	18	28	38
	220	6	13	24

We see that the April month has gone and been replaced by January, the next month in the series. We also note that the share price has gone up 20p and the £1.80/ July call premium is now quoted as 36.

If we are new to options, this might puzzle us. We could argue that, as the share price has gone up 20p, the right to buy at £1.80 must be 20p more valuable. If the old premium was 24, it should now be 44. To understand what is happening to the premium we must break it down into intrinsic value and time value and compare the positions on 27 March and 6 June. We can see this in Table 10.5.

Table 10.5   Breaking down premium into intrinsic and time value

Premium date	Market price	Intrinsic value		Time value		Premium
27 March	186	6	+	18	=	24
6 June	206	26	+	10	=	36

We can see that intrinsic value has gone up by 20 but time value down by 8, giving a net increase of 12. The time value is down simply because, at 6 June, there is less time left to expiry. If we need more time value for more time, as we saw earlier, then we need less time value for less time.

It is most important to grasp this. It means that there is an element in the premium, the time value, *which is steadily going down*, regardless of what is happening to the share price. There is an element, intrinsic value, which may be going *up* or *down* – that depends on the share price movement. Since we may *trade* the option, that is, receive the quoted premium, we must understand its behaviour.

Suppose we decide to take profit at this point, We have two choices – *exercise* the option or *trade* it. Let's examine each in turn.

If we exercise the option, we buy 1000 shares at £1.80 and sell them at the market price of £2.06, making 26p per share, ignoring dealing costs. As the option cost is 24p per share, our profit is 2p.

If we trade the option, we sell it back for 36p, today's quoted premium. As the option cost is 24p per share, our profit is 12p.

In the first case we make £20 and in the second, £120. Why was trading more profitable? When we exercise we buy at the exercise price (£1.80) and sell at the market price (£2.06). We have a term for this gap – intrinsic value. When we exercise we receive the intrinsic value, in this case 26p. When we trade, we receive the premium, that is, intrinsic value *plus* time value. The premium is 36 because 10p of time value was added to the intrinsic value. In other words, we are gaining from the protection built into the premium by the option writer. In fact, when we trade the option we *are* an option writer! However, as we previously bought the same option, we are not left with any outstanding position in the market. It follows that, at expiry, there is no time value and exercising the option or trading it will produce the same result. There is one final point regarding the time value. We have noted that it declines as time passes. However, this decline accelerates as we approach expiry. An option buyer may defer taking profit for several weeks, allowing the share price to rise even further. It may well be, however, that the time value declines faster than the intrinsic value rises and the total premium falls in value. This will be particularly true with a few weeks of expiry.

Other Terminology

We have noted the term 'intrinsic value' which is used when a call option exercise price is below the market price or a put option exercise price is above it. The option is also described here as *in the money*. If the exercise price is the same as the market price, we say the option is *at the money*. If the call exercise price is dearer than the market or the put exercise price cheaper we say the option is *out of the money*. Please note, however, that the use of standard exercise prices means that it is only rarely that one is the same as the market price. As a result, it is very common to call the at-the-money option the one which is *nearest* to the market price.

We described these LIFFE options earlier as *American* options, that is, they can be exercised at any time prior to the expiry date. The alternative is the *European* option which can only be exercised at expiry. We will give an example of this shortly. Typically, options on trading exchanges are American options but European options are quite common in the OTC Market. Both options can be *traded* at any time on trading exchanges.

Options on Indices

Having looked at options on individual shares, we can now consider options on a whole share index, for example, S&P 100, FT–SE 100, CAC 40, DAX and so on.

In principle, we can see that the idea has advantages. Now we can back a view on the whole market, not an individual share. Alternatively, we may be a market maker or fund manager owning all the top shares. The index might be a good way of hedging market risk. The practice of index options may be puzzling at first. One can readily envisage exercising an option and buying GEC shares. What if we exercise the index option and buy the FT–SE 100 index or the DAX? What exactly do we receive?

The contracts are *cash settled*. Since there isn't anything to deliver, the contract is settled by paying cash. The index must be regarded as a price. If a call option on the FT–SE 100 index is bought at an exercise level of 3700, then money will be made if the level rises to 3800 because 'the price' is higher. If the option buyer exercises, buying at 3700 and selling at 3800, then 100 points have been gained. To turn this into money, we settle at £10 per point per contract. For one contract, the gain is $100 \times £10 = £1000$. For ten contracts, it would be £10 000, and so on. The premium paid would have to be deducted in the usual way to arrive at the net profit. Alternatively, the option could be traded in the way described earlier.

A fund manager with a holding of £28m in shares might be nervous of a fall in the market but not nervous enough to actually sell the shares. If an assumption is made that their holding of shares will behave in a similar way to the FT–SE 100 (the correlation will be measured), then the manager could buy put options on the index contract. If the market falls, the puts will win some money to help compensate for the fall in the value of the portfolio.

How many contracts should the manager buy? Let us say that the index is at a level of 3500. If the contract is settled at £10 per point, then the whole index is $3500 \times £10 = £35\,000$. As this is one contract, the total number of contracts needed to cover a portfolio of £28m is:

$$\frac{£28m}{£35\,000} = 800$$

The manager buys 800 put options on the index at an exercise level of 3500 and pays the premium, say, £500 per contract or $800 \times £500 = £400\,000$ in total.

(The premiums are also quoted as *index points*. In this case 50 index points. At £10 per point, this gives us a premium of £500.)

If the index falls 10% to 3150, the value of the portfolio of £28m is reduced by £2.8m. However, the manager could exercise the put option, that is, selling at a level of 3500 and buying at a level of 3150, making 350 points. Bearing in mind that the manager bought 800 contracts and that they are settled at £10 per point, the gross gain is:

350 points × £10 × 800 contracts = £2.8m

From this we deduct the premium of £400 000 giving a net gain of £2.4m (ignoring dealing costs). This is a substantial compensation for the fall in the value of the portfolio of £2.8m. This is a classic *hedge*.

If the index rises 10% to 3850, the put option will expire worthless with the loss of the premium of £400 000. On the other hand, the value of the portfolio is now £30.8m not £28m, to help offset this loss. In particular, the manager is pleased that the portfolio was not liquidated due to nervousness about the market.

This is how options on an index are traded everywhere. At London's LIFFE, there are two FT–SE 100 options. Both have a maximum maturity of 1 year but one is an American and one a European option.

The Chicago Board Options Exchange trades the S&P 100 at $100 per point (American). The Chicago Mercantile Exchange trades the S&P 500 at $100 per point (European). The Paris MONEP trades the CAC 40 at FF200 per point with an European option as an alternative. The German DTB trades the DAX at DM10 per point (European) and so on.

In the US, the main markets for equity options are the Chicago Board Options Exchange, the New York Stock Exchange, the American Stock Exchange and the Philadelphia Stock Exchange.

In Europe, the main markets for equity options are shown in Table 10.6.

Table 10.6 *Main European markets for equity options*

Exchange	Country	No. of equities traded
Deutsche Termin Börse (DTB)	Germany (1990)	15
European Options Exchange (EOE)	Netherlands (1978)	41
London Traded Options Market (LTOM)	UK (1978)	70
Marché des Options Negociables de Paris (MONEP)	France (1987)	28
Swiss Options and Futures Exchange (SOFFEX)	Switzerland (1988)	14

Mention should perhaps be made of OM Sweden, which set up in 1985 and is very entrepreneurial. They help other exchanges to start, such as Madrid (MEFF) and Vienna (OTOB), and sell software and consultancy. They have linked with EOE, SOFFEX and OTOB to promote cooperation in selling each other's products. They also trade various Swedish options and futures through a London operation – OM London.

This is not an exhaustive list and option markets have now been set up in virtually every major European economy. The contract size of 1000 shares in LTOM reflects low UK share prices. In the Chicago Board Options exchange, it's 100 shares; in the MONEP, 100 shares; the DTB, 50 shares and SOFFEX, only five shares, reflecting the Swiss practice of high share prices!

TRADED OPTION: OTHER OPTIONS

Currencies

In this chapter so far, we have covered options on equities and equity indices. In Chapter 7, we discussed options on currencies and ways in which importers and exporters could hedge risk.

Having looked at the mechanics of options, let's return to the 'breakforward' option which we explained in Chapter 7. We showed that a buyer of dollars for sterling in 3 months might be offered a floor rate of $1.88 and a break rate of $1.91. If the spot rate in 3 months was less than $1.88, the importer will buy dollars at $1.88. If the spot rate later was better than $1.91, the importer could buy dollars at the spot rate less 3¢. Thus, if spot later were $1.98, the importer could buy dollars at $1.95 and thus benefit from an improvement in the rate while still getting substantial protection from any worsening. There is no cost to the importer.

The bank has bought a sterling put option at $1.91.

If the spot rate later is, say, $1.85 the bank exercises the option to buy dollars at $1.91 and sells them to the client at $1.88, making 3¢.

If the spot rate later is, say $1.98 the option is abandoned. The bank buys the dollars spot at $1.98 and sells them to the client at $1.95, again making 3¢.

The 3¢ cover the option premium and a profit margin. The client is happy with the blend of risk protection and profit participation and the bank makes a profit. A simple example of some of the clever ways in which options can be used.

Bonds

Options are also available on bonds. Many of the major exchanges trading equity options will also trade bonds.

Germany's DTB for example, trades the 5 year government bond and the 10 year government bond. London's LIFFE trades options on a range of government bonds – German, Italian, UK and Japanese. Here we have a situation where the German government 10 year bond is traded on both the DTB in Frankfurt and at LIFFE in London. To Frankfurt's annoyance, two thirds of the volume is traded in London.

In Paris, options on French government bonds are traded on the MATIF exchange. In the US, options on Treasury notes and bonds are traded on the

American Stock Exchange, Chicago Board of Trade and Chicago Board Options Exchange. Options on 3 month Treasury bills are dealt on the American Stock Exchange and the Chicago Mercantile Exchange.

These bond contracts work in a similar way to the options on shares we described earlier. They can be used to speculate or hedge risk.

For example, the option on the French government bond on the MATIF offers standard exercise price levels, such as 108, 109, 110, 111. The contract size is FFr500 000 and the premiums are expressed as a percentage of the bond's nominal value to two decimal places. Thus, the March call at 110 exercise price may have a premium quoted as 3.25. In money terms, this is 3.25% of FFr500 000 = FFr16 250. Each full 1% is FFr5000. If the bond price is 112, we can see that an exercise price of 110 has 2% of intrinsic value since it is the right to buy the bond at less than the market price. If the bond price rose to 114, the call buyer could make a profit of 4% = FFr20 000 *less* the cost of the premium. If there is some time left to expiry, the call option buyer may trade the option and make even more profit. If the market price is 114, the right to buy at 110 has 4.00 intrinsic value plus an element of time value. Since the contract size is FFr500 000 a bond dealer wishing to hedge a portfolio of FFr10m, will need to deal in 20 contracts.

(The above explanation has been simplified. At this point, we have ignored the complication that the bond is called *notional* and that the option is an option to have the futures contract. This is explained in Chapter 11.)

Interest Rates

The equity, currency and bond options covered above can go to delivery. That is, we can use the option to actually purchase or sell the relevant equities, currencies or bonds.

We also met index options, which cannot go to delivery as there is no real underlying product. These are called *cash settled*. Interest rate options are of this kind. We cannot use the contract to borrow or lend money at a given rate of interest. Just as the index option was settled on the basis of a value per point of index change, so the interest rate option is settled on the basis of a value per 0.01% change in interest rates.

For example, the Chicago Mercantile Exchange trades 3 month Eurodollar interest rates. The contract size is $1m. Thus, with an underlying sum at risk of $20m, the options user would be dealing in 20 contracts. Each 0.01% of interest rate change will gain or lose $25 per contract. The option user buys a call or a put on a given level of interest rates and pays a premium. If rates change to the profit of the option user by 0.50%, the gain is 50 × $25 = $1250 per contract.

In the case of index options, the price per point of FFr200 or DM10 is arbitrary. It is picked to produce a sensible contract size. In the case of the interest rate contract above, the $25 per 0.01% is not arbitrary but follows logically from the contract size of $1m. If the whole contract, that is 100%, has a value of $1m, then 0.01% has a value of $100. However, this is a 3 monthly contract, so the value is a quarter of this, that is, $25.

So far, the procedure for trading interest rates has seemed quite straightforward. The level of interest rate for 3 month Eurodollars is regarded as a price, like any other, and we either buy cheaper than we sell or face buying dearer than we sell, in which case the option is abandoned. Each 0.01% of gain on the price level wins $25 for each contract traded. We can either use the contract to speculate or hedge interest rate risk.

There is, unfortunately, a complication. This relates to the pricing of the contract. We might expect to see prices like 3.50%, 5.00% or 8.00%. What the market actually does is subtract the desired rate of interest from 100 to arrive at the price level of the contract. Thus an interest rate of 4.00% trades as 96.00 and one of 8.00% trades as 92.00.

Let's look at the effect of this pricing:

Interest Rate	Contract Price		
10.00%	100 – 10%	=	90.00
9.00%	100 – 9%	=	91.00
11.00%	100 – 11%	=	89.00

Notice that as the interest rate goes *down* from 10% to 9%, the contract price goes *up* from 90.00 to 91.00. As the interest rate goes *up* from 10% to 11%, the contract price goes *down* from 90.00 to 89.00.

We met this reverse relationship before when we discussed long-dated bonds – interest rates down, bond prices up; interest rates up, bond prices down. The Chicago markets did start trading interest rates in the obvious way (in 1975). After a few weeks, however, the traders preferred to trade the contracts in the way we have just described. It suited bond dealers who were hedging risk and it suited the psychology of traders. After all, as a generalisation, higher interest rates are seen as bad news – equity and bond prices fall. It seemed logical that with higher interest rates, the contract price fell.

This means that the call/put logic we learned earlier must be reversed in the case of interest rate contracts. If you wish to gain from higher interest rates buy *put* options – the contract price will fall. If you wish to gain from lower interest rates, buy *call* options – the contract price will rise. Other than that, it's easy really!

Let's take an example. Suppose a US corporate has a $20m loan from the bank at floating rate and reviewed every 3 months. The rate is linked to Eurodollar LIBOR. Let us also suppose that the dates for the CME 3 monthly contracts coincide with the bank's rollover of the loan. The bank has just fixed the rate for 3 months based on Eurodollar LIBOR of 3.75%. The corporate believes that rates are due to rise and seeks a hedge using the CME contract.

As the contract size is $1m and the loan is $20m, they deal in 20 contracts. As they wish to gain if interest rates go up, they buy 20 *put* options for the next expiry at a level of 3.75%, that is, a contract price level of 100 - 3.75 = 96.25. The premium is quoted as 0.30 and also must be interpreted at $25 per 0.01 per contract, the way the contract is settled. Thus 0.30 = $750 per contract and the corporate bought 20 contracts, paying 20 × $750 = $15 000.

Assume that at the expiry of the contract the Eurodollar LIBOR rate is 4.75%. The bank notifies the client that the interest charge is 1% higher on the $20m loan for 3 months – an increase of $50 000.

At the CME, the contract price is 100 – 4.75% = 95.25. The corporate bought 20 put options at 96.25, that is, the right to sell at 96.25. The contract is exercised by selling at 96.25 and buying at 95.25, a profit of 1% for each of 20 contracts. Since 0.01% = $25 the gain is:

100 × $25 × 20 contracts = $50 000

Deducting the premium of $15 000, the corporate has $35 000 to help meet the bank's extra interest charge of $50 000.

Suppose interest rates had fallen to 2.75%? The CME contract is not profitable and will be abandoned for the loss of the premium of $15 000. However, the bank notifies the corporate of a reduced interest charge for 3 months of $50 000. The corporate has bought protection from higher rates but can still gain if they fall.

This is the essential character of options to which we referred in Chapter 7 on foreign exchange. It is worth repeating.

The option purchase protects against a deterioration in the rate but the option buyer can still benefit from an improvement in the rate. There is a cost – the premium.

(Again, the complication that the CME contract is an option to have the future has been ignored.)

OPTION STRATEGIES

The experts in the option market will not content themselves with one position, such as buying a call at a particular exercise price and expiry but will combine several positions in order to carry out complex strategies.

For example, in the case of GEC in equity options above, we might buy both a call *and* a put on the exercise price of £1.80 for July expiry. If the share price rises we win, if it falls we also win. Well, in principle at least. The problem is that two premiums have been paid. The call premium is 24 and the put might be 18, that is, 42 in total. Having paid 42 for a £1.80 call, the price must go up to £2.22 (£1.80 + 42) to break even and that ignores dealing costs. Having paid 42 for a £1.80 put, the price must fall to £1.38 (£1.80 – 42) to break even, In other words, this is a strategy for a very volatile situation. A sharp share movement is expected, either up or down. It might be that there is a takeover bid struggle. The bid will either fail and the victim's share price fall sharply or the bidder will come back with a higher offer and the opposite will happen.

The most dangerous situation for the buyer is if the price remains stable at £1.86. The call option will be worth 6p and the put will expire worthless. The loss is 42 – 6 = 36: for a single 1000 share contract, £360 lost out of the premium of £420. (This has ignored *trading* the option prior to expiry in order to cut the loss and take advantage of remaining time value in the premium.)

This is quite a well known strategy called the *straddle*. The straddle buyer expects a volatile situation; the straddle writer thinks they are wrong.

Another strategy might be to buy the July £1.80 calls and write the July £2.20 calls. If the share price goes over £2.20 later, we have bought a call and also sold one at this level and so no further gain can be made, the purchase and sale will cancel out. However, we have offset the 24p premium for the £1.80 call by receiving the premium of 7p when we wrote the £2.20 call. Our net cost for a 1000 share contract is 24 – 7 = 17p per share or £170 instead of £240 had we simply bought the £1.80 call alone. We have reduced our possible loss from £240 per contract to £170 per contract and brought the break even point down from £1.80 + 24 to £1.80 + 17. What we gave up to achieve this was any profit above a later share price of £2.20.

This strategy is called the *bull spread*. We give up some of our unlimited profit potential in order to cut cost and risk. It has become so popular that the Chicago Market offers this embedded in the option product. If we are pessimistic about GEC, we do the opposite and buy the £1.80 put but write the £1.40 put – a *bear spread*.

There is no end to the permutations and variations on this theme. There are books on option strategies which will list a figure in excess of 50 possible strategies. Often they take their name from the shape of the graph showing the potential profit and loss from future changes in the market price, for example, the forked lightning, Mexican hat, Mae West, condor, butterfly and many others.

Look at all the variables there are to play with:

❑ Number of contracts
❑ Calls/puts
❑ Buy/write
❑ Exercise prices
❑ Expiry dates.

Computers are an essential tool to carry out the necessary calculations, produce the profit/loss graphs and control the total exposure contained in a trader's book of option deals.

Unfortunately, the activities of Nick Leeson, the Baring's derivatives trader who is alleged to have lost £860m and bankrupted the bank, has led many people to believe that derivatives trading is all about gambling.

It would be quite wrong to regard it all as simply sophisticated gambling. Risk management is a key topic today and options make their contribution. The description in Chapter 7 shows the ingenious use of options by banks to provide situations which are attractive to importers and exporters and which yield the banks a profit as well. Another possible tool is the *future* transaction, and that's the one which will be covered in Chapter 11.

SUMMARY

The users of derivative products are speculators, hedgers and arbitrageurs. The key products are *options* and *futures*. All the others (like FRAs and swaps) are simply variations on the same theme.

An option gives the buyer the right, but not the obligation, to buy or sell financial instruments or commodities at an agreed price and at an agreed future date or time period.

Options can be purchased on a trading exchange or over the counter. The exchange has the advantage of the protection of the *clearing house*, but the OTC market will more easily tailor a product to suit the user's needs.

Options to buy a given product at a later date are *calls*. Options to sell are *puts*. There are *buyers* of options and *writers* (sellers).

The price of the option is the *premium*, the price of the product at which the option buyer can exercise is the *exercise* or *strike price*. Options can also be *traded*.

The option buyer cannot lose more than the premium, the option writer cannot gain more than the premium.

To protect against default, the clearing house asks option writers for *initial margin* and, each day, *variation margin*.

If the option to buy or sell is at a price more favourable than the market price, the option is said to have *intrinsic value*. The balance of the premium is *time value*, which will fall as the expiry date approaches.

Trading the option will be more profitable than exercising if the option has time value.

A small percentage change in the price of the underlying asset leads to a large percentage change in the premium. This is *gearing*.

The premium is based on the past performance of the share price. The more volatile the performance, the higher the premium.

Options at a price more favourable than the market price are said to be *in the money*. If the price is less favourable than the market, they are *out of the money* and if the price is the same as the market they are *at the money*.

There are options on equities, equity indices, bonds, currencies, interest rates and commodities.

Combining option positions leads to options strategies such as a *straddle* or *bull spread*.

11 Financial Futures

Background

Transactions very similar to options and futures contracts today have existed in commodity markets for hundreds of years. There was an astounding Dutch tulip bulb mania in the 17th century. As tulips became more and more fashionable, people bought tulips several months in advance of the harvest. As the price went up, the contracts at the old prices were more valuable and could be sold to other people without waiting to take delivery at harvest time. In the end, the government had to step in when more tulips had been bought than were actually in the ground and several people made large losses.

Commodity prices fluctuate and where there are fluctuations, we find speculators and hedgers. The harvest may be good or bad and the product is only available once per year anyway. It would be natural to buy or sell ahead of the harvest. As prices went up or down, some of these contracts became more valuable and could be sold on to other people.

Metals are not crops but prices do fluctuate and it takes some time to receive a consignment from overseas. The London Metal Exchange's 3 month contract came into use after the Suez Canal was opened and metals like copper and zinc could be shipped in 3 months.

The largest commodity markets in the world settled down in Chicago at the Mercantile Exchange and the Board of Trade. It was here too, that the modern futures contracts were developed.

Before looking at the mechanism of futures as opposed to options, let's look again at the hedging technique.

Hedgers vs Speculators

A hedger is at risk if a given potential price movement happens. Hedgers seek to create a profit from this price movement in another market so as to create a gain in partial compensation for the loss.

A sugar dealer may have sold sugar short for future delivery. That is, the dealer hasn't yet bought the sugar to meet these contracts. If the price of sugar goes up before the purchase is made, a loss will occur.

Let's look at the hedge diagrammatically in Figure 11.1.

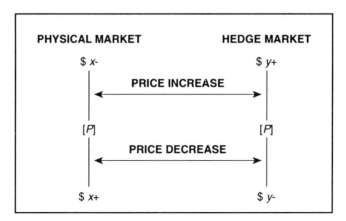

Figure 11.1 *Structure of a hedge*

If a given rise in the price of sugar will lose $x in physical trading, the sugar dealer could buy call options on sugar contracts at the Chicago Coffee, Sugar and Cocoa Exchange. This will create a profit of $y to, at least, offset the loss of $x in physical trading.

If the price of sugar falls, the dealer will have lost money on the call option but will be delighted because, having sold sugar short, even more profit is made on physical sugar trading. This explains why some traders with large losses may walk off the floor of the futures or options exchange and seem to be smiling. They must be hedgers. The price movement they feared hasn't happened. Speculators, of course, will have genuinely lost money.

This is a simple but most important principle, often misunderstood. It's worth repeating:

> *If hedgers lose money in the hedge market, they must make money in the market being hedged because the price movement they feared has not happened.*

We will find that futures, unlike options, involve unlimited risk. For the reason just explained, hedgers can accept this risk. Indeed, the bigger the loss on the futures hedge, the bigger the offsetting gain in the physical market.

There is another important principle – who is on the other side of the hedge? It may be another hedger but one whose position is the opposite – someone who will lose money if the price of sugar goes *down*, not up. This means that whatever happens to the price, both will get the hedge they are looking for. The broker will make a living, the exchange will make a profit and everybody goes home happy.

In financial markets, people are too quick to claim that it must be what they call a 'zero-sum game' – that is, what someone wins, someone else must lose. This is sometimes the case, but by no means always. There are usually plenty of opposite hedgers.

Those with loans at floating rate are hoping interest rates will go *down*. Those with investments at floating rate are hoping interest rates will go *up*.

It all seems too good to be true, and it is. The problem is that there won't be the same value of opposite positions except by a miracle. The hedger wants to do a deal and no one wants to say 'yes' or, at least, not at a reasonable price. That's where speculators come in. They provide the trading liquidity, so that trade hedgers can reduce the risk and do the deals they want. Usually, they are called *locals*, a term from the Chicago Markets, where more than half the membership is locals. Even the conservative London Metal Exchange, where no one can be a member unless they physically trade metals, agree in their literature that speculators play an essential role in providing liquidity. It's a new light on a term that most people regard as being totally pejorative.

Commodity Futures

A futures transaction provides an alternative to an option as a way of hedging risk. Its characteristics are different. A futures contract is a commitment to buy or sell a given quantity of an underlying product by a given date in the future at a price agreed now.

Let's note that a futures transaction is a *commitment,* not an option. If the price moves the wrong way, the option buyer can abandon the contract. As this is a privilege, a premium is paid. A futures contract cannot be abandoned in this way. Since no privilege is involved, no premium need be paid. For the same reason, a futures contract is riskier.

Options had calls, puts, buyers and sellers. Futures contracts only have buyers and sellers. To that extent, they are simpler.

Our sugar trader, worried about the price of sugar going up, could take a futures position in white sugar on the above-mentioned Chicago exchange (or the exchange known as the LCE in London).

Let us say that the trader commits to buy 100 tonnes of sugar by the next expiry date at $250 per tonne.

It is clear that if the price of sugar goes up to $280 a tonne, a contract that can buy at $250 a tonne has value and can create profit. That is not difficult to grasp but what people do find hard to understand is that the above trader hasn't the slightest intention of buying any sugar!

What happens then if sugar rises to $280 a tonne? The trader *closes the position* with the opposite contract – the trader commits to *sell* 100 tonnes of sugar by the next expiry date at $280 per tonne. The contracts are not settled in sugar but on the price difference of $30 a tonne, that is, our trader has gained $100 \times \$30 = \$3000$. This is to offset the trading loss which will result from having sold sugar short and being obliged to buy physical sugar at a higher price.

People tend to ask at this point – but what happens to the sugar? They have a vision of someone at expiry date trying to handle all the sugar that no one seems to want.

Let's realise that no one can contract to buy sugar unless someone contracts to sell. Equally, no one can contract to sell unless someone contracts to buy. If everyone closes their position with the opposite contract later (as we described above) there isn't anybody left at expiry, nor can there be.

If the sugar trader did not close the position, they would indeed buy 100 tonnes of sugar at $250 a tonne. But if they did remain open at expiry as a buyer, there must also be a seller with an open position. If there are three buyers left, there will be three sellers and so on.

The sugar is only the means to the end – the hedge or speculation. Either way, with the occasional exception, cash settlement is quite acceptable.

The fact that the contract *can* go to delivery, however, is crucially important. It means that the price of sugar in the futures exchange must relate to the real price of sugar. If it was cheaper, traders would use the futures exchange to buy it and sell it at profit in the cash market – arbitrage.

The contract is not an option, and we see the difference if we assume that sugar were to fall in price to $220 a tonne. If this were an option, the contract would now be abandoned – there is no point in buying sugar at $250 in order to sell it at $220. As a futures contract, the trader is committed to buy at $250 a tonne. The position is closed out by later entering the opposite contract to sell 100 tonnes of sugar at $220 a tonne, losing $3000.

This loss is not a problem. As the price of sugar has fallen, the short position in the physical sugar market is even more profitable as sugar can be purchased much more cheaply than it was sold. As we observed earlier, for the hedger a loss in the hedge market must mean a gain in the market being hedged.

Notice the symmetry in the futures contract – a rise in price of $30 a tonne gained $3000, a fall in price of $30 a tonne lost $3000. Options are not symmetrical because, when the price moves the wrong way, the contract is abandoned.

Finally, we now have two terms – forward and futures – which ought to mean the same, but don't.

❑ *Forward* is buying or selling for actual delivery at a future date at a price agreed now
❑ *Futures* is similar to forward, but usually there is no intention to take or make delivery; later, the position will be closed with the opposite contract and settled in cash.

Forward is for those who want the physical commodity, futures for those who are speculating or hedging and happy with cash settlement.

Thus, we need futures exchanges where everyone realises what the end objective is. There will be formal contract sizes, fixed delivery dates and the guarantee offered by the clearing house. The latter will take margin (deposits) from *both* parties as both are at risk. All contracts are legally with the clearing house. *Initial margin* is paid with the first contract. If the contract moves into loss, extra margin, called *variation margin*, is debited on a daily basis but if the contract moves into profit, variation margin is credited. The major players will have what is, in effect, a bank account with the clearing house. The locals will arrange to clear with someone who is a full clearing member.

Financial Futures

If options and futures are essentially driven by price volatility, the only surprise is that it took so long to be applied to financial contracts. Looking at interest rates, currency rates, equity prices, equity index levels and bond prices, there is huge volatility and also huge risk for many of the parties involved.

As we have observed, a market in futures on currency rates began in the CME with the collapse of the Bretton Woods system. Options and futures on financial contracts spread to the CBOT, the CBOE, New York and Philadelphia in particular.

In Europe, the EOE opened in Amsterdam in 1978 and London's LTOM in the same year. LIFFE opened in London in 1982. Then came the Paris MATIF in 1986, the Paris MONEP in 1987, the Swiss SOFFEX in 1988 and the German DTB in 1990.

As it has the biggest spread of international contracts in Europe, let's look at LIFFE – the London International Financial Futures Exchange (now legally the London International Futures and Options Exchange Ltd due to the merger with the London Traded Options Market – LTOM – but still calling itself LIFFE).

There are three types of contract – bonds, interest rates and an equity index. There are futures on them all and options in some cases. As we will see, they are options to have the futures contract. The contracts are listed in Table 11.1.

(The German 'Bund' is the 10 year Bundesanleihen.)

The international nature of the exchange can be seen not only from the list of contracts but from the fact that the most popular contract is the German government 'bund' contract. The top contracts at LIFFE in 1996 were:

❏ German government 'bund'
❏ Euromark interest rate
❏ Short sterling interest rate
❏ Gilts
❏ Italian BTP.

Other than the FT–SE 100, the options are options to have the futures contract. This doesn't make any difference if the buyer is trading the option but any exercise is into the futures contract. A key difference between this and a direct option is that, in the case of the direct option, having used (say) a call option to purchase the product, it can be sold at the market price. The seller of the option would have to purchase the product. If it is an option to have the futures, the buyer finds themself the buyer of the futures contract (a 'long futures' position). This can be left to go to delivery. The seller of the option is now the seller of the futures contract (a 'short futures' position). However, if they don't wish to physically sell the products they have time to close their position by buying the contract and letting someone else go to delivery. In the case of a direct option, they would have no choice.

Table 11.1 *LIFFE contracts, April 1996*

Contract type	Individual contract	Futures	Options
Bonds	Gilts	Yes	Yes
	German 'Bund'	Yes	Yes
	Italian BTP	Yes	Yes
	Japanese Govt	Yes	No
Index	FT–SE 100	Yes	Yes
Interest Rates	Sterling	Yes	Yes
(Three month)	Eurodollar	Yes	Yes
	Euromark	Yes	Yes
	Euroswiss	Yes	Yes
	Eurolira	Yes	No
	Ecu	Yes	No
	Euroyen	Yes	No

Source: LIFFE.

From the last remarks, the reader will realise that in some cases, the contracts can go to delivery if the position is not closed out. The gilts contract size is $50 000. A buyer of 20 contracts can let the position go to delivery and buy £1m of gilts at the agreed price. All the bond contracts except the Japanese Government bond can go to delivery in this way. Prices will be kept in line with cash market prices or arbitrage will take place.

The FT–SE 100 can't go to delivery (as there isn't anything to deliver) and the interest rate contracts can't go to delivery either, they can't be used to borrow money at an agreed rate of interest. This raises two interesting points. Since the contract can't go to delivery, what happens if a buyer *doesn't* close the position with the opposite sale? For the same reason, how do we know the price will relate to that of the underlying product in the cash market?

Any buyer or seller who doesn't close the position is automatically closed by the clearing house as the contract can't go to delivery. If the buyer or seller is letting the contract go to delivery, they don't need to take any action as the position will be closed for them.

The problem of correlation with the market price is solved by the convention that the expiry price is always the market price. The expiry price of the FT–SE 100 is the average of the 21 Stock Exchange FT–SE 100 values between 10.10 a.m. and 10.30 a.m. on the expiry day. The expiry price of the short sterling interest rate contract is the average of the sterling LIBOR rate of 16 named banks at 11.00 a.m. on the expiry day.

Index Futures

In Chapter 10, we discussed options on share indices – S&P 100, FT–SE 100, CAC 40, DAX and similar indices. Futures contracts are also available and make a good starting point, as we've already met options on the indices.

The futures contract is a commitment and there is no premium to pay, only margin to the clearing house.

An insurance company investment manager may be planning to sell £35m of shares in 3 weeks to meet claims for storm damage. The manager does not wish to sell at the moment as market conditions are poor. The worry about waiting, however, is that the market may fall in the next 3 weeks and the same quantity of shares raise less than £35m.

The answer may be a full hedge using the futures contract on the FT–SE 100 contract. This is a way of locking in to today's index level without actually selling the shares.

The first question is – how many contracts? Cash settlement is based on £25 per point. If the index is 3500 then the whole index is valued at $3500 \times £25 = £87\,500$. Since the value of shares to be hedged is £35m, then the number of contracts is:

$$\frac{£35m}{£87\,500} = 400$$

The fund manager sells 400 contracts for the next expiry period. The first complication is that although the stock exchange index is 3500, the figure in the trading pit may be, say, 3510 (reflecting supply and demand, market expectations and certain technical factors). So our manager has 400 contracts to 'sell' the index at 3510.

Three weeks later the market is down 10% at 3150. The manager sells the shares at this level. For the same quantity of shares that might have been sold 3 weeks earlier, £31.5m is received not £35m, a loss of £3.5m.

The position in the LIFFE exchange is now closed. If the contract in the pit is being traded at a level of, say, 3170, the position is closed by buying 400 contracts at 3170. The gain is:

Sell contracts at	3510	
Buy contracts at	3170	
Gain per contract	340	points

The contract is cash settled at £25 per point, a gain of £25 × 340 = £8500. For 400 contracts, the total gain is 400 × £8500 = £3.4m. Thus, waiting 3 weeks lost £3.5m on the share sale but the LIFFE contract gained £3.4m.

An initial margin was paid of £2000 per contract and thus £2000 × 400 contracts = £800 000. However, as this was only a deposit to cover possible loss, this sum is returned. In addition, one can usually negotiate interest on initial margin.

There will be brokers' costs to pay and a fee to the clearing house. These might be about £4 per contract or a total of £4 × 400 = £1600 in this case.

If the index rose in the 3 week period, the contract cannot be abandoned, as in the case of options. If the index rose 10% to 3850, the futures position is now loss making. If the pit level is 3850, the position is now closed by buying 400 contracts at 3850. It is the opposite of the previous case:

Sell contracts at	3510	
Buy contracts at	3850	
Loss per contract	340	points

The total loss is:

$$\text{£25 per contract} \times 340 \text{ points} \times 400 \text{ contracts} = \text{£3.4m}$$

We commented before on the essential symmetry of the futures contract. A fall in the index traded of 340 points gains £3.4m but a rise of 340 points loses £3.4m. Unlike options, the futures contract faces potentially unlimited loss. However, we are not talking here of a speculator but a hedger. When the investment manager sells the shares, the market is up 10% and the shares are sold for £38.5m not £35m. The gain of £3.5m offsets the loss of £3.4m on the futures contract. This is the point we made earlier in the chapter. For a hedger, a loss on the futures means a gain in the physical market being hedged.

Note one important point. Although the manager was protected against loss arising from a market fall, no profit can be made from a rise in the market.

Let's spell out this essential element in futures, as opposed to options:

Futures give the user protection from an adverse price movement but they cannot benefit from a favourable movement. Risk is unlimited but there is no premium to pay.

The manager could give up some of the protection to allow room for a gain should the market rise. Instead of selling 400 contracts, 200 could have been sold.

The effect would be that a loss of £3.5m due to a 10% market fall would be offset by a futures gain of only £1.7m. However, it follows that a gain of £3.5m due to a 10% market rise would be offset by a futures loss of only £1.7m.

The manager has a range of choices varying from not hedging a position at all right up to an attempted 100% hedge.

One final point. In the above case, there is an implicit assumption that the manager's mix of shares will behave in the same way as the market, that if the market fell 10% so would the mix of shares the manager is selling. It's not an unreasonable assumption but it won't be left to chance. Using computer techniques the manager measures the correlation between the volatility of the shares in the portfolio and the volatility of the FT–SE 100 – its called the *beta factor*. If the shares move in the same way as the index, the beta is 1.0. If the shares move by 90% of an index movement, the beta is 0.9. If the shares move by 110% of an index movement, the beta is 1.1. The number of contracts traded will be adjusted by the beta factor.

Bond Futures

In principle, bond futures are not difficult. The US Treasury bond contract in Chicago, for example, is based on an underlying value of $100 000. Like gilts, the smallest price movement, or tick, is $\frac{1}{32}$. If the contract is £100 000, then 1% = $1000 and $\frac{1}{32}$ = $31.25. If ten contracts are sold at a level 10 ticks higher than they were bought then there is a gain of:

$$10 \text{ ticks} \times \$31.25 \times 10 \text{ contracts} = \$3125$$

The contract need not be closed out but left to go to delivery. Certain days are *delivery days*. In the case of the Treasury bond contract and gilts, it's any business day in the delivery month. In the case of the German government 'bund' contract, it's the tenth calendar day of the delivery month (if a working day). The decision as to which day is delivery day is made by the *seller*.

The principle, then, is not difficult but the practice is more complicated. Most bond futures contracts are based on a *notional* bond – that is, one that doesn't exist. Newcomers will find the idea of trading in a bond that doesn't exist very strange but the market takes it in its stride. The exchange makes available a list of bonds which can be delivered. The Treasury bond is an 8% coupon bond as the unit of trading. Delivery can be made from a list of actual bonds with 15 years left to maturity. If one of these is a 10% bond, a 10% bond is inherently more attractive than an 8% bond and has a better price. The exchange makes available a *conversion factor* which calculates the sales value which must be used for delivery purposes. If the contract is for an 8% bond with $100 000 nominal value, then a 10% bond can deliver $100 000 nominal to meet the contract specification but receive a higher price. There will be one bond in the list which is cheapest to deliver. The price in the trading pit will be based on this *cheapest to deliver* bond – if not, arbitrage between this and the cash market will take place. For example, someone will buy the underlying bonds, sell the futures contract at the current price level and actually deliver the bonds at a profit.

As a result, the list of bonds available for delivery is significant and the exchange will make changes from time to time. In October 1992, for example, LIFFE produced a new list of deliverable bonds for the gilt contract from June 1993, reducing the list from nine existing bonds to four. Problems had been caused by the fact that the cheapest to deliver bonds were in some fairly illiquid high coupon stocks. Bonds selling above par can create problems due to capital loss at redemption.

Interest Rates

The interest rate contracts create valuable opportunities for those at risk from interest rate changes to hedge that risk. The LIFFE contracts offer short sterling, Eurodollar, Euromark, Euroswiss franc, Eurolira, Ecu and Euroyen interest rates. 3 month French franc interest rates based on PIBOR are traded at the Paris MATIF (Marché à Terme International de France and interest rates based on FIBOR at the German derivatives exchange (DTB) in Frankfurt).

Interest rate contracts are cash settled – they cannot go to delivery. At expiry, any open positions are closed by the clearing house at the expiry price, which is always the market price. As we said in Chapter 10, the pricing of the contract is based on subtracting the implied rate of interest so that, for example, 10.00% is traded as 90.00.

The normal rule with futures is that the contract is bought in the first instance if a gain is to be made from a price increase. If a gain it is to be made from a price fall, the contract is sold in the first instance. If a hedge is involved, then buying the contract is the *long hedge* and selling the contract is the *short hedge*.

Once again, interest rate contracts reverse the logic. To gain from a price increase, we *sell* the contract (because, if the price goes up, the contract level will fall). To gain from a price decrease, we *buy* the contract (because if the price goes down, the contract level will go up).

In Chapter 10, we used the example of a corporate with a $20m loan at floating rate related to Eurodollar LIBOR and reviewed every 3 months. To hedge interest rate risk, put option contracts were bought. The effect was that, when interest rates went up, the $50 000 extra bank bill was offset by a gain of $35 000 on the option contract. When interest rates went down, the $50 000 fall in the bank bill was only offset by the loss of the premium at $15 000. The option buyer still benefited.

Let's look at a futures hedge in the same circumstances. To keep it simple, we will assume that the interest rate level traded in the pit is the same as current real interest rates (since this was the assumption with the interest rate contract, we need to be consistent).

As the loan is $20m and the contract size on LIFFE is $1m, then the corporate needs to deal in 20 contracts. As they wish to gain from an interest rate rise, they sell 20 contracts for the next expiry at a level of 3.75%, that is, a contract price level of 100 – 3.75 = 96.25. No premium is paid but the initial margin is $500 per contract, so 20 × $500 = $10 000 is paid to the clearing house.

As before, we assume that at the expiry of the contract, the Eurodollar LIBOR rate is 4.75%. The bank notifies the client that the interest charge is 1% higher on the $20m loan for 3 months – an increase of $50 000.

At LIFFE, the contract price is 100 – 4.75% = 95.25. The corporate's position is closed by buying 20 contracts at 95.25. The position is:

Sell 20 contracts	@	96.25
Buy 20 contracts	@	95.25
Gain per contract		1.00

Each 0.01% is settled at $25 so the gain is:

100 × $25 × 20 contracts = $50 000

There is no premium to deduct, so the bank's extra $50 000 interest is met by the gain of $50 000 on the LIFFE contract (in the best of all possible worlds). As there was no premium to deduct, the futures contract has so far worked out better.

But what happens if interest rates fall to 2.75%? The bank notifies the corporate of a reduced interest rate charge for 3 months of $50 000.

At LIFFE, the contract price is 100 – 2.75% = 97.25. The position is closed by buying 20 contracts at 97.25. The position is:

Sell 20 contracts	@	96.25
Buy 20 contracts	@	97.25
Loss per contract		1.00

The loss is:

100 × $25 × 20 contracts = $50 000

This is, of course, the symmetry in futures. A rise in interest rates of 1% gains $50 000, a fall in interest rates of 1% loses $50 000. The result is that the corporate does not gain from the fall in interest rates as the reduced interest rate bill is offset by the loss on the futures contract. Here options gained, as the contract was abandoned when the interest rate fell for the loss of the premium, allowing the corporate a net gain from the interest rate reduction.

Currency Futures

We commented in Chapter 7 on foreign exchange on the strength of the OTC market in currency futures. Currency options and futures closed in London in 1990. Very few are now traded in Europe. The EOE in Amsterdam trades a guilder/dollar contract, the Barcelona MEFF Renta Fija Exchange trades peseta/dollars and the French MATIF a growing range of currency contracts. The Dublin exchange IFOX (Irish futures and options exchange) traded an Irish pound/dollar contract but abandoned it in mid-1991. In the US, the main trading is at the PHLX and the CME.

Some of these contracts can go to delivery (EOE, PHLX, CME) while others can only be cash settled (MEFF Renta Fija).

The trading of the futures follows the lines we have explained in this chapter. The CME Deutschemark contract, for example, is based on DM125 000 as the contract size and is quoted at an exchange rate of dollars per mark. A tick is 0.01¢ and is valued at $12.50. A contract can be bought at a dollar/mark exchange rate of $.6160 and sold at $.6260 – a gain of 100 ticks or $1250 per contract traded. Contracts can be left to go to delivery if required.

Some Problems of Futures Exchanges

In general, corporates are not enthusiastic about use of futures exchanges. The contracts are standard sizes, so a small corporate with a loan of $800 000 finds the interest rate contract size of $1m inconvenient. The expiry dates of the contract are unlikely to coincide with real life needs. Margin calls upset cash flow calculations and no interest is paid on variation margin in credit. For interest rate and currency contracts, the banks offer an attractive range of OTC products, some of which we will meet in Chapter 12.

For banks themselves, however, the exchanges have one key advantage – the security of the clearing house. At a time when counter-party risk is a major worry, this is increasingly a key benefit.

For fund managers, too, the index contracts provide secure, liquid trading and the chance to carry out asset allocation smoothly. Suppose a fund has £100m in assets. A decision may be taken to decrease exposure to equities by 2% and increase exposure to gilts by 2%. With one phone call, the fund manager can sell FT–SE 100 index contracts to the value of £2m and buy gilts contracts to the same value. Over time and at leisure, the manager can progressively sell the equities, buy the gilts and close the futures position.

Open Outcry or Computers?

A major talking point at present is whether traders will continue to buy and sell in trading pits on a floor or whether the market will move to computerised order matching.

The large US markets are based on *open outcry* trading but the last European exchange to open on an open outcry basis was the Paris MATIF in 1986. The European Options Exchange (EOE), which has traded open outcry since 1978, decided in December 1992 that some contracts would continue to be traded open outcry but others by computer. The argument for open outcry is that its the quickest way to trade high value standardised contracts. With computerised trading, however, the expensive floor is no longer needed and a firm audit trail is produced making fraud more difficult. (In 1989, 47 traders were indicted for fraud in Chicago following an undercover investigation by the FBI.)

The signalling in the pits usually follows the Chicago practice. There are three variables:

❑ Number of contracts
❑ Buy or sell?
❑ Price.

As in foreign exchange, only the last two digits of price will be quoted. If the interest rate contract level is 92.55, the price will be '55'. If the trader is buying, the hand begins away from the face and moves back to the forehead. The price is shouted with the hand away from the face and the number of contracts at the forehead. A buyer of 10 contracts at 92.55 will yell:

'55 for 10'

If the trader is selling, the hand begins at the forehead and moves away, shouting the number of contracts first and the price second:

'10 @ 55'

If there are no takers, the price may have to be moved up to 56 or 57 until a counterparty yells 'sold'! The two traders fill in dealing slips, the trades are matched by computer and matched trades are sent electronically to the clearing house.

The Chicago pits are very busy with frenzied shouting and pushing. The classic story is of the trader who died but couldn't fall over because the pit was too busy. Later, other traders who had lost on deals, filled in slips and put them in his pocket, leaving it to his insurer to pay up!

Computer systems are more boring, being based on order matching electronically. There is a CME/MATIF/Reuters system called GLOBEX. This is being used when the exchanges are closed, enabling them to continue trading and cross time zones with Europe and Japan. The CBOT already operates an evening session and the floor at the PHLX is open 18 hours per day.

LIFFE in London has a unique computer system called 'Automated Pit Trading' (APT). This is used when the exchange is closed – usually from 4.30 p.m. to 6.00 p.m. – and during the day for the poorly traded Japanese government bond contract. It is not order matching but simulates trading in the pits with little icons on the screen representing each trader!

If computer systems become popular and widely used the speculation is whether they might be used during the day instead of open outcry. The Chicago die-hards say 'never' but, then, they would, wouldn't they?

Contract Volumes

The volumes in the major exchanges in 1996 are shown in Table 11.2.

Table 11.2   *Leading derivatives exchanges, 1996 volumes, million contracts*

	Total
CBOT	222
CME	177
LIFFE	165
DTB	77
MATIF	68

Source: Various derivatives exchanges.

However, the dominance of LIFFE is under threat. On 13 January 1993, it was announced that the MATIF and the DTB had agreed to link their markets in what was meant to prove to be a significant co-operation pact. By May 1996, however, not a lot of progress had been made. The French can trade the German contracts by putting a computer terminal in the office. The French contracts are open outcry and there has been fierce resistance to taking any off open outcry and onto the computer system.

SUMMARY

Futures trading began with crops which were only available once per year and whose price fluctuated.

Buyers and sellers might seek to reduce the risk of an adverse price movement by a *hedge*.

A futures contract is an agreement to buy or sell a product at a set price at a later date. Unlike options, however, it is a commitment. Speculators, therefore, are exposed to unlimited risk but hedgers can offset losses with profits on their physical positions.

Usually, futures contracts do not go to delivery. An opening contract to buy is closed by a later contract to sell; an opening contract to sell is closed by a later contract to buy. The position is cash settled. In contracts like equity indices and interest rates, delivery is not possible anyway.

A *forward* deal is one where the intention is to go to delivery.

A *futures* deal is one which is likely to be closed with the opposite and lead to cash settlement. They are traded on futures exchanges with set contract sizes, set expiry dates and the protection of the clearing house.

Futures exist on the same range of products as options although futures on equities are rare.

Many options contracts on futures exchanges are *options to have the future*.

Some exchanges use a trading floor and *open outcry*. Others use systems of order matching by computer.

12 Other Derivative Products

INTRODUCTION

All the derivative products which we shall describe in this chapter are essentially options and futures in another guise. They are not, however, traded on exchanges but are OTC products. In addition, as interest rates, the price of money, lie at the heart of the financial markets, they are all about controlling *interest rate risk*.

FORWARD RATE AGREEMENTS (FRAs)

To begin with, we must consider the term 'forward/forward'. This is an arrangement between two counterparties to borrow or lend an agreed sum of money at an agreed rate for an agreed period which will not begin until a future date. For example, *A* will lend *B* $1m at 5% for 6 months commencing in 6 months, called '6 against 12' or simply '6 × 12'.

It may be that a corporate needs a bank loan of $1m in 6 months and is worried about rates going up. They ask the bank to quote a rate of interest now for lending money in 6 months for 6 months. This is rather like an importer asking a bank to quote a rate for buying dollars against deutschemarks in 6 months. In foreign exchange, we argued that the bank could avoid risk by buying the dollars today and putting them on deposit for 6 months until needed by the client.

In the interest rate market, if asked to quote forward/forward, the bank could equally borrow money at today's rates and put it on deposit until needed by the client. In the above case, the bank will borrow money for 12 months, deposit it for the first 6 months and then lend it to the client for the remaining 6 months. The rate quoted will depend on:

❏   The bank's cost of borrowing and return from lending
❏   The yield curve: if positive, the bank borrowing for longer periods costs more than borrowing for short periods
❏   The reinvestment of the interest it earns on the money in the first 6 months.

This is how such deals were actually handled until the 1980s, when other techniques were developed. The banks are not keen now to quote these forward rates since the borrowing/lending uses up the bank's line of credit with other banks and also the line of credit with its own customers.

The *Forward Rate Agreement* (FRA) is the bank's answer to the request for the forward/forward deal.

The FRA is not about borrowing money, but about a future level of interest rates. The future level is compared to an agreed level and the agreement is settled on the difference between the two rates. The future level in the London market will be based on the LIBOR rate – in this case, Eurodollar LIBOR.

For example, the corporate arranges with a bank that the 'target rate' of interest for 6 months ahead is 5% on a notional principal of $1 million. If, in 6 months, interest rates are 5%, then nothing happens. If rates are 4%, the corporate pays the bank 1% of $1 million (but will have lower borrowing costs elsewhere). If rates are 6%, however, the bank pays the corporate 1% of $1 million to help offset their extra borrowing costs (see Figure 12.1).

This is 'accounting for differences', and has the advantage of less credit risk. The bank, for example, is not borrowing or lending $1 million, only accounting for the difference in rates from a target of 5%.

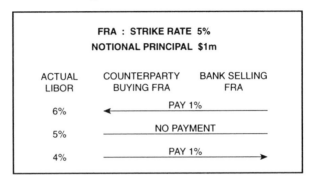

Figure 12.1   *Accounting for differences*

The corporate has fixed its rate for borrowing in 6 months in an indirect way. If rates go up, the corporate pays more for the money but is compensated for the extra cost by the FRA. If rates go down, the corporate will not benefit because the lower borrowing costs are offset by a payment under the FRA.

This line of explanation may well sound familiar. It's the same effect that was achieved by the interest rate futures transaction in Chapter 11. In selling the futures at 3.75%, the corporate was agreeing to settle on the difference between 3.75% and market rates at expiry. When rates were 4.75%, the corporate received 1% on the underlying contract value of $20m. When rates were 2.75%, the corporate paid the futures exchange 1% on the underlying $20m. The FRA is really an OTC future being arranged with a bank and not a futures exchange. It has the advantage of flexibility on both dates and amounts of money.

Typical FRA periods are '3 against 6' and '6 against 12'. This is because floating rates on loans and FRNs are revised at 3 month or 6 month intervals. A bank with a gap in its asset/liability management can thus close the exposure with an FRA. There will be a corporate market with corporates talking to their commercial banks for deals down to, say, $1m or £1m and a professional market, the banks between themselves, for typical sums from 50m to 100m and in sterling, yen, Swiss francs and deutschemarks.

How does the bank make a profit? The FRA is a product, like any other product, and sold with a bid/offer spread. Just as a market maker will buy shares and hope to sell them at a better rate, so the bank expects to buy FRAs at one rate and sell them at another. It will base the price for future interest rates on the deposit market yield curve or the prices of futures exchange contracts. At the time of writing, a '3 against 6' dollar FRA is quoted at 5.54/5.50. A bank will sell an FRA based on 5.54% but buy one based on 5.50%. If the rate at the 3 month date is 6%, the bank pays 46 basis points on the FRA it sold but receives 50 basis points on the one it bought. If rates are 5%, the bank receives 54 basis points on the FRA it sold but pays only 50 basis points on the one it bought (see Figure 12.2). Four basis points may not seem much for the administrative cost and the risk (*and* capital ratio for the risk) and it isn't. The market is very competitive and banks need to be totally efficient to make any money. As a result, the trader may choose not to offset the FRA with one in the opposite direction but believe they will receive more money than they will pay. This does, of course, now involve interest rate risk and risk limits must be set.

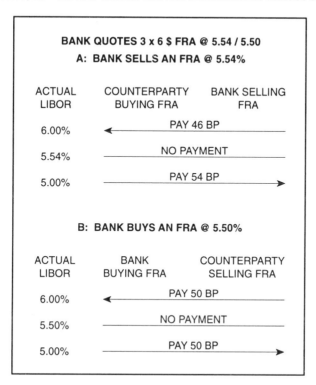

Figure 12.2 How the bank makes a profit from an FRA

(One technical point. With an FRA which is, say, in 3 months for 3 months, then the payment is made in *advance* of the second 3 month period. As a result, only the net present value is actually paid.)

It may be that an FRA buyer is unsure of the direction of interest rates. The FRA will protect against a rise in rates but no benefit will arise if rates fall. If this is unacceptable, the answer here is to pay for an *option* to have an FRA. If rates rise, the option to have the FRA is exercised. If rates fall the option is abandoned. (Simple, really!)

The FRA solves the problem of an interest rate risk for one future time, but what about risk over, say, 5 years? For this we turn to *swaps*.

SWAPS

Comparative Advantage

Interest rate swaps exploit what could be described as arbitrage opportunities, and in doing so create a market in which others can hedge or speculate on the movement of interest rates.

It begins with the 19th century economist, David Ricardo and his 'Theory of Comparative Advantage'. Ricardo argued that two countries could benefit from international trade even where one made all products more productively than the second.

Let's take two countries, *ABC* and *XYZ*, and two products, *A* and *B*. The product rates per hour for *A* and *B* in both countries are shown in Figure 12.3.

	ABC		*XYZ*
Product *A*	100	Product *A*	50
Product *B*	100	Product *B*	70

Figure 12.3   *International trade – comparative advantage*

Ricardo argued that country *ABC* should concentrate on producing product *A* and country *XYZ* concentrate on product *B* and then trade. This is because, while country *ABC* is superior in both *A* and *B*, it has a great *comparative advantage* in *A*. Country *ABC*, thus, produces all product *A* and exports the surplus to country *XYZ*. The latter produces all product *B* and exports the surplus to country *ABC*. Both countries gain as *ABC* exploits to the full its comparative advantage in producing product *A*. This will become clearer from a study of the corresponding examples from the financial markets (see Figure 12.4 and the accompanying explanation).

We translate this now to borrowing rates instead. The two products become fixed rate finance and floating rate finance. The two countries become two companies, *ABC* and *XYZ*. Investors' perception of risk is not the same in the fixed interest rate market as it is in the floating rate market. Thus, company *ABC* may be able to borrow more cheaply than *XYZ* at either fixed or floating rate but the difference is not the same – that is, there is a comparative advantage to be exploited.

Company *ABC* can raise fixed rate finance at 7% or floating at LIBOR (really wants floating rate funds).

Company *XYZ* has to pay 10% for fixed rate borrowing and LIBOR + 1% for floating rate funds (really prefers fixed rate financing).

ABC can borrow cheaper than *XYZ* in both fixed and floating rate markets but has greater comparative advantage in fixed.

Therefore:

ABC raises fixed at 7% but agrees to pay LIBOR to *XYZ*. *XYZ* borrows floating rate funds at LIBOR + 1% but agrees to pay 8% to *ABC* (Figure 12.4).

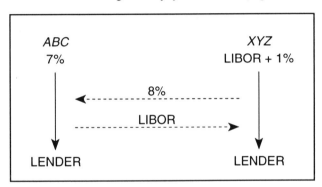

Figure 12.4 *Using the swap technique*

Thus:

ABC pays 7% fixed but receives 8% from *XYZ*. Pays LIBOR to *XYZ* but in effect is paying LIBOR -1% – less than if it borrowed at floating rate at LIBOR.

XYZ pays LIBOR + 1% but receives only LIBOR from *ABC*, thus costing *XYZ* 1%. Pays 8% to *ABC*, in effect paying 9% – but this is less than if it borrowed fixed at 10%. (This is another example of a technique that is not a 'zero-sum game'.)

ABC and *XYZ* are each saving 1% on their cost of borrowing by using the swap technique. This swap opportunity occurs because floating rate lenders do not distinguish between the credit standing of borrowers to the same degree as fixed rate lenders. We might imagine that if one borrower is AAA credit rating and one BBB, then the difference between the rates of borrowing, whether fixed or floating would be the same. In fact, this is not the case. If lesser rated credits want to borrow at fixed rate instead of floating, then the rate is not quite as attractive.

Interest Rate Swaps

In our example above, the difference in rates was a considerable exaggeration on a real life situation. This was in order to simplify a concept that always seems complex to newcomers. The principle is the same even if the real life difference is only a matter of a few basis points.

There are, therefore, two aspects to an interest rate swap. One is simply that one party agrees to pay a fixed rate on a notional principal sum of money for a period of time and the other agrees to pay floating rate. Unlike an FRA, which was only for one future time period, a swap is for several time periods ahead, for example, 6 monthly rate comparisons for say, 5 years.

The other element is a possible profit arising from the comparative advantage concept which we just described. Even without any 'profit' element, one party with a floating rate commitment may feel happier swapping into a fixed rate commitment.

The elements in the swap are:

❑ The fixed rate
❑ The variable rate
❑ The settlement periods
❑ The total maturity
❑ The underlying notional principal.

For example, the parties may agree that one pays 5.5% and the other pays Eurodollar LIBOR on a notional underlying principal of $50m. The swap is to last 5 years and the settlement periods are 6 monthly. That is, every 6 months 5.5% is compared with Eurodollar LIBOR and a net sum of money is paid over. If the difference was 1%, then 1% of $50m for 6 months is the sum to be paid over – $250 000. The money, however, is not in fact, paid over until the end of the 6 monthly period, not the beginning. That is because interest payments are paid in arrears. A bank, for example, sets the rate on an actual loan for 6 months at 5.5% but the interest is paid at the end of 6 months, not the beginning.

Making a Market in Swaps

How do these companies, *ABC* and *XYZ*, find each other? Obviously, with difficulty. So there is a role for banks to bring the parties together and take a piece of the action. In Figure 12.4, the bank could take 8% from *XYZ* and only pass on 7¾% to *ABC*. It could take LIBOR from *ABC* and only pass on LIBOR – ¼% to *XYZ*. *ABC* and *XYZ* will still profit from the deal but the bank now has ½% for its trouble.

The market began in 1982 and as it grew banks became prepared to carry out a swap just for one counterparty, pending finding another counterparty later. This is called a *warehouse* swap. The bank is prepared to 'warehouse' the swap until a counterparty can be found, in the meantime taking hedging action as we will explain later. It is called an 'unmatched swap'.

The swap, therefore, has simply become another product which the banks market with the usual bid/offer rates.

The bank may quote, for example, 5.80/5.75 for a 5 year dollar swap (Figure 12.5).

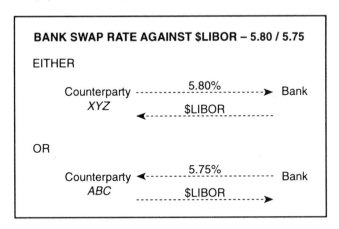

Figure 12.5 *Bank swap quotation*

If the bank stands in the middle between two counterparties (the matched swap), then the bank has no interest rate risk and a locked in 5 basis points profit. If LIBOR goes up, the bank pays more to counterparty *XYZ* but receives it from *ABC*. If rates fall, the bank receives less from *ABC* but pays less to *XYZ*. *XYZ* pays 5.80% to the bank and the bank pays 5.75% to *ABC*, keeping 5 basis points (Figure 12.6).

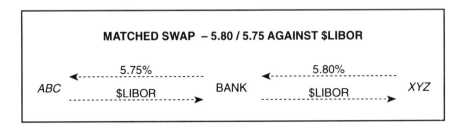

Figure 12.6 *Using matched swap*

The bank may have no interest rate risk but it does have counterparty risk. What if *ABC* or *XYZ* goes into liquidation and the bank is left with an unmatched swap? Under today's rules from regulators, capital must be provided for this risk.

In providing a market in swaps the banks are exposed to risk until they can find someone who wants to do a swap in the opposite direction. In the meantime they can adopt hedging strategies:

❏   If the bank is at risk to a *fall in interest rates* (because it has lent floating and borrowed fixed), then it will buy fixed interest securities, whose price will rise when interest rates fall.
❏   If the bank is at risk should *interest rates rise* (because it has borrowed floating and lent fixed), then it can hedge in the *futures* market by selling an interest rate future, giving the right to borrow at prevailing rates of interest. When interest rates rise this right becomes valuable and the bank will make a profit on the futures contract.

(Notice the language used above. The bank receiving LIBOR and paying 5.75% can be said to have *lent floating and borrowed fixed* (and vice-versa).) Other language used is a reference to the 'payer' and the 'receiver'. This always refers to the fixed rate element.

Actual market rates tend to fall between the rates quoted for an AAA borrower and a single A borrower for borrowing for given periods of time. If $, they are usually expressed as a given number of basis points over US Treasury bond rates for the fixed element. If £, they are usually expressed as a given number of basis points over the gilts rate. The variable rate is Euro or domestic LIBOR.

Users of Swaps

Assuming that a 5 year dollar swap rate is quoted as 5.80/5.75, who are the users of these swaps? We find that the market talks of *liability swaps* and *asset swaps*.

❏   Liability swaps are simply swaps for borrowers of money
❏   Asset swaps are simply swaps for lenders of money.

The treasurer has a bank loan based on $ LIBOR (see Figure 12.7). Worried that rates will rise, he does a swap, changing the floating rate bank loan into fixed rate by this indirect route.

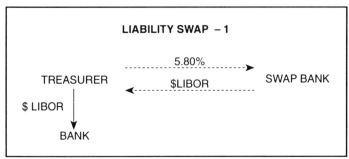

Figure 12.7   *Swap to change floating rate bank loan into fixed rate*

We can also envisage a situation in which a treasurer with a fixed rate loan could receive 5.75% and pay LIBOR, turning the fixed rate loan into floating rate. A further variation is possible. If the loan is, say, $100m, the treasurer can do the swap for only $50m – leaving half the money at fixed rate and half at floating (quite common).

Using the swap technique, a Eurobond issuer may not only change the fixed rate basis into floating but create a profit margin of 10 basis points due to the general comparative advantage concept (see Figure 12.8).

What the issuer may well do is equalise the fixed rate payment and receipt and use the profit margin to cut the LIBOR rate (see Figure 12.9).

The issuer agrees to receive 5.65% instead of 5.75% and to pay LIBOR - 10 instead of just LIBOR. What we say is that the issuer has achieved 'sub-LIBOR funding'.

The investor is receiving floating rate income based on $ LIBOR (either from a loan or FRN). Believing that rates will fall, the issuer swaps into a fixed rate return. We say that the investor has changed the FRN into a 'synthetic' fixed rate bond (see Figure 12.10).

Banks often buy fixed rate bonds from lesser rated corporates (that is, higher interest rates) to use for an asset swap to create floating rate income well above LIBOR (see Figure 12.11).

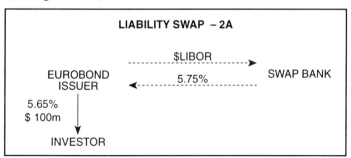

Figure 12.8 *Swap to change fixed rate bond into floating rate*

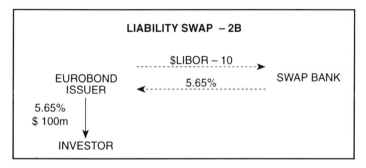

Figure 12.9 *Equalising the fixed rate payment and receipt*

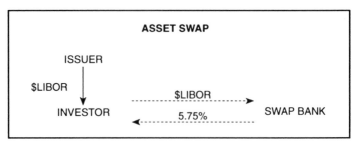

Figure 12.10   *'Synthetic' fixed rate bond*

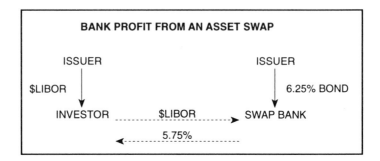

Figure 12.11   *Bank profit from an asset swap*

In Figure 12.11, the bank receives 6.25% from a bond but only pays 5.75% on the fixed leg of the swap. It also receives LIBOR and thus a total receipt of LIBOR + 50.

Swaps and Futures

Swaps are really a strip of futures or FRA contracts lasting over several years. They are, of course, OTC with all the flexibility that that involves. When the corporate sold an interest rate future at 3.75%, we saw that the effect was the same as the FRA based on 3.75%. In the same way, selling an interest rate future at 3.75% is choosing to borrow fixed and lend floating (the alternative language we used for swaps). It's a swap (or FRA) for a single time period only. Equally, the buyer of an interest rate future is choosing to borrow floating and lend fixed – the other side of the swap.

Because the language and terminology used in FRAs and swaps is different from that used for futures, newcomers think of them as essentially different products when they are really all variations on the same product. They therefore have the essential characteristic of futures – that a hedger can gain protection from an adverse rate movement but will not benefit from a favourable one.

Futures are for 3 month time periods ahead (although we could book all eight quarterly contracts for the next 2 years – called a 'strip' of futures). FRAs are for one time period ahead but not necessarily 3 months and, again, a strip of FRAs could be purchased or sold. For periods of 2 years or more, swaps are more attractive. Most swaps are in the range 2–10 years. However, the UK Halifax Building Society has issued a 25 year bond which is said to have been swapped into floating rate for 25 years!

Other Swaps

A swap buyer may want a swap but only wish to commence in, say, 6 months' time. This becomes the *forward swap*.

In 6 months' time, the forward swap buyer's view of interest rates may turn out to be incorrect. The buyer is, however, committed to the swap. Another possibility, therefore, is to pay a premium for an option to have the swap later (just like the option to have an FRA). This is called by a curious piece of jargon – the *swaption*.

It may be that the notional principal in the swap is not constant but on a 'reducing' basis. For example, a swap based on a notional principal of $10m for 5 years but the amount of the principal is reduced each year. This could apply when the swap backs a loan of which some of the principal is constantly being repaid or a bond for which a sinking fund is being accumulated to redeem the bond. This is called an *amortising swap*.

The notional principal at risk might also vary but up and down rather than on a declining basis. This is the *roller coaster swap*.

There are swaps in which both parties pay floating rate, but on a different basis. For example, one pays Eurodollar LIBOR and the other pays 3 month US Treasury bill rates. This is the *basis swap*.

A more complex variation (and very common in 1992) is for one party to pay Eurodollar LIBOR plus a premium and the other Euromark LIBOR. The assumption is that dollar rates, at historically low levels, will go up and mark rates, at historically high levels, will go down. A 5 year swap of this nature will be based on the market's view of these changes and this will be built into the premium. The swap user, however, may be backing a judgement that the market's view is wrong. What is new about this type of swap is that the user may wish to be paid or pay in dollars throughout, even if the mark rate is the higher one. The bank arranging this swap has to cope now with foreign exchange risk. This swap is the *diff* swap, that is, based on the difference between two rates.

CURRENCY SWAPS

The swaps market began with currency swaps. It may be that a US-based issuer wants French francs but is not well known to French franc investors. A French corporate or public body, well known in France, may want dollars but is not well known to dollar investors. The US issuer will have to pay a premium to raise French francs and the French issuer will have to pay a premium to raise dollars. The answer is for the US issuer to raise dollars, the French issuer to raise French francs and then swap the proceeds. This is the classic *currency swap*.

The first major case was in 1981, with the World Bank wanting a further Swiss franc issue and faced with paying a premium to persuade Swiss franc investors to hold even more World Bank paper. IBM wanted a dollar issue but faced the same problem. Salomon Bros arranged a swap. The World Bank raised the money in dollars and IBM raised the money in Swiss francs. Dollar investors were pleased to hold World Bank paper and Swiss franc investors were pleased to hold IBM paper. The two entities swapped the proceeds. On redemption (in 1986), they arranged to swap back at the same exchange rate.

In the meantime, IBM sent dollar interest payments to the World Bank who sent Swiss franc interest payments to IBM.

Again, as the market grew, banks took on unmatched deals and made a market in currency swaps. Sometimes, though, the bank can be lucky and match two investors coming to the market at the same time.

In September 1996, the European Investment Bank (EIB) and the Tennessee Valley Authority (TVA) came to the market at the same time. The EIB wanted 10 year D-marks and the TVA wanted 10 year dollars. However, the EIB could borrow in dollars 7 basis points less than TVA, but only 4 basis points less in D-marks. As a result, the EIB borrowed $1bn, the TVA borrowed DM1.5bn and they swapped the proceeds. It was a classic case of exploiting comparative advantage. In swapping directly, both parties also saved bid/offer spreads and reduced transaction costs.

CAPS, FLOORS AND COLLARS

Introduction

Sometimes, the user in this market may require protection in one direction only. For example, a corporate may seek protection from interest rates rising but seek to benefit should they fall. An investor, receiving money at floating rate, may seek protection from rates falling but seek to benefit should they rise.

This end objective can be achieved by interest rate options on trading exchanges. If the rate moves the wrong way for our market position, the option is exercised and compensation obtained. If the rate moves the right way for our borrowing/lending position, the option is abandoned and we benefit from better rates.

Exchanges, however, have drawbacks, as we have seen. The OTC market has responded with two flexible products to meet the above situations for borrowers and investors – the *cap* and the *floor*.

Caps

The interest rate cap sets a maximum level on a short-term rate interest rate. Buyers are compensated if the interest rate goes above a certain level (the strike level).

For example, the arrangement may be based on 3 months LIBOR and have a term of 3 years. The strike level is 5%, the revision of the rate is quarterly and the notional principal is $10 million. Thus, if LIBOR is 6% in 3 months, the seller pays the buyer 1% of $10 million for 3 months – say, $25 000 (see Figure 12.12).

If rates are 5% or less, nothing happens and the cap buyer can benefit from lower borrowing rates. The fee is, of course, the option premium. The OTC cap can not only offer the precise dates we require but it is a continuous arrangement, like a swap, and not just for one time period ahead.

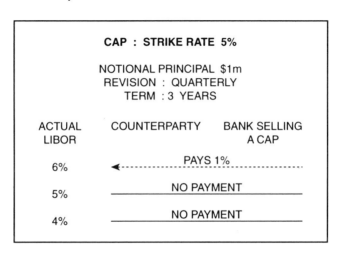

Figure 12.12 *Using the cap*

There are the usual variations on the theme that we associate with options. If the buyer is prepared to accept some interest rate risk, the strike rate in the above example could be chosen as 6%. This is 'out of the money' in options terms and the premium will be cheaper.

Floors

The interest rate floor is simply the opposite product. An investor, receiving income at floating rate, may buy a floor. This sets a minimum level to a rate of interest. The buyer is compensated if the market goes below this level (see Figure 12.13).

The terms could be exactly as described for the cap, but on the basis that payment is made if rates fall *below* the strike rate.

It may be that the user is fairly sure about interest rates for 1 year, but not thereafter. The cap or floor can be arranged to commence in 1 year's time – the *forward* cap or floor.

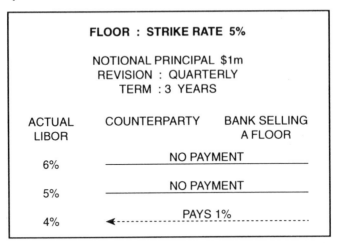

Figure 12.13   *Using the floor*

Collars

We will have seen from the above that the cap buyer pays a premium and receives payment if rates rise above a given level.

The floor seller receives a premium, but must make payment if rates fall below a given level.

Imagine simultaneously buying a cap at 6% and selling a floor at 4%.

The effect of this is shown in Figure 12.14.

The net effect is to lock into a band of rates – the *collar* – for the next 3 years.

If rates are between 6% and 4%, we borrow at the market rate. If rates rise above 6% we are protected. If they fall below 4%, we don't benefit. The effect of paying a premium and receiving one is that the cost is reduced. Rates can be chosen at which the two premiums are the same – the *no cost collar*.

This is an attractive device and very popular at the moment. All our other devices have turned around a given rate of interest. Here we select a band instead.

We have actually met this product before. It was in Chapter 7 on foreign exchange, and it was the 'cylinder' or 'collar' or 'range forward'. The future buyer of dollars will never have a worse rate than $1.85 per £ but never have a better rate than $1.95. It's just the same logic applied in a different market.

Caps, floors and collars are a series of interest rate options over a period of time. 2–5 years is the most popular range.

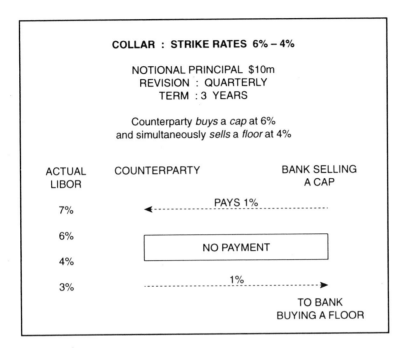

Figure 12.14 *Using the collar*

THE MARKET IN DERIVATIVE INSTRUMENTS

One of the most comprehensive surveys of the size of the market was carried out in the spring of 1995. Central banks and monetary authorities in 26 countries carried out a survey of the derivatives market activity in their local markets. The survey, coordinated by the Bank for International Settlements (BIS), is estimated to have covered about 90% of intermediaries active in the derivatives markets. It was particularly useful for the OTC market where previously rather general figures had been provided by the International Swap Dealers Association.

After adjustment for double-counting, the survey found that the notional amount of outstanding OTC contracts was $40.7 trillion. As the notional value can be a misleading figure, the gross market value (replacement cost and thus risk) was estimated at $1.7 trillion. (In May 1996, the figures were revised to $47.5 trillion and $2.2 trillion respectively.)

The survey also collected information on participants' exchange-traded derivatives business. This revealed a notional amount of $16.6 trillion outstanding in exchange-traded contracts. Unfortunately, double-counting could not be eliminated. The figures are valuable, however, in terms of the breakdown of the business.

An earlier BIS report in May 1992 estimated that in 1986 the underlying notional value of OTC instruments was $500 billion and of exchange-traded instruments was $583 billion. The 1995 survey revealed the extraordinary growth in the market.

An extract of the figures is shown in Table 12.1.

Table 12.1   Notional amounts of derivative contracts outstanding at end March 1995 in billions of US dollars

Market Risk Category	OTC	Exchange-Traded
Foreign exchange	13 153	120
Interest rates	26 645	15 674
Equity and stock indices	599	645
Commodities	317	142
Total	40 714	16 581

Source: BIS, Basle.

The OTC figures include forward and foreign exchange swaps except in the case of the UK. Of the swaps figures provided, currency swaps were $1974bn and interest rate swaps $18 283bn.

In the exchange-traded figures, futures were $12 762bn and options $3819bn. In interest rates and commodities, there are more futures contracts than options. In foreign exchange and equity and stock indices, the opposite is the case.

The growth in the market and the growth in sheer complexity has led the BIS and others to draw attention to the dangers of controlling the risks, and deficiencies in systems for controlling these risks.

To the usual counterparty and position risks we have to add legal risk and tax risk. The UK sterling swaps market was thrown into confusion by a decision that local authority swaps were illegal. Conflicting tax treatment in Australia and the US led to Westpac paying out an extra $80m in tax to the US authorities and cutting its dividend.

The outstanding example of the risk in derivative transactions was the collapse in early 1995 of the UK's oldest merchant bank, Baring Bros, alleged to be due to the activities of one trader, Nick Leeson. The bank's controls were woefully inadequate and management allowed one trader's activities to ruin the bank at a cost of £860 million. At Kidder Peabody, in the US, one trader, Joseph Jett, is alleged to have concealed losses of $350 million over a period of 2 years.

Corporates, too, have incurred losses – Allied Lyons, Codelco, Metallgesellschaft, Procter and Gamble and Gibsons Greetings Cards were well publicised examples.

The last two sued Bankers Trust and both settled out of court.

Perhaps we should not get this out of perspective. The banks lost enormous sums due to the LDC debt crisis. The bad debts of Crédit Lyonnais at the moment are estimated to total the equivalent of £6000 million. The banks are owed £8000 million by Eurotunnel and haven't a hope of getting back more than half. This makes Barings £860 million loss seem less significant! These losses were incurred in bank lending, which we've had for the last 600 years. There aren't too many weighty reports on the risk in bank lending and yet reports on derivative risk have been written not only by the BIS but by the IMF, Bank of England, General Accounting Office (US), Federal Reserve and the G30 group of bankers.

It's unfortunate that the intellectual effort required to gain an understanding of these products leads some people to dismiss it all as 'gambling'.

Suppose we have two corporates facing significant interest rate risk over the next 3 years. One buys certainty by doing an interest rate swap and electing to pay fixed. The other does nothing.

Who is gambling? Surely, it is the corporate that does nothing and leaves itself open to whatever volatility of interest rates comes along.

The paradox about these products is that the ability to use them to lay off risk means that bankers can *take* more risk. Insofar as they can take more risk, the more they can offer end users ingenious products which they find beneficial.

As the markets grow, there are more opportunities for laying off a growing variety of risks in an ever more efficient way. As a result, more and more end user products are being released which they find attractive.

This is the beneficial aspect of these markets. Of course, there are the gamblers (speculators) and the markets couldn't exist without them, but to dismiss it all as gambling is to make a serious mistake.

SUMMARY

Forward rate agreements (FRAs) are a way of fixing a rate of interest for a date in the future and for a given period of time (*forward/forward*).

The buyer is compensated by the seller if market rates on the given date exceed the given *strike rate*. The buyer, however, must compensate the seller if market rates fall below the strike rate.

Borrowers seeking protection will *buy* FRAs, investors will *sell* them. Banks make a profit through the use of a bid/offer spread.

Essentially, the FRA is the exchange-traded interest rate futures contract in the OTC market.

The FRA is for one forward period only. *Swaps* are agreements for many forward periods (for example, one per year for the next 10 years). Again, the market rate of interest (usually LIBOR) is compared with a given strike rate leading to a compensatory payment from one party to the other.

The buyer in the case of the FRA is usually called the *payer* in the swap (that is, the payer of the fixed rate). The seller in the FRA is usually called the *receiver* in a swap (that is, the receiver of the fixed rate).

The above are *interest rate swaps*; there are also *currency swaps*.

Profit may arise for both parties from the application of the theory of *comparative advantage*. Banks will make a profit through the bid/offer spread.

Swaps for those borrowing money are *liability swaps*; swaps for investors are *asset swaps*.

Swaps are essentially a series of FRAs. A swap starting at a future date is a *forward swap*; an option to have a swap is a *swaption* and a swap of two floating rates is a *basis swap*.

A borrower can be protected from an interest rate rise but still benefit from a fall using an interest rate *cap*; an investor can benefit from an interest rate rise but still be protected from a rise using an interest rate *floor*.

The combination of a cap and floor leads to a range of interest rates for future transactions called a *collar*.

Caps, floors and collars are variations on *options*.

The BIS carried out a survey of the derivatives market in 26 countries as at end March 1995. Its initial estimate of outstanding OTC contracts was $40.7 trillion, later amended to $47.5 trillion. However, the replacement cost was estimated at only $1.7 trillion (later $2.2 trillion).

The outstanding value of exchange-traded contracts was estimated at $16.6 trillion but double-counting could not be eliminated.

Interest rate derivatives accounted for much the largest category for both OTC and exchange-traded derivatives.

13 Insurance

BACKGROUND TO THE INSURANCE MARKETS

History

> But ships are but boards, sailors but men: there be land rats and water rats, water-thieves and land-thieves, I mean pirates: and then there is the peril of waters, winds and rocks.
> (*The Merchant of Venice,* Act I, Scene III)

Shylock is quite right and Antonio is soon to discover that an insurance premium is cheaper than a pound of flesh any day! While the history of insurance is lost in the mists of time, our modern history surely begins with marine insurance.

Shipowners would meet with rich merchants who would agree to jointly pay for any losses for a share of the premiums. A contract was drawn up and merchants added their name at the bottom. As they wrote underneath the text, they were *underwriters*. Apart from this, a group of shipowners might agree to raise a levy on all members and share losses between them. This principle continues today with the so-called 'P&I' club (see below).

Meetings in London for business took place in coffee houses. In 1688 we have the first mention of Edward Lloyd's coffee house in Tower Street. They moved to Lombard Street in 1691. Then, as now, information was power and, in 1734, they began a publication, *'Lloyd's List'*, which gave shipping information and also some financial data. It is still published today.

The insurance world in those days was as full of scandals as the world of stocks and shares. Just as the Stock Exchange was set up to bring respectability and rules so, in 1769, one Thomas Fielding set up a new organisation meeting in Pope's Head Alley and, in 1771, drew up a document setting up a ruling committee. A move to the Royal Exchange building in 1774 was followed in 1781 by the first constitution of Lloyd's. These were the early origins of the famous Lloyd's of London, of which more later.

Even earlier than Edward Lloyd's coffee house, the Fire Office Company was set up in 1680. The Amicable followed in 1706 and the London Assurance and the Royal Exchange Assurance in 1720.

The basic idea of insurance is the *sharing of risk*. Experience may suggest that, of an insurance population of buildings, 2% will have a fire in a given year. Dividing the anticipated claims by the numbers seeking insurance gives us the *premium* to be paid. Those who haven't had a fire have contributed to a pool to pay for those who have, while buying protection in case they were the unfortunate ones.

The Insurance Market

The biggest market in the world by premium income is the US, followed by Japan and Germany. Premiums in the US in 1993 were $564bn, $547bn in Japan and $116bn in Germany. The premiums for Europe as a whole totalled $490bn with Germany, the UK and France contributing $320bn. However, while non-life business is 50–60% of the market in the US and Europe it is only 25% in Japan. (Figures from Swiss Re Sigma publication, March 1995.)

Within Europe, the largest markets in relation to GDP are in Germany, the UK, Ireland and the Netherlands. Very weak markets for insurance are found in Portugal, Spain, Greece and Italy. The main characteristic of the UK insurance companies is the international flavour of the business. Members of the Association of British Insurers earn 50% of their premiums from abroad and 70% of Lloyd's premiums are also earned abroad. Insurance produced 'invisible earnings' for the UK of £3.9bn in the year 1993/1994.

Assurance/Insurance

Assurance is the cover for events which are certain. Since death comes to us all, life insurance (strictly speaking, 'death insurance'!) is providing cover for a claim which is certain, only the timing being open to doubt. The study of the relevant statistics and laws of probability by a profession called *actuaries* leads to an accurate estimate as to how many of an insured population will die in a given year. As a result, it would be very unlikely that the claims would exceed the premiums. In other words, the company expects to make an *underwriting* profit. In addition, premiums are paid in advance and will be invested prior to any money being paid out. The second source of profit is thus the return on the investments. Ironically, interest rate risk will be more than mortality risk! Finally, people take out a life policy and perhaps do not change this for the whole of their life. As a result, the business is stable and can invest for the long-term. The nature of this business is such that it is natural for them also to invest funds to provide pensions in the longer term. We, thus, talk of the 'life and pensions business'.

The industry has been ingenious in working out variations on the theme of a simple life policy. One variation is *term assurance*. The life cover is for a given number of years such as 10 years. As death is no longer certain, the policy is cheaper. We can have heavier protection for a vulnerable period (a young family) than later.

Endowment policies add the element of investment. Life cover is provided up to the age of, say, 50 and if death has not taken place a sum of money is guaranteed. Often the 'life' element is only 10% of the premiums or even less.

Living assurance is a new type which has become popular in the US. This policy will pay out on the diagnosis of serious diseases such as cancer, heart disease, and so on.

Life policies can be with or without *profits*. The with profits policy pays bonuses annually (*reversionary*) and at termination.

A variation on this theme, which has become popular in many countries (US/Canada/UK/France), is to link the policy to mutual fund performance (*unit linked*), as the fund is usually divided into units (see Chapter 9).

Insurance is providing cover for events which may or may not happen: for example, theft, fire, accident, storms, and so on. Judging the probability of these events is much more difficult than judging the incidence of death and frequently claims exceed premiums – an underwriting loss. In recessions, for example, the incidence of arson mysteriously increases!

At times, too, premiums are driven down to uneconomic levels due to fierce competition. The industry is cyclical. It is not difficult to start up in insurance and, when profits are good, firms are attracted in until the extra competition produces losses. Firms then depart until profits rise again and the whole cycle starts once more. We have just been through a very bad period for insurance, exacerbated by an extraordinary series of disasters – hurricanes, the Exxon Valdez spillage, and so on. There are bigger risks due to new technology and claims for pollution.

The possibility of underwriting loss means that a good profit from the investment of the premiums is essential since this may be the only profit there is. To make matters worse, premiums are specifically renewed annually and the insured party may look around and decide to switch to another company, leading to less certainty regarding future income.

The investment policy of the insurance company, therefore, has to pay much more attention to liquidity than the investment policy of companies in life and pensions.

As a result of the two sides of the business – assurance and insurance – we find companies which do assurance only, insurance only and companies which are in both markets, called *composites*.

As well as public companies with shareholders, it is very common to find companies which are not public companies but are owned jointly by the policy holders. These are called *mutuals* and this is very common across all the western markets, especially for life companies.

Regulation

The importance of insurance, and the fact that it is often bought by members of the general public, means that it is an industry which is closely regulated. The collapse of the Vehicle and General Company in the UK in 1971, for example, left 800 000 motorists uninsured overnight!

In the US, regulations are made by both the central government and the states themselves. In the UK, regulation is from the Department of Trade and Industry, in France from the Direction des Assurances and in Germany from a body called the BAV.

Regulations may cover general supervision, licensing, solvency ratios, accountancy practices and annual returns. They will also cover the question of compulsory insurance, such as third party motor insurance, public liability and so on.

Solvency ratio is similar to the concept of capital ratio in banking (see Chapter 2). In banking it was, in essence, a prudent relationship between capital and lending. In insurance, it is a prudent relationship between capital (shareholders' equity plus reserves) and premiums. Money spent buying *reinsurance* from others can usually be deducted from the premiums (up to a maximum figure), thus allowing the insurer to take more business. The rules are complicated and alternative calculations are often possible. Each country tends to have different rules but the EU single market regulations are imposing common minimum standards. Liquidity is important and the regulations may demand that part of the capital must be held as a *minimum guarantee fund*.

Distribution

The question of the distribution channel for selling personal insurance is very important. It has led to insurers linking with banks to use them as a channel for selling policies (see Chapter 4) and banks buying or starting insurance companies.

Typical distribution channels are:

- ❏ Tied agents
- ❏ Direct sales staff
- ❏ Independent Financial Advisers (IFA)
- ❏ Part-time agents
- ❏ Brokers
- ❏ Telephone selling.

Tied agents are usually self-employed and sell only the policies of one company – Allianz, for example, has 43 000. They are also very common in France, where there are about 80 000.

A *direct salesforce* is often employed, especially in assurance.

Independent financial advisers will make recommendations from a range of products. They may charge a fee for their advice or simply take a commission on the policy offered from the company concerned. In the latter case, the possibility of bias towards high commission policies may lead to the 'independence' of IFAs being questioned. The UK has struggled with this problem in recent years and regulations force IFAs to register with a 'Self-Regulatory Organisation' (SRO) and declare their commission on the recommended policy. Another rule called 'polarisation' rules out combining the roles of IFA and tied agent in any way. For example, a bank manager might act as agent for the banks mutual funds but act as adviser in other matters. This is not permitted. A seller of mutual funds and life policies must inform the prospective buyer in writing whether their status is that of IFA or tied agent.

Part-time agents are usually solicitors and estate agents who will handle personal assurance and insurance on a casual basis and take commission.

Brokers are very common in the US, UK and the Netherlands. They are much more involved in commercial insurance for businesses than personal insurance. In so far as they do personal insurance, much of it is in areas like motor and household which are not especially lucrative. For the broker, it is the contact from which they hope to sell more profitable life and pensions business.

Many mergers of brokers have taken place and six of the world's biggest set up a global electronic network called World Insurance Network (WIN) in late 1995.

There is also a type of distribution called *industrial*. This involves calling door to door to collect premiums in cash. The term was used in the last century as it was regarded as insurance for people employed in the factories. In the UK, the Prudential is famous for its industrial sales force, giving rise to a cliché , 'the man from the Pru'.

Today this type of distribution is very expensive and is dying out fast in the US and Australia. The percentage cost of premiums collected is much higher than for other types of business. It suits some policy holders who manage their lives on a week to week cash basis! For others, sadly, loneliness is a factor. There will be someone to talk to each week even if it's only the person from the insurance company. Many companies are abandoning this type of business. The UK Prudential gave up taking new policies from January 1995, at which time it employed 8000 people visiting 1.6 million homes.

Finally, mention should be made of the fact that company pension schemes (where they exist) usually provide life assurance cover automatically.

Telephone Selling

As a way of cutting costs, doing business exclusively by telephone is becoming very common. In the UK, this was pioneered by Direct Line, a subsidiary of the Royal Bank of Scotland, which now has two million motor policies, the largest private sector insurer in this market. They have now set up Linea Directa in Spain using Bankinter. Other insurance companies such as Axa and Zurich have followed suit as well as others in the UK.

Self-insurance

As insurance is essentially a spreading of risk, the rising premiums in some market sectors have led to a growth in *self-insurance*. For example, municipal authorities with their common interests might form their own pool of premiums, especially for public and employers liability. As a further example, in 1995 London Transport set up its own insurance company in Guernsey, expecting to cut £2m off premiums in the first year.

For a single entity, a large multinational company, for example, self-insurance might simply involve putting aside an amount of money each year into a fund to build up a sum to meet given insurance risks. This could apply if the company felt that it was a much better risk than the general insured population of firms for a given risk and was paying excessive premiums as a result. It also saves on insurance commission and expenses.

In marine insurance, an association of shipowners will organise mutual aid for risks not covered under a marine hull policy. Each member will contribute to a pool to cover losses up to a given sum. Above this sum, reinsurance will be used (see below). These associations are known as *Protection and Indemnity Associations* or P&I clubs.

REINSURANCE

Definitions

Reinsurance is the form of insurance by which an insurance company can transfer to another company all or part of its liability for claims of a given type. This reduces the risk that excessive claims could seriously weaken the company.

The company transferring the risk is the *reinsured* and is also known as the *ceding* company. The company accepting the risk is the *reinsurer*.

The reinsurer may themselves pass on some of the risk to another company – this is a *retrocession* contract. Often two companies will each reinsure the other on a swap basis for particular types of risk.

The reinsured company now has protection against excessive claims or a large accumulation of claims and can write more business than if it was standing 100% of the loss.

The amount of business it can take is limited by the solvency margin. The reinsured company can deduct premiums due to reinsurers when calculating this (although EU regulations restrict this to 50%).

Generally, reinsurance is divided into *proportional* and *non-proportional*.

Proportional and Non-proportional Reinsurance

Proportional The reinsurer takes an agreed share of the risks ceded in return for the same share of the premiums less a *reinsurance commission*. This latter is to offset commission paid to intermediaries and also the expenses incurred.

In the case of *quota share reinsurance*, the reinsurer takes an agreed proportion of all insurances of a given type written by the ceding company.

Surplus reinsurance occurs where risks above a given retention limit are insured. For example, the limit or *line* for a risk like fire might be $1m. Reinsurance is fixed with a group of reinsurers to cover an agreed multiple, for example 10 lines, that is $10m.

The arrangement with the group of reinsurers is called a *treaty*. In the above case, the original company will take the risk until the sums insured exceed $1m. Then the risk is reinsured up to a maximum of $10m when a new treaty may be drawn up. If the sums insured total $4m, the reinsured is accepting risk for $1m and the reinsurers for $3m, that is 75% and, thus, proportional. Occasional risks, not covered by the treaty, may be reinsured on an ad hoc or *facultative* basis.

Non-proportional The reinsurers contribute to losses in excess of a given figure in return for a premium. This may be *excess of loss* or *excess of loss ratio*.

Excess of loss Here the reinsurers agree to pay any loss in excess of a given figure up to a maximum stated amount. This may be on a *per risk* basis (that is specific to, say, a ship or building) or on an *event basis* (for example, a hurricane, and often called *catastrophe* cover).

Excess of loss ratio Here the excess of claims over an agreed loss ratio is reinsured. The loss ratio is the ratio of claims to premiums. For example, a reinsurer might cover 90% of losses above a loss ratio of 75% to a maximum of 110%. Suppose the premium income was $10m. A 75% loss ratio would arise for claims of $7.5m. A 110% loss ratio arises with claims of $11m. The difference is $3.5m. A reinsured might agree to cover 90% of this figure, leaving the reinsurer to bear some of the loss (an important principle).

Financial Reinsurance

This has three key features:

- ❏ A ceiling on the liability for the reinsurer
- ❏ A recognition of the time value of money
- ❏ A sharing of profits through premium rebates.

The first policies were the *time and distance* policies of Lloyd's syndicates in the 1970s. The reinsurer undertook to meet a number of future claim payments. The reinsured undertook to pay a premium equal to the net present value (that is, the discounted value) of the above payments. The reinsurer, in a tax haven, would make a profit by reinvesting the premium at a higher rate of interest than that used in the discounting calculation.

The reinsured was left with no responsibility for the correct investment of the premium and might still benefit from a rate of return it could not achieve by itself. There was no transfer of risk and the arrangement was purely financial.

Today's financial reinsurance contracts do involve a transfer of risk, for example, timing risk, that is, that claims payments may be made earlier than expected. They might also agree to cover a sum higher than that implied by the premium (*finite risk*). Financial insurance contracts can be:

- ❏ *Retrospective* – the schedule of future payments is guaranteed in respect of business already written
- ❏ *Prospective* – providing cover for future losses on business currently being written
- ❏ *Loss Portfolio Transfer* – a transfer of liability for losses from policies already written up to a maximum figure.

The Reinsurance Market

Lloyd's (to be discussed below) covers reinsurance, as do many insurance companies. It is, however, a specialist international business rather dominated by specialist companies like Munich Re and Swiss Re. The German and Swiss firms are helped by being allowed to build up catastrophe reserves which can be offset against tax.

As in most financial markets, consolidation is taking place. Employers Re from the US, the world's third biggest, has taken large stakes in Frankonas and Munich Re in Germany. The US General Re, the world's fourth biggest, has also taken a majority holding in Cologne Re.

Reinsurance Brokers also operate internationally and play a very important role in non-proportional reinsurance and also in handling unusual risks. The large US broker Marsh and McLennan declared income in 1991 of $269m from its reinsurance subsidiaries, now grouped into two operations – as Guy Carpenter in the US and Carpenter Bowring elsewhere. two of the largest UK brokers, Sedgwicks and Willis Coroon, also have large reinsurance businesses. Reinsurance broking is especially strong in the UK.

Financial reinsurance is a growing area and Zurich Insurance is probably the largest specialist. Its subsidiary is Centre Re and it has bought the Pinnacle company in Bermuda, which has underwritten many reinsurance policies for Lloyd's. Bermuda is the centre for financial reinsurance due to its tax free status.

The banks have also become involved in financial reinsurance and Bankers Trust have set up a subsidiary to handle this in Jersey (Channel Islands). J.P. Morgan and Marsh and McLennan have set up a joint venture catastrophe insurer based in Bermuda.

The excess of loss market has been particularly badly hit by a string of recent disasters. This includes Hurricanes Gilbert, Hugo and Andrew; the Philips Petroleum explosion; the Piper Alpha oil rig disaster; the San Francisco earthquake; the Los Angeles riots; the Exxon Valdez oil spill and the storms in Southern England in October 1987 and January 1990.

This spate of catastrophes has even led the Chicago Board of Trade to set up futures and options contracts for 'Catastrophe Insurance'!

LLOYD'S

Organisation

Lloyd's of London is a special case and merits special treatment. The Corporation of Lloyd's (formed in the 1771 reorganisation) does not itself insure anyone. The council of Lloyd's lays down the regulations for members' financial status, provides premises and general central support services. The insurance itself is provided by individual members called *names*.

There are at present about 12 800 names and they risk their personal wealth in providing insurance underwriting as they have unlimited liability. The theory is that, with unlimited liability, people will behave more prudently. The problem is, that with 12 800 names and only 170 professional underwriters actually doing the work, controlling their actions is difficult. Much of the debate in Lloyd's over the last 20 years has turned on the question of giving the names more control.

The actual underwriting is carried out by professional underwriters organised into 170 *syndicates* (in 1980, there were 437). Each syndicate is run by a *managing agency*, of which there are 65. As is often the case, they are dominated by the biggest (Sturge, Merrett, Wellington, Murray Lawrence) and the top 10 manage 42% of the capacity.

The syndicate runs for a year and is then reorganised. The accounts for that year are published 3 years later. For example, the accounts for 1992 were published in 1995. This allows time for claims to be made and settled. Even then, there may still be potential further claims, so these are reinsured so that the books can be closed – *reinsurance to close*. More recently, Lloyd's has proposed a move to 1 year accounting but this will need EU approval.

Each name is looked after by a member's *agent*. They advise the members on the rules, risks and which syndicates to join. There are 33 agents, of which the biggest are Sturge, Sedgwick, London Wall, Fenchurch and Willis Faber Dumas.

Lloyd's will use brokers but only those who are the *Lloyd's brokers* (some 270). They have to be able to distribute premiums to several syndicates and collect payment of claims from several syndicates. There are also some direct sales, especially for motor insurance.

To facilitate dealings between underwriters and brokers, there is a central service provider, the *Lloyd's Policy Signing Office* (LPSO). This not only handles the distribution of money for premiums and claims but will also prepare the wordings of policies and check them.

The names must have personal disposable wealth of £250 000. They will deposit 30% of their maximum premium capacity. If the capacity is £1m, they will deposit £300 000. At this level, the risk will probably be spread over some 10/15 syndicates.

The big attraction for the aristocracy and wealthy sports and pop stars has always been the threefold opportunity for income:

- ❏ The investment revenue from the deposit
- ❏ The investment income from the premiums
- ❏ The share of underwriting profit.

In addition, the attitude of the tax authorities in previous years was not as strict as it is today.

Among the names are the Duke of Marlborough, author Jeffrey Archer, jockey Lester Piggott, golfer Tony Jacklin and former Prime Minister, Edward Heath. The late Robert Maxwell, too, was a name.

The names contribute 0.5% of premiums to a central fund for the protection of the insured and can themselves insure against excessive claims (although this has become more difficult and costly in recent years).

Lloyd's is run from the £160m Richard Rogers building which was opened in 1986. At the heart is the *room*. This is the area where underwriters sit on uncomfortable desks and are visited by brokers seeking cover for particular risks. A broker gets agreement from a prominent underwriter first – this is a *line*. They then visit other underwriters (who will probably follow this example from one of their eminent colleagues) until they have enough 'lines' to cover the policy.

In the room is the famous Lutine Bell. This was salvaged by Lloyd's from HMS Lutine during the Napoleonic wars. In the days when communications were not as good as today, one ring was bad news (a delayed ship was lost) and two rings was good news (the delayed ship had arrived safely in harbour). It is now rung on ceremonial occasions only. The bell was rung when the Queen opened the building in 1986. In view of the many scandals which surrounded Lloyd's at the time, one wit asked whether it would be one ring or two!

Lloyd's is run by the Lloyd's Council of 14 members – active names, non-active names, the Chairman and Chief Executive and six others nominated from outside. There is also a regulatory board and a market board.

The Chief Executive of Lloyd's is Ron Sandler, previously special projects director. His appointment came in 1995 when Peter Middleton resigned. David Rowland, Chairman of the largest broker, Sedgwick's, took over as Chairman of Lloyd's in January 1993.

Lloyd's is a major centre for world reinsurance, of key importance for marine insurance and has pioneered policies for new risks such as AIDS and computer fraud. It has also always specialised in unusual risks such as multiple births, a famous film star's legs (Betty Grable, many years ago) and the world's largest cigar! Its reputation in the US was enormously enhanced by its prompt settlement following the 1906 San Francisco earthquake, in contrast to many other insurers.

The London Market

Lloyd's is part of what is usually described as the 'London Market'. This consists of three bodies:

- ❏ Lloyd's itself
- ❏ The Institute of London Underwriters (ILU) – a trade association for marine, aviation and transport business
- ❏ The London Insurance and Reinsurance Market Association (LIRMA) – a trade association specialising in reinsurance and non-marine business.

These last two bodies share policy processing and claims facilities and tend to use the London Underwriting Centre (set up in 1993) as a convenient base.

Two electronic networks are relevant. The London Insurance Market Network – LIMNET – enables data exchange, electronic mail, and provides various information services. The Lloyd's Outwards Reinsurance Scheme – LORS – has processed reinsurance debit and credit notes electronically since late 1993.

Electronic placing of business has commenced and is making slow but steady progress.

Early Problems

From the late 1960s onwards, the operation of Lloyd's began to attract increasing criticism. The accounting information was weak (and prevented names from realising the true facts); managing agencies shared profits but not losses; some syndicates were exceeding premium limits; periodically huge losses arose; and finally, the ownership of managing agencies by brokers led to conflicts of interest.

The Fisher Report   In 1980, the Lloyd's committee asked a judge, Sir Henry Fisher, to prepare a report. The Fisher report made three key recommendations.

❏   The Lloyd's Committee be widened to a Lloyd's Council with outside members
❏   The Council to have new, tough, disciplinary powers
❏   Underwriting agencies should no longer be permitted to own brokers.

The point about the last recommendation is that the broker wants to cover the worst risk for the lowest price. The underwriter wants the best risk for the highest price. So what happens when the underwriting syndicate is owned by a broker?

The new changes were to be embodied in an Act of Parliament – the Lloyd's Act 1982. Although the third change aroused great opposition, the Act was passed in mid-1982 and became law in January 1983.

Before it even became law, Lloyd's was hit by two scandals which made everything that had happened so far seem minor.

Alexander Howden   The large American brokers, Alexander and Alexander, took over Alexander Howden, a UK Lloyd's broker. The audit showed that $55m was missing. It was alleged that Howden directors had set up reinsurance syndicates abroad and paid higher premiums than necessary, keeping the extra profit for themselves. The chairman and four directors resigned. One was Lloyd's star underwriter, Ian 'Goldfinger' Posgate. Auditors found that £5.2m in premiums had been paid to Southern International Re in Panama. 'Re' always stands for reinsurance – in this case it stood for 'real estate'!

With one death and severe illness in two other cases, only Ian Posgate and Kenneth Grob remained later to face charges. They were arrested in July 1987 but acquitted at Southwark Crown Court in August 1989.

Minet/PCW   The PCW Managing Agency, owned by Minets, was found to have transferred some $40m to offshore reinsurance companies in which the directors had personal interests. The chairman of Minets, John Wallrock, resigned. As he was a pillar of Lloyd's establishment, this caused shockwaves.

These two events coming together were the last straw. The Bank of England 'persuaded' Lloyd's to accept a chief executive from outside. Ian Hay Davison, from Arthur Anderson, was appointed.

Although Davison had a difficult time and finally resigned after clashes with Lloyd's Chairman, Sir Peter Miller, he did much good work. In particular the accounting standards of the syndicates were considerably improved.

Further revelations about PCW made things even worse. It was alleged that two underwriters, Peter Dixon and Peter Cameron-Webb, had filtered money abroad to offshore companies controlled by themselves. They both fled abroad and, in December 1988, warrants were issued for their arrest by the Serious Fraud Office. It was a hollow gesture as the time had passed for extradition.

The Minet losses finally reached £300m – some due to bad underwriting and some due to fraud. Lloyd's created a special fund and settled a large percentage of the losses from this fund in June 1987.

The Financial Services Act, imposing new regulations on the financial markets, became law in 1986. Lloyd's was excluded. Many felt that the Howden/PCW affairs had shown that the 1982 Lloyd's Act had not gone far enough.

The Neill Report   Sir Patrick Neill started an enquiry into the workings of the Lloyd's 1982 Act in January 1986. The key recommendation of the report in February 1987 was that outside members of Lloyd's Council and nominations of the non-working names should be in a majority. It also recommended that managing agencies share losses as well as profits. It did not suggest that Lloyd's be covered by the Financial Services Act.

Commercial Problems

The problems that hit Lloyd's in the late 1980s and early 1990s were commercial problems, due to poor underwriting rather than fraud.

The names have, of course, unlimited liability and began to find themselves facing huge losses, in many cases involving personal ruin.

This was particularly true in the excess of loss market (LMX). Here one syndicate reinsures the losses of another or of a company outside the Lloyd's market. At first, syndicates specialising in excess of loss were very profitable and attracted new and undercapitalised names. The old wealth minimum level of £100 000 had been kept at this figure for far too long and was only raised to £250 000 in 1990. Gooda Walker syndicate 290 went from underwriting capacity of £6.2m in 1982 to £69.4m in 1989. As the string of catastrophes occurred, to which we have already referred, names faced huge losses. Accusations began to be made that 'insiders' only put money into the safest syndicates and that some agents packed innocent names onto weak syndicates as cannon fodder. In particular, there had been excessive passing on of reinsurance risks from one syndicate to the other.

Members of the Oakley Vaughan syndicates brought a unique court case against the Corporation of Lloyd's itself, claiming that it had failed in its duty to protect the names. In June 1992, the High Court came to a decision. It was decided that Lloyd's had a duty to regulate the market and act fairly, but no specific duty of care to the names.

Another problem was caused by huge payments for compensation as a result of litigation arising in the US. The cases concerned pollution and asbestosis. In some cases, the law was even changed with retrospective effect. The uncertainties this created led to a large number of years accounts being left 'open' – a highly undesirable state of affairs. Normally, the accounts are closed after 3 years by 'reinsurance to close'. If the value of potential claims is so uncertain that they cannot be reinsured, the accounts are left open. The names then face unlimited future claims on their resources.

The Rowland Report   David Rowland, Chairman of Sedgwicks, was asked to head a task force and produce a report on how Lloyd's could be a safer place for the names and respond to the latest difficulties.

Rowland reported in January 1992 and made 65 recommendations. The key ones were:

❑   Lloyd's must cut costs and reduce the numbers of agencies and syndicates
❑   A stop-loss scheme should be set up to put some limit to the apparently unlimited liability; a new fund should be set up financed by an extra 0.25% levy on premiums
❑   A system like unit trusts should be set up to allow names to put money into a 'pool' of multiple syndicates (an idea rejected in 1990)
❑   Limited liability companies (including insurance companies) should be allowed to join syndicates
❑   The size of the council to be reduced and a new separate regulatory body set up
❑   Reverse the rule not allowing brokers to own managing agencies.

On the question of costs, Rowland showed that costs had been 7% of premiums in 1982 and were 13% in 1990. Since the 1960s, premium income had risen 45% in real terms but Lloyd's had three times as many people. (Ironically, some increase in costs was due to regulation.)

In 1900, Lloyd's had 50% of the world's non-life business and now has 2%. It is still, however, the second biggest reinsurer and has 20% of the marine and aviation market. Rowlands looked to a 30% reduction in costs to improve their competitiveness.

Although Lloyd's had unused capacity in 1991 (premium income £8bn, capacity $11bn), the number of names leaving meant that Lloyd's would need more capital in the 1990s. (The 1992 figure of 22 300 names fell to 12 800 by 1996.)

Three separate bodies were proposed to replace the existing Lloyd's Council:

❏   The Lloyd's Council, to be reduced to half its size by end 1993
❏   A market board of 18 members to be responsible for the development of business and to be led by a group of working members, the Chairman and Deputy Chairman
❏   A regulatory board, led by an outsider, to be responsible for the regulatory structure; the Chairman of Lloyd's and the working members group are to be on this board.

The new Lloyd's Council supervises the work of the market board, but has no say in the regulation of the market.

These new arrangements started in January 1993 and the first Chairman of the new regulatory board is Brian Garraway, Deputy Chairman of BAT Industries. External members of the marketing board were named in mid-December 1992.

1992 was clearly a busy year for Lloyd's! Aggrieved names called an extraordinary meeting on 27 July. 5200 names attended this meeting. Chairman David Coleridge confirmed a loss of £2.06bn for the year 1989 and that further losses were likely for 1990 and 1991. two markets, aviation and motor, did make a profit. In addition, 34% of the loss was concentrated on five syndicates managed by the Gooda Walker and Feltrim agencies. They involved 4000 out of 30 000 names. An attempt was to be made, Coleridge announced, to set up a voluntary fund of £50m to help the worst losses.

Following his earlier report, David Rowland published a business plan in April 1993 with a concentration on two elements:

1. Corporate members with limited liability to be admitted in 1994
2. The formation of a new reinsurance company (NewCo), to which all the 1986 potential claims would be transferred; this would enable a cap to be placed on names' losses.

As the essence of Lloyd's has always been unlimited liability, the admission of corporate members was a decisive but necessary change. Many new corporates were set up to trade at Lloyd's. There are 165 and they already contribute 30% of underwriting capacity.

There is, in general, a new professionalism around. The number of syndicates and managing agencies has fallen. Members' agents in 1996 were 33 where there had been 250 in 1984. There is also a suggestion that this role could be carried out by a new central services agency at Lloyd's.

Wellington Underwriting Agencies (the largest managing agency) launched a £30m listed investment company to support its seven syndicates. The Wellington members' agent business is to merge with Stace Barr to form the largest members' agent. Murray Lawrence are to merge their seven syndicates into one 'umbrella' syndicate with the capacity to write business with premium income of £500m. These two moves are very much a sign of the times.

The second part of the business plan is the proposal to concentrate all old business into one new company and cap names' losses. In addition, an out-of-court settlement offer is needed for the many organisations set up by names to take legal action. These 'action groups' have had some success. In mid-1994, the High Court decided that names on the Gooda Walker Syndicate should be compensated to the value of £500m for incompetent underwriting. In October 1995, the High Court decided in favour of members of Merrett Syndicate 418 who brought a case against Agencies, Underwriters and Auditors.

The name NewCo was changed to Equitas and losses up to and including 1992 (not 1986) are to be transferred to it. In May 1995, Lloyd's produced a plan by which names' losses would be offset by a special credit of £2.8bn but £1.9bn would be needed to be contributed to set up Equitas.

Many names felt that this credit was not enough and, one year later, Lloyd's announced an increase in the credit to £3.1bn and a reduction in the Equitas premium to £1bn. The offer was put to 34 000 names who were affected. It was approved by 90% of the names by 30 August 1996, when the offer went unconditional. The DTI then gave the go-ahead for the Equitas plan and on 4 September David Rowland, Lloyd's chairman, rang the Lutine bell – not twice, but three times! Clearly, the hope was that the nightmare was over.

The plan will put a cap on names' losses prior to 1993 and enable an out-of-court settlement of claims. In addition, a new 'auction' system will enable names to sell places on syndicates to others. In 1995, £246m of underwriting capacity (2¼%) was traded. Those wanting places on syndicates paid up to 14p for each pound of the syndicate's underwriting capacity. These schemes, together with a pooling system for syndicates – MAPA – which operates like a unit trust, will finally pave the way for the new Lloyd's into the next century.

THE MARKET TODAY

The US has not suffered as badly as Europe from some of the problems we have mentioned. Nevertheless, new rules and higher solvency ratios from US regulations will make life difficult. We are also seeing a growth in mergers as in Europe. American State Insurance has taken over American Union Re and Mony Re was acquired by Folksamerica. Attempts to get around rules forbidding banks to sell insurance have also failed, making life easier for the insurance companies.

Europe faces more competition due to the new EU directives. We have already seen (Chapter 4) the banking and insurance link ups; cross-border mergers and alliances in insurance have also become more common.

In France, there are three large insurers – UAP (Union des Assurances de Paris), AGF (Assurances Générales de France) and GAN (Groupe des Assurances Nationales). These and others have become very aggressive in cross-border activity.

Axa has a 49% stake in the US Equitable, a former mutual which turned itself into a shareholding company in 1992.

UAP has bought stakes in Royal Belge (Belgium), Allsecures (Italy) and Guarantia (Portugal). It now has a joint 59.9% stake in the UK's Sun Life with Liberty Life of South Africa. The French Victoire, however, was acquired by the UK's Commercial Union in 1994.

GAN bought the UK's General Portfolio Group and Athena a stake in the UK's Refuge. Compagnie du Midi acquired Equity and Law (UK) in 1989.

Domestically, the French scene may be about to alter. Distribution is largely in the hands of direct agents but Axa, the second largest insurer, has set up Direct Assurance to use direct marketing in addition to a network of agents. Other French companies, too, are looking at direct marketing.

Allianz, Europe's biggest company, made a loss in 1991 of DM1.78m compared to a profit of DM182m in the previous year. There were problems following the acquisition of the US Farmers' Fund in 1990 and the acquisition of the East German State monopoly.

Allianz is building links with banks elsewhere, as we saw earlier. It has linked up with Dresdner Bank to meet the challenge of Deutsche Bank in insurance. Allianz also has a 22% holding in Dresdner. It has also linked with Crédit Lyonnais. Deutsche has set up its own insurance subsidiary, has bought a 30% stake in the East German insurer, Gerling, and has bought Deutsche Herald which specialises in private client business.

A pan-Europe alliance of insurance companies has also been set up. Topdenmark (third in Denmark), Wasa (third in Sweden), AVCB (fourth in the Netherlands) and Friends Provident (third largest mutual in the UK) have formed a joint company to develop European business.

Apart from Lloyd's, in the UK the scene is most marked by banking moves, with banks and building societies setting up insurance companies and insurance companies (for example the Prudential) announcing moves to set up a bank! In addition, mergers continue, the most dramatic being the proposal to merge Sun Alliance and Royal Insurance, the two composites, if regulatory approval can be gained.

A large ultimate impact may come from the gradual implementation of EU directives. This will be especially true in the countries weak in premium income – Portugal, Spain, Italy and Greece.

EU REGULATION

While some progress has been made with EU Directives on general insurance, progress with life assurance has been very slow. However, in June 1992, two key directives were finally passed – the Third Non-Life Insurance Directive and the Third Life Assurance Directive. These became law on 1 July 1994. From this date, insurers need only be authorised once, in their own country. This is the same 'single passport' idea that will apply in banking. However, marketing and selling practices will still be regulated by the country in which the insurance is sold. For example, cold calling is banned in Denmark and Germany.

There will still, of course, be problems with foreign insurers, especially at the retail level – language, distance, law, local support. Will policy holders wish to pursue a case in a foreign Court? Following a European Court decision in 1992, it was ruled that a German, living in Belgium, could not claim tax relief from the Belgian government on insurance policies he was buying in Germany. For this and other reasons, the Chairman of Allianz said in October 1995 that the single market in insurance was a 'myth'! What was needed first was harmonisation of legal, tax and social security systems.

The 'Bureau Européen des Unions des Consommateurs' produced a report on comparative premiums in the life market. Using 100 as the cheapest cover, they produced the following figures:

Ireland	100
UK	102
Germany	118
France	151
Portugal	345

There is clearly scope for more competition!

SUMMARY

The biggest insurance markets in the world are in the US, followed by Japan and Germany.

Assurance is cover for events which are certain (death). *Insurance* is cover for events which may or may not happen (accident, fire, catastrophe).

Offering insurance protection is *underwriting*.

Some companies do assurance only, some insurance only, and some (called *composites*) do both.

The equivalent of capital ratio in banking is *solvency ratio*.

The distribution of the insurance product is a key issue with the possibility of agents, direct sales staff, independent financial advisers, part-time agents, brokers and telephone selling.

Sometimes a large multinational or a group with similar interests will cover their own insurance – *self-insurance*.

Reinsurance occurs when the underwriter spreads the risk with other insurers or specialist reinsurers. There are various terms used such as *proportional, non-proportional, quota, share, surplus* and *excess of loss*.

A reinsurer may offer to reinvest premiums to provide future cover. This is *financial reinsurance*.

There are reinsurance companies, reinsurance brokers and a large reinsurance market at Lloyd's of London.

The so-called *London Market* consists of *Lloyd's*, the *Institute of London Underwriters* (ILU) and the *London Insurance and Reinsurance Market* (LIRMA).

Lloyd's of London is an organisation of individual members called *names* who offer insurance. They have traditionally had unlimited liability. The actual underwriting is carried out through *syndicates* and syndicates are run by *managing agencies*. Names are advised by *members' agents*.

Syndicates run accounts for 1 year but they are left open for 3 and may then be terminated by *reinsurance to close*.

Lloyd's uses *Lloyds's brokers* and a central service provider, the *Lloyd's Policy Signing Office* (LPSO).

Lloyd's has faced increasing problems in the last 20 years. These have arisen from fraud, careless underwriting, a disregard for the names' interests, huge claims due to pollution cases in the US and a string of natural catastrophes. This has all led to names facing huge losses.

Lloyd's is in the process or reorganisation on the following lines:

- ❏ Allowing corporate membership with unlimited liability
- ❏ Setting up a system like unit trusts to pool money across syndicates (MAPA)
- ❏ Reorganising the Lloyd's Council
- ❏ Forming a new reinsurance vehicle called Equitas to which all claims up to the end of 1992 will be transferred; this will set a cap on names' losses.

The key move is Equitas. Detailed plans were approved by the members in the late summer of 1996.

Like banking, the insurance market is seeing consolidation, mergers and cross-border initiatives. Some are buying banks, some setting up their own banks and some forming joint ventures with banks.

The EU has passed the *Third Non-Life Insurance Directive* and the *Third Life Assurance Directive*. These provide the single-passport concept that we have seen in banking but the results have been less than dramatic.

14 Key Trends

INTRODUCTION

The Western financial markets experienced total upheaval in the 1980s and in the first half of the 1990s. The pace of change slowed a little with recession in several key markets and the banks struggling to contain balance sheet weakness, but continued again from 1994 onwards as the banks (except Japan) left their major problems behind them. A number of key trends continue to shape and reshape the financial world into new patterns.

It is the purpose of this final chapter to highlight a number of major factors for change.

DEREGULATION

Artificial restrictions continue to be abandoned. As part of the Single Market commencing in 1993, the countries of the EU have abandoned exchange controls.

Stock markets have seen the ending of the monopoly position of privileged brokers, the introduction of competition for commissions, a move to computer screen trading and (in the EU) growing cross-border competition. Switzerland has seen its first hostile cross-border takeover (the takeover of Holvis by the UK's BBA) and, slowly but surely, moves to allow foreign shareholders voting rights and foreign firms access to the markets.

In the US, country-wide branch banking will soon be a reality (unless local state law forbids it) following the repeal of the McFadden Act. The expected repeal of Glass–Steagall has not followed (for the third time in 8 years) nor have banks been allowed complete access to insurance markets. Nevertheless, the Federal Reserve has used powers under the Glass–Steagall Act to allow several commercial banks limited permission to deal in municipal bonds, commercial paper and equities.

The Japanese are making more progress with their equivalent of Glass–Steagall, Article 65. In 1993, some commercial banks were allowed limited dealings in bonds and in 1994 the list of banks allowed these powers was widened. In 1993 also, brokers were allowed to deal in investment trusts, land trusts and foreign exchange. Prohibitions of local dealing in London-issued eurobonds have been relaxed, foreign banks are being given greater access for fund management and the regulations limiting the local repo market are being lifted in 1996.

The need for the German government to increase its borrowings has led to a relaxation of limits on foreign participation in the government bond auctions. Reserve requirements for local banks at the Bundesbank have been lowered and money market funds are now permitted.

The privatisations carried out by the Thatcher government in the UK have led to widespread privatisations, full or partial, of state-owned enterprises across Europe – France's BNP, UAP and Crédit Local de France, Spain's Argentaria, Italy's ENI and telecommunication authorities everywhere, culminating in Deutsche Telekom at the end of 1996.

In the last edition, we commented on the liberation of markets in East and Central Europe and Russia. We mentioned the threat of political backlash and we have already seen former communists returned to power in several countries. Russia has proved in many ways to be a disappointment and Hungary, which started off so well, has begun to retreat. The bright stars are the Czech Republic, with its convertible Korunna, and Poland. Both have now reached investment grade. Regarding the former Yugoslavia, one can only hope that we are seeing an end to the depressing racial, religious and nationalistic strife.

REREGULATION

Following the deregulation comes reregulation – that is, how do we control the markets that have just been freed?

For example, as the markets become international, bank supervisors wanted international rules and this led to the so-called Basle agreement on capital ratios. This was implemented in 1993. With the improvement in the banks' trading positions since 1993, most western banks have ratios comfortably in excess of the BIS figures. Indeed, some have spent money buying back their own shares. In Japan, however, there is a feeling that a correct write off of bad debts would lead to many banks' ratios being seen as unsatisfactory.

The early warnings of 'credit crunch' were special pleading on the banks' part. However, no less an authority than Richard Breeden of the SEC has attacked the agreement as distorting investment patterns away from corporate lending and towards government bonds.

For all the criticisms, the key question is: 'would the banks be in a better position today if these rules had been in place in 1980?' Surely, the answer must be 'Yes'.

In stock markets, new rules have already been drawn up to control the markets (for example, France, Italy and Germany). The rules govern fair treatment for investors, insider dealing and takeover regulations. In the UK, a whole new bureaucratic apparatus was set up by the 1986 Financial Services Act. It is rightly criticised for substantial weakness but it is, at least, encouraging to see severe fines imposed on large insurance companies for failing to ensure that their agents did not sell totally unsuitable policies.

The process of change within countries' domestic laws has been reinforced by the EU directives on capital adequacy, insider dealing and mergers and takeovers.

RISK MANAGEMENT – COUNTERPARTY RISK

The high value of payments being processed as a result of interbank loans/deposits, foreign exchange deals, derivatives and securities trading, has led to a growing concern about 'systemic' risk. This is the risk that one bank's failure to settle could result in a domino-like collapse throughout the entire banking system.

BIS figures show that the value of interbank payments in many countries has doubled since 1985. Its 1995 Central Bank Survey of foreign exchange dealing revealed a net value of trades to the tune of $1.2 trillion every day. Tom Labreque, president of Chase Manhattan, has calculated that the money going through the world's payment and settlement systems adds up to $6 trillion each day.

Banks still talk of 'Herstatt risk' following the failure of the German Herstatt Bank in 1974. It went into liquidation after settling in deutschemarks but before settling the dollar equivalent of $620m (due to the time difference). More recent events have added to their worries – the huge bad debts of Japanese banks; the appalling losses of Crédit Lyonnais ($4.2bn in 3 years); the Barings collapse, wiping out £860m; the LDC debt crisis, following loans to Latin America in the 1970s; the US savings and loan bank fiasco with losses of $150bn; the widespread rescues of Scandinavian banks in the early 1990s; and, in March 1996, the announcement of a rescue for Banco di Napoli.

There are four areas of concern – foreign exchange, electronic interbank payment systems, securities trading and derivatives. Derivatives we will look at separately, but consider the other three in turn.

In March 1996, the BIS published a paper on the risk in foreign exchange settlements, claiming that not enough was being done to control the risk. A start has been made with netting systems. FX Net in London started several years ago and is bilateral netting. The payments between two banks in a single currency are netted as one payment (see Chapter 7). This has now been followed by a multilateral netting system called Echo, involving 15 banks. In the US, a similar system, called Multinet, began in 1996.

At the same time, in April 1996, a group of 17 banks calling themselves G20 (for some reason) announced plans to create an organisation for 24 hour foreign exchange real time settlement within 3 years.

On the question of interbank electronic settlement systems, there have been worries for many years. Payments to individual accounts are processed in real time as they arise, but the net impact on each bank has, in the past, been calculated at the end of the day, leading to worries about the effect if one bank were unable to settle. In November 1985, for example, the New York Fed lent $23bn to the Bank of New York (equivalent to 20 times its capital) after a computer failure had led it to run up a daylight overdraft of $30 billion.

Since then, the New York Fed has set up a system of charges for daylight overdrafts and requires collateral from banks that regularly run up large credit positions.

Elsewhere, systems have been rewritten to charge banks in real time for the money credited to other banks' customers – a process called Real Time Gross Settlement. This is the approach being taken in Japan, the Netherlands, the UK and France. Banks are usually asked to provide liquid assets as collateral before their settlement accounts can be overdrawn or (in the case of Japan) daylight overdrafts may be forbidden.

Realising that international trading and competition in securities is slowed down by disparate and inefficient settlement systems, the bankers' so called 'think-tank', the G30 group, drew up their report on settlement. We have referred to this once or twice in the text but, as it is a classic example of a move to reregulation and has exercised considerable influence, it is worth listing its recommendations and their (optimistic) target dates (Table 14.1).

Table 14.1 Settlement: G30 recommendations

❏ Trade matching by T + 1		1990
❏ Institutions to be included		1992
❏ Book transfers only		1992
❏ Trade netting systems		1992
❏ Delivery versus payment		1992
❏ Rolling settlement	T + 5	1990
	T + 3	1992
❏ Increase in stock lending/borrowing		1992

Faster trade matching has been implemented generally with the arrival of new electronic trade confirmation systems. Gradually, the passing round of share and bond certificates is being replaced either by the use of depositary systems or the elimination of the certificate – dematerialisation. Netting systems are widespread and delivery versus payment becoming the rule. The French system RELIT enforces delivery versus payment and has eliminated the use of share certificates. In March 1996, the Amsterdam Stock Exchange linked its electronic share register with accounts at the Dutch central bank to enforce delivery versus payment. Settlement on the basis of an accounting period is being replaced by rolling settlement and faster settlement. The eurobond market, the US equities market and many others moved from T+5 to T+3 in mid-1995. The UK, having lagged behind on settlement due to the collapse of TAURUS, has abandoned its 200 year old trading account in favour of T+5 rolling settlement. The long-awaited new system CREST commenced in the second half of 1996. For all but small shareholders, share certificates are being replaced by entries on the CREST share register and delivery versus payment is now enforced. T+3 settlement is to follow in 1997. The French RELIT system allows T+3 settlement but, interestingly, most trades still settle using the old règlement mensuel. Finally, stock borrowing and lending systems are becoming universal.

RISK MANAGEMENT – DERIVATIVES

Derivatives were a cause for concern long before Nick Leeson was alleged to have caused the crash of Barings, the UK's oldest merchant bank. There have been reports from the BIS, IMF, G30 and the US General Accounting Office and many others warning of the risk to the banking system. Again, the fear has been that market losses could lead to a failure to settle and thus 'systemic' risk.

Several corporate losses have also hit the headlines – Allied Lyons, Metalgesellschaft, Kashima Oil, Codelco and Procter and Gamble.

Action in the industry has concentrated on more sophisticated calculation of the market and counterparty risk and moves to lessen counterparty risk anyway.

The G10 committee (usually called the BIS committee) and the EU have laid emphasis on 'value at risk' analysis. This consists of marking positions to market daily and then applying statistical techniques to calculate a value at risk in extreme circumstances. In 1995, J P Morgan caused a stir by making its own internal system – Riskmetrics – generally available. In May 1996, came the news that Reuters was working with them to enable users to pick up figures via Reuters and input to Riskmetrics.

The counterparty risk worries are at their most extreme with swaps when contracts are often 10 years or more. Measures taken include margin calls (like a clearing house) and use of netting systems to reduce settlement risk.

It may be that, in the end, the risk is exaggerated. The BIS study of OTC trading revealed that the outstanding value of contracts at the end of March 1995 was $41 trillion. However, replacement values were only $1.7 trillion (4%). (These figures were revised in May 1996 to $47.5 trillion and $2.2 trillion respectively.) The collapse of Barings (£860m) caused only a minor ripple. The Singapore exchange settled the Barings deals over the following 2 weeks through its clearing house and didn't have to go back to the members for more capital.

We ought, perhaps, to put the figures into perspective. The spectacular Barings loss of £860m should be compared with the LDC debt crisis losses in excess of $50bn, the saving and loan crisis of $150bn, the bad debts of Crédit Lyonnais (about Ffr50bn) and the debts of Eurotunnel – £8bn of which the banks won't get more than half. All this is due to ordinary bank lending which has been around for the last 600 years.

MERGERS/COOPERATION

Appendix 2 of Chapter 2 (p.38) listed examples of bank mergers and cooperation. The most spectacular recently was the merger of the Bank of Tokyo and Mitsubishi, which created the world's largest bank. The US has seen the dramatic merger of Chase Manhattan and Chemical Bank. In April 1996, there was even talk (soon denied) of a merger between the Union Bank of Switzerland and Credit Suisse.

The process is partly driven by fear of competition, partly by weakness due to an excessive number of banks, and partly by weakness due to losses. The process will continue, and we see its immediate effect in further staff redundancies and reduced expenditure on IT by the new single bank compared with the previously separate organisations.

Cooperation continues and it was encouraging to see in November 1992, advertisements for 'Eurogiro', as 14 European Post Office and Giro banks got together to launch a new cross-border payment system. Cooperatives are already making reciprocal facilities available, and savings banks selling three sets of mutual funds on a joint basis. The joining together of the Eurocheque organisation and MasterCard to produce a single debit card, widely acceptable across Europe, is another move which can only benefit consumers.

If we can emerge from the process with stronger banks, with prudent capital ratio backing, it can only provide an element of stability for the years to come.

BANCASSURANCE/ALLFINANZ

This is the joining together of banks and insurance companies to sell each other's products. This may be by a complete merger or takeover (such as NMB Postbank and, later, Barings by the Internationale Nederlanden Group) or by setting up joint subsidiaries or just by having a cooperative agreement.

It goes further than this. The German term is more general and suggests the idea of what some people call the 'financial supermarket'. Interestingly, we commented in Chapter 4 on the way certain US banks are actually setting up small branches in supermarkets! The basic idea is that the branch of the future will have a series of desks at which staff, supported by computer terminals, are equipped to sell and advise on a whole range of products – bank loans, mortgages, savings accounts, mutual funds, pensions, life insurance, general insurance. The arrival of the ATMs, home banking and telephone banking has made the traditional role of the branch redundant. Just as we might visit a 'computerworld' type of outlet to buy a personal computer so we might visit a 'financial world' type of outlet to make personal financial arrangements. On the other hand, the arrival of the 'information superhighway' may mean that we simply do it from home using the television as a terminal!

DEMOGRAPHIC FACTORS

The ageing populations of Europe will lead to a wide spread of 'funded' pensions. This, in turn, will have a considerable effect on stock exchanges in countries like Germany and France where pension funds have not been the norm. Their investments in equities and bonds will lead to an increase in trading and this will almost certainly lead to a rise in mutual funds, often used by pension funds themselves as an investment.

THE EU

Monetary union in Europe is due to commence in 1999. Opinion has swung back and forth, from a belief that a monetary union will begin as planned to scepticism that it will ever happen, back to belief again. In May 1996, the European Commission published an optimistic report suggesting that France would achieve the desired budget deficit reduction as required, that Germany would overcome problems due to low growth and that, generally, everything in the garden was lovely.

That does rather overlook the widespread opposition in France and Germany to social security cuts, wage freezes and tax increases. There is also the barely concealed concern at the Bundesbank at the prospect of being submerged in a wider European central bank. Finally, there are elections in Germany in 1998.

Assuming that monetary union is achieved and that Europe moves to its single currency, the euro, in 2002, there will be a considerable impact on bank profits. There will be the high cost of preparation and the awkward 6 month dual currency period. There will also be the loss of the nice foreign exchange profits currently being earned.

The UK will stay out initially, as with the Treaty of Rome in 1957, but gradually come to feel that its isolation is a mistake and seek to join later. What will be the effect on the markets of the City of London of persisting with the pound sterling? No one quite knows for certain but the effect may be less than some currently think.

On a wider front, the directives on banking, securities, insurance, capital adequacy, insider dealing, mergers and takeovers, all add up to a formidable amount of new legislation. There is disappointment in some areas, such as the effect of the insurance directives and the failures on pensions, but slowly but surely the financial face of Europe is changing.

ASIAN EMERGING MARKETS

One key trend which cannot be ignored is the near double-digit growth levels of Asian markets – China, Hong Kong, Singapore, Thailand, Philippines, Indonesia, Malaysia and South Korea. Their own banking and financial institutions face the need for change and it presents a challenging opportunity for western bankers.

These high growth rates bring high demand for capital. The World Bank has calculated that east Asian countries alone will need to spend $1500bn over the next 10 years to develop their infrastructure. It has also calculated that the value of outstanding bonds in Asian markets will triple to $1100bn over the next 10 years. Generally, their domestic markets, however, are under-developed and must progress at an extremely fast pace over the next few years if they are to intermediate the funds required. There are formidable obstacles in some countries – delays in developing regulation, political instability and tiny government bond markets. Nevertheless, we are going to see an increasing involvement from western commercial and investment banks. There will be opportunities in retail banking, securities markets, project finance, foreign exchange, fund management and pensions.

SUMMARY

Key trends in the financial markets are:

Deregulation   This covers relaxation of restrictions in banking, insurance and securities markets and a reduction in protectionism. It also includes widespread privatisations and the liberation of markets in Russia, East and Central Europe.

Regulation   Examples of this are international banking rules on capital ratio, new stock market laws and the effect of EU directives.

Risk Management – Counterparty Risk   There is concern about the risk of settlement failure due to the high value of payments being processed in foreign exchange, electronic interbank payment systems and securities trading. This has led to changes such as *netting* and *real time gross settlement*.

Risk Management – Derivatives   The huge value of derivatives transactions and much-publicised losses have led to fears about *systemic* risk. New risk management systems using *value at risk* analysis have spread widely.

Mergers/Cooperation   Increasing competition, an excessive number of banks and weakness due to losses have led to a fresh spurt of bank mergers and takeovers.

Bancassurance/Allfinanz   This is the desire of banks and insurance companies to offer a wide range of products across all the financial markets.

Demographic factors   Ageing populations are leading to a spread of funded pensions with implications for bond and equity markets.

The EU   Possible monetary union in 1999 will impact banks with changed systems and loss of foreign exchange profits. Politically, preparations are already having serious consequences in France and Germany. The various EU directives are also affecting the way banks and insurance companies operate.

Asian Emerging Markets   Double-digit growth levels across Asia have considerable implications for the changes needed in their financial markets, often under-developed.

Glossary

ACCEPTING	Signing a Bill of Exchange signifying an agreement to pay. Subsequent or alternative signature by a Bank virtually guarantees payment.
ACCOUNT	For equity settlements, exchanges may have an account period, for example 2 weeks, 1 month, etc. with payment due on 'account' or 'settlement' day. The alternative is a rolling settlement system.
ACCRUED INTEREST	The interest accrued so far on a bond and payable by the purchaser. Quoted separately from the 'clean price'.
ADR	American Depositary Receipt – the form in which foreign shares can be traded in the US without a formal listing.
AIBD	Association of International Bond Dealers, changed in 1992 to International Securities Market Association.
AIM	Alternative Investment Market – a new market for smaller companies' shares set up in the UK in June 1995.
ANNUAL YIELD	*See* Flat Yield.
APACS	Association for Payment Clearing Services – controlling cheque clearing, BACS and CHAPS in the UK.
APT	Automated Pit Trading – a computerised trading system used at LIFFE in addition to open outcry.
ARBITRAGE	Taking advantage of an anomaly in prices or rates in different markets – e.g. buying in one and simultaneously selling in the other.
ARBITRAGEURS	Those looking for arbitrage opportunities. Applied especially in the US to those trying to exploit takeover possibilities.
ARTICLE 65	Article of the Japanese Financial Code – prevents commercial banks from engaging in some investment banking activities (and vice-versa).
ASK RATE	*See* Offer Rate.
ASSETS	The side of the bank's balance sheet dealing with lending.
ASSURANCE	The business of life insurance and pensions.
ATM	Automated Teller Machine.
BACK OFFICE	Accounting and settlement procedures.
BACKWARDATION	When one market maker's offer price is less than another's bid – a clear opportunity for arbitrage!
BACS	Bankers' Automated Clearing Services (UK).

BANK BILL	A Bill of Exchange accepted by a bank on the central bank's 'eligible' list. The central bank itself would rediscount a bill of this type. Also called an 'eligible' bill.
BARGAIN	Any Stock Exchange transaction.
BASIS POINT	One-hundredth of 1 per cent.
BEAR	A pessimist, selling securities in the belief of a falling market, hence a 'bear market'.
BEARER BOND	A bond payable to whoever is in possession – that is, no central register.
BED AND BREAKFAST	Selling shares one day and buying them back the next – at the end of the tax year to maximise CGT allowance or claim losses against profits.
BID RATE	Rate of interest offered for deposits in banking. Generally, the dealer's buying price for equities, bonds, foreign exchange, etc.
BIG BANG	Deregulation of the UK Stock Exchange, 27 October 1986.
BILL OF EXCHANGE	A signed promise to pay by a receiver of goods or services and kept by the supplier. May be sold at a discount.
BIS	Bank for International Settlements (Basle). The central bankers' central bank.
BLUE CHIP	The most highly regarded shares. (Metaphor is from gambling casinos!)
BOBL	Short name for the short-term German government bond contract on the DTB.
BOND WASHING	Selling a bond prior to the ex dividend date to take a capital gain instead of receiving income.
BOND	A certificate issued by a borrower as receipt for a loan longer than 12 months, indicating a rate of interest and date of repayment.
BOND STRIPPING	*See* Coupon Stripping.
BONOS	Bonos del Estado – Spanish government bonds.
BONUS ISSUE	A free issue of shares to existing holders.
BRETTON WOODS	Meetings at Bretton Woods (US) in 1944 set up the World Bank, IMF and foreign exchange system for the period following the Second World War.
BROKER	An agent for buying/selling securities or intermediary for a loan or sale of foreign exchange.
BTAN	Bons du Trésor à Intérêt Annuel. French Government 2 and 5 year notes.

BTF	Bons du Trésor à Taux Fixe. French Government Treasury bills.
BTP	Italian government bond (Buoni del Tesoro Poliennali).
BULL	An optimist, buying securities in the belief of a rising market, hence a 'bull market'.
BULLDOGS	Sterling Bonds issued in the UK by foreign organisations.
BULLET REPAYMENT	The whole of a bond or bank loan is repaid at maturity (instead of staged payments in the last few years).
BUND	Short name for the medium-term German government bond contract on the DTB and LIFFE.
BUNDESBANK	The German central bank.
CABLE	Shorthand for dollar/sterling rate.
CALL MONEY	Money lent by banks to other banks or discount houses which can be recalled at noon each day.
CALL OPTION	An option to buy a share/bond/index/interest rate contract later at a price agreed today.
CAP	An agreement with a counterparty which sets an upper limit to interest rates for the cap buyer for a stated time period.
CAPITAL ADEQUACY	The need to maintain adequate capital to cover counterparty risk and position risk.
CAPITAL MARKETS	The market for medium- and long-term securities.
CAPITAL RATIO	The ratio of a bank's primary capital to a weighted value of assets (for example cash = 0 weighting).
CAPITALISATION	Market capitalisation of a company is the number of shares multiplied by the current price.
CBOE	Chicago Board Options Exchange.
CBOT	Chicago Board of Trade.
CERTIFICATE OF DEPOSIT	Issued by banks to raise money – strong secondary market. (Also Eurocertificate of Deposit.)
CGT	Capital Gains Tax.
CHAPS	Clearing House Automated Payments System – for electronic clearing of payments the same day (UK).
CHINESE WALL	A theoretical barrier between different sections of a firm to avoid conflicts of interest or insider dealing.
CHIPS	Clearing House Interbank Payments – electronic bank clearing system in New York.
CLEAN PRICE	Price of a bond not including the accrued interest element.

CLEARING HOUSE	Central body guaranteeing contracts in a traded options/ futures market place.
CLOSING OUT	For futures market – taking the opposite contract, for example, having previously bought 100 tons of cocoa for June delivery, the buyer now sells 100 tons for the same delivery (or vice-versa).
CME	Chicago Mercantile Exchange.
COLLAR	A combination of a cap and floor. Setting a band within which interest rates will apply, for example 10–12%, for a given period. Also used for currency rates.
COMMERCIAL BANKING	The 'classic' banking business of taking deposits and lending money, either retail or wholesale.
COMMERCIAL PAPER	A short-term security issued to raise money, usually by corporates. (Also Eurocommercial Paper.)
CONCERT PARTY	A group acting together (secretly) in a takeover situation, for example three people each buy 2.9% of shares to avoid no longer being able to hide behind nominee status.
CONSOLIDATION	Reorganising share holdings so that, for example, 10 shares at 10p nominal are replaced by one at £1 nominal.
CONVERTIBLE	A convertible bond may be converted later into equity, some other bond, or even a commodity, for example gold, as an alternative to redemption.
CORPORATE FINANCE	The department of a merchant/investment bank dealing with takeovers, mergers and strategic advice to companies.
COUNTERPARTY RISK	The risk involved if a counterparty fails to settle.
COUPON RATE	The annual rate of interest on a security noted on coupons issued with bearer bonds.
COUPON STRIPPING	Detaching the coupons from a bond and selling the coupons and the principal as individual zero coupon bonds.
COUPONS	Issued with bearer bonds to enable the holder to claim the interest.
COVER	The amount of dividend paid (net) divided into the amount of profit after tax available for distribution.
CREATION OF CREDIT	Banks' ability to lend money, facilitated by the use of notes and coin for a small percentage of transactions only.
CREDIT RATINGS	For example AAA, issued by companies like Standard and Poor's and Moody's to rate the level of security of a bond or note issue.
CREST	The new UK paperless equity settlement system which commenced in July 1996.

CROSS-RATES	Rates between two currencies neither of which is the dollar.
CUMULATIVE	Applied to a Preference Share – if dividend is missed it is still owed to the holder.
CYLINDER	Name used for a collar in currency markets.
DEBENTURE	In the UK, a bond secured on assets. In the US and Canada, a bond not secured on assets!
DERIVATIVES	Products whose price is derived from the price of an underlying asset – for example if ICI shares are the underlying asset, an option to buy or sell them at a given price is the derivative. Applied to options, futures, swaps, etc.
DIRTY PRICES	Bond prices including the accrued interest element.
DISCOUNT HOUSE	Takes the liquid money of the banking system and uses it to discount bills of exchange, buy Treasury bills, etc. Have the privilege of approaching the Bank of England as 'lender of the last resort' (UK).
DISCOUNTING	Buying/selling a security at less than face value.
DISINTERMEDIATION	Direct market borrowing or lending by companies without going through a bank. A bank is traditionally the 'intermediary' between depositors and borrowers.
DIVIDEND YIELD	The annual percentage return on a share price represented by the current dividend – usually gross.
DOCUMENTARY LETTER OF CREDIT	A documentary letter of credit is the written undertaking of a bank made at the request of a customer (for example an importer) to honour the demand for payment of a seller (for example an exporter) if terms and conditions are met.
DOUBLE	See Straddle.
DRAGON BOND	A Eurobond issued in Hong Kong or Singapore and targeted for primary distribution to Asian investors.
DTB	German Futures/Options Exchange (Deutsche Termin Börse).
EARNINGS YIELD	Earnings per share (after tax) expressed as a percentage of share price.
ECU	European Currency Unit – a weighted basket of EMS currencies to give an 'average' value, especially against the dollar.
EFT-POS	Electronic Funds Transfer at Point of Sale.
ELIGIBLE BILLS	Bills of Exchange eligible for sale to the central bank when acting as 'lender of last resort'.

EMS	European Monetary System – general agreement on monetary cooperation. Includes official use of the Ecu, 20% of central banks' reserves held in a European Monetary Cooperation Fund and exchange rates of member countries kept within a stated range, one to another (ERM). Set up in 1979.
EMU	European Monetary Union – a long-term aim, possibly resulting in a single currency.
EOE	European Options Exchange (Amsterdam).
EQUITY	General term for shares.
ERM	The Exchange Rate Mechanism of the EMS.
ESOPS	Employee Stock Ownership Plans (US).
EUROBOND	A bond sold in a market outside that of the domestic currency.
EUROCERTIFICATE OF DEPOSIT	*See* Certificate of Deposit.
EUROCOMMERCIAL PAPER	*See* Commercial Paper.
EUROCURRENCIES	Any currency held by banks, companies or individuals outside its country of origin.
EURONOTE	Short-term security denominated in a Eurocurrency.
EXERCISE PRICE	The price at which an option can be exercised. (Also called strike price.)
FACTORING	Buying trade debts on a regular basis to assist cash flow – usually done by subsidiaries of banks.
FCP	Fonds Communs de Placement. French 'closed ended' fund.
FEDWIRE	Electronic payments system between Federal Reserve banks in the US.
FLAT YIELD	The annual percentage return on a bond taking into account the buying price, for example if £100 nominal worth of an 8% bond is bought for £50, the yield is 16%. Also called 'annual', 'running' and 'interest' yield (see Redemption Yield).
FLOATING RATE	A loan with the interest rate varied at agreed intervals, linked to a base rate, for example LIBOR.
FLOOR	An agreement with a counterparty which sets a lower limit to interest rates for the floor buyer for a stated time period.
FORFAITING	Buying export trade debts on a non-recourse basis to assist cash flow. The debts must be in the form of a Bill of Exchange or Promissory Note.

FORWARD CONTRACT	A contract to buy or sell a commodity or security for future delivery at a price agreed today.
FORWARD/FORWARD	1. An agreement to lend money at a future point in time for a given period of time, for example, in 6 months for 6 months.
	2. A forward foreign exchange deal not dated today but at a later date.
FORWARD RATE	A rate agreed now for a future purchase or sale of a currency. Derived from the difference in interest rates in the two currencies.
FOX	London Futures and Options Exchange (commodities) – former name of the London Commodity Exchange (now merged with LIFFE).
FRA	Forward Rate Agreement. An agreement with a counterparty which agrees on a stated rate of interest to apply to a notional principal sum at a future time to last for a stated time – for example, in 6 months for 6 months.
FRN	Floating Rate Note. An issue where the interest is at floating rate.
FRONT OFFICE	Dealing room system to facilitate buying and selling.
FUNGIBLE	Exchangeable – for example, a contract of one futures exchange and another will be identical. Can be opened in one and closed in the other exchange (or vice-versa). Also used for further issues of bonds on exactly the same terms (and accrued interest) as those issued earlier.
FUTURES CONTRACT	Similar to Forward but not expected to go to delivery as the position will be closed out with the opposite contract.
G7, G10, etc.	Meetings of International Finance Ministers – 'Group of 7', 'Group of 10', etc.
GDR	Global Depositary Receipt – a form in which foreign shares can be traded outside their domestic markets.
GEARING	Carrying out financial transactions on the basis of a deposit or borrowed money. US term is 'leverage'.
GEARING RATIO	Ratio of equity and long-term debt.
GENERAL CLEARING	Part of APACS – the normal 3/4 day cheque clearing (UK).
GILTS	Term applied to UK and Irish government bonds. From 'gilt-edged' or virtually guaranteed. In general use for UK government stock from the 1930s onward.
GLASS–STEAGALL ACT	Passed in the US in 1933 preventing Commercial Banks from engaging in certain Investment Banking business (and vice-versa).

GLOBALISATION	The movement to integration of world markets regardless of national boundaries.
GROSS REDEMPTION YIELD	*See* Redemption Yield.
HEDGING	A technique for limiting risk. For example, if a price movement would cause loss, a purchase is made of an options or futures contract giving the opposite result; if a rise in interest rates causes loss, a position is taken with interest rate options/futures so that a rise in interest rates will yield a profit.
ICCH	International Commodities Clearing House – clears contracts for LIFFE, LCE and LME and some exchanges elsewhere. Main operating company: the London Clearing House.
IDB	Inter Dealer Broker – facilitates deals between market makers who can deal in confidence and anonymity.
IMF	International Monetary Fund. Set up in 1946 to help nations in balance of payments difficulties.
INDICES	Like the S&P 500, the CAC 40, DAX, FT–SE 100, etc.
INELIGIBLE BANK BILLS	Bills of Exchange accepted by a bank, but one not on the central bank's list (see Bank Bill).
INITIAL MARGIN	Initial deposit required by a Clearing House (as opposed to variation margin).
INSURANCE	If contrasted with assurance, this is business other than life insurance.
INTERBANK MARKET	Bank lending/borrowing one to another.
INTEREST YIELD	*See* Flat Yield.
INTERNATIONALISATION	*See* Globalisation.
INTRINSIC VALUE	The amount by which a call option exercise price is below the market price (or a put option exercise price is above it).
INTRODUCTION	A method of obtaining a Stock Exchange quotation. No new shares are issued. Usually they are foreign shares seeking a listing on a domestic market.
INVESTMENT BANKING	Banking implying a high involvement with securities – new equity issues, rights issues, bond issues, investment management, etc. Also advice to either party for mergers and acquisitions.
INVESTMENT TRUST	A company whose whole business is running a wide portfolio of shares. A 'closed ended' fund.
IPMA	International Primary Markets Association (for Eurobond dealers).

IPO	Initial Public Offering – American term for Offer for Sale.
IRREDEEMABLE	Same as perpetual.
ISDA	International Securities and Derivatives Association.
ISMA	International Securities Market Association (new name for AIBD).
ISSUING	Offering a security to the market in the first instance.
JOINT STOCK	Having shareholders.
JUNK BONDS	Specifically bonds with ratings of BB or less. Generally high risk, high yield bonds.
LCE	London Commodity Exchange – cocoa, coffee, sugar etc. Merged with LIFFE in 1996.
LDC	Less Developed Countries.
LEAD MANAGER	Bank(s) taking a key role in a syndicated loan or issue of securities like Eurobonds.
LEVERAGE	American term for gearing or 'making a small amount of capital go a long way'!
LIABILITIES	The side of a bank's balance sheet dealing with borrowing – that is, deposits, formal loans from others. Also share capital.
LIBID	London Interbank Bid Rate. Rate paid by one bank to another for a deposit.
LIBOR	London Interbank Offered Rate. Rate charged by one bank to another for lending money. Hence PIBOR in Paris, FIBOR in Frankfurt, etc.
LIFFE	London International Financial Futures Exchange.
LIMEAN	Average of the LIBOR and LIBID rates.
LIQUIDITY RATIO	Usually a percentage relationship between a bank's liquid assets and its eligible liabilities.
LLOYD'S	The Corporation of Lloyd's provides insurance through pooling the resources of individual members (the 'Names') operating in syndicates.
LLOYD'S BROKER	Lloyd's will only deal with a 'Lloyd's Broker' – there are 270 of them.
LLOYD'S REGISTER	Shipping classification society dating back to 1776.
LME	London Metal Exchange – deals in six non-ferrous metals.
LOCALS	Traders dealing for themselves as speculators.

LONDON CLEARING HOUSE	The main operating company of ICCH.
LONG	To be 'long' in shares, bonds or foreign exchange is to own more than have been sold.
LORO	Alternative term for 'Vostro'.
LTOM	London Traded Options Market. Merged with LIFFE in early 1992.
MANAGING AGENTS	Run and administer Lloyd's syndicates on behalf of the names.
MARGIN	The deposit required by a Clearing House.
MARKET MAKER	The dealers in stocks and shares as principals – that is, taking the risk in their own name.
MATADOR BOND	Peseta bonds issued in Spain by non-residents.
MATIF	French Futures Exchange (Marché à Terme International de France).
MEDIUM-TERM NOTES	A flexible facility to issue notes of varying maturity, varying currency and either fixed or floating – all within one set of legal documentation.
MEFF	Spanish Futures and Options Exchange in Madrid and Barcelona (Mercado de Futuros Financieros).
MEMBERS' AGENTS	Advise members on Lloyd's syndicates regarding tax, spread of risk, etc.
MERCHANT BANKS	UK term for Investment Banks.
MEZZANINE	Just as a mezzanine floor is a floor in between two others, so mezzanine debt is subordinated debt lying between equity and senior debt.
MLA	Mandatory Liquid Asset – the charge for a sterling loan in the UK to cover non-interest bearing deposits at the Bank of England.
MLR	Minimum Lending Rate – the rate at which the Bank of England will lend to discount houses. Only published as an 'official' rate in emergencies, for example January 1985 during the fierce run on sterling, October 1990 when the UK joined the ERM and the ERM crisis in September 1992.
MOF	Multiple Option Facility. A revolving facility from a syndicate of banks permitting the raising of finance with various options – bank loan, banker's acceptance or commercial paper.
MONEP	French Options Exchange (Marché des Options Negotiables de Paris).

MONEY BROKER	Intermediary putting borrowers in touch with lenders for a small commission.
MONEY MARKET	The market for money instruments with a maturity of less than one year.
MUTUAL	A bank or insurance company not a public company but owned by the members.
MUTUAL FUNDS	General name for pooled funds, such as investment trusts and unit trusts.
NAMES	Members at Lloyd's.
NASDAQ	North American Securities Dealers Automated Quotations – computerised dealing system for US 'over the counter' (OTC) trade outside recognised exchanges.
NATIONAL DEBT	The total of outstanding debt of the central government especially bonds and national savings.
NIL PAID	A new issue of shares following a rights issue on which payment has not yet been made. Rights can be sold 'nil paid'.
NMS	'Normal Market Size'. This is the classification concept replacing the three classes alpha, beta and gamma. It is based on a percentage (currently 2½%) of an average day's trading. There are 12 bands and they are used to decide the minimum quote size, the maximum size for immediate publication of trades and the maximum size handled by the SAEF system (UK).
NOSTRO	'Our' – the overseas currency account of a bank with a foreign bank or subsidiary.
OATS	Obligations Assimilable de Trésor. French Government bonds.
OFF BALANCE SHEET RISKS	Risks for bankers other than activities which end up as an asset on the balance sheet. For example, standby loans, standby letters of credit, derivatives generally.
OFFER FOR SALE	A method of bringing a company to the market. May be at a fixed price or by tender.
OFFER RATE	Rate of interest charged for lending money in banking. Generally, the dealer's selling price for equities, bonds, foreign exchange, etc. Also called 'Ask' Rate or Price.
OPEN OUTCRY	Face to face trading.
OPEN YEAR	When an accounting year cannot be closed due to uncertainty about claims (the Lloyd's market).
OPTION DATED FORWARD RATE	A forward rate (foreign exchange), but the date is more flexible.

OPTIONS	The right but not the obligation to buy/sell equities, bonds, foreign exchange or interest rate contracts by a future date at a price agreed now. 'Traded options' means the options themselves can be bought and sold.
OTC	Over the counter market. Dealing outside a trading exchange, for example a currency option purchased from a bank.
OVERFUNDING	The issue of government bonds or Treasury bills not for immediate government borrowing needs but as an instrument of monetary control.
PAR	The nominal value of a security, for example $1000 for US Treasury bonds or £100 for UK government bonds.
P/E RATIO	Ratio of share price to earnings after tax.
PERPETUAL	A security without time limit for redemption.
PITS	Trading areas in options, futures and commodity exchanges.
PLACING	A method of bringing a company to the market. The shares are placed with institutional investors and some private investors, that is, not 'offered for sale' generally.
PLAZA AGREEMENT	An example of international cooperation. Following a meeting in October 1975 at the Plaza Hotel, New York, international finance ministers agreed to take measures to reduce the exchange rate for the dollar.
POSITION RISK	The risk involved in holding any financial market position (equities, bonds, currencies, options, futures, etc.) should the relevant rates/prices change.
PREFERENCE SHARE	Dividend is paid as a fixed percentage. They have preference over ordinary shareholders for dividend payment and in case of liquidation. Usually non-voting. (Preferred stock in the US.)
PRIMARY MARKET	Markets where securities are sold when first issued.
PRIVATE BANKING	Specialist banking services for high net worth individuals.
PROMISSORY NOTE	A signed promise to pay a sum of money.
PSBR	Public Sector Borrowing Requirement – excess of public sector spending over revenue.
PSDR	Public Sector Debt Repayment – excess of public sector revenue over spending.
PUT OPTION	An option to sell a share/bond/index/interest rate contract later at a price agreed today.
REDEEMABLE	Applied to a preference share or bond – may be redeemed by the issuer on terms stated at the outset.

REDEMPTION	Final payment to holders of bonds.
REDEMPTION YIELD	The gross redemption yield takes into account the gain or loss to redemption as well as the flat yield (also called yield to maturity).
REINSURANCE	Laying off the original risk with others.
RELIT	Règlement Livraison de Titres. French Stock Exchange settlement system.
REPO	Sale and Repurchase Agreement. Securities are sold but must be repurchased later.
RETAIL MONEY	High street deposits/borrowings.
REVOLVING CREDIT	A commitment to lend on a recurring basis on pre-defined terms.
RIGHTS ISSUE	An offer of shares for cash to existing shareholders in proportion to their existing holdings.
ROLLING OVER	Renewal of a bank loan with alteration of interest rate as per the agreed formula, for example LIBOR + 1%.
ROLLING SETTLEMENT	For example '5 working days' – that is deal on Tuesday, settle next Tuesday; deal Wednesday, settle next Wednesday, instead of all deals within a given 'account' being settled on a given day.
ROOM	The 'Room' is the area at Lloyd's where brokers meet underwriters.
RUNNING YIELD	*See* Flat Yield.
SAEF	SEAQ automated execution facility – the automated share sale/purchase system introduced in early 1989 (UK). It is to be discontinued in late 1996.
SAMURAI BONDS	A yen bond issued in Japan by non-residents.
SCRIP ISSUE	Same as bonus issue.
SEAQ	Stock Exchange Automated Quotations – the system that came in with 'Big Bang' (UK).
SEATS	Stock Exchange Alternative Trading System. A dealing system for smaller companies' shares (UK).
SEC	US body controlling regulation of the market (Securities and Exchange Commission).
SECONDARY MARKETS	The buying and selling of a security after its primary issue.
SECURITISATION	The borrowing of money through issue of securities on international markets (in particular) instead of through a bank loan. Also, converting an existing loan into securities, for example mortgage bonds.

SERIES	All options of the same class, exercise price and expiry dates.
SETTLEMENT DAY	When the money for a given trade is due to be paid (and the securities handed over).
SHARES	Shares are shareholdings in companies with reward by way of dividend – usually called equities.
SHORT	To be 'short' in shares, bonds or foreign exchange is to have sold more than have been bought.
SIB	The Securities and Investment Board – UK body controlling regulation of the market.
SICAV	Société d'Investissement de Capital Variable. French 'open-ended' mutual fund.
SIGHT BILL	A Bill of Exchange payable on acceptance.
SOFFEX	Swiss Options and Futures Exchange.
SOFT COMMODITIES	Sugar, coffee, cocoa, etc. – as opposed to metals.
SPLIT	Existing shares are reorganised ('split') into more shares, for example two shares @ 25p are exchanged for each one @ 50p (nominal values).
SPOT	Today's rate for settlement in 2 days.
SPREAD	Difference between a bid and offer rate. More generally between one rate and another.
STAG	One who applies for a new issue in the hope of selling for a premium – no real interest in the share.
STOCK BORROWING	When a dealer has a short position, an alternative to buying the stock is to *borrow* it from another dealer or institution. The original dealer surrenders full collateral and pays a small fee.
STOCK LENDING	*See* Stock Borrowing.
STOCKS	Fixed interest securities, for example bonds, debentures, preference shares.
STRADDLE	A traded option strategy – simultaneous purchase/sale of both call and put options for the same share, exercise price and expiry date.
STRIKE PRICE	*See* Exercise Price (alternative term).
STRIPPED BONDS	*See* Coupon Stripping.
STRIPS	Stripped government bonds in the US – Separate Trading of Registered Interest and Principal of Securities.
SUBORDINATED DEBT	A bond that, in the event of liquidation, can claim only after other senior debts have been met.

SUPERDOT	Automated execution system on the New York Stock Exchange.
SWAPS	Exchange of debt obligations between two parties, either exchange of currencies or fixed to floating rate (and vice-versa) and sometimes both. The latter applies to a notional principal sum and the agreement lasts for a stated time period.
SWAPTION	An option to have a swap at a future point in time.
SWIFT	The banks' international message switching system – Society for World Wide Interbank Financial Telecommunication.
SYNDICATE	Managers, underwriters and selling agents of a bond or bank loan.
SYNDICATES	Organisation of the names at Lloyd's. Each of some 300 syndicates has their own professional underwriter.
TALISMAN	Transfer Accounting Lodgement for Investors Stock Management for Principals – the SE Computerised Settlement System (UK). Being replaced by CREST.
TAP STOCK	In general, in bond markets further issues of a previously issued bond.
TAURUS	A new service due to start in 1994 to allow for settlement by book transfer and not exchange of share certificates, but abandoned in March 1993 (UK).
TENDER	A bank loan or new security is offered to dealers who must compete for the business. If settled on a striking price basis, all pay the same price. If offered on a bid price basis, all pay the price they bid.
TICKS	Smallest price movement of a contract, for example 0.01 or 1/32.
TIME VALUE	That part of an option premium which is not the intrinsic value.
TOMBSTONE	Formal notice in the press of a syndicated loan, bond issue, commercial paper programme, etc.
TOPIC	Teletext Output of Price Information by Computer. The standardised display of SEAQ information (UK).
TOUCH PRICES	The lowest bid price and lowest offer price for a particular stock or share.
TOWN CLEARING	Same day clearing of cheques over £500 000 issued within the City – abandoned in February 1995.
TRADE BILL	A Bill of Exchange not endorsed by a bank and not eligible for rediscount at the central bank.

TRADE DATE	The date a trade is agreed, as opposed to settled.
TRADED OPTIONS	An option to buy or sell a share/currency/index/interest rate contract later at a price agreed today. This is a standardised market and the options can themselves be sold.
TRADEPOINT	A UK share trading system using computerised order matching. Began in September 1996.
TRANCHE	Further (large) issue of an existing bond to meet the needs of the market.
TRANCHETTE	Further (small) issue of an existing bond to meet the needs of the market.
TREASURY BILL	Issued by governments to raise money. Typically, 3 months, 6 months, 12 months.
UNDATED	Same as perpetual.
UNDERWRITE	When a group of financial concerns agree to subscribe for a proportion of a new issue to ensure its full subscription. The other use of the term is in insurance.
UNDERWRITER	Anyone offering insurance cover for a premium.
UNIT TRUST	A portfolio of holdings in various companies, divided into units which are bought and sold directly. An 'open ended' fund, for example, the French SICAVs.
UNIVERSAL BANK	A term for a bank that is equally engaged in commercial and investment banking, for example Deutsche Bank, UBS, etc.
USM	Unlisted Securities Market – a market since 1980 for companies that do not meet the requirements for a full listing. 138 firms at mid 1995. Will cease operation at the end of 1996 (UK).
VARIATION MARGIN	Further amounts of deposit (debit or credit) calculated by a Clearing House.
VENTURE CAPITAL	Capital provided for high risks which would not normally attract conventional finance.
VOSTRO	'Your' – the domestic currency account of a foreign bank with a domestic bank.
VRN	Variable Rate Note. A floating rate note where the margin above LIBOR is not fixed but reset at intervals.
WARRANT	A certificate attached to a bond or security giving the holder the right to buy equity/bonds later at a set price. May be issued on its own without attachment, for example gilts warrants, currency warrants, CAC 40 warrants, Eurotunnel warrants, etc.

WHITE KNIGHT	In a takeover situation, a more acceptable bidder may be sought – the White Knight.
WHITE SQUIRE	Alternatively, key blocks of shares are bought by friendly contacts – the White Squire.
WHOLESALE MONEY	The borrowing and lending of large sums of money – usually between banks, large companies and the institutions.
WORLD BANK	The International Bank for Reconstruction and Development. Set up in 1945.
WRITING AN OPTION	Selling the option. A margin is paid to the Clearing House.
XD	'Ex Dividend'. If a share or bond is marked 'XD', this means that the purchaser is not entitled to the forthcoming dividend/interest payment as the cut-off point has passed.
XR	'Ex Rights'. In rights issues, if a share is marked 'XR', this means that the purchaser is not entitled to the rights as the cut-off point has passed.
YANKEE BOND	A dollar bond issued in the US by non-residents.
YARD	Foreign exchange term for 1000 million.
YIELD	*See* Flat Yield.
YIELD CURVE	A graph showing the relationship between short-term and long-term yields for a given security or type of borrowing. Upward-sloping = positive yield curve; downward-sloping = negative yield curve.
ZERO COUPON BOND	A bond issued without interest payments but at a deep discount.

Index

A

ACH, Automated Clearing House 59, 60, 174
ADP, actions à dividende prioritaire 117
ADR, American Depository Receipt 213
advance payment 176, 184
advance payment guarantee 184
advising bank 177, 179, 181
agent bank 73, 74
Allfinanz 65, 300
American Express Card 56
Amtliche Kursmakler 204
APACS, Association for Payment Clearing
  Services 60, 62
APT, Automated Pit Trading 256
arbitrage 153, 168
Article 65 88
asset backed bonds 112, 115
assets 6, 21, 22, 24, 25, 28, 32, 75, 125,
  140, 163
assignment 76
ATMs, Automatic Teller Machines 12, 53,
  54, 57, 59, 62, 64, 300

B

BACS, Bankers Automated Clearing Service
  60
Baker Plan 123
balance sheet 6, 21, 22, 23, 26, 28, 102,
  163, 228, 295
Bancassurance 65, 300
banco 9
bank draft 176
Bank of England 6, 11, 24, 25, 41, 42, 43,
  44, 45, 46, 47, 49, 55, 60, 66, 71, 72, 89,
  104, 108, 109, 110, 114, 122, 132, 138,
  142, 151, 163, 165, 169, 170, 173, 219,
  220, 288
Bank of France 40, 49, 59, 151
Banking Act, 1826 41
Banking Act, 1924 40
Banking Act, 1979 42
Banking Act, 1987 25, 42
banks
  clearing 20, 22
  commercial 11, 13, 45, 52, 55, 60, 78,
    81, 85, 86, 87, 88, 102, 107, 133, 223
  cooperative 13, 15, 15, 63
  credit unions 13, 19, 34, 43, 186
  giro 13, 19, 300

industrial 20
international 7, 21, 31, 32, 121
investment 10, 13, 14, 21, 29, 52, 65,
  76, 78, 82, 85, 87, 130, 133, 223
merchant 10, 13, 78, 82, 87
national savings 20
post office savings 19, 20, 300
private 11, 13, 86
public 20
savings 13, 14, 15, 16, 53, 61, 93, 300
savings and loan associations 14, 15, 61
state 20, 42
thrifts 14
Bardi 9
barter 186
basis point 69, 91, 102
Basle Committee 25, 223
Bausparkassen 18
BCCI collapse 43, 166
bearer bond 113, 125
beneficiary 177, 179
bid bond 184
bid rate 102, 265
Big Bang 58, 85, 219
bill of exchange 79, 80, 81
  accepting 78, 79
  bank 81
  discounting 79
  documentary 177
  eligible 81
  sight 177
  tenor 177
  term 177
  trade 81
  usance 177
BIS, Bank for International Settlements 25,
  31, 32, 44, 54, 72, 105, 106, 121, 122,
  137, 150, 151, 168, 169, 171, 181, 274
block trades 204, 210, 224
bonos del estado 111, 114
book-runner 73
bought deals 210, 224
Brady Plan 123
Breeden, Richard 223, 296
Bretton Woods 50, 142, 143, 170, 248
British Bankers' Association 68
BTAN, Bons du Trésor à Interêt Annuel 113
BTF, Bons du Trésor à Taux Fixe 113
BTP, Buoni del Tesoro Poliennali 115, 248
building societies 17, 53, 58, 61, 94
Building Societies Act 1986 17, 18
bulldog bond 118
Bundesanleihen 113, 220, 248
Bundesbank 12, 13, 24, 40, 41, 44, 45,
  46, 72, 105, 108, 109, 113, 142, 148,
  152, 169

S

SAEF, Stock Exchange Automated Execution Facility 207, 208
samurai bond 118
Schatzwechsel 104
scrip dividend 216, 225
scrip issues 58, 214, 215
SDR, Special Drawing Rights 144
SEAQ, Stock Exchange Automated Quotations 206, 207, 220
SEATS, Stock Exchange Alternative Trading System 206, 208
SEC, Securities and Exchange Commission 219, 223, 296
Second Banking Directive 28, 222
securitisation 27, 124
share buy-backs 210
shareholders' funds 6, 21, 22
short-term financing facilities 151
SICAV, Société d'Investissement à Capital Variable 19, 58
SIM, Societa di Intermediazione Mobiliare 222
SIS, Système Interbancaire Suisse 60
SIT, Système Interbancaire Télétransmission 13, 59, 60
smart card 57
SOFFEX, Swiss Options and Futures Exchange 237, 238, 248
specialist 208, 209
speculator 127, 137, 142, 226, 244, 245, 246, 251, 275
splits 215
stamp duty 204
Standard and Poor's Corporation 99, 100, 124, 192
standby credit 67, 68, 69, 72, 74, 179
stock borrowing 209, 298
stock index arbitrage 168, 202
stock lending 125, 209, 210, 298
sub-participation 76
Supercac 203
superDOT *see* DOT
SVT, Spécialiste en Valeurs du Trésor 113
swaps 26, 87, 126, 262
  amortising 269
  asset 266, 268
  basis 269
  CIRCUS 127
  currency 126, 163, 269
  diff 269
  foreign exchange 163
  forward 269
  interest rate 126, 163, 262, 264

  liability 266
  roller coaster 269
  swaption 269
  unmatched 264
  warehouse 264
SWIFT, Society for Worldwide Interbank Financial Telecommunications 168, 174, 175
swingline 69
syndicated facilities 70

T

Talisman, Transfer Accounting Lodgement for Investors and Stock Management for Principals 211
Taurus, Transfer and Automated Registration of Uncertified Stock 211
Telegraphic Transfer 174
telephone selling 280, 281
tender bond 184
term loans 67, 70, 72, 74
Third Life Assurance Directive 292
Third Non-Life Insurance Directive 292
Tier 1 capital 26, 27, 29, 33, 118
Tier 2 capital 26, 27, 118
TIPA-NET 60
titres participatifs 117
tombstone 121
tomnext 137
touch price 208
traded options *see* options
Treasury bills 3, 22, 23, 24, 45, 47, 91, 103, 113, 150, 151, 201, 239, 269
Treasury bonds 110, 113, 123, 238, 252, 266
Treasury notes 110, 113, 238

U

UCITS, Undertakings for Collective Investments in Transferable Securities 58, 201
uncommitted facilities 66
undated 111
Uniform Customs and Practices for Documentary Credits 177
unit trusts 58, 200, 289

V

Visa 55, 56, 59
Volcker, Paul 50, 122
vostro account 166, 181
VRN, variable rate note 27